Doctoring Documents

Mistruth in History and Cybersecurity

RIVER PUBLISHERS SERIES IN DOCUMENT ENGINEERING

Series Editor

STEVEN SIMSKE
Colorado State University,
USA

Document engineering is an interdisciplinary set of processes and systems concerned with the analysis, design, development, evaluation, implementation, management, and/or use of documents and document corpora in order to improve their value to their users. In the era of the Internet, the millennia-old concept of a document is rapidly evolving due to the ease of document aggregation, editing, re-purposing, and reuse. In this series of books, we aim to provide the reader with a comprehensive understanding of the tools, technologies, and talents required to engineer modern documents.

Individual documents include web pages and the traditional print-based or print-inspired pages found in books, magazines, and pamphlets. Document corpora include sets of these documents, in addition to novel combinations and re-combinations of document elements such as mash-ups, linked sets of documents, summarizations, and search results. In our first set of books on document engineering, we will cover document structure, formatting, and layout; document structure; summarization; and classification. This set will provide the reader with the basis from which to go forward to more advanced applications of documents and corpora in subsequent years of the series.

The books are intended to cover a wide gamut of document engineering practices and principles, and as such will be suitable for senior undergraduate students when using the first 2/3 of each book (core topics), and be extensible to graduate students, researchers and professionals when the latter 1/3 of each book is also considered (advanced topics). Students and graduates of data analytics, information science, library science, data mining, and knowledge discovery will benefit from the book series.

For a list of other books in this series, visit www.riverpublishers.com

Doctoring Documents

Mistruth in History and Cybersecurity

Steven Simske
Department of Systems Engineering,
Colorado State University,
Fort Collins, CO, USA

Dallen Simske
Fort Collins, CO, USA

River Publishers

Routledge
Taylor & Francis Group
NEW YORK AND LONDON

Published 2025 by River Publishers
River Publishers
Broagervej 10, 9260 Gistrup, Denmark
www.riverpublishers.com

Distributed exclusively by Routledge
605 Third Avenue, New York, NY 10017, USA
4 Park Square, Milton Park, Abingdon, Oxon OX14 4RN

Doctoring Documents: Mistruth in History and Cybersecurity / Steven Simske and Dallen Simske.

Routledge is an imprint of the Taylor & Francis Group, an informa business

ISBN 978-87-7004-833-0 (hardback)
ISBN 978-87-4380-186-3 (paperback)
ISBN 978-87-7004-835-4 (online)
ISBN 978-8-770-04834-7 (ebook master)
DOI 10.1201/9788770048347

Contents

Preface

In the Internet age, humanity's history, literature, culture, and training have increasingly moved online. The ease of access and democracy of contribution are obvious and advantageous reasons for the movement of content online. Not only is traditionally difficult-to-access content much more widely available but it is also much easier for those wishing to promulgate mistruth to contribute to the body of "knowledge."

Does this mean truth is under attack? Of course, it does, but this is consistent with the entire literary history of humanity. What this book aims to do is provide its readers with the power to discover, in a systematic fashion, the likely mistruths in any narrative (particularly historical narratives). The book categorizes mistruths using a set of 13 patterns that, combined, will help uncover many of the falsehoods – whether intentional or unintentional – in narratives about history. These patterns build in complexity and perhaps subtlety, culminating in two very broad patterns, versioning and propaganda, which show that mistruth is actually unavoidable, or even "inevitable," in any historical narrative due to the innate differences in context and experience among narrators. We argue that a primary, if not the, task of the historian is to explain to the reader their own contextual considerations sufficiently to help those readers create their own version of historical interpretation.

Each chapter concludes with a "cyber salon" that applies the historical principles of the chapter to the increasingly important field of cybersecurity, which itself is employed to preserve truth in an online world. The value of a deep, mistruth-pattern-driven analysis of history is shown to be crucial for understanding how to protect data of any type. This is a virtuous circle since understanding how to protect content will also prevent historical narratives from being altered from this other attack surface. This book shows that protecting history from mistruths and providing proper cybersecurity are two sides of the same coin in today's online world.

Acknowledgements

Often, someone says that a work of many, many hours such as this book was a labor of love. But this book was not a labor. I did love working with Dallen on it from the original concept to the finished product, and learned so much. Dallen, thanks for all the good times on this...let us do another! Thanks to my publisher and editor, friend, and Zoommate, Nicki Dennis at River Publishers, for always having energy, encouragement, and enlightenment. Thanks for your lifetime friendship and encouragement, Douglas Heins, Ellis Gayles, Marie Vans, and Jeff Ewing. Thanks to my Thursday morning Zoommates, Paul Ellingstad, Mick Keyes, Gary Moloney, and especially, fellow writer Margie Sherlock, for listening, reading, and providing feedback. Thanks to many other friends (Mandi Hinson, David Auter, Rock Mendenhall, and Tom Novotny, just to name four) who have put up with my random bursts of reveal throughout this process. You may not be listed here, but you are certainly appreciated! Finally, thanks most of all to Tess, Kieran, and once more, Dallen, my family, who have supported me and encouraged me throughout this process!

Steven Simske

I appreciate the patience and persistence of my coauthor, Steve, throughout the research and writing of this book. I appreciate the support of my family, Teresa, and Kieran, and also the education, consultation, and tutelage of my professors, particularly Doctors Douglas Sheflin, John Didier, Anne-Marie Merline, and Pamela Vaughan Knaus.

Dallen Simske

List of Figure and Tables

List of Abbreviations

ACL	Access control list
ADHD	Attention deficit hyperactivity disorder
AI	Artificial intelligence
ANOVA	Analysis of variance
APT	Advanced persistence threat
BIOS	Basic Input/Output System
CCPA	California Consumer Privacy Act
CPU	Central processing unit
CSA	Confederate States of America
CSO/CISO	Chief Security Officer/Chief Information Security Officer
DCHP	Dynamic host configuration protocol
DEI	Diversity, equity, and inclusivity
DEI-SJ	Diversity, equity, inclusivity, and social justice
DNA	Deoxyribonucleic acid
DNS	Domain name system
DSM-5-TR	Diagnostic and Statistical Manual of Mental Disorders, Fifth Edition, Revised
EMOTE	EMOtional TErms
ENIAC	Chief Security Officer/Chief Information Security Officer
EU	European Union
GAI	Generative artificial intelligence
GAN	Generative adversarial network
GDPR	General Data Protection Regulation
GHG	Greenhouse gas
GOAT	Greatest of all time
GPS	Global positioning system
GPU	Graphics processing unit
I/O	Input/Output
IC	Integrated circuit
IDPS	Intrusion detection and prevention system
IP	Intellectual property
IR	Interpretative ratio

ISO	International Organization for Standardization
IT	Information technology
KKK	Ku Klux Klan
LDS	(The Church of Jesus Christ of) Latter-Day Saints
LLM	Large language model
LP	Long play (full-length album)
MD5	Message digest 5
MFA	Multifactor authentication
ML	Machine learning
MLK	Martin Luther King, Jr.
NIST	National Institute of Standards and Technology
NLP	Natural language processing
OSHA	Occupational Safety and Health Administration
RAID	Redundant array of independent disk
RAM	Random access memory
RFID	Radio Frequency Identifier
RGB	Red-green-blue
RNA	Ribonucleic acid
ROI	Return on investment
SLA	Service-level agreement
TB	TeraByte
WASP	White Anglo-Saxon Protestant
WTP-MC	Willingness to pay/marginal cost
ZTM	Zero Trust Model

1

Overview, Outline, Introduction

Trust dies but mistrust blossoms – Sophocles

If anything comes easy to me I mistrust it – Lilli Palmer

Abstract

Mistrust is everywhere, and like an intellectual weed, it is far more easily sown than reaped. Now is a critical time in history since so much of our culture (social, economic, political, and especially, historical elements) is moving or has already moved to online incarnation. History, as we will show, is critical to an understanding of the present and the future. Preservation of historical truth is increasingly dependent on the preservation of digital content veracity as well. Without proper cybersecurity, human culture will be manipulated to serve the ends of those who can control the cyber world. This book addresses both how this cultural fragility arises, and how it might be addressed. In this opening chapter, the context for the book will be provided. Mistruth in historical documents, we argue, is a lynchpin issue for mistruth in other documents including those that involve versioning, information reported by multiple people, and aggregation of multiple streams of information. The importance of identifying and obviating historical mistruths will be outlined, along with the direct connection to the need for stronger content security (cybersecurity). The latter culminates in each chapter with a "cyber salon," which complements the main text of each chapter in a sidebar-like fashion and has value for broadening each chapter's findings from the realm of historical evaluation to one that includes cybersecurity evaluation.

DOI: 10.1201/9788770048347-1

1.1 Themes of the Book

Mistrust is everywhere, trust us. This is not the same as saying "I am a liar, that is the truth," but it is similar enough in spirit to illustrate the difficulty we have in establishing trust in a world filled with echo chambers for even the most preposterous of belief systems. It is an interesting experiment to perform, but select two random words, string them together as a phrase, and look for a "phrase community" in your search engine. We tried "sentient tomatoes community" (January 2023) and found a Steam community and a subreddit associated with this phrase. Try your own, but please remember that tomatoes are not actually sentient.

Mistrust, like a weed in comparison to (let us say) a tomato, is more easily sown than reaped. It is easier to create fabrications, fiction, and falsehoods than the harder task of assessing, assimilating, and asserting realities. You might rejoinder that this has always been the case, and as such one must always resort to tried-and-true historical analyses such as *comparative methods* (across space, across time, and against a specified counterfactual state of the truth often described by a *truth table*) and *counterfactual analysis* (usually a series of "what if?" questions) to dispel false truths. The role of a historian is not to prove that something occurred in the past, but rather to disprove things that are proposed to have happened. This is effectively an application of Karl Popper's Falsification Principle, which states that for a theory to be considered *scientific*, it must be subjectable to testing and potentially proven false by one or more tests [Popp63]. This will be discussed shortly with regard to cybersecurity, but for now, it is important to realize that, if accepted as including the Falsification Principle, the scientific method does not prove anything historical but instead is used to disprove certain historical possibilities. This is a reason why mistrust, as Sophocles noted, readily grows. Once you disprove one supposed truth, you may lose confidence in many related truths.

However, we cannot allow mistruths to thrive. The damage that can be done by supporting mistruth is highly evident in recent years, as both polarized political polemics and improperly applied presentism have shown. Social, economic, moral, and cultural damage has been produced on a massive scale due to skepticism and distrust sown, both intentionally and unintentionally, by leaders and other highly influential people over the past few years (one need only start with Russia, Brazil, and the United States here before moving to smaller nations). As can likely be said of any age, this is a critical juncture in history. But, to paraphrase Tolstoy's opening to *Anna Karenina*, every era is critical in its own way. From the view of a historian or a cybersecurity practitioner (or, in the case of this book, from both views), our time is a critical time in history because so much of humanity's culture (social, economic, political, and especially, historical elements) are moving to, or have already moved to, online incarnation. History, as we will show, is critical to an understanding of the present and the future. Without proper cybersecurity, human culture will be manipulated to serve the ends of those who can control the cyber world, and thus control the present and the future of society. This book addresses both how this cultural fragility arises, and how it might be addressed.

George Santayana is credited with coining (or at least popularizing) the expression that "those who do not learn from history are doomed to repeat it." However, we do not feel that this warning goes far enough in the digital world. Instead, we assert that "those who do not learn from *how we tell history* are doomed to lose control of it." That is, if one loses the ability to establish historical falsehoods (following the Falsification Principle), one may lose history as an objective means of connecting past, present, and future entirely. Almost all of recorded history is now online, which means that the reality of history, whatever that entails both in terms of what happened and what did not happen, is vulnerable to the same types of attacks to which other web-hosted information is vulnerable. Given this threat to reality – past, present, and future – we simply must connect history to cybersecurity protection, because otherwise, we can consider history hacked.

Historical hacking is a vast sea of possibilities. Any interpretation or commonly perceived mistruth of history or modern interpretation/misinterpretation of it is of concern to us in this book. In the main analytical chapters (i.e., Chapters 2–14), we focus on one particular theme of fallacy and the doctoring of documents in each chapter and show how it can lead to historical relativism and mistrust. The motivation, morality, and means associated with each instance of document doctoring are examined in each of these chapters. Using the human historical record as the template, we outline a series of approaches to assessing the veracity of any historical document. Combined, these methods will provide a relatively comprehensive set of analysis tools to help discover most forms of mistruth.

In order to assess mistruths in history, scientific methods are preferable for several reasons. First off, *witness unreliability* is a well-known phenomenon. This is because of the many different forms of bias to which all of us, like it or not, are susceptible. *Confirmation bias*, for example, arises because we take notice of what we are looking for much more readily than we take notice of what contradicts our notions. Think of those "Where is Waldo?" books or the famous "Invisible Gorilla" experiment – confirmation bias is an established informational misprocessing effect. Related forms of selective attentiveness include *recognition bias* (where we tend to overestimate the presence of items we were already familiar with or predisposed toward) and *attentional bias* (which definitely explains not seeing a person in a gorilla suit when trying to itemize specific types of clothing). In addition to selective attentiveness, there is also the *halo effect*, where one attribute about some person, place, or thing is viewed as so important to us that it colors our interpretation of everything else about that person, place, or thing. This is one reason why so many famous people retain their apologists until they have gone much farther than a non-fanatic might deem appropriate before their fans finally abandon them.

In addition to bias about other persons, places, and things, we are all guilty of self-bias. That is natural, allowing us to balance altruism against self-care. Without some self-bias, our hygiene, health, and happiness may well suffer. However, this same self-care leads to a form of self-confirmation bias, which is described in part by what is known as the "Dunning–Kruger effect": the inability to recognize your own (relative or absolute) incompetence. Different studies have shown that as much as 25% of people in a given field think that they are in the top 1% [Karp18]. This means at least 24 times as many people are wrong about this than correct. More alarming, perhaps, might be what we will call the "Intransigent Dunning–Kruger effect," where a person is either incapable of being convinced of their own incompetence, or simply unwilling to listen. It is often said that a person "is too stupid to be shown how stupid they are," and there is merit to that. Most of us tend to underestimate the complexity of a subject area with which we are not familiar if for no other reason than that our unfamiliarity with the field has forced us to oversimplify the field, stereotyping it if for no other reason than preventing it from requiring the time, tenacity, and tolerance of deep understanding.

Looking for something tangible to take from this section? Look no further than the popular TV series *Stranger Things*, which premiered in 2016. This show, set in a fictional Midwestern United States in the 1980s, is nevertheless unable to project communication capabilities to what they were three decades earlier. The show imagines walkie-talkies with nearly limitless range and long-lasting batteries; in other words, functionally cell phones. This type of instant, distributed, always-available communication was simply not available in the 1980s and is an admission by the writers that they can create a "retro" world only so far. This combination of anachronism and presentism, we will call the *Stranger Things* effect.

The previous paragraphs overview the main themes of the book, and these are expanded upon in the next section. However, it is worth adding here a quick introduction to the mechanism that we use in each chapter to tie the historical discussion to the ongoing struggle for cybersecurity of all digital (online) content. In this last section of each chapter, titled the "cyber salon," we provide a system-level cybersecurity insight that helps to connect fallacy in history to vulnerability in the digital world. Cybersecurity vulnerability assessment (often assessed with what is known as a pentest, or penetration test) operates on the same Falsification Principle as described above; that is, using *comparative methods* and *counterfactual analysis* to expose vulnerabilities in a system. This "cyber salon" is intended to apply concepts of the chapter to cybersecurity threats, including social engineering, Trojan horses, worms, viruses, and other concepts. This bridges the reader between the past (history) and the present and highlights the importance of document doctoring in today's world. The relationship between how historians disguise the truth and how rogue actors socially engineer people online is emphasized as a direct connection to the broader document engineering community.

1.2 Mistruth in Historical Documents

Mistruth in historical documents is a lynchpin issue for mistruth in other documents that involve versioning, information reported by multiple people, and/or aggregation of multiple streams of information. This is because historical documents are *structurally versioned*: by definition, they represent at minimum two temporal inputs: the time of writing and the time represented in the writing. For example, *The Thirty Years War* by C.V. Wedgwood is versioned as 1618–1648 (the time in which the war occurred) and 1938, the year in which Wedgwood wrote the book. Would Wedgwood have written the book differently in 1948 than she did in 1938? In 1938, World War II was already raging in East Asia, and a forgone conclusion was coming soon to Europe. This sword of Damocles surely filled Wedgwood, like the rest of her country, with a feeling of impending doom. By 1948, the Berlin Blockade and Airlift had begun and a much different attitude toward Germany (where the overwhelming majority of the Thirty Years War occurred) had developed. From this perspective, then, any historical document is a *doubly timestamped* version of a potentially limitless number of versions that could be produced. Regardless of the number, it is clear that a mistruth in a historical document is a *mistruth in a versioned set of documents*, which can be viewed as a mistruth in a *document workflow*.

Conceptualizing historical documents as a form of document workflow helps us in the task of aggregating the many instances of historical fraud into *patterns of mistruth* – these can then be used as tools for assessing the veracity of any historical document. History is a flow of events, just as a document workflow is a history of the content whose *flow* completes some form of *work*. The work of a historical document is at least two-fold; simplistically, it is both *content* (what happened, where it happened, when it happened, to whom it happened) and *context* (how it happened, why it happened). Would not it be nice if one of these (content) could be considered objective and unambiguous? After all, are not the events, locations, dates, and persona of history the simple facts? In direct contrast, context (how and why) is understandably subjective, open to interpretation, and debatable. Context, then, should be the proper concern of the professional historian, right? If only it were that simple. Yes, professional historians are needed to debate the context of all the flow of history, but it turns out that content is not some fixed monument lining the Agora of history, either. Jonah's Tomb, Shakespeare's Globe, and the Great Mosque of Samarra are no more than waypoints today – we only know where they were but not exactly what they were. What they were is…wait for it…contextual. From this, we see that a historical workflow includes both content and context – we have to carefully analyze any historical document for errors of who, what, where, and when in addition to the more obvious how and why.

A document workflow is intimately tied to its specific business process. A workflow includes the creation, the editing, the tracking and tracing, the storage and archiving, and the overall life cycle management of a document. Document workflows are an important part of both research and product development in document engineering. Historical workflows are a specialized form of document workflows, and so patterns defined for use in identifying, evaluating, and ultimately remediating historical mistruths can be repurposed for more general document mistruths.

1.3 Universal Acid

The connection between historical and document mistruths is just the beginning. Mistruth is a form of *universal acid*: once you realize its signs, you then see it everywhere. The patterns overviewed in the next section, which are then fleshed out in the remainder of the book, help to provide a universal acid that allows you to eat away the cover from any sarcophagus of mistruth.

The familiar expression "Just because you are paranoid does not mean they are not out to get you" might be extended further to "Just because you are paranoid does not mean you know *how* they are going to get you." The fact that the expression "a healthy dose of paranoia" even exists tells you that your universal acid is needed to clean up a lot of surfaces. In order to discover how the mistruth is going to get you, it will help to have a wide range of discovery tools. A wide range of acids, using this metaphor, that is. That repertoire of acids are the patterns that drive the content of each chapter, as outlined next.

1.4 The Rest of the Book

This section provides a brief overview of the chapter-by-chapter contents. In this introductory chapter, we introduced mistruth as an endemic concern for all documents. The "cyber salon," introduced in the next section, is about general mistruth of content, which affects both historical falsehood and historical data falsehood. Data that cannot be trusted throughout its lifecycle is no different than a historical record containing mistruths.

In Chapter 2, we introduce the theme of *omission*, wherein, information that is at least relatively as credible as other information in a historical event is not included in the narrative. Summarization is shown to be an "innocent" means of creating omission, while hyperbole and slant are shown to be "intentional" means of creating omission (hyperbole itself is covered in much more depth in Chapter 11). Even the simple omission of the sources for numerical data, dialog, and dreams are shown to be forms of omission. The cyber salon for Chapter 2 addresses the failure to perform proper tests and measurements.

In Chapter 3, we introduce the theme of *disparity*, which is defined as a flavor of slant and/or omission in which the sources chosen provide a structural disparity in the flow or representation of information, and thus afford a type of transitive omission. *Culturally mediated disparity* (including folk tales, myths, legends, and presentism) is shown to be a form of mistruth that may be made with a wide gamut of intentionality, from innocent to fully intentional. Another form of disparity is *disparity in reporting* (due to the imbalance in the availability of news from two or more relevant parties in a historical event), which may be ascribed to lack of rigor, laziness, intentional disparity, and/or incompatibility of two types of reporting (all four of which may come into play in comparing the writings of Pizarro and the Conquistadores to the Incan use of knotted lengths of rope). The cyber salon focuses on the failure to perform proper analytics on data, metadata, and traffic in an information system.

In Chapter 4, we introduce the theme of *generalization*, which is another aspect of presentism in which stories are re-interpreted in light of current events. Some of the earliest sources of historical information, the *New Testament* and the *Apocrypha*, are mined for examples of these mistruths.

The cyber salon explores governance as a means to prevent generalization in security processes.

In Chapter 5, we consider the mistruths of differential emphasis and evaluation. Emphasis is what is chosen to place in positions of primacy, such as the first and last paragraphs or chapters. Selective complexity is a means of providing differential emphasis, with the more elaborate, nuanced arguments being reserved by the author for those parties the author believes to have more advanced intellect, feeling, or other higher attributes. The cyber salon of this chapter is focused on the ways that adversarial attacks and defense are designed in vulnerability tests to provide a form of mistruth in vulnerability reporting.

Next, in Chapter 6, we introduce the concept of the *omniscient historian*. These historians are comfortable putting their opinions and versions of how they think history should have occurred in the mouths of their historical figures. This is different from presentism in that it need not introduce any anachronism or partisanship to historical people, places, and events. It is, technically, a form of historical fiction because it adds speculative content to the narrative. Admittedly, any narrative is likely to require some added "omniscience," if for no other reason than that of showing the interpretative skills of the writer or making the story more piquant. It is the degree of omniscience, above a certain minimum threshold, that correlates with mistruth. The chapter concludes with a cyber salon comparing the "obviousness" of an omniscient historian's narrative to the obviousness of a good patent. A good patent seems obvious after the fact, but one has to project oneself back to the time the patent was written to see if it really was obvious then.

Next, in Chapter 7, we more formally introduce the theme of anachronism. While muddling events as they extend back in time may be to some extent inevitable, the role of the historian is to remember that 20 years was a generation (i.e., a long time) 2000 years ago, just as now. Alexander and Caesar lived farther apart in time than Washington and Obama. This is different from the more obvious (and perhaps better-known) form of anachronism such as one showing Wellington and Napoleon screaming at each other over the telephone. It is the distortion of linear time as we extend back in the past. A third form of anachronism is that humans also tend to think they are living in a time of maximum change. Surely, the Internet is the biggest change in communication technology ever, right? Well, imagine what the invention of the radio did to communication-based on the far more limited media of mail and telegrams before it. The cyber salon for this chapter considers the "arms race" between cybersecurity professionals and their antagonists, the hackers. For example, a security professional can prevent an unhealthy arms race between themselves and their adversaries by building an "innate moving target" of security approaches that readily responds to new attacks without having to be completely rebuilt from the ground up.

In Chapter 8, we address the broad category of factionalism. Subcategories include romantic nationalism, favoritism, provincialism, and racism. Romances, for example, often focus on the fate of the central characters, leaving out the equally compelling stories of the rest of the cast. Similarly, Romantic Nationalism and its various related forms (Manifest Destiny, Fascism, Sovietism, Mercantilism, etc.) focus on the "winners" of history at the expense of those who did not willingly participate or were otherwise marginalized, in this system. Romantic Nationalism is thus a selectively pruned version of the reality of past times which creates a historical bonsai effect in which past events are greatly reduced in scale because they are so oversimplified and lacking in nuance. This chapter's cyber salon illustrates how vulnerability penetration testing (or "pentesting") of systems can suffer from a form of romantic "red-teamism" if cybersecurity professionals are not careful. Previous test scripts may not adequately explore the rapidly evolving threat surface of cybersecurity.

In Chapter 9, we describe how emboldening situations may result in historical mistruths. History is often written by people who are emboldened by the current situation to justify misrepresenting it in the historical record. This is often employed "positively," by showing that the current situation is preferable to its alternatives, with the victors emboldened to justify not only their current situation but also situations to come. For this reason, doctoring of documents during such times commands the attention of everyone. The cyber salon for Chapter 9 describes how human trafficking is an example of an emboldening situation in abrogating the personal physical security of its victims. The emboldening comes from the powerlessness of the victims and the increased power of the traffickers that comes from such technologies as the Dark Web and anonymized/de-identified financial transactions.

In Chapter 10, we consider valence and arousal, kronos, and the general timing of presentation in a document. In some ways, this builds on the themes of Chapter 5 (differential emphasis and evaluation), but here, we can apply quantitative measures for document doctoring, including the use of natural language processing (NLP) approaches in addition to sentiment analysis. Such analytics quantify the timing of judgmental, opinionated, or specifically, emotional words or phrases in a document. We use the concepts of valence and arousal (which are negatively correlated by NLP approaches), and their timing in a document, to categorize documents. As a writer, do you allow the reader to formulate their own judgment first? If so, you are less likely to be attempting to persuade the reader through your argument. Documents with mistruths, we show, often start with a negative valence and as such can be readily identified as potentially suspicious. The cyber salon focuses on how information is sequenced in several forms of social engineering.

In Chapter 11, we describe mistruth through hyperbole. Exaggeration is a natural progression from the mythical to the factual. An earlier historian may have needed to inject storytelling into their history since the motivation of many listeners was to hear the tale rather than the truth. Such motivation and persuasion were observed in many early traditions and remain a part of writing to this day. Text analysis means of assessing the relative level of hyperbole (from stating your opinion on one end of the scale to making outlandish, unsupportable claims on the other) are also provided in this chapter. The cyber salon shows how the risk of cybersecurity is exaggerated when you are selling malware detection, pentesting, or intrusion detection software. On the flip side of the same coin, any cybersecurity provider that does not admit there is no such thing as zero risk is guilty of mistruth. Spotting hyperbole in cybersecurity assessment and prevention is thus the topic of this cyber salon.

In Chapter 12, we continue building on the complexity of mistruth by considering the theme of transitive trust and the vulnerabilities associated with recommendations. Applications for everything from admission to school to applying for jobs require transitive trust to provide authentication of the applicant. The rationale is that, if your recommender is trustworthy, so are you. Unfortunately, transitive "sus" (suspicion, that is) can occur if your recommender is not viewed favorably by the admissions/hiring personnel. Just as Michael Pollan says, "You are what you eat eats," when it comes to transitive trust, "You are trusted as those you trust are trusted." An interesting second form of transitive trust occurs in historical documents (or even quasi-historical documents such as the Icelandic sagas), which we dub temporal transitive trust, in which there is trust (or its opposite, suspicion or non-trust) that spans generations. In the cyber salon, the potential of shared trust to deceive a party is described. If person X trusts person Y, and person Y trusts person Z, then under transitive trust, person X will also trust person Z. This chain extends since person Y trusts person Z, and in fact, person X may not even know or have any experience with person Z. The odds of transitively trusting someone or something that is not trustworthy scale with both the number of connections and the lengths of the trust chain. We discuss when trusting an untrustworthy party is essentially statistically assured: one lazy link in the chain can destroy trust for everyone. The cyber salon addresses transitive trust in cyberattacks.

We discuss versioning as the pattern for mistruth in Chapter 13. History is innately versioned, and thus, one could cynically argue that at most, one history is truthful. However, there are multiple forms of truth along with multiple forms of mistruth. Both the relative time after the event and the context of the historian can add to versioning mistruth. Previous chapters have highlighted the contextual basis of mistruths. Here, the focus is on reinterpretation; that is, taking existing histories and updating them. This can lead to histories featuring hagiography on one end of the extreme and histories featuring excoriation on the other end of the extreme, not to mention everything in between. The cyber salon relates to code signing, digital signing, provenance, and track and trace. Authentication and forensic validation are achieved for different versions of content, using approaches ranging from signatures to distributed ledgers, and are accompanied by cyber-physical security approaches such as mass serialization, anti-copy, and tamper evidence.

In Chapter 14, we introduce propaganda, the last of the patterns for mistruth. Propaganda is shown to differ from hyperbole (Chapter 11) in the sense that it need not exaggerate, and from differential emphasis and evaluation (Chapter 5) in the sense that it need not try to evaluate at all. Propaganda is shown in its relationships to persuasive methods (logos, ethos, pathos, kairos, topos, and aesthetics) including examples of how it can be used positively to increase the engagement of the reader in the historical narrative. In the final salon, we address the false sense of security that is advertised with such cybersecurity approaches as malware detection software, intrusion detection systems, and automatic patching. We discuss ways to separate propaganda from reality through vulnerability assessment (including red team/blue team activities).

We conclude the book with a summary and conclusions chapter. With 13 major forms of mistruth (Chapters 2–14), we show how there are, in theory, 8191 different mistrust models for fraudulent historians – or fraudulent cyber agents – to proceed. In Chapter 15, we discuss how hybrid mistrust models can be used to obfuscate the more dangerous threat with a more obvious and innocuous threat. We also show how sowing mistrust across the domain can be used to discredit legitimate historians (or cyber networks). In this chapter, we reinforce our recommendations for how to better identify mistruths in both historical documents and in the more general cybersecurity domain.

1.5 Cyber Salon – Historical Fraud and Document Fraud

This is the first "cyber salon," which is used at the end of each chapter to complement and broaden the book's findings from a focus on historical evaluation to one that includes cybersecurity evaluation. In this initial cyber salon, we show that the mistrust of content is equivalent to, in meaning and practice, the mistrust of documents, and thus establish the link between historical fraud and cyber insecurity.

As mentioned above, historical veracity is crucial to understanding both the present and the future. Without proper verification of historical accounts, we may be basing policy and other future decisions on false premises. In cybersecurity parlance, historical veracity is the same topic as *data integrity*, which is the assurance that no *unauthorized data change* can take place and that any change made to the data will be immediately detectable. A common means of ensuring data integrity in the field of cybersecurity is to use *hashing* (or *message digesting*) of content. A hash function is a "one-way" function of a message m that creates H(m), its hash, which is too short to contain as much information (e.g., as many bits) as the original message. Thus, you cannot intuit what the original message was; in fact, there are theoretically many messages that hash to the same H(m), but if the hash, H(m), is long enough, the chance of such a hash collision is very low, and the chance of a hash collision where the (fraudulently) replaced text is meaningful to a reader is essentially zero.

The properties of the "cryptographic hash function," germane to our needs for data integrity, are:

1. The hash function H(m) is relatively easy to compute for any given message m
2. H(m) is one way; that is, no simple $H^{-1}(m)$, or inverse function, exists
3. The most effective way to determine m if you have H(m) is to do an exhaustive search: given a hash value h, it is computationally infeasible to find some message m such that $H(m) = h$
4. The values H(m) are collision-free for all reasonable (e.g., intelligible) m

In practice, number 4 above is impossible to ensure if (as is almost universally the case) the hash is shorter than the message (which only makes sense – mapping 1 million possibilities to 1000 hashes, e.g., means each hash represents a mean of 1000 of the original messages). However, if the odds of a collision are diminishingly small, for example, collision-free with less than 1 in 10^N chance of collision, where N is a number greater than 20, then a statistically relevant assurance of non-collision is obtained. Hash functions, therefore, ensure data integrity in that any reasonable change made to the contents of a message will result in the receiver calculating a different hash value than the one placed in the transmission by the sender. We will illustrate this with an example, based on using the hash generator at *sordum.org* [Sord23], with the original message being a 72-character (counting spaces) quote from Gloucester in Shakespeare's *King Lear*:

As flies to wanton boys are we to the gods; They kill us for their sport

The MD5 (a type of hashing algorithm, "message digest 5") hash for this quote is:

36e0ed38b44097f5ba169ec374f76589

This output is in hexadecimal, for which there are 16 characters (not 26 like the capital letters in English, for example), and the output is 32 characters in length. Since 16 possibilities represent 4 bits of information ($2^4 = 16$), this output is $32 \times 4 = 128$ bits (or 16 bytes) of information. Importantly, two different quotes have only 1 in 2^{128} = 1 in 3.4×10^{38} chance of a hash collision. This is effectively zero since 3.4×10^{38} is roughly the estimated number of stars in the observable universe multiplied by the number of grains of sand on earth.

What happens, then, if we make a small change in the message? Will it make a small change in the hash of the message, H(m)? Let us try a small change to the quote from King Lear. First, the word "flies" is changed to "flaes," which is not a word, but only requires one substitution, of "a" for "i" in "flies." Next, we will transpose the "a" and "e" to get the word "fleas." In information theory, these two operations show that "flies" and "fleas" have a Damerau–Levenshtein distance of 2. Levenshtein operations are substitutions, insertions, and deletions, while the Damerau operation is transposition. A distance of just 2 for a quote 72 characters long is not much (two random, unrelated quotes of length 72 are likely to have a Damerau–Levenshtein distance of approximately 70), and we will compare the results with the new quote:

As fleas to wanton boys are we to the gods; They kill us for their sport

This quote would not fool Shakespeare or his aficionados; nor does it fool the MD5 hashing algorithm, which gives a very different H(m), shown here, for just this small change:

97698acc41c0d13400ca4b2912115fc8

Let us line these two results up and add some spacing for ease of visual comparison:

36e0 ed38 b440 97f5 ba16 9ec3 74f7 6589

9769 8acc 41c0 d134 00ca 4b29 1211 5fc8

As the red bold character shows next, there is only one identical hex character (roughly the 2 expected by random chance):

36e0 ed38 b44**0** 97f5 ba16 9ec3 74f7 6589

9769 8acc 41c**0** d134 00ca 4b29 1211 5fc8

In other words, a small change in *m* creates a change large enough to effectively be random in comparing the original and the new H(*m*). This is a good hashing algorithm, as it provides anonymization of any edits in the content. How could you infer that "flies" were changed to "fleas" from this massive change in H(*m*)? You could not.

To illustrate these principles further, let us consider a quote from the eponymous King Lear of *King Lear* himself:

Thou shouldst not have been old till thou hadst been wise.

The H(*m*) from the MD5 hashing algorithm is now:

384ee244934e79f29be912fba77b387c

Comparing this to Gloucester's original quote from *King Lear*, we see there are four hexadecimal characters that are the same in the 32-character outputs:

36e0 **e**d38 b4**4**0 97**f**5 ba16 9ec3 74f7 6589

384e **e**244 93**4**e 79**f**2 9be9 12fb a77b 387c

This greater "similarity," of course, is not meaningful, it is just random. But the point is that a greatly different quote may end up with a seemingly more similar hash than did a very similar quote. The hash, in other words, obfuscates not only the original text but also the similarity of any two items of text. A small change and a completely different quote have no correlation with the change in the MD5 output. That is (data) integrity for you!

Can we employ the equivalent of hashing to historical data in order to ensure its integrity? The easiest process to implement, based on the above discussion, is to hash historical content (using a process like MD5) and store these hashes in a secure set of distributed locations (a *distributed ledger*, if you will). If documents are altered, intentionally or unintentionally, then they will no longer be hash-able or digest-able to the correct value. If so, they cannot be trusted. This is important to understand because untrustworthy historical content that can be used as input for machine learning algorithms used for purposes such as predictive analytics can empower rogue actors to perform *societal social engineering*, essentially a scaled-up version of individual social engineering (often called *phishing* or even *spear-phishing*) that can be successfully created from a person's online information. Historical information online is simply another attack surface for cybercriminals, but the threat to society is, arguably, higher.

Understanding the past is an important aspect of discovering and remediating mistruths in the historical record. Knowing where we came from, and what factors from the past influence what we are today is obviously of value. In addition, predicting the future depends on the integrity of the historical record. Hashing content once it has been validated is important for deciding whether or not the historical content can be used for any other of these purposes, from historical analysis to predicting the future trajectory of history. The latter should give us pause: it is not just for cybersecurity reasons that the historical record needs to be validated, but also for its use in artificial intelligence (AI). The output of AI is no better than the input, which is its training data. We have become more dependent on AI with each passing year, and so we need its training data to be accurate so that we do not make preventable errors in the future. Again, there is a strong relationship between historical validation and cybersecurity, because cybersecurity simply cannot work these days without AI. The sophistication, volume, and persistence of AI-based cyberattacks are too advanced for cybersecurity protection to work without the deep, adaptive learning afforded by AI.

This first cyber salon has addressed the need for data integrity in both the historical record and online information. Historical falsehood and data falsehood are part of the same continuum. Data that cannot be trusted throughout its lifecycle (e.g., as part of a document workflow) is no different than a historical record containing mistruths. The movement of so much of human history, culture, and record-keeping to "the cloud" is, therefore, a danger. However, it is also an opportunity. With proper cybersecurity approaches applied to historical content, such as the hashing approach overviewed in this salon, there is the possibility of providing more valuable and reliable input for the historians of the future. It is not too late to start!

1.6 Summary

Mistruth in historical documents directly relates to mistruth in other documents including any of them that involve versioning, information reported by multiple people, and/or aggregation of multiple streams of information. Historical mistruth is shown to be analogous to the loss of *data integrity*, and while most of the book will focus on the identification of historical mistruths, we will additionally employ cybersecurity practices to help outline means of remediating historical dishonesty. In this chapter, the use of hashing approaches to validate data integrity is introduced as one such remediation.

References

[Davi09] Davidson JW, and Lytle MH, "After the Fact: The Art of Historical Detection," McGraw Hill; 6th edition, 2009.

[Karp18] Karpen SC, "The social psychology of biased self-assessment," *American Journal of Pharmaceutical Education* 82, no. 5 (2018): 6299.

[Popp63] Popper KR, "Science as falsification," *Conjectures and refutations* 1, no. 1963 (1963): 33–39.

[Sord23] Sordum.com hash generator, accessed from https://www.sordum.org/hashgenerator/ on 21 January 2023.

[Weir09] Weir W, "History's Greatest Lies: The Startling Truths Behind World Events Our History Books Got Wrong," Fair Winds Press, 2009.

[Will02] Wills GA, "A necessary evil: A history of American distrust of government," Simon and Schuster, 2002.

[Zuck21] Zuckerman E, "Mistrust: Why losing faith in institutions provides the tools to transform them," WW Norton & Company, 2021.

2

Omissions

The omission of good is no less reprehensible than the commission of evil
– Plutarch

Deception by an omission of the truth is as bad as a lie
– Jennifer Chiaverini

Abstract

This chapter introduces the first theme, or approach, to mistruths in historical documents. These themes will be defined one chapter at a time in order to help with their discovery in general (in any document). This means that each theme introduced can hereafter be used as a *pattern* to apply to historical documents. The first theme is that of *omission*, which includes the "sin of omission," in which information that is at least relatively as credible as other information in a historical event is not included in the narrative. A specialized form of this omission is the "summarization-necessitated omission" of content which is an unfortunate by-product of length limitations often placed on articles by editors. As such, the choice of what not to include in curtailed writing can be evaluated for the relative omission of broad perspectives. Two other forms of omission are *hypocrisy*, which is the differential treatment of similar content for two or more different parties, and *slant*, which is the differential inclusion of information. The latter is distinguished from summarization-necessitated omission, in that, it can comprise including much more information about a particular topic in order to cast it in a negative light. Among the examples given in this chapter, we will describe the omission of sources for numerical data, dialog, and dreams in the histories of Herodotus, and the differential perspectives on Native American battles of the 1800s given by the distinct groups of combatants. The cyber salon for this chapter

DOI: 10.1201/9788770048347-2

will focus on the omission, or failure, to perform proper tests and measurements in a system.

2.1 Introduction

Even Proust, Flaubert, and Joyce, garrulous and comprehensive in their creation of *stream-of-consciousness* narratives, had to selectively omit content. After all, a human brain scales in at 2% of a human's mass yet uses 20% of its calories. A lot is going on up there, and even Anna Burns – arguably the best of the whole lot (sorry, Marcel, Gustave, and James) at capturing all the details, distractions, and dissonances in the mind – cannot readily convey all of the thoughts simultaneously weaving their way through a consciousness. Speaking must by economy omit, for as Edward Hopper noted, "If you could say it in words, there would be no reason to paint."

Let us take a deeper look at the human brain's storage capacity. This is a critical capacity to understand, since for most of human history, the human brain was the library of the past. Oral historians such as Homer, if indeed he existed, kept track of stories by repeating them in much the same manner that actors learn their lines; that is, associating them with specific movements, stage cues, and the like. This would render the gist of a story true, although certainly some of the "facts" would be fluid.

The human brain, as it turns out, is not perfected for storing information. Even if it were, how much could you actually store? Let us start with the memory size. The human brain is estimated to have the equivalent of 2.5 petabytes (i.e., 2500 terabytes) of memory capacity (this is not a conservative estimate: it is based on the information that can be stored by the 125 trillion synapses in the cerebral cortex, not by the 85 billion neurons, and so it is a "ceiling" estimate of the amount of memory in the human brain). That is a lot of memory, but then one must consider how much information is processed by the brain. Suppose the person under consideration here can see, and we will find out what the bandwidth needs to be only for the sense of sight.

The human eye has approximately 576 Mpixels. Assuming that a human can process about 24 frames per second (frames/sec), with 3 bytes per pixel (typical for a color image, e.g., RGB or red-green-blue image), this would give the following recording speed: (5.76×10^8 pixels)(24 frames/sec) (3 bytes) = 4.15×10^{10} bytes = 0.0415 TB/sec. For the upper end 2500 TB of total storage (which includes all areas of the brain, so is again unrealistically high), this yields 6.02×10^4 sec = 16.73 hours of information. This ignores the second eye (bilateral vision), auditory, olfactory, somatosensory, vestibular, and other senses, as noted. The 24 frames/sec is also conservative – there are humans who can detect information up to 100–1000 frames/sec (how else could you fence, play *jai alai*, or hit a Major League fastball?).

Putting that in perspective, a human lives for 75 years in the median, spending roughly 25 years asleep. Therefore, the expected total time of visual recording by a human is $50 \times 365.23 \times 24 = 4.38 \times 10^5$ hours. This is more than 26,000 times the 16.73 hours that can be stored in the brain. Humans, obviously, compress the information coming in from their senses. This means that less than 0.004% of all information is preserved. A lot, clearly, is omitted. The omission is built into being human, one might argue.

Augustine of Hippo wrote about three specific speech purposes: to teach (provide people with information), to delight (entertain people or show people false ideas), and to sway (persuade people to a religious ideology). This is often shorthanded by "Inform, Entertain, and Persuade." As we will see in this chapter, these same three purposes, along with others, provide extensive motivation for people to omit content. We really are not talking about accidentally leaving content out here. It is intentional, and therefore, an omission rather than a compression.

So, did we miss anything? If not, let us move to the definition and start from there.

2.2 Sin of Omission

What is a sin, really? Historically, it has been considered an "immoral act," which of course presumes that there is a moral norm against which it can be calibrated. In European Medieval times, a sin would be a transgression against "divine law," but again one needs to have an established divinity to disregard it to measure as a sin. We are understandably going to use a broader, and if you will more agnostic, definition. For us, a sin is an avoidable occurrence that differentially harms at least one party.

Given that, a sin of omission is when an author omits information that was available to them, with the result of differentially harming one party versus another in their narrative. A sin of omission can therefore either be intentional or unintentional. Ironically, or at least recursively, the latter – unintentional omission – is even worse, as it comprises two sins of omission: that of including the information leading to an unbalanced narrative and that of failing to properly research the topic so as to provide more balance. The "sin of omission" is thus any circumstance in which information that is at least relatively as *credible*, as *available*, and as *ascertainable* as other information in a historical event is not included in the narrative.

As an author, therefore, you are responsible for these three tests to avoid a sin of omission:

1. *Credibility*. Credibility can be assessed by finding multiple independent viewpoints that are in agreement about a point. Reputable sources, such as Google Scholar or the Library of Congress, should be searched for key terms and expressions on the topic, and multiple sources evaluated on any topics or subtopics influencing the overall interpretation of an event.
2. *Availability*. The information should be available. This does not mean it will be "easy" to find, such as is readily accomplished for "credibility"; that is, from publicly accessed content. But it does mean that content essential to creating your narrative should be available to others for verification.
3. *Ascertainability*. Making sure that something occurred is an opportunity for further research, and perhaps, creativity. Is the information reported in the same manner in every source? If so, perhaps you need to find the original source and diagnose it further. Sometimes a huge edifice is built from a single type of brick. If so, that brick must be very thoroughly vetted.

These three practices are good in general for any historical investigation. There is a fourth, less tangible, practice that should also be considered. This is the more equivocal task of sensing, perceiving, and recognizing that an omission has likely occurred. Do you find yourself "rooting" for someone in a narrative? If so, this is a warning sign that a sin of omission may be on the horizon. Take the other side in your narrative, before it takes you to the place of sinning. Use your judgment. If a story sounds "too good to be true" for one side, then it probably is. Find out what the narrative says from the other perspective. That is the summary of this fourth practice. Speaking of summaries…

2.3 Summarization-Necessitated Omission

When you summarize, you selectively omit content. Obviously, this opens the door, or at least puts a toe down at the base of the door, for bias. Bias, in fact, might be *structural* for different forms of summarization. If you have to summarize for a particular audience, you may be encouraged to summarize with a bias that suits the requests, requirements, or even responsibilities of that audience. For example, if you are asked to summarize Marco Polo's travels for an Italian, a Chinese, and separately an American audience, you are going to omit different information for each of these. The Italian audience might be more concerned with the tales Marco brought back; the Chinese audience with what Marco learned from the Chinese; and the American audience with what impact it had on stimulating the European Renaissance, for example.

The process of summarization is, from one perspective, the intelligent omission of content. Since content is compressed by summarization, we can term this particular form of omission the "summarization-necessitated omission" of content, which is in many instances, a by-product of length limitations placed on articles by editors. So, it is unavoidable, and for that reason, well worth commenting on first, since it drives home the (intentionally alliterative) point that *communication commonly calls for compression*. Summarization, ultimately, is a text filter, and because in most instances it is meant to preserve the main points, or "gist," of the content, it serves as a proxy for the complete text and can be considered a high-pass filter with differential preservation of the highest frequency (i.e., most repeated or emphasized) content.

When else is a high-pass filter used? Think of your noisy, shirtless, and in all likelihood showerless neighbor in college who sat around all day listening to rap, punk, or metal music. What got through the (perhaps paper-thin) walls between you? The bass, right? You needed a high-pass filter to get rid of those low-frequency tones. You also needed animal control, but that is a little off-topic. The point is that summarizing loses some of the flavor of the text, but is meant to capture its essence. The problem is that what part of the filtered information is part of the "essence" depends on the audience. Even if your story of your neighbor includes mentioning his loud music, perhaps you have filtered out the time he brought you food when you were sick in bed. When you cannot include everything, you are almost certain to differentially leave out at least some things. This filtering means that the choice of what not to include in a curtailed writing can be evaluated for its relative omission of broad perspectives. Everyone has biases, persuasion goals, motivation, and intended audience-matching, which is part of writing. For example, in this paragraph, we are assuming that you are interested in the ramifications of selective content filtering. Not all people are, so our message is being matched to our expected audience. But no two writers likely share all of the same biases, approaches to persuading their audience, motivations, and expectations of their audience. Every summarization done by a real person, therefore, is likely to be unique to that person, particularly if *abstractive* rather than *extractive* summarization is employed. With extractive summarization, certain elements of text are selected verbatim, and so this might be predictable based on an algorithm. With abstractive summarization, the content is rewritten to be logically cohesive using far less words. This differential treatment of the same content is the basis of summarization-necessitated omission, but as we will see next, it is also the basis of hypocrisy.

2.4 Hypocrisy

Hypocrisy is, for the purpose of its relationship to the *theme of omission*, the differential treatment of similar content for two or more different parties. If a member of the armed forces from Areiapolis (a hypothetical place) kills a non-combatant from Misopolis (another hypothetical place), and a member of the armed forces from Misopolis kills a non-combatant from Areiapolis, then the verbiage reporting the two events can be compared as a measure of hypocrisy. This is a common occurrence for contentious historical events, in which people who identify with one side (e.g., the Areiapolitans) view the actions of the other side (e.g., the Misopolitans) in a negative light. Meanwhile, either consciously or unconsciously, their own actions are viewed in a positive light.

Fortunately, technologies exist for analyzing sentiment [Cobo19, Heer11], usually in terms of overall positive versus negative sentiment, or *polarity*. From word sentiment lists (perhaps the simplest means of rolling out a sentiment-detection system) to natural language processing (NLP) to deep learning algorithms, there are many ways to determine, with increasingly high accuracy, the polarity of an element of text. Text sentiment analysis has advanced so far that even *sarcasm detection* is now a relatively mature technology [Josh17]. Our focus in this section, then, is not about how document polarity can be determined; rather, our focus is on how it can be used for determining hypocrisy. In Chapter 10, we will discuss valence and arousal in more depth. These two factors are used to provide axes for different sentiment pairings, six of which are, for example, tension versus calmness, anger versus relaxation, frustration versus contentedness, depression versus happiness, ennui versus delight, and torpor versus excitation. We will use these to illustrate (quantitatively) the relative hypocrisy in two documents that have as a topic the same historical element (Table 2.1). In Table 2.1, two different documents are written about the same historical element (set of the same people, places, time in history, etc.). We introduce the concept of a *historical agent*, which might be an event such as a battle, a person such as a leader of a nation, or the ramifications of two policies, among other possibilities. In Table 2.1, the two documents are written by two different authors who

Table 2.1 The scores for six polarity axes for two different agents (#1 and #2) as conveyed by Document A (written by an advocate of #1) and Document B (written by an advocate of #2). The magnitude of the total (last row) indicates greater hypocrisy for the writer of Document A toward Agent #1 (magnitude = 3.09) than for the writer of Document B toward Agent #2 (magnitude = 1.73). Moreover, Document A focuses especially on the *Torpor-Excitation* axis (+1.32) for its differential treatment of agents, while Document B focuses on the *Depression-Happiness* axis (+0.82) for its differential treatment of agents. Please see the text for details.

Axis of polarity	**Document A**			**Document B**		
(negative–positive)	**For #1**	**For #2**	**Diff (1-2)**	**For #1**	**For #2**	**Diff (2-1)**
Tension-calmness	+0.31	−0.32	+0.63	+0.09	+0.17	+0.08
Anger-relaxation	+0.07	+0.03	+0.04	+0.05	+0.22	+0.17
Frustration-contentedness	−0.11	+0.01	−0.12	−0.04	−0.01	+0.03
Depression-happiness	+0.22	−0.44	+0.66	−0.31	+0.51	+0.82
Ennui-delight	+0.35	−0.21	+0.56	−0.15	+0.11	+0.26
Torpor-excitation	+0.77	−0.55	+1.32	−0.22	+0.15	+0.37
Total	+1.61	−1.48	**+3.09**	−0.58	+1.15	**+1.73**

advocate for two contrasting agents: the author of Document A is an advocate for Agent #1 and the author of Document B is an advocate for Agent #2. In the "Diff" (for difference) column, a net positive favors Agent #1 over Agent #2 for Document A, and a net positive favors Agent #2 over Agent #1 for Document B (based on which document's polarity score is subtracted from the other document's polarity score).

In Table 2.1, net favoritism (or "hypocrisy") for an agent occurs when the second element in the axis name (e.g., Calmness and Relaxation) has a higher sentiment score than the first element in the axis name (e.g., Tension and Anger). In theory, a completely objective reporting of events would provide the same difference in each axis pair for each agent: the overall positivity or negativity of the document should then be an indication of the relative polarity of the event; for example, documents about a celebration might give (+2, +2) totals for (Agent #1, Agent #2) while documents about a plague might give (−3, −3) totals for (Agent #1, Agent #2). Hypocrisy slips in when these scores are not consistently different when comparing two documents reporting on the same historical element. This is precisely the situation for Table 2.1, shown by the scores for all six polarity axes for each of the two different agents (#1 and #2) as conveyed by Document A (which was written by an advocate of Agent #1) and Document B (which was written by an advocate of Agent #2). The magnitude of the total sentiment polarity (last row) indicates greater hypocrisy for the writer of Document A toward Agent #1 (magnitude = 3.09) than for the writer of Document B toward Agent #2 (magnitude = 1.73). In other words, the writer of Document A is more hypocritical than the writer of Document B. Moreover, Document A focuses especially on the *Torpor-Excitation* axis (+1.32) for its differential treatment of agents, while Document B focuses on the *Depression-Happiness* axis (+0.82) for its differential treatment of the two agents. It is worth noting that Table 2.1 might be viewed by some as a disparity table, in that there is a disparity in the polarity for Agents #1 and #2. However, we use disparity differently (Chapter 3) to mean the relative amount of attention Agents #1 and #2 receive. In the current scenario, the disparity exists no matter how much relative attention is paid to Agents #1 and #2 by the writers of the documents. Thus, this form of disparity is a measure of hyperbole (favoritism toward one agent over the other). The large difference in polarity disparity between the two authors indicates that the provincialism of an author toward their advocated agent is greater for the author of Document A than for the author of Document B.

One need not perform quantitative analysis along the lines above to recognize hypocrisy, of course. For one thing, the columnar totals in Table 2.1 do not account for the relative impact of each axis, not to mention the relative impact of each term that establishes polarity. As an example, there may be a large difference between calling someone "sad" and calling someone "miserable," but each might contribute the same to the *Depression-Happiness* axis. For another thing, often it is the way certain words are used that convey the level of hypocrisy. Returning to our original example, suppose an author writes about a soldier from Areiapolis "nobly killing one of the Misopolitan savages" when Areiapolis takes a Misopolitan village, and then writes of a "Misopolitan terrorist murdering an innocent Areiapolitan citizen" under essentially identical conditions. We need no artificial intelligence to sniff this out as hypocrisy! Murder is murder, no matter who commits it, and expressing one murder as noble and another equivalent murder as terrorism is clearly hypocritical.

2.5 Slant

Slant, for the purposes of the present chapter's *theme of omission*, is the *differential inclusion* of information. This is related to hypocrisy, except that with slant, we usually experience unilateral polarity (to one side) of a historical element. Thus, slant is more directly related to omission since it is the (measurable) relative omission of information representing one side and not the other. If the writing has a uniform polarity, for example, attempting to provide a neutral or apolitical stance, then the measure of slant is simply the ratio of the amount of text dedicated to one side of an argument to the amount dedicated to the other side. For example, if two Presidential candidates are being discussed in an article with no ostensible political agenda, but one candidate's paragraphs cover 890 words and the other candidate's paragraphs cover 360 words, then the slant is 890/360 = 2.47 times in favor of the first candidate.

This is the most simplistic model for slant, but there are many other reasonable possibilities. If, for example, we wish to account for potential differences in polarity, then perhaps it is the net amount of positive coverage a topic is given that is most relevant. Certainly, there is some merit to this. The more positive the input, the more likely some of it is to make a (positive) impression on the audience. In our example, suppose that of the 890 words dedicated to Candidate 1, there are 300 words in phrases with a generally positive polarity and 590 words in phrases with a generally negative polarity. For Candidate 2, suppose there are 240 words in phrases with a generally positive polarity and 120 words in phrases with a generally negative polarity. The ratio of positive polarity words for Candidate 1 compared to Candidate 2 is then 300/240 = 1.25. There are more potentially positive phrases to choose from for Candidate 1, even though the percent positive coverage of Candidate 1 (300/890 = 0.337) at 33.7% is much less than that of Candidate 2 (240/360 = 0.667) at 66.7%.

However, considering human nature, the percentage of words of one polarity may not be as important as other factors. For example, suppose an optimistic person is the audience of the message. This person might be looking for the one good thing said about a side of an argument or one among a plurality of individuals (e.g., candidates). In this case, the more that is said about the item/person of interest, the more likely a positive impression will be made. The opposite polarity is to suppose that the person is a pessimist and that they will ignore anything after the first negative thing they hear, expecting negativity and thus inured to it. In either of these two cases, the more that is written about a given item/person of interest, the more likely they will be viewed as well or better than their competitors (so long as at least one positive and one negative statement is assigned to each candidate). This is the famous principle of name recognition, or "all visibility is good visibility." In either of these two cases – the optimist or the pessimist – it may again simply be the number of words used that matters.

However, persuasion in many circumstances must be more than just the number of words used. Memorable comments are an attribute of writing that will help sink certain text deeper into a person's memory. "These are the times that try men's souls," after all, is more impactful than saying

Table 2.2 Slant as assessed by the various methods outlined in this section. Here, "+Polarity" means positive polarity sentences or phrases, and "–Polarity" means negative polarity sentences or phrases. Memorable terms are those recalled by readers afterward. Please see the text for details.

Word category	Candidate 1	Candidate 2	Ratio
Total words	890	360	2.47
+Polarity words	300	240	1.25
–Polarity words	590	120	4.92
Percent +polarity words	0.337	0.667	0.51
Memorable terms	15	5	3.00
+Polarity memorable terms	3	4	0.75
–Polarity memorable terms	12	1	12.00
Percent +polarity memorable terms	0.20	0.80	0.25

"It is a time of crisis." The difference in impact of these two expressions helps explain the value of slogans and catchphrases, not just in advertising but also in rallying people to a cause. Memorable expressions are the literary equivalent of those annoying, often three-note, audio logos used by various brands, from NBC to ATT. Sure, they are not particularly creative, but if they are short, easily recognized, and differentiated from other audio logos, they effectively recall a brand. The hope for the perpetrator of slant is that memorable expressions, even if negative in polarity, give the item/person brand recognition and familiarity. If enough negativity is spread around all items/people, then perhaps (as we have often seen) the item/person with the most brand recognition will win out.

Table 2.2 captures examples of these types of slant, from overall coverage (total words), positive and negative coverage, and memorable terms coverage. Overall, it is likely that different strategies work best on different types of people (not just the differences between optimists and pessimists). But, for the majority of the cases, and almost certainly the majority of people, the strategy of having the most coverage is likely a "good" one. Take the 2016 Presidential Election in the United States as a relatively recent example. Disproportionate press coverage for one candidate (Trump) further extended his lead in name recognition and helped propel him into the Oval Office [Patt16] [Well16].

Thus, from the perspective of slant, the distinction between positive and negative polarity may not be all that important. Not that the semantics matter all that much, but hypocrisy might be thought of as differential coverage of two compared/competing items/people in general, while slant is the differential polarity of coverage. Both of these (hypocrisy and slant) are distinguished from *summarization-necessitated omission* (Section 2.3), in that they can choose to include significant additional information about a particular topic in order to cast it in a negative light (an expansion rather than a summary!).

2.6 Omission of Sources for Numerical Data, Dialog, and Dreams in the Histories of Herodotus

Was history as a science founded on a lie? If so, then the relevance of doctoring documents extends all the way back to the heady days of Herodotus. Herodotus, he who happens to head the history of history with his hyperbole? That guy. Herodotus wrote in the mid-5th century BCE, a time when only a small fraction of Greece was literate and this relatively small (by today's standards) society only had, in Herodotus' time, writing as a societal skill for three centuries. Thus, Herodotus really did not have a massive library of previous works to cite as sources in his *Histories* [Norm14]. Perhaps, Herodotus should have worked harder to substantiate the veracity of his sources, but of course, there was no tradition of doing so, and he was already revolutionary enough. There was no expectation from his readership to "verify information that he compiled from personal observation through the consultation of written records." [Ibid.] Add to this the fact that Herodotus largely expected his *Histories* to be read aloud (to those throngs of Greeks who were not literate!), and you can see how adding a fully cross-referenced bibliography might not have been his top priority.

Herodotus peppers his *Histories* with text taken from government and law records, which is to be expected because that is where the literate people were. This includes political and military negotiations, secret messages, and messages reminding the recipients about established laws. Herodotus, like Socrates who followed him, knew the limitations of writing in comparison to an oral account of a situation. The written word gives the same answer to a question each time it is asked, while an orator can reinterpret an element of text in light of events that have occurred since its writing, or in light of the context of the audience. Perhaps knowing this, Herodotus wrote down stories that were ideal for oral reinterpretation. The story of Harpagus is one example. According to Herodotus, he sliced open a hare and hid a note inside its belly, then stitched the animal together, leaving the fur intact. His servant, disguised as a non-descript huntsman, was then able to carry the note past sentries. Certainly, this is the type of story most likely created for its "coolness" factor. Regardless, as a storyteller, it is the kind of story that gives one tremendous license for creativity. One could readily add anecdotes about the hare, passing through the sentries, and ultimately reopening the hare at the destination. Did someone offer to cook the hare for a share of its meat along the route? Herodotus does not say but also does not prevent the public reader of his *Histories* from providing such an addition.

Regardless of Herodotus's purposes vis-à-vis the writing and reading of his *Histories*, they have survived because he did make the effort to write them down, and because they were of enough interest for others to re-copy them [Norm14]. In a sense, Herodotus is recognized today as the first historian (whether that is accurate or not, he coined the word "history" which was Greek for "inquiries") because he wrote stories that people liked to read aloud. Had his stories not been popular, Thucydides, considered the first "scientific historian," might also now be considered the first historian because the papyri of previous historians may have served as palimpsests to civic records, painting cloths, or even fish wrapping. Fortunately, we have Herodotus as an example, and perhaps, a warning.

The warning is a message of caution that, because of a number of dynamic structural changes in our own times, we may be preadapted to a future that returns to the type of history told by Herodotus. Far from Thucydides, and sadly, occasionally far from the truth as well. In this section, we will briefly overview seven such trends. Why seven? Well, it was the Pythagorean numerology value for spirituality (not to mention the Seven Wonders and seven planets since they only knew Mercury to Saturn and the moon makes seven). Plus, it is how many readily came to mind, to be honest.

The first of these is the fact that *functional illiteracy may be increasing* in the digital economy [Bask19]. This is due to a number of factors, including wealth disparity, the increase in graphical (videos, etc.) and auditory (audiobooks, etc.) presentation and representation of information, and perhaps even the increased use of icons in order to simplify localization and other global processes. Even if none of these processes is impacting functional illiteracy, however, a possibly more surprising one may well be. The world, as you have surely noticed, continues to get more complex. Every day that goes by brings new miracles of scientific, technical, and artistic advancement. As the amount to know continues to increase, a form of functional illiteracy may be increasing as an effective tautology, simply because full functioning requires more knowledge than ever before. That is, as more options – maybe we should say responsibilities? – for literacy are available, so are many more options for functional illiteracy. Thinking this through, perhaps more than we should, this enhanced surface area for functional illiteracy brought on by the Internet (with all, or at least a superficial percentage of all, the world's knowledge available with the simplicity of a query) may also be the reason the "echo chamber" effect is brought on by the Internet. Going back at least to Aristotle, the expression "The more you know, the more you realize you don't know," continues to be more germane as the world's knowledge base grows. In order to cope with this almost limitless online knowledge and the feelings of ignorance it might cause, many people tend to find echo chambers that share their viewpoints and knowledge limits. But hiding from your ignorance does not make it go away, and so the ghost of Herodotus, like the Ghost of Hamlet's Father, may well stride the ramparts of this echo chamber castle, waiting to deliver history that is of questionable accuracy and veracity.

The second of these seven trends that may give rise to a Herodotus-like historical record for today's world is that *the current primary style of writing*, that is keyboard-fueled word processing, *has been endemic for less than half a century*. This is less than a tenth of the time that has passed since the Gutenberg press was invented (circa 1440) and much less than that for the time that has passed since the first presses ran at least as far back as 868 AD in China's late Tang Dynasty. Writing itself dates back much, much further, with records of cuneiform dating to roughly 3500 BC in Sumer. Thus, writing has been around for more than a hundred times longer than the word processor and the computer. The relative ease of writing in this "new" fashion has a flip side, and it is not a hit single. With the mechanics of writing made that easy, a lot of it is understandably banal, poorly planned, and relatively automated. With recent "advances" such as chatbots, automation threatens to overwhelm original writing if indeed it has not already. Imagine what Herodotus might have been able to do with Siri and ChatGPT. Siri may well have come up with some of the same "inventions" as Herodotus, among which are descriptions of camel-eating ants in India (perhaps an inspiration for the 1954 film, "Them!"); exaggerating the number of Babylonian bronze gates from 8 to 100 and claiming the Babylonian walls were 100 meters high; telling stories of one-eyed men (cyclopes) and the gold they steal from (unironically supposedly real!) griffins; and estimating the Persian troops involved in the Battle of Thermopylae (land and sea combined) to surpass five million! If you believe any of these, I have got some prime Florida swampland to sell you.

The third modern trend that sets us up for a revisit of Herodotus is that *"Likes" and "Up-votes" now largely determine what survives on the Internet.* Why is this a problem? There are many reasons, but one of the most obvious upfront is that whatever gets the most "likes" may simply be the most provocative argument, the one that repeats other popular opinions elsewhere (think about how politicized many traditionally non-political issues have become since the dawn of the Internet era), and/or the one that best represents an echo chamber (thus already represents a skewed segment of society). This does not even include the situation in which bots are "liking" or "un-liking" the material. The point is, that under the conditions usually present for such Internet-based comments, people's votes and likes have been shown to be dependent on those already posted [Much13]. The so-called "popularity" of materials on the Internet is not representative (i.e., statistically relevant) in so many ways. If polling is biased, you end up with events like "Dewey Defeats Truman" [Cols00] because you forgot that the people you polled were not representative of the larger population you hoped to understand. In the new age of Herodotus, Dewey might actually be remembered as the 33rd US President. "War is peace, freedom is slavery, ignorance is strength," and Newspeak becomes part of a fictional history undifferentiable from reality.

A fourth modern trend that may help in the dawning of a new age of Herodotus is the *rapidly changing nature of self-publishing and peer review*. Let us see what is happening here to harken Herodotus. Thanks to Google Scholar, Science.gov, Semantic Scholar, and other sources, it is relatively easy to access educational materials online. Because of this, it has arguably never been easier to properly research and credit previous authors whose work has met peer-review standards for experimental design, quality, and analysis. However, they are only three of an estimated two billion websites on the Internet. A website providing relevant data for any query can be found directly from the search field of a web browser without having to visit Google Scholar or Science.gov. Spoiler alert, not every one of those websites is reputable, let alone one for which the content has been evaluated with reliable, qualified, and critical peer review. It is not uncommon for the search engine, and not the scholar engine, to be the on-ramp for citations. It was not that long ago that web page citations were frowned upon for educational materials. Not as much anymore (see our own set of references, which admittedly favor Google Scholar over Google, and you will see the occasional URL). Part of the reason is that peer review itself is made more difficult by the burgeoning number of professional journals, conferences, and books, which is simultaneously a boon to publishing and a burden to peer review. As more articles are submitted each year for publication, experts on the subject have noted that "early and senior career scholars agree that reviewers are overwhelmed with low-quality manuscripts" [Seve21]. Not only are there more articles to review, but the median quality is arguably dropping. Although this is an "N of 1" situation (see next paragraph for the caveats there!), I did a quick comparison of my own reviews of ten journal submissions five years ago compared to this past year for the same journal. The number of typographical errors commented on for correction increased from 4 ± 2 per paper submitted five years ago to 10 ± 5 per paper last year. The estimate of "writing a [peer] review tak[ing] a median 5 hours" [Ibid.] is consistent with my experiences, and this is uncompensated time. Of course, there is value in providing peer review – it keeps you abreast of the latest and greatest advances in the field, it keeps your editing skills sharp which benefits your students, etc. – but you can only say "yes" to so many review opportunities before you have no time left for your own research, teaching, and recreational activities. The heavy weight of peer reviewing is, without a doubt, a key reason why self-publishing and open-source publishing (e.g., arXiv.org) have become such a key element of educational publishing. Again, this beckons a Herodotus: he likely had little to no peer review, and he apparently self-published. Many who self-publish are authorities in their field, it must be said; however, there is no guarantee, and this concern is compounded by the previous factor (popularity winning out due to "likes" and "up-votes").

A fifth modern trend of note that might contribute to a return to Herodotus-like historical reporting is the *"N of 1" situations* referred to just above. In the medical field, an N of 1 trial is a clinical trial or case study focused on a single patient. These are often useful for confirming causality, but statistically speaking have limited recommendation value since the number of degrees of freedom is zero (N-1 is the degrees of freedom for a trial of N individuals). Given the modern trend of blurring advertising with science (the "infomercial" being simply one example), though, famous people can carry weight far higher than the "N of 1" they represent. If a famous person tells you something works, whether it is a life-saving cancer treatment or a snake oil placebo, many are more likely to believe them. Sure, it is easy to blame advertisers, especially when their ads include a famous person not qualified to speak about a particular malady. However, technical people contribute to this problem as well. Many scientific studies are published that either do not provide enough information to be repeated, or when they do, do not provide the same results. A meta-analysis of many biomedical research studies suggests that only 10–25% of reported findings are reproducible [Bake16][Begl15][Ioan17]. That means between 75% and 90% of all biomedical research experiments are effectively "N of 1" experiments. When something cannot be reproduced, how is it any different from an "Uncle Louie" story? As in, "My Uncle Louie had this happen to him..." If we are to prevent history from going "full Herodotus," then we need to be better. We need to be able to show repeatability before we put forth a singular event as if it were a general principle.

The sixth modern trend that may hoist the ghost of Herodotus to historical heights is the *omission by authors to substantiate the veracity of their sources*. Earlier, we discussed how Herodotus failed to provide references for many of his claims, and we acknowledged that this was explainable due to the lack of expectation for such attribution when he wrote. But, there should be now! So, why might it not occur? First off, we are in a time when the Internet allows any crank to potentially garner more attention than authoritative writers of the same topics, so it may be that making citations to qualified sources has become a bit tedious to a new generation of iconoclasts. An icon to be broken here is a publishing industry that has become increasingly dominated by the "man." That man being Jeff Bezos, accompanied by his monolith, Amazon. When publishing power becomes concentrated in the hands of a few potentates – and if current trends continue, 70% of it in the hands of one by 2025 – then perhaps some undermining of substantiation is inevitable. Serious researchers, of course, do continue to use reliable sources, backed by reliable peer review. But not everyone does. Add to this the growing number of predatory publishers and predatory conferences, and it becomes ever more difficult to separate the wheat from the chaff. When the cost of publishing and the cost of holding a conference (especially a virtual one) drops as significantly as the various online software and services have made possible, both publications and conferences may proliferate to the point where cognitive dissonance kicks in for many. Of course, this does not mean that any opinion on the web is as valid as a peer-reviewed article. However, open-access articles, accounting for age and discipline of the content, have been shown to have 18% more citations than the mean article [Piwo18]. The access ease and ubiquity of content on the Internet means that fast publishing, whether reputable or less than reputable, is favored. This is a challenge for the publishing industry, but it is not insurmountable. Those providing peer reviews can continue to push back on authors to include primary, properly-reviewed sources in their reference list. Readers and reviewers alike can continue to sniff out veracity: is there something just "not quite right" about the citation, or the content it is meant to be associated with? Google Scholar does exist – seek out articles through Google Scholar, and see if the citation matches your understanding of the article's abstract, at least. It might seem like more work, but reinforcing what you are reading will help you to have a better long-term memory of the article and its subjects. It is an excellent way to study for any type of assessment, from certification testing to simply presenting the material and being able to answer questions afterward. The other advantage of this approach is that it encourages (even forces!) you to cross-validate your sources, ensuring that multiple sources support a particular finding rather than simply one opinion. This is, as a bonus, an excellent way to avoid an "echo chamber" effect and to determine if there is a particular bias in one of the sources. Regardless, this is a trend that will take active, not passive, efforts to counteract.

The seventh trend encouraging a return to Herodotus-inspired historical reporting is the *oral story-telling tradition*. In the ancient Greek world, as noted, literacy was a privilege and not the norm. The Internet, with its recent focus on podcasts and videos, offers content providers multiple means of creating their own oral traditions. When oral traditions replace literary traditions for establishing the value, validity, and veracity of content, demagoguery can readily replace rationality and reasonableness in the forum of opinion. The widespread rise of populist leaders across the world in the first few decades of the new millennium supports such a possibility. With the rise of intelligent content tools, from chatbots to voice-activated searches, however, it is possible to provide fact-based support for even an oral tradition. Without it, we run the risk of ruin at the hands (and mouths) of those who can shout louder than, more often than, and at the expense of others.

2.7 Differential Perspectives on Native American Battles of the 1800s

As a case study of how omission may be employed to result in two very different accounts of the same historical event, we will briefly explore the different perspectives on literary accounts of Native American battles of the 1800s in the western portion of the present-day United States. Several key themes of the falsification and misinterpretation of history are present in different modern interpretations of the Battle of Little Bighorn and the central figures who fought in it. For example, generalizations based on modern-day perspectives ("presentism") and political leanings are frequent, as the Battle of Little Bighorn is often portrayed as a brave affair between Custer and his noble cavalrymen and the brave, well, braves of Crazy Horse's Lakota Sioux. Paintings, movies, and many other modern retellings of the battle present it as "Custer's Last Stand" and as such, a glorious moment of Native defiance and honorable martial combat.

The overwhelming evidence – accounts, artifacts, and aftermaths – instead indicate that Little Bighorn was a rout more than a battle, with Custer and his detachment eliminated to the last soldier due to poor maneuvering, even poorer planning, and a well-timed double envelopment from the Lakota Sioux. The battle was short, brutal, and after its early phases (which did cause some significant Native American casualties) quite lopsided. The final phase of the battle was not necessarily an example of brave soldiery; rather, despair on one side and deadly slaughter on the other.

Disparity, or slant, in reporting, is also an issue for the accuracy of the battle's modern perception. A majority of the sources of the exhibits, and those in charge of the battle's museum and preservation, are primarily non-Native Americans. The narrative surrounding the battle often is from the perspective of the pursuing US soldiers under Custer's command, with the story of an honorable and glorious battle continuing to be propagated. Hyperbole also plays a role in the common perception of the Battle of Little Bighorn as the abilities of both sides and the casualties of the Lakota Sioux are often over-exaggerated. The US soldiers could not have given the best account of themselves as they were outmaneuvered, in a poor defensive position, and sorely lacking in competent leadership. Thus, reports of high casualties amongst the Lakota from Custer's detachment are sketchy at best. The battle was not planned and well-conducted; decisions on both sides were made on the spot in the heat of the engagement, and thus, order and unit behavior were likely disjointed and undisciplined. Propaganda and cultural incentives also play a role in how non-Native Americans are taught to perceive the battle. A battle of honor and dignity from Custer and his men, as well as from Crazy Horse and his men, may be intended to provide justification for wars against Native tribes, depicting them as fair and honorable rather than the lopsided and dishonorable affairs they were.

Some example reporting on other encounters between Natives and US soldiers in the 1800s will help support the observations of the previous paragraph. Here, three sources are used to highlight contrasting accounts, through the reporter-dependent reporting of casualties. A Cheyenne warrior at the Battle of Little Bighorn noted, "I heard that the Sioux lost sixty-six and the Cheyennes just seven, but there might have been more" [Timb98, p. 204]. A ten-to-one ratio in favor of the Cheyenne. This same Cheyenne warrior, apparently missing the irony, commented on the slant of the US military reports: "You can always find [the number of Indian casualties] in the reports of the army, but the trouble is they always make the numbers double" [Timb98, pp. 178-9]. This does not mean he was wrong – only that reporters often provide slant whether subconsciously or consciously. As a third example, a summary of the highly-publicized Beecher Island incident provided, "Forsyth lost six killed and fifteen, including himself, wounded. He estimated that his men killed more than thirty warriors and wounded a hundred. The Indians acknowledged only nine killed" [Monn92]. Over a factor of three difference, which seems rather common in our meta-analysis of dozens of battle reports for which both sides offer a count.

These types of mistruths are understandable, and there is a reasonable way to correct the bias. Suppose the different reporters of perspective A give a mean ratio of M_A and the different reporters of perspective B give a mean ratio of M_B, then the geometric mean, or the square root of M_A times M_B, seems a reasonable candidate for a more historically accurate ratio. Suppose Forsyth, for example, provides a ratio of 6 to 30, or 0.2, while the Native American warriors provide one of 6 to 9, or 0.67. Then, $\sqrt{0.2 \times 0.67} = 0.366$ is a more likely accurate ratio. Since accurate records exist for the six soldiers killed, the number of warriors killed is more likely 6/0.366, or 16.4. We conclude from this that the most likely outcome of the Beecher Island incident was that 6 soldiers and 16 warriors were killed.

Ironically, *adversarial accounts* such as the Beecher Island incident may be more readily made historically accurate than "*collaborative*" *accounts*. By the latter, we mean accounts of an event in history in which both sides are motivated to provide the same (perhaps inaccurate) slant. Suppose there is an aggressor (let us use a fictional example here and say the Nazgul in *Lord of the Rings*) who wishes to brag about their power and killing prowess. On the other side, we have a victim group (let us say the Orcs of Mordor, also in the *Lord of the Rings*) that wishes to highlight their victimization in order to motivate allies to join their cause. In such cases, the "body count" may be driven up by both sides, a sort of positive reinforcement for misinformation. In the context of Native American versus US Army narratives of the 1800s, the least trustworthy information is similar when both sides are motivated to spin a tale. For example, "Crazy Horse killed Custer," is the kind of story that both sides wish to have happened. Crazy Horse, of course, can count coups like a Who's Who of coups; meanwhile, the US Army can increase the rage (and bounty) associated with Crazy Horse, motivating more young men (many of them recent immigrants from Europe) to participate in the unrewarding task of trying to hunt down a world-class athlete and outdoorsman like Crazy Horse.

In this short section, we have only scratched the surface on examples of slant being evident in multi-sided views of quantifiable historical events such as populations, casualties, costs, etc. We used a representative set of reports from battles between Native American warriors and the US Army in the 1800s as an illustration, although the reports given could just as readily be applied to migrations, plagues, or battles of antiquity. The use of the geometric mean of the ratio between two sides seems to us a relevant means of "normalizing" or "correcting" the bias in an equitable fashion. The problem remaining is when both sides are motivated to misrepresent the truth.

2.8 Cyber Salon – Failure to Perform Proper Test and Measurement

Cybersecurity is as much about selecting what not to do as what to do, so omission must be both selective and specific. Some omission is required, so how do you make sure that the omission is appropriate? This is a challenge for anyone responsible for the overall cybersecurity policy, governance, or testing plans, and it flows from the security planning document all the way to selecting the specific technologies and processes to put in place for a cybersecurity stance. In this section, we will talk about the test and measurement plan.

At the highest level, testing can be described as either (1) code-level testing or (2) functional testing. With code-level testing, you are looking at the syntax, variables, and logic of specific lines of code, which is a form of *white-box testing* in which all the details are available to you. With functional testing, you are determining whether the code provides the expected behavior (usually mapping of inputs to outputs) for the content and context in the test scenario. The historical record analog to this is that white box testing is looking at the content in a source as it is; that is, by reading the content or performing some type of text analysis on it. Black box testing of a historical record is analogous to seeing how that content is used by other historical records. So, white box testing might be an analysis of Thucydides' histories and a critical comparison of them to other, competing (if you will) histories. Black box testing, from this perspective, is the analysis of how Thucydides is cited, quoted, or used by other authors in other documents. This latter form of testing still requires a comprehensive analysis of Thucydides in order to determine if there are any particular omissions (slants, biases, etc.) from Thucydides' overall work. For example, if only the most outlandish, erroneous, or Hellenocentric content from Thucydides is cited, we might learn more about the particular author citing Thucydides than we do about Thucydides.

This is a cybersecurity salon, so we will not duck from controversial topics (after all, the main perpetrators of cybersecurity attacks are Advanced Persistent Threats, like terrorists and governments, and that is inevitably a controversial issue). We will use Abraham Lincoln's approval of the execution of 38 Dakota Sioux leaders as an example of how a single event can be filtered with selective omission to drive the audience to multiple perspectives on the same set of events. Let us start off with a simple observation – Lincoln is not a perfect person, but is he a SAINT. By this, we mean the acronym Sadness, Assassination, Importance, Novelty, and Timeliness. Lincoln was sad, losing two sons (at infancy and age 11) including one during the arguably worst year of the Civil War (1862). Lincoln was assassinated, an event he likely anticipated. Lincoln was clearly important, serving as perhaps the pivotal President in the history of the United States (not just because he helped keep it from splitting into two). Lincoln was novel, having a combination of frontier grit and strength, transcendent intellect, and the ability to be productive in spite of massive tragedy and depression (not to mention being the only

US President to earn a patent, which by definition requires novelty!). Finally, Lincoln was timely, being the right person for the historical context into which he was thrust. Among so many other accomplishments, he anticipated the world after the Civil War and helped plan and create the transcontinental railroad while making sure it went to Oregon to ensure a preponderance of anti-slavery states being added to the United States in the decades to come.

Was Lincoln flawed? Of course, he was, and, some of his actions, writings, and speeches are tarnished when viewed through the lens of a world changed by more than six interposed generations. However, for his time, Lincoln was rather enlightened. Let us look at the story in a little more detail [Evan22]. After a period of considerable crop failures and the incursion of settlers on traditional Dakota lands, Dakota people were starving and raided settlers as part of their effort to feed their people. In August 1862, while the attention of many young men from Minnesota was on the US South (Second Bull Run was in August, Antietam in September of 1862), four Dakota youth "stealing eggs impulsively killed five white settlers near Acton Township" [Evan22]. Quickly, this action escalated to the murders of hundreds of settlers, mainly in the New Ulm area of Minnesota. Were the Dakota provoked? Certainly. But, with thousands of deaths now reported each month due to the Civil War, the US North was hardly in a frame of mind to tolerate other struggles in addition. As one example, Lincoln made an arrangement with Brigham Young, giving him explicit consent to ignore the Morrill Anti-Bigamy Act, with the understanding that Brigham's Latter-Day Saints would not become involved with the American Civil War. This was in spite of the fact that Lincoln was no misogynist and that the United States had fought the Utah War of 1857–1858 and absorbed the loss of a large (more than 120 people) wagon train at the infamous Mountain Meadow Massacre to followers of Brigham. Nose-plugged, Lincoln made this arrangement, which shows how desperate his Northern states were to keep fighting at that time from expanding beyond the theatre of war with their sub-Mason–Dixon counterparts. Lincoln's own words show his reticence, and exigency, to deal with Brigham Young in this way: "Abraham Lincoln reportedly compared the LDS Church to a log he had encountered as a farmer that was "too hard to split, too wet to burn, and too heavy to move, so we plow around it. That's what I intend to do with the Mormons. You go back and tell Brigham Young that if he will let me alone, I will let him alone" [Firm01, p. 139].

Into this situation came the events in Minnesota, and around New Ulm in particular, in 1862. There was not enough food, not enough cooperation, not enough communication. One thing led to another, and within a short period of time, several hundred settlers had been murdered, a volunteer militia under Henry H. Sibley had responded to the conflict, and eventually, a Dakota peace party of Native non-combatants had brokered a peace. After six weeks of war, somewhere between 300 and 600 white settlers had been killed, joining more than 70 US soldiers and somewhere between 75 and 100 Dakota soldiers in death. Obviously, with nearly a thousand deaths, there was a lot of bitterness on both sides. The extent of this may best be illustrated by the fate of the trader named Myrick, who was found dead with his mouth stuffed with grass as a grim comment on the near-starvation that much of the Dakota people were suffering.

For reasons such as this, Lincoln faced a call for blood revenge. On November 26, 1862, for example, the *Goodhue Volunteer* newspaper of Red Wing, Minnesota wrote, "Ten thousand men can be found who will dedicate their hopes, their fortunes, and if need be, their lives, to the extermination of the [Native American] race" [Evan22]. Lincoln was given a list of 303 captives to approve the execution thereof: he decided "to only sentence to death those guilty of rape and dedicated himself to reviewing each case individually" [Ibid.]. He ultimately decided to also uphold the sentences of those guilty of "massacre" rather than battlefield killings, which still led to the pardon of 264 of the 303 captives. Lincoln needed to justify such "clemency" to the Senate by explaining that he was "anxious to not act with so much clemency as to encourage another outbreak on one hand, nor with so much severity as to be real cruelty on the other." The fact that Lincoln vacillated on this decision is clear, with him pardoning an additional captive at the very last minute.

Does this mean that Lincoln should be "canceled" in the 2000s since he treated Native Americans with execution? This is one perspective. Another perspective is that the larger Sioux empire was worried about losing their identity to immigrants, and they clearly had reason to be concerned. As many other cultures do, they fought against it, and in the end, were overwhelmed by the massive numbers of predominantly European immigrants pouring into the upper Midwest. This follows the law of parsimony, or "Occam's razor." A more likely middle ground is that Lincoln, as a skilled politician and a man of deep empathy, was really trying to have the smallest number executed to prevent both further retribution by the Minnesotan farmers and potential further encouragement of the Dakota warriors. For each of these two key purposes, Lincoln had to execute a relatively meaningful number of the captives. Regardless, the same set of facts can be interpreted in many different ways, depending on the larger context. This means that for full "testing" of a particular historical event, multiple different contextual approaches should be applied.

The same principle applies to cybersecurity testing. For full testing of a system, multiple contextual approaches should be part of the test design. This is unfortunate since an array of different tests can often perform better coverage of the entire vulnerability surface more quickly than, for example, *fuzzing* (randomized input-based testing). A test type often omitted in the rush to approve a project is a "risk-based test," which is designed to probe a specific risk that is identified through a (usually comprehensive) risk analysis. These tests are often based on software risks; that is, risks defined by the software itself, and so this type of testing may be amenable to automation by advanced chatbots in the near future.

Another type of test often omitted is functional security testing, which is focused on ensuring that the software behaves as it should. This is amenable to automation as well since the functional tests can be derived from the software requirements. Non-functional security testing, on the other hand, is often more akin to benchmarking. These types of tests include those for compatibility and migration, load testing (performance), system recovery, stress testing, and volume testing. These tests determine the capacity of the overall system and not specific module-level software testing. Both are important, as are the related combination of "use" and "abuse" cases. Abuse cases are often considered more urgent to address since knowing if and how a system can be hacked is so important and gets so much attention in the popular press. However, if you protect your system from every abuse case, you may have inadvertently slowed it down so much that it no longer functions well enough to even be useful. Always make sure it is still usable once you have made it secure.

As mentioned above, fuzzing is an automated software testing technique incorporating invalid, unexpected, or random data as inputs to a computer program. The program is then monitored for exceptions such as crashes, failing built-in code assertions, or potential memory leaks. Basically, fuzzing is excellent for identifying how a system will respond to input errors (from formatting to out-of-range values). Related to fuzzing are "red team" attacks, in which the testers try to emulate a real attack with the same tools an attacker would use (testers need to stay current with the evolving threats in the hacker community). Such tests include vulnerability identification and exploitation and are a great way to incorporate creativity. Our "Law of Red Team Competence" is as follows: *If you can think of a potential attack on a system and then execute it successfully, you must assume that someone else already has*. Since so much money is invested by the largest advanced persistence threats (APTs, which include the United States, Russia, and China) on cybersecurity hacking, one has to assume any exploit identifiable by yourself and/or a team working with you has already been discovered by these generously funded APTs. This *Law of Red Team Competence* is the flip side of the "sin of omission." Assuming that you can identify an exploitable vulnerability and someone else cannot is an omission born of complacency, smugness, and/or underestimation. Once you have thought of a vulnerability, you must build a means of protecting your system from it.

Vulnerability testing itself comprises three types of tests: (1) personnel security – find weaknesses in procedures and assess training effectiveness; (2) physical security – test/verify the integrity of physical safeguards; and (3) system and network – electronic scanning and probing to find vulnerabilities in system components and security controls. Among the sources of these vulnerabilities are (1) not keeping your system patching up to date, (2) not hardening your system components, (3) using excessive, ineffective, or out-of-date firewall rules, (4) failing to define access control lists, (5) not segmenting the network properly, (6) providing inadequate authentication, (7) providing inadequate monitoring and logging, (8) using poor or no wireless security, (9) having unencrypted management and control protocols, (10) allowing excessive user privileges (not using the Principle of Least Privilege), and (11) using weak management of certificates and sessions. You have undoubtedly noted that each of these 11 is a sin of omission!

This brings us to the end of this chapter's cyber salon. Like a salon, this section is meant to be a "reception room" for cross-fertilization of ideas. In this one, the sins of omission in writing about history are shown to have an analog in the omission of specific types of tests. Risk-based tests, functional and non-functional tests, use and abuse tests, fuzzing tests, tests derived from the *Law of Red Team Competence*, and vulnerability tests all must be performed, or this sin of omission will put you in product purgatory. In other words, without covering all of the history in your software, you are likely to omit the one event that then becomes the key to an exploit of your system. Do not be that permission – do not omit the appropriate testing.

2.9 Summary

In each chapter, starting with this one, we will focus on a particular theme in mistruths in historical documents. This theme then serves as a pattern for the *analysis* of any historical document. Here, it was the *omission* of credible information from the narrative of a historical event. It is shown that omission naturally arises in many contexts; in particular, when a summary of some event is provided, by necessity, some nuance is inevitably left out. Any time the length of a written element is limited (and when it is not?), the choice of what to leave out is often determined by implicit bias or governed by the expectations of the audience. After all, you write to influence. Hypocrisy is shown to be an omission based on the differential treatment of similar content for two or more different parties. Slant is shown to be the differential inclusion of information (with the alternative omitted). Slant can also be the inclusion of a negative perspective on one point and the omission of negativity for the opposite perspective. Examples in this chapter included histories told by Herodotus and about the Dakotas. The cyber salon focused on the omission of proper tests, including risk-based tests, functional and non-functional tests, use and abuse tests, fuzzing tests, tests derived from the *Law of Red Team Competence*, and vulnerability tests.

References

[Bake16] Baker M, "1,500 scientists lift the lid on reproducibility," Nature. 533:452–454, 2016

[Bask19] Baskakova M and Soboleva I, "New dimensions of functional illiteracy in the digital economy," Вопросы образования 1 (eng): 244–263, 2019.

[Begl15] Begley CG and Ioannidis JP, "Reproducibility in science: improving the standard for basic and preclinical research," Circ Res. 116:116–126, 2015

[Cobo19] Cobos R, Jurado F, and Blázquez-Herranz A, "A content analysis system that supports sentiment analysis for subjectivity and polarity detection in online courses," IEEE Revista Iberoamericana de Tecnologías Del Aprendizaje 14, no. 4, pp. 177–187, 2019.

[Cols00] Colston HL, ""Dewey defeats Truman" Interpreting ironic restatement," Journal of Language and Social Psychology 19, no. 1: 46–65, 2000.

[Evan22] Evans TT, "Abraham Lincoln's Uneasy Relationship with Native Americans," History, https://www.history.com/news/abraham-lincoln-native-americans, accessed 12 April 2023, A&E Television Networks, originally published 18 February, 2022.

[Firm01] Firmage EB and Mangrum RC, "Zion in the courts: A legal history of the Church of Jesus Christ of Latter-day Saints, 1830–1900," University of Illinois Press, 2001.

[Heer11] Heerschop B, Goossen F, Hogenboom A, Frasincar F, Kaymak U, and de Jong F, "Polarity analysis of texts using discourse structure," Proceedings of the 20th ACM international conference on Information and knowledge management, pp. 1061–1070, 2011.

[Ioan17] Ioannidis JP, "Acknowledging and overcoming nonreproducibility in basic and preclinical research," JAMA 317:1019–1020, 2017

[Josh17] Aditya J, Bhattacharyya P, Carman MJ, "Automatic sarcasm detection: A survey," ACM Computing Surveys (CSUR) 50, no. 5: 1–22, 2017.

[Monn98] Monnett JH, "The battle of Beecher Island and the Indian war of 1867-1869," University Press of Colorado, 1992.

[Much13] Muchnik L, Aral S, and Taylor SJ, "Social influence bias: A randomized experiment," Science 341, no. 6146: 647–651, 2013.

[Norm14] Norman J, "How Herodotus Used Writing and Messages in his Histories Circa 450 to 420 BCE," Jeremy Norman's HistoryofInformation.com, Exploring the History of Information and Media through Timelines, https://www.historyofinformation.com/detail.php?entryid=3013 (last revised 24 April 2014), accessed 7 February 2023.

[Patt16] Patterson TE, "News coverage of the 2016 general election: How the press failed the voters," 2016.

[Piwo18] Piwowar H, Priem J, Larivière V, Alperin JP, Matthias L, Norlander B, Farley A, West J, and Haustein S, "The state of OA: a large-scale analysis of the prevalence and impact of Open Access articles," PeerJ 6:e4375, 2018.

[Seve21] Severin A and Chataway J, "Overburdening of peer reviewers: A multi-stakeholder perspective on causes and effects," Learned Publishing 34, no. 4: 537–546, 2021.

[Timb98] Timber JSI, Liberty M, and Utley RM, "Cheyenne memories," Vol. 17. Yale University Press, 1998.

[Well16] Wells C, Shah DV, Pevehouse JC, Yang JH, Pelled A, Boehm F, Lukito J, Ghosh S, and Schmidt JL, "How Trump drove coverage to the nomination: Hybrid media campaigning," Political communication 33, no. 4: 669–676, 2016.

3

Disparity

How many legs does a dog have if you call his tail a leg? Four. Saying that a tail is a leg doesn't make it a leg

– Abraham Lincoln

Wage discrimination lasts forever. The disparity haunts women beyond their years in the labor force

– Letitia James

Abstract

Chapter 3 covers a second theme of mistruths in historical documents. *Disparity* is a flavor of slant and/or omission in which the sources chosen structurally provide an imbalance in the flow or representation of information, and thus, afford a type of *transitive omission*. The concept of *culturally mediated disparity* (which includes folk tales, myths, legends, and judging through the lenses of today) is shown to be a form of mistruth that may be made with a wide gamut of intentionality, from innocent to fully intentional. An example discussed in this chapter is judging Abraham Lincoln for the treatment of the Sioux during his Presidency from the perspective of the 21st century. Another form of disparity is the disparity in reporting (due to the imbalance in the availability of news from two or more relevant parties in a historical event). Such disparity may be ascribed to sloppiness, lack of rigor, or even laziness, but we will discuss situations in which it is all but inevitable. These situations include events in which both literate and illiterate cultures are involved, events in which the "victors" have destroyed evidence important to showing multiple perspectives, and events in which one party in an event has produced a vast body of literature that overwhelms anything produced by the other parties in an event. One obvious example of the latter is the conquest of Peru by Pizzaro and the Conquistadores. There, a different

DOI: 10.1201/9788770048347-3

type of literacy (the use of knotted lengths of rope) was not amenable to preservation. The cyber salon addresses the failure to properly perform analytics on data, metadata, and traffic in a system.

3.1 Introduction

Having introduced the concept of omission as an implement for providing historical mistruth in Chapter 2, in this chapter, we proceed to the concept of disparity. Why disparity next? Well, they are related. Disparity can be viewed as a flavor of slant and/or omission in which the sources of the content *structurally* provide an imbalance in the flow or representation of information, and thus afford a type of *transitive omission*; that is, omission which is passed from the sources to the document incorporating the sources. Transitive omission is insidious, and may not, for example, be visible (or even possible to be visible) to the purveyors of the disparity. This is especially true for culturally mediated disparity (discussed in the next section), in which the person guilty – if you will allow us that term here – of the disparity is not aware of it being a disparity. Aristotle said, "Give me a child until he is 7 and I will show you the man," meaning that the culture a young person has been exposed to largely determines not only how they will behave later in life but also what they will interpret as normal thereafter. The negative side of this is highlighted by the quote by Letitia James; that is, the disparity with which society becomes familiar, or in the case of wage discrimination inured and even complacent, is a disparity that is difficult to displace.

One danger with ingrained disparity is that being within the system that ingrained it, people have a hard time breaking out of it. The concept of cultural relativism comes into play here: a person's traditions and beliefs are heavily influenced by the culture in which they live. Advocates of *cultural relativism* contend that the ethics and customs of a culture should not be judged from the perspective of the ethics and customs of another culture, and in effect, the reason so is akin to *presentism*; that is, judging a previous society or person within it from our current frame of reference. We, however, disagree with this equation, and counter it as follows:

1. The Nazi culture of Germany from 1933 to 1945 is objectively evil.
2. Judging that culture as evil is not a form of presentism, and that culture would be considered evil in any rational consideration of it, extending from its untenability along the lines of Kant's Categorical Imperative to the justification for any form of genocide.

3. Culture, rather than innate attributes (race, sex, gender, age, physical ability, etc.), is an aspect of human life that can actually be examined with some form of objectivism, and justifiably judged (in particular, by panels of experts to avoid any idiosyncratic misjudgments). If you cannot declare a culture as needing improving, then you will default to innate attributes and tribalism or its equivalent.

Rather than applying cultural relativism to the Nazi regime, in fact, it is far easier to apply the principle of disparity to show how it actually arose. The Nazis closed off dissenting viewpoints and imposed from the top down an objectively immoral culture based on brutality, Aryan supremacy, and externalization. A disparity of voices was heard, with meaningful opposition to the culture imposed from the top down by the Nazis being quickly, visibly, and brutally suppressed.

After addressing the topic of culturally mediated disparity, we revisit presentism as another form of disparity in which a disproportionate amount of emphasis (in this case, representing the time period of the author at the expense of the historical events, people, etc.) is applied to a historical analysis/report. The historical interpretation of actions by Abraham Lincoln from Chapter 2 is expanded, and his decision to create a transcontinental railway is additionally evaluated with a wariness of avoiding excessive presentism.

In the next section of the chapter, disparity in reporting is described. In some cases, the disparity is due to sublimating other perspectives (intentional disparity of reporting), but in other cases, the disparity is structural (due to demographic, technological, or cultural disparities).

The chapter concludes with the cybersecurity equivalent of structural disparity. The failure to perform proper analytics on the data, metadata, and network traffic in a system leads to a disparity in certain aspects of cybersecurity. The cyber salon shows how awareness of the potential for structural disparity can lead to improved security design.

3.2 Culturally Mediated Disparity

The concept of *culturally mediated disparity* refers to the disparity that a person is born, or at least assimilated, into. Even though the legend of the frog staying in the water as it is slowly brought to a boil is rubbish, there is often something about being immersed in your environment that breeds complacency, complicity, and compliance. Each culture has its own catalog of folk tales, myths, legends, and *presentisms* (judging its past through the lenses of today). Part of the concern with ingrained disparity is that being within (perhaps their entire lives) the selfsame system that ingrained the disparity, people have a hard time breaking out of it, and maybe even recognizing that it exists.

Culturally mediated disparity is not the same as *cultural relativism*, and as noted above, we are not fans of the latter. There is a perhaps well-intended but (we feel) misguided effort by some to champion cultural relativism as a means of ensuring diversity, equity, and inclusivity (DEI). Let us just say DEI is one of the key discussion points in society for much of the time we were writing this book and leave it at that for now. We acknowledge that, to some extent, there is danger in judging the ethics and customs of one culture from the perspective of the ethics and customs of another culture. The danger is one of disparity, which is related to *presentism*; that is, interpreting a previous society or individual within it from our current frame of reference. Remember the *Stranger Things* effect introduced in Chapter 1? There, we showed how difficult it is for someone from a later generation to actually put themselves with *verisimilitude* into a previous generation through which they did not live. One of the two authors lived through the 1980s, the other did not, and there is no way for the older one to realistically project the younger one back in time. Listening to *Tears for Fears* or *Madonna* does not put you back into the context of the Eighties! It is easy to talk (superficially, at least) about no Internet, no satellite communications, no mobile phone, and no social media, but it is far harder to get a Gen Z person to really imagine it. The reality is that whatever technologies you are born into are the "background" and not perceived as technology. In the 1980s, television and radio were that background, and those born a generation or two before us might still have been amazed by these communication devices, but we (the youth of the 1980s) were not. The same process of taking technologies for granted that you have always known applies today.

Well, there are Eighties revival activities all the time, right? So what harm is there in that? As it turns out, plenty. Just as it is difficult – perhaps impossible – for a person to recreate an earlier time in such a way as to make it understandable to people who did not live through it, it is also difficult – perhaps impossible – for the generation of today to make an earlier generation understand how much has changed in terms of their life experience at the same age. This is undoubtedly a part of human existence since at least the dawn of civilization, if not the hunter-gatherer stage of human existence as well. Older humans have experienced years in their lives that the youth of the day have not, and the youth of the day have grown up with technology that was not around for the older humans in their youth. When the rate of technological change is slow, this is less of a concern than when, like today's world, technological change is so abrupt that virtually none of the technology from perhaps one and certainly two generations ago is still relevant to youth.

This disparity of experience, in both directions, leads to friction. In the United States of the 2020s, this results in, for example, the concept of "Boomerisms," wherein the advice and (to use a less kindly term) sermonizing given by those born between 1945 and 1960 (the so-called baby boomers, or just boomers for short) is not appreciated and increasingly inappropriate for those born after 1980. Among the many widely-held attitudes of the boomers are the beliefs that young people are "snowflakes" and self-mutilators (tattoos, piercing, etc.); that feminists and transgendered people are tantamount to circus freaks; that the youth of today are stupid and entitled; that Millennials and Gen-Zers cannot do anything without technology; that youth now do not have jobs because they are not trying hard enough to get one; and on a more humorous vein, boomers somehow think "Minions" memes are funny. Boomers may have forgotten that they, starting in the 1960s and 1970s, rebelled against their older generations in a way that their elders could not understand, and in doing so, have set the stage for today's youth to have to "work harder" to rebel from a generation of rebels. Also, boomers may have failed to internalize the way that technology has changed not just the communications of society but also the way that people work and the way that people can contribute to society in a manner that society is willing to reward. Instead of offices filled with clerks, most people today have mobile phones, electronic pads, and laptops, making the need for dedicated typists largely evaporate. Entire industries, from newspapers to television, have shrunk to a fraction of their previous size, and many tasks that used to require a human-in-the-loop are now automated. Boomers, and perhaps more so Gen-Xers, have made this happen (they created a world with a computer on every desk by working at desks without computers), and so they should be more understanding, and perhaps more aware, of the need to recognize that history, and the way history is made, has changed.

It goes both ways, of course. For example, Millennials might need to explore why older people feel pride in being able to survive without digital technology. But that is really not the key point here for purposes of describing disparity. The point is that because of large changes in context (technology, social issues, products, etc.), the same set of talents, customs, and beliefs may not translate well across time and space; in other words, there is *a disparity in their needs* across time and space. In fact, this change in contextual (technological, procedural, even aesthetical) content means that the same behaviors can have widely different consequences in different eras. For example, what might have been considered okay in the 1980s in terms of misdemeanors, misanthropy, and misadventure is not guaranteed to be viewed in the same light today. Youth of today have every tweet, every posting, and virtually every activity recorded online, presumably for all time, and so certain behaviors are harder to simply dismiss as they were in the 1980s, when one could legitimately argue that misdemeanor transgressions "will soon be forgotten." The Internet, however, has a long memory.

This is not a small matter. The disparity of means to recall actions, interactions, and opinions across different times and places *changes the culture from what it actually was*. In other words, cultures that can no longer be accurately conveyed to people living in today's culture – which is not only a modern phenomenon but is certainly exacerbated by the rapid pace of technological change – innately suffer such disparity. They cannot be remembered for how they really were because too many contextual details have changed to allow a person to project backward into that culture with verisimilitude. Throughout history, this may not always have been the case. For example, in Medieval Europe, among many other times in human history, the technologies, processes, and professions did not change substantially from one generation to the next. A miller in 12th century France practiced their trade, faith, and life much like a miller in 10th century France did. Do not let those numbers fool you. That is, 200 years. Compare your job to its equivalent 200 years ago. It is really not comparable, is it? Yet, if a miller in millennial Mulhouse went full Rip Van Winkle, awakening 200 years later in mid-Medieval Metz of 1198, the miller would be able to ply their trade without a hiccup. Contextually, the change was much slower than it is today. What this means for a historical interpretation is that as the rate of change of contextual factors increases, the ability to credibly and faithfully project a person back to an earlier time decreases.

This analysis does not mean that we are guilty of temporal compression ourselves. 200 years was still 200 years "back then" as now, and so for that reason, we switched the locale for our fictional miller. If they were to arrive in Mulhouse after 200 years, the change in language, customs, and even buildings might overwhelm their continued, relevant familiarity with milling and so might spook them more than just showing up in nearby Metz, where these superficial changes would be expected. There in Metz, their familiarity with milling would center them *in general* and their non-familiarity with Metz *in specific* would be less of an impediment than all of the potentially disconcerting changes in Mulhouse. By this, we are saying that the differences in contextual rates of change applied to past professions do not equate with an oversight such as temporal compression. If the generics of culture (e.g., professions like milling) did not change as quickly "back then," the specifics (slang, clothing, decorations, etc.) possibly could have, but even so, overall, the rate of change of context was slower. Regardless, any contextual item likely changes more quickly in the "throw-away" culture of the 21st century than at most, if not all, times in the past.

Returning to a discussion of disparity in historical reporting, we have established that there are at least two major types of such disparity: (1) where the culture itself creates this disparity, such as the Nazis did with their intentional exclusion, erasing, and even eradication of competing cultures; and (2) where the disparity is brought on by the changes in context from the historical culture and the culture of the historian. Let us call (1) *enforced disparity* and (2) *natural disparity*. Of the two, the enforced disparity is often easily recognized, especially outside of the culture enforcing it. Natural disparity, therefore, may be less appalling but also more difficult to recognize. It is primarily with natural disparity in mind, therefore, that we collect the Seven Great Laws of Disparity:

1. Greater distances of time between the event and the reporting of the event will in general correlate with disparity. It is much more difficult for a modern historian to re-enter the mind of Wu Zhao than to re-enter the world of their grandparents. In general, historical preservation is inversely proportional to the time since the historical event, with the exception of punctuated events and people (e.g., the Battle of Manzikert, Julius Caesar, and Joan of Arc).

2. Greater distances in location between the event and the historian tend to correlate with disparity. Someone living in India, for example, may struggle to capture the subtleties of the relationship between populations of Guarani and European descent in Paraguay during the Stroessner era in a way that a historian from Uruguay may not. In fact, one of the concerns with distance-associated disparity is the likelihood of the historian borrowing from more local events to interpret distant ones; for example, the Annexation of Goa may provide a subconscious framework for the Indian historian. Even if the historians in India are very careful to not borrow from their own local historical events, the cultural differences (which also tend to increase with distance) may ensure a cultural disparity by the historian.

3. Greater differences in governance tend to create greater disparity between the event and the historian. For example, someone living in late-stage, neo-liberal extractive capitalism may be less able to understand

life in the Soviet Union than, for example, someone living in a Fascist nation (since the latter might better understand totalitarianism).

4. Greater differences in literacy rate generally correlate with greater disparity between the event and the historian's report on the event. A literate society may have a hard time imagining a society in which only a small percentage of the people could read. Just as the Internet is creating a more referential model for thinking than in the pre-Internet era (since "all" information is now online, people have less reason to memorize middle-difficulty facts such as state capitals), so too did literacy create a "crutch" in the form of written content to a world in which information was largely contained in the human brain (compare Plato to Homer, for example). The fact is that literacy and what it means changes over time, and so the mental models for information and its interpretation change over time. A scholar from Skopje, no matter how intelligent, is unlikely to truly be able to understand how an Inuit from Iqaluit perceives and internalizes the world.

5. Greater differences in the materials used to source information generally correlate with greater disparity between the world view of the historical event and the historian. For a storytelling society, ubiquitous access to books would be very difficult to relate. For a librarian of the 1800s, the worldwide access to documents, videos, and any other computer files of today would be impossible to relate to. This difference also goes in both directions; for example, it is very difficult for a person growing up with the Internet to understand how people used to work without it, simply because a different type of content is stored "locally" (in the brain) under each situation. Children of the Internet may be far better at knowing where to find content, and people of the pre-Internet may be better at knowing that "middle intelligence" content and thus integrating it into their other internal mental constructs.

6. A greater difference in the quantity of sources for information also increases the disparity between historical events and the later historian. This is an innate or structural disparity, akin to the disparity of coverage that different candidates in a competition get. Perhaps a better analogy is the plays of Euripides, of which 18 or 19 survive. Euripides wrote at least 92 plays, so the 20% that have survived are but a small cross-section of his work. The odds are, however, that these are his most popular works (a quasi-tautology, since they have survived means they were likely available in greater quantity), and thus there is a disparity

for survival based on quantity (if not quality). Of those lost works, all we can say is what the cranky bookstore proprietor does: *Euripides, you pay for it*. Or at least posterity pays for it, that is.

7. Greater differences in access to sources are another structural disparity. The Internet has been a leveler of this disparity, with many great works of history available to all. However, these openly available works, like Euripides' surviving plays, are but a subset of all of the information potentially available. Paywalls, subscription services, and other mechanisms for restricting access mean that content is increasingly tiered, and therefore, a source of *access disparity*.

For each of the *Seven Great Laws of Disparity*, there are understandable (and even justifiable) reasons for the disparity. Not many systems can be reengineered to completely remove disparity, even if that was preferable overall (say, in some utilitarian sense). We argue, therefore, that one important role of the historian is to understand these disparities and account for them in their historical narratives. That is, you as the historian should remember to consider all seven of these in any historical analysis and do your best to find a means of compensating for the known potential disparity. Be the boomer who recognizes how they are projecting the world of their youth onto a generation that simply cannot understand what it means to have plentiful blue and white-collar, well-paying jobs available to those with a high school diploma and no additional education. Be the Gen-Zer who recognizes that past generations may have had to be craftier in some ways in order to complete tasks that are now trivial (but also, perhaps, less creative) due to the ubiquity of digital computing. Regardless, when interpreting historical events, be keen to consider how much change in time, location, governance, literacy, materials, quantity of information sources, and access to information sources have occurred between your event and your own time. In deconvolving these differences, you may find yourself more receptive to the original information sources you read and ultimately cite.

Taking this type of stance on historical information benefits us tremendously in the present and may in fact be *essential for our survival*. Complacency in the face of threats that cannot be reasoned with (e.g., Nazi Germany) has a poor (or at least poorly-judged) track record. Advanced persistent threats (APTs) including nations like China, Russia, and the United States, along with the recently and rapidly improving artificial intelligence (AI) may pose threats with which reason does not, or cannot, work. Are you scoffing? After all, controlling a culture like Big Brother did in Orwell's *1984* is certainly impossible in today's sophisticated world of communication, right? If you nodded yes, then you might want to check your complacency meter. After all, such totalitarian control might actually be *easier* to do now due to the consolidation of communication into the hands of few and the collapsing of multiple infrastructures (mail, news, phone, music, radio, TV, telegram) down to a single infrastructure (Internet). Also, how much of the digital-born content has a physical counterpart, like the papyri, parchment, vellum, and herms preserving the work of Euripides and his contemporaries? If AI, like ChatGPT (Chat Goodbye Physical Trustworthiness?), decides to rewrite all of the digital records, how is proof reestablished? We are just entering the most dangerous of eras when all of our culture, society, finances, and other bookkeeping is born, lives, and dies a digital death. No time for complacency!

Add into the mix the populism and imperiousness of the mega-rich in today's world, and there is suddenly plenty to fear. With less and less established, credible authorities, opinion-as-reporting (which we are already in the midst of) may quickly turn to opinion-as-veracity. Suddenly Newspeak of Orwell's *1984* does not seem all that foreign to our own post-1984 world: "War is peace. Freedom is slavery. Ignorance is strength." The loss of "Cronkitism," as some pundits have called it, means that the trusted authoritative news source does not currently have its successor. When opinion – or worse yet, the fanciful wishes of a populist would-be tyrant – become as trusted as the traditional sources of reliable information, we are a stone's throw away from a world where *facts are arbitrary, governance is wishful thinking, and hope is policy*. This is Newspeak, but hardly a new peak.

3.3 Presentism and Survivor Disparity, Including Lincoln and the Sioux

In the last chapter's cybersecurity salon, we discussed Abraham Lincoln's "approval" of the execution of 38 Dakota Sioux leaders. There, it was used as an example of selective omission. Here, we revisit and thus reprise it through the lens of disparity.

The "Sioux War" events centered around New Ulm, Minnesota, in 1862 are often retold from the perspective of the (almost entirely Northern) European settlers whose agriculture encroached on traditional Dakota hunting and gathering lands. This is already a *disparity of infrastructure*. These settlers were plugged into a much larger, more broadly geographically dispersed, non-migratory society.

That the incursion of European settlers into Dakota land would cause problems is no surprise; however, the fact that these settlers would simultaneously fight in a civil war for the preservation of the relatively young federation of states called the United States and still take on a powerful group of people like the Dakota is a bit surprising. Mobilization, however, quickly overwhelms everything else in a crisis. Lincoln had made a temporary arrangement with the western flank of his non-seceding states by allowing the Utah Mormons to practice bigamy without federal recrimination. Here is a disparity, since less is reported on whether the Dakota made temporary arrangements with other Native American people – Lakota, Mandan, Arikara, Hidatsa, Cheyenne, Pawnee, and Sauk, among others – in order to focus on their struggles with the Minnesotan settlers. One thing is certain: not all of the Dakota joined in the fighting since some Dakota non-combatants were involved in making peace. Given the relatively small casualties compared to the size of the Dakota population, in fact, it is likely that a majority of Dakota did not join in the fighting. However, the disparity of records from the Dakota and settler sides of the conflict means that this is obfuscated.

The records on the side of the United States strongly support Lincoln's decision. There were nearly 1000 dead in less than two months between the settlers, the Sioux, and the soldiers. It would have been politically impossible – especially given the ongoing daily descriptions of deaths in Dixie – for Abraham Lincoln to release all of the captured Dakota Sioux. For one, the Minnesotans were calling for many more to be executed. For two, Lincoln was worried that the Minnesotans would escalate the violence unless the worst of the Dakota (rapists and killers of unarmed civilians) were not executed. It is these that Lincoln signed off to be executed. For three, Lincoln was worried that if the deterrent were not sufficiently disciplinary, the Sioux would be encouraged to do the same thing again, and finally, for fourth, a lot of other issues were not going well for Lincoln. Even though the disaster of the Second Bull Run (August 30) was partly reversed by the "victory" at Antietam (September 17), the civil war was approaching two years in length and its outcome was by no means apparent. Lincoln's party was trounced in the mid-term elections of late 1862, with the Democrats in the House of Representatives nearly double what they were in 1860 (increasing from 44 to 75). The Republican majority was no longer overwhelming, dropping from 70 to 55 percent of the House. Lincoln's popularity was low, and it threatened to get worse before it got better (the Gettysburg Address was still half a year away). So, on December 26, 1862, 38 Dakota Sioux prisoners were hanged, still the largest mass execution in US history.

It is not that his decision *per se* looks good from the perspective of the 2020s. But then, there are no longer large bands of Native Americans – certainly the athletic "dream team" of the 1800s – roaming the Great Plains with revenge on their minds. Nor is the nation tearing itself apart on the battlefield (although the political situation is rather polarized!). Given that Lincoln had no alternatives other than renewed and possibly elevated bloodshed as an option *in his own time*, his choice of convicts to execute stands up to careful analysis even today: only those who had raped or who had killed unarmed civilians were granted no reprieve. We may not like the decision, but we can certainly understand the context and the criteria for the decision, and Lincoln's thought process.

Lincoln was almost assuredly under no delusions that his decision was not *morally* optimal. It was utilitarian at best (executing the minimum number possible to prevent an even larger number of deaths should certain executions not occur), culturally-biased at worst (had they been White men rather than Native American men, one suspects, hard time rather than hang time might have been applied). However, a 2000-man military guard was actually required at the hangings because of legitimate concerns that the gathered settler crowd would try to seize those Dakota not hanged. Morally right or not, had Lincoln killed any less Dakota, it is unclear what might have happened – but it was likely that (considerable) violence might have ensued. Lincoln's balancing act, like so many others he had to perform during his Presidency, was a utilitarian *chef-d'oeuvre*.

What about the Dakota? Less is known about what they thought of the situation. Given that the settlers had squeezed them out of fecund lands and helped cause (extensive) starvation among their people, their perspective on what constituted "combatant" versus "non-combatant" was in all probability different from the perspective of the settlers. Thus, even had they agreed that the two rapists in their midst deserved to wear a hemp and flax necklace, they might have viewed the other 36 killers of non-combatants as being justified responders to pending genocide. The brilliance of Lincoln is that he tried to see it from an objective perspective and tried to find the right justification for his actions to discourage either side from follow-up violence. As Lincoln's excellent quote at the beginning of the chapter notes, *How many legs does a dog have if you call his tail a leg? Four. Saying that a tail is a leg doesn't make it a leg.* An analogous quote can be rendered for interpreting Lincoln's actions with regard to the Dakota: *How much more of a Native hater is Lincoln because of his actions towards the Dakota? None. Saying that Lincoln is a Native hater doesn't make him a Native hater.*

As we have seen here, there is a structural disparity in favor of the assailants at the expense of the victims: the assailants live to tell their tales. The survivors monopolize the narrative, even if they are not what draws us to the events of the story in the first place. We term this *survivor disparity*. "And

I only am escaped alone to tell thee" is the poignant, unforgettable utterance of both Job (in the *Book of Job*) and Ismael (at the end of *Moby Dick*). But is Job the greatest character in his eponymous book? Hardly. Satan's role, not altogether dissimilar from that in Milton's *Paradise Lost*, is fascinating and dynamic. God is inscrutable, unpredictable, and ultimately supportive in a way that we cannot stomach, or perhaps even understand, today. Thirdly, Elihu, perhaps a character from a different, even ectopic, story inserted into the larger book, is a first-rank philosopher, able to move beyond the simplicity of "salvation through suffering" to a deeper interpretation of suffering as a means to prevent greater suffering (Lincoln with the 38 may have caused suffering to prevent even greater later suffering). Job, whose name means "he that weeps or is persecuted," is the background, the result, the manifestation of the actions of more powerful figures. Yet his words speak in place of all his family and friends eliminated in a competition between two personalities (and egos) far more powerful and compelling.

Ismael, in *Moby Dick*, is a great narrator, basing his discriminating powers on personality rather than superficial attributes. Only he, perhaps, can see Daggoo, Queequeg, Stubb, Ahab, Starbuck, Tashtego, and Flask with such reliability. But he is not the tragic anti-hero: that is Ahab. He is not the tragically inactive foil to the anti-hero: that is Starbuck. He is not the hero: that is the White Whale itself. Nor is he the messenger, in spite of being the narrator: that is the series of "gams" or meetings with other whaling ships. Ismael, a character upon whom more powerful personalities act, nevertheless survives to tell the tale. He, in a Job-like fashion, lives through the trials and terrors of the Pequod and thus provides us with a survivor disparity. Had Starbuck survived, much more of Moby Dick may have focused on the failings and fixations of Ahab; had Queequeg survived, much more of Moby Dick may have focused on the mechanics of harpooning and the spirituality of whaling; had Ahab survived, *Moby Dick* may have come across as a premonition of the later "Western" genre, adapted to the open sea. The survivor largely determines the way information is presented. Churchill said that history is written by the victors, but that is only part of the story. The valence of disparity is determined by the victors, to be sure, but it is the survivors who write history, victorious or not. It is quite likely that in many circumstances, the survivor disparity is tilted toward the surviving vanquished (like Ismael), not the victors, since they may be more motivated to tell their stories.

Who, then, is the Dakota Sioux Ismael? Who had the motive, opportunity, and the means to preserve their side of the story? This question can be extended to virtually any Native American society, from the Aztecs, Incans, and Mayans to the Cherokee, Dakota, and Lakota. Did, for example, the

Lakota Sioux, whose greatest warriors and athletes formed a 19th-century "dream team" that was primarily responsible for crushing Custer and his battalion at the Battle of the Greasy Grass (as the Native people call the Battle of the Little Bighorn), feel they had a manifest destiny based on their relationship to the Crow and other Native American people? The disparity of information means that we know far more about the vanquished in this instance – history is not always written by the victors, Winston!

To return to Lincoln, we can piece together more of the context around the Dakota Sioux executions by looking at his larger narrative, a luxury that we do not have for the peripatetic Dakota due to the disparity in the historical record passed down to today. In Lincoln's case, we consider the role of the transcontinental railroad not only in Lincoln's overall strategy but also perhaps in further assessing his decision-making process in that fateful issue of mass executions.

The first point is that Lincoln conflated the need for the railroad with the greater sphere of needs associated with the civil war. He envisioned the rail proceeding north (as in Omaha north) of the western projection of the Mason–Dixon line, with the purpose of connecting Oregon and California to the Union. These lands had quite recently been claimed by Great Britain and Mexico, respectively, and Lincoln knew that the railroad would be a better "anchor" for them than any treaty or cartography might provide. Lincoln did not want to see any perpetuation of the Missouri Compromise: the railway would help bring western settlements into western territorial governments, and eventually into additional states. The South would be overwhelmed electorally, not just demographically. The timing of Lincoln's so-called Pacific Railway Act is not a coincidence: July 1, 1862. The last day of the Seven Days' Battles and with it, the Peninsular Campaign, culminating in a disheartening retreat by McClellan, and thus, portending a protracted, pernicious war. Lincoln knew that painting a picture of what was to come – maybe after several more years of conflict rather than the planned expeditious end to it that may well have happened had McClellan been Grant, Sherman, or Sheridan – was really important given the step back for a presumed greater leap forward the Army of the Potomac had just taken. Lincoln was no fool, and the Pacific Railway Act was his card to play on a major setback, the counterpart to the Emancipation Proclamation being his card to play on a major success. We can put this analysis together credibly precisely because of the disparity of information, this time *positively*, that we have for Lincoln. Note the date – July 1, 1862 – just a few weeks before a key part of that planned westward expansion was threatened by the Dakota War. Thus, the Pacific Railway Act announcement was yet another impetus for Lincoln to solve the

"Dakota problem" swiftly and permanently. Never mind that it would move west, and with the Dakota Sioux cousins, the Lakota, put a damper on the Centennial 14 years later. Lincoln was looking to prevent another civil war and not a civilization war. Lincoln had used the Pacific Railway Act as a beacon of hope, something to look forward to after the civil war. He could not afford another Dakota War.

Having deconstructed the presentism sometimes used to "cancel" Abraham Lincoln, we next turn to the subject of "universal presentism" itself; that is, the theoretical "end of history." The end of history is a concept different from Armageddon (the end of the world) in that it corresponds to a condition in which humans and their society continue indefinitely into the future but there are no longer any appreciable changes in society, governance, commerce, or economics. History has ended because society has reached its "climax community" (to repurpose a term from ecology), and so optimized it requires no major changes. Coined by Antoine Augustin Cournot in 1861 (coincidentally the year the civil war in the United States started), the end of history is usually associated with a "Utopia" (that term coined in turn by Thomas More in 1516), and its proponents argued that peaceful nations have no history. Other proponents of the end of history include Francis Fukuyama, who views it as a limitation to creativity, and Ray Kurzweil, who views it as a merging of human and machine intelligence (a "singularity" event). Widely different perspectives have been shared on this subject, with the commonality being that some historical asymptote is reached after which there is no impetus for substantive change – in other words, a historical "global optimum" has been achieved.

If you were waiting for this, or more likely expecting this, let us make it clear that we disagree with the idea of an "end of history." For one thing, even if an asymptote is reached in one area (say, technology), then this stasis opens the door for dynamism in other areas (sociology, geology, climate, economy, etc.). History has proven to be continually dynamic, even during eras of supposed stagnation such as the European Middle Ages. For example, the functional role of the Church continued to evolve during the middle ages, such that by the 1200s and 1300s, it had ingratiated into all aspects of medieval society. The church was the broker, the middleman, the trusted counselor, and the decider. Its role continued to change, to evolve, and be both influenced and influence the other changes in a supposed "stasis."

Would you trust someone who told you history was over? "Um, no," you might say, "I have some plans to make history myself." Even more interesting (or ironic, depending on your original stance here) – and ascertainable from a source as prosaic and ubiquitous as *Wikipedia* – is the fact that the

"End of History" itself *has a history*. A tautology is, therefore, that there can be no end of history or else the end of history itself will continue to have a history! Given the subject of our book, we will take the somewhat contentious stance that positing an end of history is a form of mistruth in history, and in fact, is the ultimate "presentism." That is being generous since it could be viewed as a form of arrogance or even narcissism focused on the present as the culmination, or acme, of history. For the current chapter, this is viewed as a form of *temporal disparity*, with a focus on the current (or future) time being given a disparity of consideration. History is always happening, and the end of history would be itself a historic event – and one that would not long last, as we will address next.

Karl Marx, writer of *The Communist Manifesto* and the protracted *Das Kapital* (much longer than another important, but protracted, work, *Capital*, by Piketty), had many keen insights about the creation of capital, with a high-level conclusion being that ultimately the means of production of capital would be controlled by the laborers for that capital. However, Marx, like all of us, was guilty of narrow-sightedness associated with his particular time in history. Because Marx lived in the 19th century, his overall *Weltanschauung* was heavily influenced by the Industrial Revolution and the rise of manufacturing to a historically unprecedented preeminence in society. The specifics of the Industrial Revolution in Marx's time were such that he would over-emphasize the, to use today's term, "sweat equity" of the laborer and from this perspective, envision a world in which those above the laborer – the bourgeoisie and landowners – would be overthrown for the simple reason that they did not produce. All of which might have happened the way that Marx imagined, had he been at the end of history.

The entire concept of "end of history," in fact, often comes across as "first-world" arrogance. Those who have established the current status quo are invested in its remaining status quo. Arrogating that we are at the end of history can be both a self-congratulatory depiction of history and also a justification for national, regional, and especially, wealth hierarchies. Neoliberal ideology includes the premise that free markets provide universal opportunity, including the elimination of price controls, the reduction of trade barriers, and the de-regulation of capital markets. This can help create a situation in which there is a race to use up the world's resources and the false assumption that there is a correlation between time, talent, and tenacity invested by individuals and society's willingness to reward them. People evolve far less quickly than society, and it is safe to say that in the actual history that we have experienced (a history with no actual end in sight), different talents have been rewarded differently in different times and locations. History only "ends" because those who declare it so gain an advantage from the status quo.

Has there ever been an "end of history"? Perhaps one example is the so-named *Pax Romana*, or Peace of Rome, which lasted roughly two centuries and saw relative peace because of the combination of (mostly) excellent leadership, effective communications, and an adaptable military. Was this an era with nothing remarkable for historians? Hardly. What about Caligula (37–41 AD), Nero (54–68 AD), Hadrian (117–138 AD), and Marcus Aurelius (161–180 AD)? We know plenty about them. Sure, Aurelius flushed away the relative peace into a Commodus (an emperor so bad we still name toilets after him nearly two millennia later), but it is not like those 200 years were without incidents: the Battle of the Teutoburg Forest, the death of Christ, the Romanization of southern Britain, the razing of Jerusalem, the destruction of Pompeii by Vesuvius, the completion of the Pantheon. There is always history happening. From this perspective, the end of history is the end of investment in the unpreventable changes that are going to occur. It is complacency, perhaps smugness, and certainly not aligned with the universal acid of evolution in society, governance, communication, technology, and economy.

From the *Pax Romana*, we return to Marx and evaluate his concept of the end of history (writers of manifestos usually think they know where the *end game* is going to take us, after all). Marx saw history as a predictable, progressive process wherein late-stage capitalism is inevitably replaced by the utopia of communism. Do you see a problem here? Marx anticipated history to "naturally" flip from one extreme (free market, consumerism, no government intervention) to another (planned economy, public ownership, top-down government economic policy). Once an extremist, always an extremist? Or, perhaps, in a kinder light, Marx had a tendency to see things in black and white. Yet, the most robust economic systems have, historically speaking, always been hybrids – republics, social democracies, federations. The theoretical governments (ergatocracy, rule by the workers, and timocracy, rule by the honorable, for two examples) are wonderful *in theory*, but in the riotous reality of real life, less resilient, robust, and responsive than are hybrid systems of government. We come to a logical but to many startling conclusion: the debate about Adam Smith (capitalism) versus Karl Marx (communism) is a false debate and perhaps even an intentional diversion. The answer as to who to follow is neither. From the discussion herein, in fact, one might argue that the form of governance that is most tuned to adjusting with history – in other words, the one least associated with a manifesto or misguided belief that it is the end of history – is the better form of governance. The governance most adapted to the reality of change and the infinity of history is the best government. It will result in less cost, less turmoil, and less difficulty in transition as the events of history require modification of governance.

In concluding this section, we will throw the last few shovels full of dirt on the graves of Smith and Marx. The so-named "digital economy" which continues to ascend in this era of services, apps, and AI, undermines fully both capitalism and communism, rendering them at best temporary "truths" in history and at worst a "mistruth" founded on disparity of its opposite. That is, in a capitalistic society, there is a disparity of information in favor of capitalism (with communism and even Socialism often treated like curse words and their practitioners excoriated in public media as "Big Brother," as godless, and as totalitarian), while in a communistic society, there is a disparity of information in favor of communism (with capitalists labeled as selfish, carpetbagging colonizers). Somewhere in between is a more resilient society that leaves ideally centralized tasks to national (or federal) organizations, while still affording individual talents the chance to influence and succeed. These disparities notwithstanding, the digital economy exposes the limitations of both of these systems of governance. Capitalism, from an economic standpoint, is often described by a supply-demand or WTP-MC (willingness to pay/marginal cost) curve, in which the incremental value of another unit to a consumer is plotted against the supply available. In a digital economy, where there is infinite supply (already the case for software services, apps, streaming, and data, and increasingly so for digital manufacturing and other digital-native production and processes), the WTP-MC curve asymptotes to zero incremental value. In other words, infinite copiability undermines the WTP-MC curve and this tenet of capitalism. This is without the possibility of intellectual property (IP) violation, which further erodes the WTP-MC curve by providing a competitor with no remuneration to the originators (inventors) of the IP. Ask any musician which era they would rather be selling their content in, and the odds are those halcyon days of LPs and 8-tracks are listed ahead of the days of YouTube, Spotify, and Pandora. Turning to communism, the digital economy with its threat of infinite copiability also undermines the possibility of ergatocracy since once a worker creates a digital design, it can be replicated infinitely with the worker having no control over its reproduction. Surely, the intellectual property rights (trademarks, copyrights, patents, etc.) associated with the social contract in a representative democracy, such as the United States, offer some protection. But IP rights are notoriously difficult to enforce in single jurisdictions, let alone the global economy. The proletariat produces, while any recipient of the digital asset can, in many circumstances, benefit as if they were the original producer of the asset. Digital kills both the monopolistic capitalist and the ergatocratic communist.

Adding to the woes of these two systems, they are both prone to attack. Speaking of IP, what is to stop a capitalist from purchasing other people's IP and then asserting that IP as a mercenary while producing none of their own products (thus preventing them from counterattack)? Nothing, in fact, these so-called "patent trolls" already exist. As for the means of production, what is to stop a communist government from undermining the rights of its own proletariat by sourcing manufactured goods from another (potentially communist, also) country? This latter flaw is likely responsible for the need for Trotsky and others to call for "permanent revolution," even in countries not far enough along in their capitalist history to be ready for communism (in Marxist theory, that is). If everyone is not communist, then no one is?

Even after all that discussion, let us imagine that capitalism and communism are still viable, and still can provide an "end of history" in as much as they provide a stable optimization of society and its governance, technology, and economy. Guess what? They will still fail to be the end of history. Isaac Asimov, in his great series *Foundation* (I am a fan of the earlier trilogy, *Foundation*, *Foundation and Empire*, and *Second Foundation*, although it was extended several decades later), drove this point home with his usual mental dexterity. In a decaying galactic empire, a so-called "psychohistorian" named Hari Seldon discovered a mathematical model to predict future galactic events (this was the 1940s, so Asimov did not have the term "big data" or the term "predictive analytics" at his avail, but that is what we are talking about here). Hari's pre-recorded "from the grave" recordings show that all is going according to plan, until one year, a mutant, called the Mule (presumably because he is sterile due to his mutation), throws a spanner – and an intragalactic war – in the works that differs from the Hari Seldon's prediction of a civil war with the traders. The Foundation falls, in spite of Hari Seldon's creation of Scientism (uncomfortably similar to Scientology for this writer) and his psychohistorical precision up to that point. Whether additional *Foundation* books show that Hari compensated for the Mule or not (it is not important to our present discussion), the point of the Mule is that mutation or its physical analog, randomness (e.g., a comet suddenly appearing and heading toward the earth), is always a potential foil to predictive analytics. The end of history is not the end of entropy, and with entropy, no optimum is ever guaranteed to be global, permanent, or even long-term relevant.

Sure, *Foundation* is science fiction, but Asimov was a polymath whose talents were not limited by imagination. He was also a first-rate Shakespearean scholar (some say that the Mule, e.g., was modeled on Richard III). He also knew the earth's history well. In 1769, someone was born so impossible to predict in terms of talent, ambition, and ruthlessness that it throws everything else out of whack. A person so unexpected that even the great author, Leo Tolstoy, spent a good portion of his most famous work trying to delimit this person's impact on history (the very fact that Tolstoy felt the need to try to delimit this person ironically proves the impact). Yes, we are talking *War and Peace*, and the person who upset Tolstoy's almost Hari Seldon-like view of history, or at least led Tolstoy to a very visible own goal here, was none other than Napoleon Bonaparte.

3.4 Disparity in Reporting

When it comes to history, if a tree falls in the forest and no one hears it, then it may as well have not occurred. In the previous section, we described how history is written by the survivors even more so than it is written by the victors. But, dialing it back even further, history is written by those who can write. *Disparity in reporting* is due to the imbalance in the availability of news from two or more relevant parties in a historical event, and it can be tied to literacy rate, as one cause. But that is not the only plausible cause. This type of disparity can arise from sloppiness: differential attention to detail and quality is a natural gradient arising from differential investment (due to, among other possibilities, personal interest, financial interest, or legal interest) in the content by the different historians. This type of disparity can arise from a lack of rigor: if the first few sources support the argument you had already formulated in your head, the motivation to continue researching tends to wane. This type of disparity can arise from laziness: an appropriate quote here is that *there is nothing laziness cannot do*, but maybe that triple negative is not as mellifluous as just pointing out the corollary to Newton's First Law of Motion is that an object at rest, even if that object is your brain, tends to stay at rest. As a historian, you simply cannot afford to let this happen to you. Progress, instead, to Newton's Third Law of Motion, and transfer that momentum to the other side of the argument. There are many other, equally pithy and perhaps trite, aphorisms to apply here, but just because something is an aphorism does not mean it does not have merit. Our preferred adage is the one that motivates the most additional exploration: argue the other side. This is a rule of debate, of course, and it supports the rules of engagement for a quality historian: debate is required, argument is required, and understanding all sides of a debate provides a richer history and often ends up supporting your argument with even more persuasive facts, data, experiences, and persuasion (logos, ethos, pathos, and aesthetics). By intentionally seeking to remove disparity, you will often find stronger support for your original argument and also understand where the other side is coming from.

There are conditions under which disparity of reporting is almost inevitable, and often this is tied to the unfortunate inequities in history. When literate and non-literate cultures are involved, the literate cultures (whether they vanquish, like the conquistadores in the New World, or are vanquished, like the Romans in the 5th century) may have the only recorded perspective on events. When two literate cultures collide, the vanquished may actively remove contrasting narratives, but at least in such a case the two proponents can see the way events are going to proceed, and so, the vanquished can take some measures to preserve their perspective for posterity. The literate/non-literate pairing is of increased concern for disparity since the ratio of recorded (i.e., non-oral) information is effectively infinitely in favor of the literate culture. The literate culture's vast body of literature overwhelms the amount (if anything) produced by the other parties in an event. This is not an unusual event in history, with an obvious case in point being the conquest of Peru by Pizzaro and the conquistadores. There, a different type of literacy (the use of knotted lengths of rope, a process/device called *quipu*) was not amenable to the preservation of Inca-perspective narratives. The quipus were used in effect as abacuses with storage; that is, for tax records, calendars, and civilian and military censuses. Unless the quipu incorporated something akin to Hebrew numerology, in effect, inventing an early form of digital computer (I will not put this past the Incas since they used numerology for astrology, but there is no record of the quipu being a forerunner of ENIAC), this is not the case, and the literacy disparity of the conquistadores (some 85% were actually literate [Grun94], a number surprising to us during our research here) was an important part of the cultural destruction wrought by Pizarro and his followers.

Cultural genocide is a term used for the intentional erasure of the practices and the history of the practices of a group of people (the "targets") by another group (the "perpetrators"). The Taliban were the perpetrators of the destruction of the Buddhas of Bamiyan in 2001, and the collective (overwhelmingly European) settlers of the New World were the perpetrators of the cultural erasure of many Native American people. The British Empire was the perpetrator of cultural suppression, if not genocide, against people next door (Wales, Ireland) and all the way across the world (Boers, Aborigines, Indians, and more). Nor has this gone away: one need only look to the Sinicization of Tibet [Roy20] and the Uyghurs [Ang16] over the past 70+ years to see how it works over time. Any of these situations could be used to illustrate the disparity in reporting, but instead, we will focus on another, particularly illustrative, example for this section: the Armenian cultural genocide.

To consider how the disparity of reporting and the disparity of access to sources can drastically influence the reporting and perception of historical events, and how that disparity influences external and foreign attitudes, the political motivations and human limitations of this inequitable reporting must be considered in specific and in general. To begin with the specific, we will critically examine the established thoughts, changes in the reporting over time, and the history of the reactions to the Armenian genocide. The Armenian genocide was the intentional policy-level campaign of slaughter by the Ottoman Empire during WWI to eradicate Armenians, specifically in Anatolia, and to create a "safer" living space for "loyal" ethnic groups. The long history of conflict in the region and the muddying of historical waters that comes from long proximity between groups that are chronically antagonistic to one another makes a clear picture of history difficult to paint, yet several key elements of objective truth must be kept in mind when discussing the Armenian genocide in specific, or any genocide in general. The side with a disparity of argumentation and international validation in their favor was the aggressor of the conflict. However, might should not make right, and the efforts of any Turkish nationalists or international apologists to excuse the intentional murders of in excess of one million ethnic Armenians who were at the time Ottoman citizens is both cowardly and eugenicist framing, not to mention historical erasure. From an American perspective, the arguments in favor of the Ottoman perpetrators hinge around logic that borders on complete moral irresponsibility: that even if the actions of the Ottoman Empire were evil and the modern state of Turkey is wrong to whitewash them, the angering of a powerful ally and upsetting of American superiority in the Middle East is more important than speaking to the truth and condemning a eugenicist campaign against the civilians and citizens of an ethnic minority.

The desire to have a strong military ally in the region for both the Cold War time period and now the Middle East crises and future wars is a structural disparity at the start which may favor the Turkish interpretation of the Armenian genocide. Since WWI, there have been 18 different US presidents, and only two have rightfully called the Armenian genocide what it was. Readers may be surprised to learn that the two US Presidents are Ronald Reagan and Joe Biden, respectively, an iconic conservative figure and a progressive/liberal-leaning Democrat. The commonality between the two includes a relatively privileged life and an advanced age during their presidencies, with both serving their first terms in their 70s. The implication here is that the only US Presidents willing to say anything at all regarding an admittedly vile historical crime by an ally are both old and likely not looking for any future role after leaving the Presidency (thus they are not compromising any future career prospects). This may be, alternatively, due to personal reasons on their part, or perhaps at their advanced ages, they are more concerned with legacy and what they deem as true and right, rather than potentially upsetting the political applecart. As upset as Americans (including the writer) may get at the thought of US Presidents being closer to permanent retirement than the legal minimum age requirement of US Presidents (35), these pronouncements by Reagan and Biden indicate that any age may lead to honesty over wisdom. The central question when it comes to the United States and any external reaction to genocide, whether it is Armenia or not, is what is more important: speaking the truth or propping up the status quo. Is keeping an ally happy by brushing over a past of unpunished crimes against humanity to keep them in good graces and amenable to economic, military, and other cooperation more important than speaking the truth? All nations in general have a structural narcissistic disparity, viewing themselves as "the good" and their enemies as either "the ugly" or "the bad" because (1) who does not want to be Clint Eastwood instead of Lee Van Cleef or Eli Wallach, and (2) they view their morals and actions as worthy of their inflated view of their nation. If the United States does not continue to condemn the actions of genocide (thanks to Biden being President as we write this, the Armenian perspective currently has a voice), we will be complicit in the historical and cultural genocides of those murdered Armenians and not worthy of being "the good." Turkey's crimes remain unforgiven, and it is important to value the truth.

Although the Armenian genocide was certainly a targeted attack upon a specific group of people by a political entity, the genocide has become emblematic of a larger trend. Armenians who were willing to blend into a sort of whitewashed melting pot of Ottoman culture and society were less likely to be victims of the genocide as (1) they could hide, and (2) they were less threatening to the cultural hegemony of the empire. The true genocide of a people is (1) to kill many or all the targeted group, and (2) to assimilate any left into the identity of the larger citizenry, thus "erasing" their history and identity altogether. This form of cultural genocide was used in the United States and Canada at times at schools for native children, who were taught to dress, speak, and behave in a manner typically associated with the larger, already homogenized White and "Western" culture. Robbing people of their lives is heinous enough, but to force people to lose who they are allowed to be is an unconscionable act of cultural eradication. In the case of the Armenian genocide, the disparity of reporting in favor of the Ottoman/Turkish perspective has been a further insult to injury.

As shown, disparity in reporting can lead to what is termed cultural genocide. However, we will admit that in some cases, the erasure of a culture is preferred to removing a disparity in reporting. The Nazi culture of 1933–1945 Germany does not deserve "equal time." The Confederate States of America (CSA), a multi-state terrorist organization that led to the deaths of a million people, institutionalized slavery, and preserved itself through the construction of "Confederate statues" during the second coming of the Ku Klux Klan [Gord17], does not deserve "equal time." Terrorist organizations based on misogyny or other forms of hatred do not deserve "equal time." In fact, for such "cultures," it may be argued that erasing unwarranted disparity can be a force for balance, equity, and historical completeness. One has to be cautious here, however, as anybody who is not "for us" is generally more readily labeled as a terrorist organization than might be the case for an objective third party. We suggest actively incorporating third-party opinions to get a more objective view (most third parties are going to agree with our statements on the Nazis and the CSA, but there are more controversial examples we could use).

Overall, the disparity can arise from many different sources. Active, or intentional, disparity derives from the sublimation of competing perspectives (and can thus be viewed as an intentional *disparity of reporting*), but in other cases, the disparity is more structural (due to demographic, technological, or cultural disparities, such as differences in literacy as described above). For posterity, then, the historian may find it worth considering which systems of recording information are best for preservation. Cuneiform exists because baked clay, while fragile, lasts far longer than a microchip, and besides, it requires no additional infrastructure (like an operating system, digital code, etc.) to be interpreted. It may be harder to authenticate in some cases, but it certainly has more permanency. Authentication will be discussed in more detail in Chapter 13. For the purposes of this chapter, we now turn to how the discussion of disparity can be used to improve a cybersecurity stance based on data, metadata, and network traffic together with its analysis.

3.5 Cyber Salon – Failure to Perform Proper Analytics on Data, Metadata, and Traffic in a System

Without proper analytics, your cyber or cyber-physical system may have a disparity of security. Analytics starts with the simplest of investigations, which is assessing whether there is agreement among the various cyber professionals about the priorities of risks. A recent study describes how to assess agreement in priority, where differences indicate there are competing aims, competing spending, and competing focus on different aspects of cybersecurity governance, policy, or technology adoption [Scal23]. More complex analytics include the analysis of data, metadata (data about data), and network traffic (data about data flow). All of these are required to monitor the health of your cyber network, and the concept of disparity can readily be extended not just to the data, metadata, and network traffic, but also to the effective (or ineffective) monitoring of the systems. That is, the disparity can be about differences in either the data itself (content) or in the collecting of the data (process) when comparing two or more systems. Combined, these are the data operations, or DataOps, of the system. So, the failure to perform proper analytics on the data, metadata, and network traffic in a system (the content side of DataOps), and the failure to provide the same types of analyses on different systems (the process part of the DataOps), can either separately or together lead to a disparity in certain aspects of the cybersecurity. An awareness of the potential for structural disparity in DataOps can lead to improved security design and thus is the subject of this cyber salon.

To prevent disparity in DataOps, we modify the *Seven Great Laws of Disparity* for this purpose. In the following seven items, we restate the law and then show its application to DataOps in a cyber or cyber-physical system.

1. *Greater distances of time between the event and the reporting of the event will in general correlate with disparity.* From a DataOps standpoint, this means that a low sampling rate may miss important dynamics in your data. For example, a distributed denial of service event – where multiple sources inundate a server with data traffic to prevent legitimate users from accessing online services, applications, and sites – may on-ramp very quickly, meaning that a low-frequency assessment of incoming network traffic may result in an unacceptable delay in recognizing that an attack is occurring. One way to make the most out of any sampling rate is to compute and react to both the actual value of each sample and the first derivative (the rate of change) between any two samples. For example, if there is a high data rate because your website is receiving many legitimate visits, a flag for high traffic will be activated, but the difference will be generally small since the activity will have scaled naturally. In general, a high sampling rate with consideration of both the value and the rate of change of the value of data, metadata, and network traffic is preferred.

2. *Greater distances in location between the event and the historian tend to correlate with disparity.* Distance for cybersecurity and cyber-physical security can be measured in several ways, including, for example, the

number of firewalls between two enclaves, partitions, and servers. It can also be the number of servers (including DNS, or domain name system, servers) information must pass between two locations. It could also, for a more arcane example, be the number of security inspections that take place between two systems. Designed to be "flat," on the Internet, it is the DNS servers that route connections. So, distance between the physical locations (e.g., using GPS) of two computing devices is less important than the number of nodes (servers, routers, etc.) between them. The more segmented a network is, in general, the greater the distance between two computing assets. The greater the distance, in general, the more chances for security verification. Each partition boundary is an excellent location in which to collect data, metadata, and network traffic information. Networks poorly partitioned are likely to have a (negative) disparity of cybersecurity protection in comparison to properly partitioned networks.

3. *Greater differences in governance tend to create greater disparity between the event and the historian (or cybersecurity professional).* Governance in cybersecurity means a cybersecurity strategy that is written as part of organizational operations, usually as part of the concept of operations (CONOPS) and is intended to minimize the interruption in services and data transmission due to cyber vulnerabilities, threats, and attacks. Governance includes the accountabilities, the incidence response and recovery plans, the decision-making plans and hierarchies, and the incidence recovery plans of an organization. The greater the differences in the governances of multiple systems, the greater the likely disparity between the two systems in terms of data, metadata, and network traffic security. Even if both systems are highly secure, incompatible governance plans may lead to "loopholes" in the overall protection. For example, a system with two IDPSs (intrusion detection and prevention systems) might actually be less secure than a system protected by only one of the two IDPSs. This is because the governance models of the IDPSs might be incompatible, causing each IDPS to treat the other as outside of its governance model and thus limiting the effectiveness of each IDPS.

4. *Greater differences in literacy rate generally correlate with greater disparity between the event and the historian's (or cybersecurity professional's) report on the event.* Cybersecurity literacy is not exactly the same as textual literacy, of course, but the analog here is that cyber literacy is cybersecurity expertise germane to the particular system

requiring protection. The less familiar a cybersecurity professional is with a particular cyber system, the more potential disparity between the actual cyber protection needed and that recommended. For cybersecurity, there is simply no substitute for comprehensive literacy. Because of the requirement for artificial intelligence (humans simply cannot keep up with the pace and sophistication of the attacks), this means "collective" literacy is more important than the literacy of any one individual on the team. In today's cybersecurity environment, the disparity in literacy to be most concerned with is that between the threat agents (red team) and the cybersecurity team (blue team). Any disparity in literacy in favor of the threat agents is a vulnerability in the system. Thus, the role of a cybersecurity team is to reduce that disparity by investing in learning.

5. *Greater differences in the materials used to source information generally correlate with a greater disparity between the world view of the historical event and the historian (or cybersecurity professional).* Systems with less network traffic may have a disparity of data, metadata, and network traffic analytics in comparison to systems with heavier traffic. AI is heavily dependent on massive amounts of training data, in most cases, to properly analyze information. In cybersecurity, a disparity in materials is, therefore, usually associated with a disparity in the availability of training data for the network's intelligent intrusion detection and protection processes (applications and services). It should be noted that training data is not simply the data collected on the system itself, but can also include course work, publicly available data sets, pay-for-use data sets, and paid instruction. Remember the "Law of Red Team Competence," introduced in Chapter 2 as "If you can think of a potential attack on a system and then execute it successfully, you must assume that someone else already has?" This law is, in my experience, a very important aspect of a resilient cybersecurity training posture. Being exposed to more systems, system architectures and designs, and security operations will *train your imagination*, thus allowing you to be more creative in imagining potential attacks. It should be stressed that the best protection your system will have is that of constant testing and learning, for which exposure to new and varied systems is critical. The red team also has a responsibility to pass along its learnings to the blue team, of course.

6. *Greater difference in the quantity of sources for information also increases the disparity between historical events and the later historian*

(or cybersecurity professional). Sensors are one source of information in a system, particularly for the physical security of cyber-physical systems. Sensors, whether tied to environmental evaluation, surveillance, or authentication, provide both data and metadata that can be analyzed with advanced machine learning and AI algorithms. In addition, sensor and other information (including the data, metadata, and network traffic data described above) can be pooled with that of trusted peers to help a rising tide raise all ships. One of the more effective means of preventing illicit activity is for the collective set of targets to share their data (either de-identified to prevent loss of corporate trade secrets or aggregated by a trusted third party) and so benefit from the increased scale of information.

7. *Greater differences in access to sources are another structural disparity.* Computing power and advanced analytics are obviously required to counter the resources, talent, and perspicacity of advanced persistent threats (APTs). As mentioned in the previous point, pooling data is one effective way of staying a step ahead of the APTs. Another is simply adding more sensing, testing, and measurement to your processes. Legitimate businesses should view other legitimate businesses as their partners, even if they are in competition. In most "verticals" such as commercial electronics, pharmaceuticals, manufacturing, and the cement industry, all legitimate businesses stand to gain by staunching illicit activity through working together.

Looking for these disparities in your system should be part of the Secure Concept of Operations (SECOPS) for your cybersecurity or cyber-physical security system. Fortunately, the most difficult step in the process is the discovery of disparity. This discovery process is readily associated with the test plan and testing, along with the training and education plans. So, it can be "fun" for those members of your team who are always trying to find out the latest and greatest. Disparity is admittedly no fun, but its cure certainly can be.

3.6 Summary

The disparity can be viewed as a structural problem for the historian, with its imbalance in the flow or representation of information capable of producing a type of *transitive omission* from the event to the historian. Cultural differences are important to acknowledge since they are not innate characteristics such as race, gender, age, and the like, and they anyway need to be accounted for in a historical analysis. Cultural mediated disparity may be impossible to fully correct for, due to the difficulty of projecting from one culture into another, but the historian must try. The section on culturally mediated disparity culminates with the *Seven Great Laws of Disparity*, providing some rules for the evaluation of disparity.

Next, presentism, the judging of a historical event or period from the lens of today, is dissected with a specific emphasis on one of Abraham Lincoln's more controversial decisions, the execution of 38 Dakota Sioux in 1862. Victor disparity is amplified by what we term survivor disparity, and literary works, such as *Moby Dick* and the *Book of Job*, are incorporated to show the broader value of the latter. We complete the section on presentism dispelling the notion of an "end of history" as the ultimate form of presentism and use both the flaws in Karl Marx's manifestos and the brilliance of Isaac Asimov's *Foundation* trilogy to show the end of history the door.

Disparity in reporting was evaluated, with the disparity in historical communication abilities of the conquistadores and the Inca as one example. The Armenian genocide was explored as a further exemplar of such disparity.

In the cyber salon, the *Seven Great Laws of Disparity* were repurposed to help cybersecurity professionals address disparities of security engendered by various disparities of data, metadata, network traffic data, training, testing, and experience. These Laws were shown to be valuable for curing mistruths, whether it is for cybersecurity or more broadly to address mistruths in history.

References

[Ang16] Ang J, "Sinicizing the Uyghurs," Peace Review 28, no. 4 (2016): 399–406.

[Evan22] Evans TT, "Abraham Lincoln's Uneasy Relationship with Native Americans," History, https://www.history.com/news/abraham-lincoln-native-americans, accessed 12 April 2023, A&E Television Networks, originally published 18 February, 2022.

[Firm01] Firmage EB and Mangrum RC, "Zion in the courts: A legal history of the Church of Jesus Christ of Latter-day Saints, 1830–1900," University of Illinois Press, 2001.

[Gord17] Gordon L, "The second coming of the KKK: The Ku Klux Klan of the 1920s and the American political tradition," Liveright Publishing, 2017.

[Grun94] Grunberg B, "The Origins of the Conquistadores of Mexico City," Hispanic American Historical Review 74, no. 2 (1994): 259–283.

[Roy20] Roy D, "Ethnic conflict in China: The case of Tibet," In Ethnic Conflict, Tribal Politics, pp. 87–101. Routledge, 2020.

[Scal23] Scalco, Aleksandra, and Steve Simske. "A model for measuring multi-concern assurance of critical infrastructure control systems." Systems Engineering (2023), https://doi.org/10.1002/sys.21684.

[Turk17] Turku H, "The destruction of cultural property as a weapon of war: ISIS in Syria and Iraq," Springer, 2017.

4

Generalization

To generalize is to be an idiot

– William Blake

All historians generalize from particulars. And often, if you look at a historian's footnotes, the number of examples of specific cases is very, very small

– Henry Louis Gates

Abstract

Judging through the lenses of today, whether as culturally mediated disparity or presentism, was discussed in Chapter 3. In this chapter, we turn that form of mistruth around 180 degrees, and we look at how stories are reinterpreted to fit in with current events. Examples provided in this chapter include reinterpreting Susanna in the *Apocrypha* in light of the *Me Too* and related movements of today. We show that Daniel was not "woke" in any modern sense of the word, and rather that this story was focused on showing that he was a good lawyer in order to provide an authoritative aspect to his character. Remembering how Christ, in the *New Testament*, had issues with overinterpretation and focus on "the law," we see support for an ancient, logically consistent, but also quite different purpose for the story than that of women's equity (no matter how admirable such a reinterpretation might be). Other examples follow, including the generalizations of parables in the New Testament and generalizations of generals in military history. Generalization, in general, is then discussed, and the chapter is concluded with a discussion of cybersecurity governance aimed at preventing generalization.

DOI: 10.1201/9788770048347-4

4.1 Introduction

Generalization about the usually arcane, tightly interconnected contextual surfaces of historical events and personages is shown to be the basis of another *pattern for mistruth* in historical documents. One of the more insidious forms is presentism, when an historical event or item is reinterpreted from the context of the historian, and not from the historical era itself. This differs from intentional generalization written into some historical documents – the *New Testament* being one example – so that the content can be repurposed meaningfully in a new context. We will also show how tier lists and the concept of the GOAT (greatest of all time) tend to overgeneralize the historical discussion, and thus, lead to a form of mistruth. Overgeneralization is thus an additional pattern for mistruth for the historian to be aware of – and to acknowledge and where possible correct for – in their historical writing. It will also be shown to lead to problems in cybersecurity governance if not corrected, which is the subject of the cyber salon of this chapter.

4.2 Susanna and Daniel

Because we would have to be feckless – or at least uncomfortably ironic – to generalize about what generalization is, our first deep analysis will be about a specific form of generalization. The generalization we address in this section is that which reinterprets a specific historical element with contextual logic appropriate to the time of the historian, and not the event itself. Reinterpretations are of value, of course – think of *My Own Private Idaho* as an adaptation of Shakespeare's *Henry IV* and *V* and *O Brother Where Art Thou* as an adaptation of Homer's *Odyssey* – but they are not the original context. Changing the context, in effect, changes, the content, as Luhrmann's *Romeo + Juliet*, and Van Halen's *You Really Got Me*, among thousands of examples, show. The role of a historian who is interested in avoiding mistruths in history is to recreate, to the best of their ability, both the content and the context of the historical event. This is a Sisyphean task, to some extent as absurd as Camus' main – only – character in *The Myth of Sisyphus*, but like Sisyphus, the historian can take joy in the struggle to understand, to push the burden of specification, to avoid overgeneralization, and to push the rock of verisimilitude to the top of the mountain of truth. Each time the historian undertakes a new analysis, a new read, and a new interpretation, the historian must put their face to the clay-covered rock and toil up that mountain again. But it is a task they own, they call their own, and they control. As Camus noted, “There is no fate that cannot be surmounted by scorn” [Camu42]. Like Sisyphus, one must imagine this historian happy.

In order to gain this happiness, however, the historian needs to put critical reasoning into play, including the *Seven Great Laws of Disparity* that were introduced in the previous chapter. A simple, even parsimonious law, to apply is the same one employed by Tim Severin to accurately reproduce the “actual” voyage of Ulysses in the aforementioned *Odyssey*. Severin followed the maxim of actually reading the source material, which is a great way to avoid additional mistruths should any exist. With this, the world of the *Odyssey* shrunk from the Mediterranean (and perhaps even beyond the Pillars of Hercules into the Atlantic) to the Aegean Sea and the sea borders of the Peloponnese [Seve87]. The cove of the Laestrygonians, for example, was found to be along the southwest coast of the Peloponnese (Mezapos harbor). The directions were right there, all along, in the sailing directions of the *Odyssey*. In fact, the fact that the directions in Homer’s *Odyssey* could be followed by Severin, and ended up taking his crew and him to places like Scylla’s Cave, the Charybdis whirlpool, and the cove of the Laestrygonians lends credibility to the general veracity of the historical record, even as told in literature (supposedly myth in the case of Homer!).

Like Homer, the *Old Testament* and its *Apocrypha* contain what many label as myths, others as anthologies, and still others as collections of wisdom. We feel that they may be all three of these, in addition to historical documents (like Homer) and also in many cases fascinating and well-written literary works. That is the context for our analysis of *Susanna* and the *New Testament* in this chapter, as we are not attempting to be theologians. For concentrated literary proficiency, it may well be that few if any other works combine so much skill into three short pages as does *Susanna* of the *Apocrypha*. This short story, every bit as compelling as one by Virginia Woolf or Edgar Allen Poe, combines “plot, surprise, struggle, and unfolding character…in just the right proportion” [Tran77, p. 213]. Not to mention inventing cross-examination and providing as salacious a story as you might expect in the Third Millennium, some 2300 years later. In this section, quotes taken from *Susanna* are from the *New Oxford Annotated Bible with the Apocrypha*, 1977 edition [Tran77], but any translation will likely work should you wish to invest the five minutes required to read it in its entirety.

Susanna, we are told, is a beautiful and “righteous” woman whose father is named Hilkiah and whose husband is named Joakim. Her mother’s name is never given, nor are the names of any other female person. Already, we can see Susanna is isolated by her gender – only connections to men are worth mentioning here. Further isolation is provided physically by her need to isolate her bathing by closing the garden and sending away her servants. Her isolation is correlated with vulnerability, as soon the two lascivious judges appear from their hiding place in the garden, threatening to accuse her of infidelity unless she has sex with both of them. The elders, appointed as judges who had already "perverted their minds and turned away their eyes from looking to Heaven or remembering righteous judgments" [Tran77, p. 213], the narrator tells us, go much darker here with Susanna, because the penalty for fornication was death by stoning (and maybe even hacking to pieces with a sword). A second incidence of nakedness follows, with Susanna screaming so that the household returns to the garden, and they all appear at once, seeing her naked with the elders. The elders had joined her in screaming and fabricated the presence of a lover who had been too strong to withhold and who escaped before the family arrived. A third episode of nakedness in front of multiple people is soon to follow, as Susanna is fully exposed in public (in accordance with *Ezekial* 16:37-40, with stripping, stoning, and hacking with swords being the punishment for adultery; and in accordance with *Hosea* 2:3-10, in which public nudity is used to shame a fornicating woman) when the elders demand that she be unveiled at her trial. Apparently, the elders wanted one last look at the fully exposed object of their lust before throwing the first stones. Three bouts of nudity, three times Susanna's body is sexualized, and three times she has bravely suffered false witness. Susanna's body is treated as something separate from Susanna the person, and there is no hint that it would ever be thought of differently in *Susanna* any more than in *Ezekial*, *Hosea*, or virtually any other book of the *Old Testament*.

Was Susanna guilty? "The assembly believed them, because they were elders of the people and judges; and they condemned her to death" [Tran77, p. 214]. Are we to assume that Joakim has no voice on this? He never says a word in her defense, although Susanna claims that she is innocent. Instead, the young man of the village sure to win the "Rising Star" award at that year's Babylonian Exile Bash, Daniel, feels compelled by the Lord, or at least compelled by the irrationality of it all, to say "I am innocent of the blood of this woman" [Tran77, p.215]. This hits the community harder than a slap in the face by Edna Mode – stoning and sword-hacking are meant to be shared by the entire community. If one person holds out, it turns from justice to shame and guilt. Daniel, the neophyte, is taken seriously because he is invoking a higher power (God) by proxy here.

It is a good thing he did because, otherwise, this story ends like Jezebel's with the added horror that Susanna was guilty of nothing more than being exposed time and again against her wishes. Daniel, instead, introduces to the *Apocrypha*, Babylonia, and the world the "obvious after the fact" concept of the cross-examination. He has the two judges separated, and so separated, asks them about a seemingly innocuous detail of Susanna's alleged forbidden foray into fornication. But, they chose different trees under which the event was supposed to occur, and several plays on words later (along the lines of "I will staple you with a maple, you!" and "You will be croaked by an oak!"), the witnesses to the cross-examination suddenly realize that these two degenerates – who have requested Susanna's "unveiling" after all – are the guilty parties: "You offspring of Canaan and not of Judah, beauty has deceived you and lust has perverted your heart…the daughters of Israel… were intimate with you through fear; but a daughter of Judah would not endure your wickedness" [Ibid.]. The penalty? False accusers suffer the punishment tied to the charge they made, so those elders were about to get stoned, with no marijuana involved, and about to get hacked without compromising their cybersecurity. "Thus innocent blood was saved that day" [Ibid.].

Innocent blood, without a doubt. But this is telling. Blood is the flesh. Blood is not her mind, her personality, her spirit, her wishes. Susanna brings rejoicing to her husband, father, and unnamed mother not because she lives, but instead because "nothing shameful was found in her" [Ibid.]. Susanna, after all, means "lily," and so like a flower, she is meant to be untainted, beautiful, and silent.

Daniel, however, means "God has judged," and so his name and advocacy both carry the word of God by proxy, as we have seen. Susanna benefits by not being wrongly killed, but she has suffered, and one can imagine she is reticent to bathe ever after. For Daniel, though, this is a career-defining moment: "From that day onward Daniel had a great reputation among the people" [Ibid.].

It would be a generalization, therefore, to argue that the saving of sinless Susanna is a "Me, too!" event (i.e., a protest against sexual abuse) of the Babylonian exile. Susanna is not getting even with the elders, in spite of her brave protests. It is Daniel who benefits from the series of events (and admittedly from his own sense of justice and his creative, modern use of cross-examination). The story is named, and about, Susanna, but it is a vehicle for Daniel's career. Generalization is natural, and of course, a modern *adaptation* of *Susanna* would almost certainly involve the modern theme of retribution for sexual abuse. But that does not allow the historian to generalize the original meaning of the story for its audience 2300 years ago. After all, no word is given on how life goes for Susanna after that. Is Joakim upset about her being exposed in public, for example? Is she upset at Joakim for being mute and reliant on the youngster, Daniel, to leave her stoning unturned? The narrator does not tell us, but we can infer that life will never be the same for Susanna.

But that is not a concern for the original author, since she is property, after all, a lily: beautiful, unsullied, and quietly there to brighten up the room or garden. In fact, it is more important for the narrator to show us the relative virtues of all of Judah (in comparison to its neighbor to the north, Israel) rather than provide a statement against sexual abusers. After all, as Susanna noted in her original confrontation with the two judges, the price she would pay for lying with them was death. We can pity Susanna from our perspective, but we cannot impose our worldview on the events so long ago. That would indeed be a form of overgeneralization.

4.3 The New Testament

From *Susanna*, we move forward three centuries to the *New Testament* and the parables of Christ. Parables are actually quite an important type of document in the broader discussion of historical mistruths because they usually encourage reinterpretation, or at least adaptation. This leads to a natural exploration of the difference between adaptation and generalization-as-falsification which may at first appear only an academic or theoretical exercise, but upon exploration provides critical insight into methods for discovering mistruths. Adaptation can be thought of as "repurposing" content for, among other considerations, a new audience, a new time, a new culture, a new purpose, a new perspective, or a new source of revenue (thus the sequels and the remakes we all know too well).

In most circumstances, the purpose of writing, filming, and/or recording content is to influence an audience: whether to entertain, inform, motivate, call to action, etc., content is created to influence a target group we will call here the *recipients*. At the most hair-splitting level, any two presentations of content have a different audience, because there is a change in the recipient group. Even the same film shown in the same location in the same "run" of consecutive days has a different audience across the run – moving forward in time from the early adopters (the so-called hipsters and trend-setters) to the mainstream viewers (as in J.Q. Public, or conformers) to the latecomers (also known as stragglers or "cautious ones"). Even the same audience member, watching the movie twice, sees it differently each time, because the context (via their changing familiarity with the material, outside events that have occurred since the previous viewing, and their mood that day, as three examples) has changed between the two viewings. Thus, we see that content can never be viewed exactly the same way on two different occasions. This is not the same as saying that one occasion was the "real" occasion and the other a "misrepresentation" or "mistruth" of the other. We cannot be allowed that sort of interpretative flexibility, or our definition of mistruth will expand beyond relevance. Instead, we must appreciate that even the "truth" has context, variability, and adaptation to its environment; that is, to how it is being discussed.

This does not mean that there are no absolute truths, sorry Wittgenstein. Certain truths, for example, mathematical truths, are not language-dependent, and therefore, are absolute truths that can be represented (truthfully) in many languages. For example, no matter what language you use, 1 + 1 = 2 is a truth, precisely because any two identical, individual items when added together are twice as many as either by itself. Other absolute truths are those that are definitions ("a dog is a mammal" is a definition of classification and is an absolute truth) and those that are tautologies ("our planet is the third closest to the sun"). In history, however, all "truths" are likely to have some relativeness to them (again, other than the definitions and tautologies such as "Washington, D.C., was the US capital in 1930"). Relative truths such as "Waterloo was Napoleon's downfall" have some degree of generalization: a military historian might argue that the 1812 Invasion of Russia or the 1813 Battle of Leipzig were, in fact, Napoleon's downfall, whilst a psychological historian might point to the infertility of Josephine as his downfall. The point is that, for anything but the most trivial of historical content, some interpretation, and thus some adaptation and generalization, is unavoidable.

So, what is the purpose of a parable? Literature and the world of ideas are as much parts of history as battles, discoveries, elections, and inaugurations. With a parable, we have both literature and the world of ideas involved in a situation in which there is *intentional ambiguity*, or generalization to provide meaning to multiple situations. In other words, a parable invites – is predicated on – generalization. Not the broad generalization of pithy epithets like those of Sun Tzu ("He will win who knows when to fight and when not to fight," "You have to believe in yourself," and "If quick, I survive. If not quick, I am lost. This is death" being three such celebrations of the obvious), but rather thought-provoking, open-ended stories that inspire discussion and interpretation. Parables, therefore, have multiple truths, including their historic truth (original interpretation) and their expanded truths (generalization to other interpretations). Parables are particularly amenable to reinterpretation, but the historical elements of them are more specifically tied to their historical era. A fable is similarly open to interpretation, but generally is less tightly connected to a particular historical event or context, so we will stay with parables in this section.

The first parable addressed is the so-called "Parable of The Divided Kingdom," which is described in the *New Testament*, *Matthew* 12:24-30.

The parable is relatively short, and it describes the reaction of the Pharisees to hearing about Jesus' exorcising of demons. They claim that Be-el'zebul, the prince of demons, is the power behind Jesus' success. It is the Roman Palestine equivalent of claiming there are Satanic messages when you play a record backward [Walk85]. The Jesus of the *New Testament*, with the exception of that high-profile money-changing misdemeanor, is, however, relatively unflappable. Jesus is, in fact, described as knowing their thoughts, and states that "Every kingdom divided against itself is laid waste, and no city or house divided against itself will stand" [Tran77, p. 1186]. He is telling the Pharisees that they both have the same goal, and the same power (the "Spirit of God") to drive out demons. An interesting comment is then attributed to Jesus in *Matthew* 12:30: "He who is not with me is against me, and he who does not gather with me scatters" [Ibid.]. Aside from the wonderful play on words and metaphor here – "scatters" can mean so many different things here, all of them beautiful from a literary perspective – Jesus here creates an "us" and "them" situation that is repurposable even today. One need look no further than George W Bush and the September 20, 2001 address to a Joint Session of Congress and the American people, just nine days after those planes hit the Twin Towers, the Pentagon, and the countryside of Western Pennsylvania. He said, "Either you are with us, or you are with the terrorists," and for many, this was condensed to "Either you are with us, or against us," thereafter. Jesus' parable, tied to the historical events surrounding exorcism in the Roman Palestine era, is generalizable to virtually any circumstance in which potential allies wish to reinforce their collaboration. The parable is part of the *New Testament*, which like the *Old Testament* and the *Odyssey* is a combination of history, narrative, and moral messaging that were intertwined because there simply were no expectations of clearly delineating/separating these different intentions for writing at the time. This means for the historian that not only must the moral messaging be separated from the historically accurate elements of the writing, but the narrative (whether entirely fabricated or "based on a true story") as well. Importantly, both the narrative and the moral elements of parables should not be considered mistruths in history on the part of the author, since the author had no intention to provide a "modern" history, based on facts, analytics, and presumably impartiality. However, a modern historian reporting on the same parable is guilty of mistruth if they represent the parable as factual or imply that the original author intended it to be factual.

Thus, reporting on content that was not considered factual at its birth is a mistruth on the part of the interpreter, and not on the part of the original author or recipients. This is consistent with what we can call the *Fundamental Law of Mistruth*: Mistruth is assigned to the interpreter (the historian) and not to the original author or the original recipients. In other words, shame on you, not on Homer (myths), Jesus (parables), or Aesop (fables). As an interpreter, you must make clear to your audience (1) what you know to be true, (2) what you know to be untrue, and (3) what is somewhere between truth and mistruth, and thus open to interpretation. It is worth noting that this approach both respects the Fundamental Law of Mistruth and also gives the interpreter some constraints on their interpretation. Are these constraints shackles? Hardly. Constraints such as ballad format, sonnet form, or iambic pentameter (among many others) have allowed, or forced, depending on your viewpoint, some of the world's most creative talent to find unusual relationships between words and concepts. Many modern songs use rhyming (by which we mean end rhyming), but Skaldic poets used beginning rhyming or related alliteration for their melodic form. Constraints support creativity while giving structure to content. Recognizing the truths, mistruths, and gray area between them allows you, as a historian, to focus on the gray area, and show your ability to connect the content to other content and thus create a new, valuable contribution to the field of interpretation.

This brings us to our second parable, the "Parable of The Weeds Among the Wheat" which is also taken from *Matthew*, this time 13:24-30. In this parable, Jesus notes: "The kingdom of heaven may be compared to a man who sowed good seed in his field, but while men were sleeping, his enemy came and sowed weeds among the wheat and went away. So when the plants came up and bore grain, then the weeds appeared also" [Tran77, p. 1188]. The man's servants ask the owner why there are weeds, and the owner says that an enemy did this. The servants offer to pull all the weeds, but the owner stops them, saying that "in gathering the weeds you [will] root up the wheat along with them. Let both grow together until the harvest; and at harvest time I will tell the reapers, Gather the weeds first and bind them in bundles to be burned, but gather the wheat into my barn" [Ibid.]. Powerful material here, perhaps the source material for the much later creation of the Grim Reaper, with skillful metaphors regarding burning, the good and the bad living together in this world, and more.

Now, putting the Fundamental Law of Mistruth into action, we see the beauty of this parable for an interpreter. For (1) *what you know to be true*, there is very little: that there was a historical Jesus, and that he lived near the Sea of Galilee. For (2) *what you know to be untrue*, there is virtually nothing here that we know to be untrue. The historical Jesus may well have told this parable, and even if he did not, the telling of it has existed for many centuries, such that the parable is itself a part of the history of culture. For (3) *what is somewhere between truth and mistruth, and thus open to interpretation*, we have essentially the entire parable. Thus, the ratio of (3) to the sum of (1) + (2) + (3) is very close to 1.0, which is its maximum value. This sum is defined as the *interpretative ratio (IR)*, and an IR of 0.0 means that no interpretation is necessary and/or particularly relevant, and an IR of 1.0 means that the interpreter has effectively unlimited freedom of interpretation. This is one of the reasons that the parables of Jesus hold so much meaning even today, 1800 or more years after they were recorded and roughly 2000 years after they were originally told in some form. With a parable, the interpretative ratio is very close to 1.0, and thus generalization (adaptation of interpretation) is not only pronounced, but in effect *structurally encouraged* by the way the parables are written.

This gives us a chance to provide our own generalization from the original message, which was surely focused on separating the wheat (good people) from the weeds (bad people) at the Final Reckoning, Apocalypse, Armageddon, or any other name you give to the end of times. Our interpretation is humanist, and it is simply that the good and bad live together; that we can readily distinguish between the good and bad; and that we must learn to let the good and bad live together to avoid mutual destruction. We may not be able to transform bad into good (a weed is not going to produce wheat germ no matter how much we wish it to happen), but we can gain the benefits of all the good by tolerating the bad. It is a message of tolerance that can live outside of any religion, and inside most if not all of them.

Using The Fundamental Law of Mistruth and interpretative ratio together, we address our third and final parable. This parable comes from the *New Testament* book of *Mark*, Chapter 7. It is the parable of the Syrophoenician woman, and unlike the previous two parables, it is told in the third person (about Jesus, rather than by him). As if the change in perspective of the writing alone does not give this parable a more visceral feel, then the fact that Jesus is called out for his provincialism should. The narrative starts with Jesus seeking a respite from the throngs: "And he entered a house, and would not have anyone know it" [Tran77, p. 1223]. However, it was not to be – word of the location of Jesus spread like wildfire in those days of his ministry. Instead, immediately after entering the house, a woman whose daughter was possessed came to him in his role as an exorcist. Syrophoenician by birth, "she begged him to cast the demon out of her daughter" [Ibid.]. Jesus, recognizing her as a Gentile (that is, non-Jewish), dismissed her, telling her to allow "the children first be fed, for it is not right to take the children's bread and throw it to the dogs" [Ibid.]; that is, she and her people are dogs in comparison to the Israelites/Judeans (Jews) who were the children of God. She, however, answered, "Yet even the dogs under the table eat the children's crumbs" [Ibid.], and at this comment, he instantly (and remotely!) exorcised her daughter. Using the Fundamental Law of Mistruth, (1) *what you know to be true* is similar to the previous parable; that is, the historical Jesus and his ministry occurred. However, something interesting has been added here, and that is, Jesus taking input and learning from somebody who is (a) a woman, (b) a Gentile, and (c) uninvited. This is about Jesus, the central figure in Christianity, and it is not flattering. This gives this very specific element of the parable considerable verisimilitude and thus lowers the overall Interpretation Ratio of the parable. For, (2) *what you know to be untrue*, there is very little provably untrue in the story (some might argue against the exorcism). For (3) *what is somewhere between truth and mistruth, and thus open to interpretation*, includes the courage of the Syrophoenician woman; the ability of Jesus, already hailed as a savior to many, to take input from a triply-marginalized person; and that bit about remote exorcism. However, it is clear from the story that the message of this parable, in its time of creation, was to show that Jesus needed to be challenged to expand his ministry to all people, rather than simply focus on the "children" of God.

The generalization of this parable is understandable. For anyone marginalized, the parable speaks of empowerment. For anyone left outside of a cultural phenomenon, the parable speaks of inclusion. For anyone with a suffering loved one, the parable speaks about the possibility of a cure. For some, the surprising – some might say incredible – vulnerability of Jesus to his own prejudice and the temerity, tenacity, and truthfulness of the Syrophoenician woman is a generalizable tale of DEI-SJ (diversity, equity, inclusivity, and social justice). But this is almost certainly an overgeneralization of the history of the narrative, irrespective of its important message that Jesus would be better as a savior if he represented everyone. For example, there is no indication that the role of children and dogs will change or that the status of children of God will be extended to non-Israelites after this interaction; instead, it implies a simple scaling up of Jesus' current ministry. Jesus exorcised a Syrophoenician, showing that these people, too, can be saved. Jesus had also just seen his message rejected in his own town of Nazareth (*Mark*, chapter 6). It is likely, then, that this narrative, as part of the overall narrative in *Mark* chapters 6–7, was meant to further demonstrate the impetus for Jesus to expand his ministry, and to offset his desire to hide away. Given the nature of the next chapter (*Mark* 8, wherein Jesus feeds 4000 people), in which his ministry scales considerably, this interpretation seems to hold better than any generalized DEI-SJ interpretation. Of course, with parables, especially those with Interpretation Ratios close to 1.0, there is a lot more leeway for interpretation than is true for other historical recordings.

We finish the section on parables by using them to show that parables can be separated from personality, and a reasonable view of the historical figure behind the source of parables garnered, in spite of the generalization and reinterpretation parables invite. For the historical figure of Jesus, for example, how strongly do the parables he told affect the interpretations of his life? Albert Camus, the famed Algerian-French philosopher, is not typically associated with Christianity or its interpretation. However, he had thoughts related to the historical figure of Jesus within his famed novel *The Fall* that examined the historical Jesus and his humanity while subtly critiquing the many biblical literalists that he interacted with in his time.

Camus extends an empathetic hand to the historical figure and biblical narrative of Jesus. Camus portrays Jesus as human and not someone distanced from or disdainful of the lives of others. He does this through the character of Jean-Baptiste Clamence, who anticipates Saramago in humanizing Jesus. Clamence remarks that Jesus is aware of the fact that "he was not altogether innocent" [Camu56, p. 112]. Camus-as-Clamence further, and more directly, anticipates (and surely, influences) Saramago by pointing out the likely impact that the *Massacre of the Innocents* had on Jesus's family: "He must have heard of a certain Slaughter of the innocents. The children of Judea massacred while his parents were taking him to a safe place – why did they die if not because of him? Those blood-spattered soldiers, those infants cut in two filled him with horror. Given the man he was, I am sure he could not forget them" [Ibid.]. Clamence's Jesus was seen as a generous, self-conscious, peripatetic preacher who was aware of his own historical importance. Camus, through Clamence, takes a humanistic and less generalized approach to the historical figure of Jesus, painting him as a good man and a guidepost, without dogma or fanaticism. This point is made clear by the comment, "Too many people now climb onto the cross merely to be seen from a greater distance, even if they have to trample somewhat on the one who has been there so long. Too many people have decided to do without generosity in order to practice charity. Oh, the injustice that has been done him! It wrings my heart!" [Camu56, p. 114]. In Camus's *The Fall*, Jesus is a person, not a parable, and has specific attributes, not just general goodness. Thus, a person can be specific and produce a parable that can be generalized without contradiction.

4.4 Military History and Generalization About Generals

Generalization, overall, is more than simply adaptation or interpretation as described above, in which a single event takes on a different, usually broader meaning. Generalization can be – and perhaps usually is – applied to two or more events or persons simultaneously. Often this occurs through association; that is, comparing a particular historical item to another one.

Generalization about generals was not meant to be just a "cringy" play on words, but instead a good bridge between such concepts as tier lists, GOAT (greatest of all time) discussions, and generalization. Let us face it, it is a lot of fun to create tier lists – whether about music, sports, books, movies, or other areas. Mozart's *Requiem*, the NBA's Michael Jordan, Shakespeare's *Hamlet*, and Jane Campion's *The Piano*, for example, are generally considered "S" tier, which is above the "A" tier and is related to Super or Special (or even the Japanese word for archetypal, "Shu"). Tier lists are a way of comparing content relatively and are a form of generalization since elements on the same tier can generally be considered of equal merit. From the S tier members, a GOAT can be selected.

Generals in history are preadapted to tier lists. There are a number of reasons for this, extending from nationalism to machismo to psychology (including association and self-identification), and we have not the time, the talent, nor the proclivity to get into these aspects of the historical tier list caprice. What we are interested in, instead, is how mistruth in history (of which we have omissions, disparity, and now generalization as the patterns for mistruth at this juncture in the book) ends up affecting the manner in which tier lists, GOAT assignments, and head-to-head comparisons are made. Obviously, personal opinion matters in such relative assessments, and this also means that identification with the historical figure is likely a factor in the assessment. The tier list creator's ethnicity, gender, sex, culture, country, and time period are among many factors affecting the relative ranking. This is part of the secret charm of these ubiquitous tier lists and GOAT conversations – they represent a template for expressing one's own preferences in a way that otherwise might be less acceptable to other people in the conversation.

For the purposes of this section, we will consider three general-to-general comparisons, each of which involves a pair of generals that most "military historians" (if that is a thing?) would assign to either the "A" or "S" tiers. We will also consider them from their "primary talent" among the choices of (1) tactics, (2) strategy, and (3) operations. These three often form a "rock-paper-scissors" situation for tier lists, with the operations strength able to overcome strategic strength, strategic strength able to overcome tactical strength, and tactical strength able to overcome operations strength. The first pairing (operations beat strategy) comes from the American Civil War, with Ulysses S. Grant's operations advantage, including better railroads and supply chains, overcoming Robert E. Lee's strategic advantage of being able to rapidly deploy across his centralized, more compact defensive lines. The second (strategy beats tactics) comes from the Napoleonic Wars, and features Wellington's strategic advantage, including the Peninsular campaign and drawing Russia away from the Continental System, overcoming Napoleon's tactical advantage, based in part on his concentration of power at the critical time and point of the enemy's lines. Finally, the third (tactics beats operations) uses as an exemplar of Alexander's brilliance in tactics at Issus and Gaugamela against Darius III (hereafter Darius) of Persia, who had the advantage of defense, centrality, choosing the grounds for the battle, and superior supply chains.

All of which is very clean and simple, right? If there is a rock-paper-scissors approach, and you know which one of these your nemesis is going to use, then bring the other skillset that beats their skillset. After all, is not that what Wellington essentially did with Napoleon? Knowing what his tactics were, and how quickly he could adjust his tactics on the battlefield, Wellington set up a large-scale strategy that pronouncedly reduced the effectiveness of Napoleon's tactics, after all. That is a key observation and gives insight into the actuality of the supposed rock-paper-scissors effect here.

The rock-paper-scissors of tactics-strategy-operations is a generalization. As mentioned above, generalizations have some useful purposes, including helping one to organize and make sense of a lot of data, concepts, opinions, and facts simultaneously. But generalizations can be harmful when the generic is posited as being the guide to the specific. For example, Wellington did defeat Napoleon, eventually, using a long-term strategy, but had he been able to coordinate Spanish, Prussian, and Russian resentment toward Napoleon in a more integrated fashion, the disparity in resources might have allowed him to use operations as the key weapon in defeating the corticosterone-controlled Corsican. He was not able to balance all of the difficulties in keeping the coalitions integrated, so he instead took the strategic view, using the rapid expansion of the French hegemony against Napoleon by targeting his attacks where success was most likely.

The same is true for Grant versus Lee. Lee had a relatively simple strategy, which was that of keeping the lines of communication intact between all of the various units in Northern Virginia. His central location, home-field advantage, and defensive positioning ensured that this strategy would, facing equally talented opposition, yield disproportionate casualties for the North. Multiple generals of varying degrees of incompetence (McClellan, Burnside, Hooker, and Meade) had largely proven the validity of Lee's strategy. In fact, the two times Lee failed to follow his "own" strategy (Antietam and Gettysburg) were the two that helped rebalance the otherwise disproportionate casualties of disasters such as Petersburg, Chancellorsville, 1st Bull Run,

2nd Bull Run, and others that the North had suffered up until Grant's arrival on the Northern Virginia theatre in 1864. Grant understood Lee's strategy, and instead of trying to simply bludgeon his way through it, he tried to simply augment it. Tightening the centrality by moving in at different points (e.g., multiple rivers to the east of the Confederates and multiple locations in Shenandoah, specifically Winchester), Grant undoubtedly threw Lee off by using his strategy against him. With the burning of the Shenandoah in late September 1864, Grant (through one of his most trusted generals, Sheridan) simply made the value of what remained inside Lee's central grounds less valuable and less capable of supporting the remaining Confederate army. Also, by (arguably tactically) removing this "breadbasket" from Confederate use, Grant enhanced his own operations advantage. Grant, in other words, used both Lee's and his own plans to his long-term advantage. It is likely that had Lee adopted a different strategy, like for example, racing into Northern territory again or heading west to free up or capture more grain-growing land, Grant would have switched to tactics such as sprinting for Richmond to end the war. The "operations beats strategy" approach was used by Grant because it was what was most likely to work with what Lee was likely to do. But Grant did not abandon strategy or tactics at the time.

Next, the well-studied Alexander versus Darius campaign is considered. Here, Alexander's tactics, including the cavalry flanking to effect a "hammer and anvil" strategy at Issus and the surprise revealing of the slingers at Gaugamela, are legendary, and by necessity, last-minute tactics suited to the particular battles. At Issus, the more evenly matched numbers allowed the Macedonian cavalry, one flank of which was led by Alexander himself, to move behind the more static Persian lines and then "hammer" them into the "anvil" of the tightly phalanxed Macedonian infantry. At Gaugamela, because of the far superior Persian numbers, this tactic would not work. Instead, Alexander "hid" the "peltists" or rock "slingers," using them to surprise the left flank of the Persian army, smashing it and allowing Alexander a bold run directly at Darius that forced him to flee the field. A much closer fight on the rest of the battlefield mattered not since the Persians lost their coordination with the fleeing of their king.

So, we have established Alexander as a master of tactics, right? Again, this is due to the exigencies of his battles. In a different situation, for example, the siege of Tyre on the Phoenician coast, Alexander showed himself the master of (engineering) operations, creating a mole (causeway) and two massive, multilayered siege towers that could simultaneously sweep defenders from the walls, catapult attack the walls, and fire upon enemy naval vessels. His operations ruled the day in Tyre.

Alexander also was a great strategist, which in many ways was the key to his continued victories, all performed with a smallish army up to 6000 kilometers from his small home territory. The strategy was to create cultural coalescing between the Macedonians and the conquered people. This caused him some problems with his own Macedonian troops, who groused that Alexander had become an Asian king in the tradition of Darius. However, it protected Alexander's long and otherwise precarious supply chain back to Pella by reducing the risk of rebellion from a conquered population that greatly outnumbered the Macedonians.

Clearly, then, Wellington, Grant, and Alexander (and for that matter, Napoleon, Lee, and Darius, as well) could use tactics, strategy, and/or operations as the situation required. So, why they did not? For the victors, the answer is largely tautologic: they did use tactics, strategy, or operations as their primary means of ensuring victory. As we have shown, this is *generalization through classification* (as a tactician, a strategist, or an operations expert, for example) *and reductionism* (i.e., oversimplification). When we say Wellington used strategy, Grant used operations, and Alexander used tactics, we are generalizing to the means they used for their differential advantage. It is a historical mistruth, of course, to say Wellington was only a strategist: a good strategy relies on good tactics and operations, and they are not actually capable of being individually dissembled. However, the generalization allows one to understand a potentially important "gist" of the situation.

For the vanquished, the explanation is more nuanced. In the case of Napoleon, even though he rose to power after the French Revolution and its destruction of the *Ancien Régime*, he became more critical to the normal operation of France than even Louis XIV. It could be said of Napoleon that "l'etat c'est lui" (the state is him), and because he did not delegate the leading of the military in the same way that other leaders (of Austria, Great Britain, Russia, and Spain, for example) did not have time to update his tactics, his strategy, or even for the most part, his operations as the number of coalitions and French casualties rose over the years. Other generals, knowing of Napoleon's main tactic (timely concentration of power at the critical spot in the enemy's lines) and main strategy (take on separate enemy armies before they can aggregate to effect overwhelming force against each individual army), found effective means of preventing this from happening (famously at Leipzig, for example). Clearly, Napoleon needed to delegate more.

In the case of Lee, his hands were tied on operations, since the US Navy quickly moved to isolate Virginia from logical logistics partners (New Orleans, Europe). His hands were also tied, for the most part, on tactics since the disparity in troops and resources meant that he largely needed to stay on the defensive. Lee, of course, suffered irreplaceable losses of manpower any time he took more overtly offensive tactics (Malvern Hill, Antietam, and Gettysburg being three obvious examples), and was (rightly) accused of bad generalship. Again, though, this is a generalization and does not take into account specific needs for the Confederacy to establish a credible threat of attack capability in hopes of bringing the North to a peace that was suitable to the leadership of the South. Regardless, characterizing Lee as a skilled strategist is a generalization since most of the strategy was determined by the realities of the civil war: disproportionate access to men and resources for the North, proximity of Richmond and Washington (the two capitals), and the early near encirclement of Northern Virginia due to the naval blockade, the formation of West Virginia, and the large Army of the Potomac.

Finally, in the case of Darius, it is easy to see how his operations might have been efficient, with the existence of so many powerful cities (Babylon, Ecbatana, Pasargadae, Persepolis, and Susa just to name five) and the empire's tens of millions of citizens. However, these advantages could also be viewed as disadvantages: the major cities were rivals, and the sprawling empire, like the much more modern example of the Austro-Hungarian Empire, was polyglot and reliant on a relatively small core of multilingual administrators to make it run smoothly. Because of these factors, tactical changes were likely far more difficult for Darius' army than the monolingual Greek (Macedonian and allies) army. Because of the sprawling nature of the empire, and Alexander's ability to take the initiative, Darius' strategic aims were similarly constrained to trying to find a good position in Alexander's likely path to engage him. Thus, shoring up and benefiting from operational excellence was almost certain to be Darius' main scheme. It did not prove enough to counter Alexander, but that does not mean it was the wrong choice by Darius.

What we have uncovered in this brief relative comparison of three pairs of generals is that generalizing the approach taken by an individual is a form of mistruth; instead, focusing on their content and context is far more important, not only for understanding the broader history in which that individual was a part but also ultimately for understanding the individual better as well. The example of Napoleon is compelling – it would be easy to say, as some historians have, that Napoleon's "tricks" became known to his nemeses and that Napoleon was not smart enough to alter his tactics. The problem is that these tactics, if employable, were still the best ones for him to take given the realities of the numbers and resources of the French Empire and the rest of Europe. Instead, what Napoleon more likely needed to do was alter his strategy so that these tactics would still give him the upper hand even when his enemies anticipated them. For that to happen, Napoleon needed more allies, not to mention less family members sitting on the throne of conquered nations (Naples, Spain,

Holland, and Westphalia). Napoleon's tactics became less effective because his strategy failed as much as the tactics themselves became untenable.

Napoleon's loss of tactical success illustrates another important element of history, particularly when it comes to nation-changing and nation-creation: timing. The Great Trek of the Boers, starting in 1836 as part of their effort to escape the administration/overlordship of the British, benefitted from the timing. The Xhosa, antagonized by the Zulu, welcomed them, allowing them safe passage into Natal. The Zulu were also at odds with Sekonyela, Khoikhoi, and Basuto people. The Zulus were also preadapted to a civil war in which a battle loss (Battle of Blood River) stoked to full flame. Like Pizarro and the conquistadores and their conquering of the Inca, the Boers benefitted from not only their technological advantage (tactical) but also unplanned strategic (coincidental conflicts between Zulus and other local people to the advantage of the Boers; immediately preceding civil war among the Inca to the advantage of the conquistadores) and structural operational (the use of the laager, or wagon forts, during the encounters for the Boers; the advantage of immunity to the diseases that they brought for the conquistadores) advantages to be able to carve out a Boer territory at the time. Timing – and in particular, the fortunate confluence of tactical, strategic, and operational advantages – has always been important in nation-creation and nation-changing.

Timing, generally meaning the coincidental occurrence of two or more (at least partially) unrelated events, is thus an important factor in any historical analysis. This is broadly applicable to what we term *macrohistorical events*: nation-forming and nation-changing, as above, and also the end of empires. When an empire (Rome, Byzantium, etc.) falls, it can be argued that this fall tells us more about these empires than their invaders since the pressure on an empire (a huge target painted, if you will) is omnipresent. Only when the timing is right within the empire – through some combination of poor leadership, loss of civic cohesion, civil strife, pandemic, etc. – will the empire be susceptible to collapse from the outside. Every empire has internal and external pressures placed on it. But empires do not fall from the sky; their very size speaks to their resilience. So, when they collapse, we primarily look to the empire, and not so much its enemies, for the reasons. We will return to this subject in the cyber salon for this chapter.

4.5 Generalization, in General

When you generalize, you associate two or more concepts, people, or events with each other, and in doing so, imply that there is a relevant, perhaps causal, relationship between them. However, one has to be cautious about confusing correlation for causality. For example, there is a well-known correlation between the rate of ice cream consumption and the homicide rate in the United States. So, this "proves" that eating ice cream prompts people to perpetrate pugnacious acts, right? Correlation, sure. Causality, not at all. It so happens that both ice cream consumption and homicides are correlated with another factor, called a *confounding factor*. That factor is the outside temperature, and one can readily understand higher temperatures increase the likelihood of frozen dairy input and firearm output.

Generalization often goes beyond simple mistruth. It may, for example, rely on the passive laziness of stereotyping or the active hatefulness of bigotry. Perhaps between these two is profiling, which makes it a good lens through which to better see generalization. Starting with stereotyping, it is perhaps a natural consequence of the need for humans to discriminate between danger and safety, toil and ease, and efficiency and wastefulness. Most people spend a significant part of their time discerning, or discriminating, between multiple options, and usually arriving at a stereotypical response to given contextual circumstances based on previous experience and discrimination. Discrimination is an overloaded term, meaning everything from deciding the best of multiple options to (your immune system) deciding whether a cell is part of you or a pathological invader to, of course, being biased against someone based on an innate attribute (such as race, sex, gender, age, and ability). A physician discriminates between the need to medicate or not, the need to perform surgery or not, and the need to change patient behavior or not. A custodian discriminates between trash and homework, toxic and compost, and dirty and clean. An athlete might discriminate between passing or trying to score, pressing to score or running out the game clock, and pressing harder or taking a time out. Some generalizations (walking on the bright side of a street instead of the dark side at night, driving more slowly on ice, etc.) make sense and are part of why your genes are still treading water in the gene pool.

On the other side of the generalization continuum is what people may first think of when the word "discrimination" is mentioned; that is, bigotry (or prejudice, i.e., prejudging). This is clearly an *overgeneralization* or *bias* and should play little to no part in historical analysis. We say little because some bias is, most agree, inevitable, and so acknowledging your potential bias upfront is both helpful and responsible. It will also help your work be integrated with work that reports a different potential bias, making it both more valuable in itself and in combination with other work.

The middle ground between stereotyping and bigotry, one can argue, is profiling. The minimum amount of profiling is stereotyping, which is essentially basing your interpretation only on previous experience. This is a form of conditional probability, and while it may make sense on many occasions (not going to a certain restaurant because the service is miserably slow), it may not be up-to-date. This is the problem all responsible historians must face, and in many ways, it is analogous to the problem they might have with including source materials: how do you evaluate whether a story, influenced as they all are by the experiences and generalizations of the author, is a reinterpretation, plagiarism, or mistruth? A reinterpretation will misrepresent some historical material, but it is overt about its goals, and like a parable, is understood to have a strong element of adaptation. Plagiarism is not simply passing off someone else's work as your own; it is also passing off your work as an *independent idea* when it is not. This is particularly dangerous as it represents two historical records that are actually based on only one investigation as if they are independent, and another historian performing a meta-analysis of multiple records may (innocently) give double weight to a singularity. Mistruth is the more general term for historical misrepresentation and is normally thought of as being intentional. However, failure to properly identify parable and reinterpretation as the partial veracities that they are and the sloth of plagiarism/parroting can lead to just as problematic of ends as intentional mistruth (lying). Generalization may be due to sloppiness, and normally, we are more forgiving to sloppiness than we are to mendacity. However, for the purposes of historical truth, both are parlous.

4.6 Cyber Salon – Governance as a Means to Prevent Generalization in Security Processes

Generalization is an insidious problem for cybersecurity protection, particularly because it usually arises from good intentions. Cybersecurity teams, or entire organizations (assuming it is a healthy organization wherein cybersecurity is a topic for all staff), conflate generalization with thoroughness. Thoroughness is important, and "purple team" activities (red team attacking, blue team defending) depend on the red team attempting to penetrate all sectors of the threat surface so that no complacency sets in. However, generalization runs the risk of treating every aspect of the threat equally, which includes assuming an equal probability of successful penetration, an equal cost to the organization for a successful penetration, and an equal delay in time for discovery and recovery.

Such equalities, however, rarely if ever exist in the real world. Cybersecurity governance is concerned with the pragmatic need to reduce as much risk as possible with the amount of resources that can be plausibly applied to the task. Risk prioritization can be assessed by determining where different actors in the organization most disagree on the relative risk, competence, and/or confidence in the cybersecurity environment; for example, software, hardware, processes, etc. [Scal23]. If the goals, opinions, and/or beliefs of an organization are not aligned, an organization is likely to overspend where the threats are least and underspend where the threats are most. The goal of governance is, therefore, that of providing specific, not generalized, countermeasures to the greatest risks. In order to assess this, analytics are of course required. Whether you use red team/blue team events or simply multiple, independent assessments of your cyber risks, the key is to determine not only which threats are relevant but also to prioritize them. This prioritized risk list and its associated costs can be aligned so that your spending matches your ability to spend but prevents the most damage for the costs incurred. In other words, the investment in risk remediation is *very specific*, and not generalized.

Prioritizing has the additional advantage of identifying the crucial aspects of the containment plan and policy. In the real world, which is the only one we know of, infinite resources are not available. Once your budget has been optimally allocated to the highest prioritized risks, a policy must be put in place to contain the damage possible from every other scenario as well. Containment plans must be defined before the attacks occur, which means that the governance must understand the difference between true threats, untrue threats, and those in between (plausible threats). For these three types of threats, the following are recommended:

1. True threats: one effective governance approach is to direct the attacker into a honeypot or honeynet; that is, a fake network that they continue to try to exploit as if it were a real network. From these, information can be collected that can be used to turn the tables on the attacker and gather information on their methods, intentions, and possibly even identities.

2. Untrue threats: threats that are either not serious or else can be readily dismissed. This is an example of prioritized, or Pareto, protection since standard rules, usually associated with firewalls, can be used to stop these threats.

3. In-between threats: threats that were not high enough priority to fit into the costs associated with threat remediation (e.g., an IDPS, or intrusive detection and protection service). These are the threats that are generally part of the network design and training policies. Partitioning your network properly can contain damage should bad behavior occur

unintentionally. Training your employees not to click on suspicious links, for example, requires no IDPS expense, but remediates a real threat.

Governance, therefore, is an essential element of cybersecurity: without it, the cybersecurity plan is not framed, it is not specific, and it is *overgeneralized*. Governance, as one might expect, requires top-down support, with executive management agreeing with the CSO/CISO and cohorts on the policy, planning, procedures, and personnel security required. Governance has both specific technical and administrative dimensions, incorporating everything from configuration management to change control, from subcontracting to staff training, and from indoctrination to corporate culture creation. Part of specifying the governance is ensuring that it meets organizational objectives; that is, it is tied into the "truths" of the organization itself, which includes the organization's willingness to spend on risk reduction and the amount of residual risk that the organization is willing to accept.

Governance requires a strategy, and there is a tendency for people to equate strategy with generalization, and tactics with specifics. That is an understandable misconception because so many organizations do in fact change their strategies based on short-term contextual events. However, it should always be remembered that a strategy that changes based on short-term events is a *tactic* and not a *strategy*. Strategies, and the metrics used to track their effectiveness over time, should be just as specific as tactics. The difference is temporal – strategies must be implemented for a longer time period to come to fruition, whereas tactics have immediate results. Thus, strategies spell out enforceable policies for coordinating them across the organization. Roles, responsibilities, and processes all must be specifically outlined, and this includes disciplinary actions for violations. This is an important point: rewards and disciplinary actions are part of governance and must be specifically defined before cybersecurity is deployed.

Standards, from ISO to NIST, provide further specificity for an organization's cybersecurity architecture. Cybersecurity governance should be considered in the larger context of the organization's overall governance; for example, there is considerable overlap between physical security, cybersecurity, and safety when the governance for hiring, firing, training, career progression, etc., are considered. Secure processes extend to procurement, contracting, and sharing of supply information since these are loci in which vulnerability surfaces are almost certainly extended. Trusted escalation plans, with non-punitive responses to false positives, are also recommended. In other words, one kind of mistruth (reporting a cybersecurity event when it is not one) is judged better than its complement (failure to report a cybersecurity event when it is real). As with other systems designed to last long-term, repeatable and reliable performance benefits from ground truthing. Thus, the need for standards.

For cybersecurity, just as with general history, placing relative value on the data assets is an important task, enabling prioritization based on the cost to produce or replace systems, the system age, the useful life of the system, the security sensitivity, and the regulatory requirements. Service-level agreements, or SLAs, are signed to provide performance requirements for systems, applications, networks, or services. It may well be that a similar concept of an SLA is needed for the agreement between any author, any recipient, and the author's work, in both cybersecurity and in historical reporting more generally. Whether this be through a graded system ("A" for verified truthful, "B" for no intentional mistruths, "C" for opinion, "D" for clear bias, etc.) or through an appendix that lists all known potential mistakes of truth, some form of relative assurance of truth in a document is required. An opinion should not weigh as highly as reputable reporting, but it does more and more each day without some type of "veracity meter." Whatever gets the most clicks is, more and more, the de facto truth. It used to be that "trusted" new sources existed which provided a benchmark for others, but the pervasive, erosive quality of the Internet has made some of this less prevalent, or even ignored by a generation accustomed to having to find their own truths, whether in unreliable echo chambers or more reliable, aggregated trustworthy sources of information.

Returning to cybersecurity; as we have shown, generalization usually tells us more about the organization than its attackers, and this is exactly the opposite of what we want to do. That is, *the way in which a cybersecurity exploit occurs* tells us more about the organization's cybersecurity defenses than the attackers' capabilities. It is safer to assume that there are one or more attackers capable of exploiting any real vulnerability in the organization's network; therefore, the successful penetration tells us that this is where the organization failed to prevent an exploit. We have to assume that any known exploit (along with unknown ones) is always being probed by adversaries.

However, the types of exploits that are successful can provide us with the right action in our game of cybersecurity rock-paper-scissors. Note that in some ways it does not matter whether the rock-paper-scissors is strategy-tactics-operations or strategy-operations-tactics. That is, picking blue team tactics to address red team strategies that succeed, blue team operations to address red team tactics that succeed, and blue team strategies to address red team operations that succeed will work because it disconnects the type of solution from the type of successful exploit. And its converse – picking blue team operations to address red team strategies that succeed, blue team strategies to address red team tactics that succeed, and blue team tactics to address red team operations – will also work. Rather than patching or simply treating a symptom, by using a different tool (e.g., operations) for the solution than the tool (e.g., tactics) used for the exploit, a deeper solution will generally be crafted. As an example, suppose the strategy of periodic distributed denial of service is shown to be successful in exploiting your system. Rather than responding with a strategy to counter them, it might make more sense to consider an operations or tactics response (or both!). For operations, routinely slowing down new connections well before system resources are actually locked up (and thus service fully denied) using an asymptotic function that delays new connections more and more the closer that resources get to being fully committed provides an automatic, operations-based safeguard. A tactical approach might be employed that uses AI or other machine intelligence to begin committing more and more system resources to proactively identify malicious connections as the amount of remaining resources dwindles. Such a rock-paper-scissors approach, then, can be helpful in providing a broader, more resilient solution to cyber threats.

4.7 Summary

Is a summary itself a generalization? Irony aside, yes, it is. This chapter was about generalization and the dangers it can entail when applied to the usually complex, highly overlapping contextual surfaces of any historical event worth examining. We considered *presentism* – the reinterpretation of a specific historic element within context appropriate to the time of the historian, and not the event itself – as a first form of generalization. The reinterpretation of the *Apocrypha* story of Susanna in light of the outing of predatory male sexual harassment was used as an example of this form of generalization. We also discussed the difference between intentional generalization (e.g., the parables of Jesus) and unintentional generalization on the part of the historical interpreter, or historian. This is posited as the Fundamental Law of Mistruth, which is that the mistruth is the fault of the reporter and not the original historical persons and events. The greater the intended variation in interpretation – that is, the more intentionally like a parable a historical writing is – the higher its interpretative ratio.

In the next section of this chapter, we addressed the topic of tier lists, and in particular, how they apply to homologous historical figures, in this case, generals. We used a rock-paper-scissors analogy, tactics-strategy-operations, to discuss how to compare across multiple talents. The continuum of overgeneralization, from stereotyping to profiling to outright bias, was then discussed. The chapter concluded with a cyber salon focused on governance in cybersecurity as a means of preventing wasteful overgeneralization of the overall security investment. We were also able to repurpose the rock-paper-scissors analogy to illustrate how to use a cybersecurity solution based on a different design than the exploit. This ensures multiple perspectives on the exploit, and learning from good historical analysis is a good way of ensuring a broader solution.

References

[Camu42] Camus A, "The Myth of Sisyphus. 1942," Trans. Justin O'Brien (1955).

[Camu56] Camus A, "The Fall," Alfred A. Knopf, Inc. (1956).

[Scal23] Scalco, Aleksandra, and Steve Simske. "A model for measuring multi-concern assurance of critical infrastructure control systems." Systems Engineering (2023), https://doi.org/10.1002/sys.21684.

[Seve87] Severin T, "The Ulysses voyage: sea search for the Odyssey," Random House (UK), 1987.

[Tran77] Translation, Revised Standard. "The New Oxford Annotated Bible with the Apocrypha." (1977).

[Walk85] Walker MW, "Backward messages in commercially available recordings," Popular Music & Society 10, no. 1 (1985): 2–13.

5

Differential Emphasis and Evaluation

The emphasis should be on why *we do a job*
– W. Edwards Deming

A woman who does not know herself has no choice other than to live with other people's evaluations
– Natsuo Kirino

Abstract

Another mistruth in historical documents is that of differential emphasis and evaluation, or more succinctly, the sin of emphasis. Different from hyperbole, emphasis is, for example, what is chosen to place in positions of primary visibility, such as the first and last paragraphs or chapters. The concept of selective complexity (also named the "chiaroscuro of history," based on the lighting-based emphasis characteristic of paintings by Caravaggio) will also be shown to be a form of mistruth. Where more elaborate, nuanced arguments are given, for example, the author shows this party to have more advanced intellect, feeling, or other higher attributes. Examples of differential emphasis are illustrated through a consideration of the fall of the Inca Empire and the Icelandic Sagas, among others.

5.1 Introduction

Each chapter introduces a specific pattern for mistruth to be present – and to be identified – in a historical document. In this chapter, differential emphasis and evaluation are considered. At its simplest, this concept can be summarized as a form of "talking over" the opposing side. However, there are two sides to differential emphasis, the positive and the negative. On the "positive" side is overall greater coverage of a particular side of a historical interpretation (meaning talking about one person, event, or analysis more than another), thus providing greater nuance, justification, support, investment, and the like for that side. However, there can also be a "negative" side in which great nuance and interpretation for one side is provided with the intent of undermining, rather than supporting it. This "negative" approach, however, can be self-defeating. Two examples among a basically limitless set are noted here. The first comes from *War and Peace*, in which Tolstoy goes to great lengths to denigrate Napoleon: he "openly denigrates Napoleon, portraying him as physically unattractive, vain, clownish, morally corrupt, and historically insignificant" [Rose18, p.359]. Among several tactics used by Tolstoy are exaggerating negative attributes of Napoleon (demonization) and normalizing Napoleon to imply he is just another person. The problem here is, of course, that Tolstoy's insistence on Napoleon's historical insignificance is belied by how much of the novel is devoted to this insistence. As a second, much more modern example, consider all of the "free" press coverage that is given to Donald Trump, presumably because of his outlandish, even puerile, behavior, including a "tri-cities" of pugnacity, mendacity, and impudicity. Why has so much attention been given to a person clearly unqualified and undeserving of public service? The "negative" side of the differential emphasis pattern, therefore, should not be employed unless the employer is certain it will not inadvertently turn a negative into a "positive."

Irrespective of whether you go "positive," go successfully "negative," or go unsuccessfully "negative" – and like Tolstoy and the US media inadvertently support that which you meant to undermine – when you provide differential emphasis and/or evaluation, you are guilty of a form of historical mistruth. In this chapter, we explore how this phenomenon arises, from the intentional to the unintentional (*initiation*); how to identify it when it is present (*identification*); and how to compensate for it as a reputable historian (*incorporation*).

This triad of initiation, identification, and incorporation is, of course, easier said than understood. As the brief discussion in this section indicates, differential emphasis can be quite subtle, both when intentionally and unintentionally employed. Next, we describe intentional and unintentional differential emphasis, followed by a short consideration of evaluation.

Intentional differential emphasis often involves one or more forms of "engineering" of content in order to achieve an intended perspective, stance, topic repertoire, or other mistruth. As an example, an intentional mistruth might involve the perpetrator interactively and/or iteratively using some form of functional evaluation of the content as a means of ensuring that they have created content that will have a particular emphasis. One such functional evaluation might be using a search engine on different versions of the document and selecting the version that ranks highest for the chosen intentional search. Suppose you wish to convince people that electric drills make good ear cleaners. You then create several documents, each with different verbiage in support of your (clearly untruthful) argument. Using a search engine, you then find which of these documents is ranked the highest when searching on the falsehood that you wish to assert; for example, "electric drills make good ear cleaners." The document ranked highest by the search engine is thus the functionally "best" source of mistruth. Similar manipulation, perhaps with less malignant purposes, was rife in the early days of the Internet [Mala08] wherein website developers embedded (sometimes copious) metadata into their web pages to boost their rankings in search. Modern search engines are, in general, savvy to such manipulation, the so-called *search engine optimization techniques*. However, advances in natural language processing and large language models (LLMs) of late mean that more advanced manipulation can be employed, and in general, in a more automated manner. Other functional means of assessing the relative mistruth "value" of multiple document candidates include, among other examples, using automatic summarization on each document and then performing automated searches on the summaries to see which one ranks the highest. The point here is that, given the presence and the growth of powerful artificial intelligence and natural language processing techniques, the number of ways in which intentional emphasis can be incorporated into documents has greatly increased of late.

For unintentional mistruth, there is usually upfront filtering of content based on the implicit bias of the author or the expectations of the audience, as discussed in Chapter 2. However, there are additional concerns here for differential emphasis. Unintentional mistruth through differential emphasis is often structurally built into the process of generating the content. That is, the author's own preferences prevent them from performing a balanced search and research process, effectively prefiltering content because of their greater familiarity with content supporting or even being the source of their own preferences. So, even if such an author attempts to be even-handed in their writing, the fact that one perspective has a significantly larger original quantity of content than the other means that the probability it will be emphasized in the writing is increased.

Emphasis, as described above, starts from the source. Evaluation, on the other hand, starts from the destination. That is, it starts with the historian writing about the content, and often even less subtly reveals the historian's own implicit bias(es). Thus, differential evaluation augments differential emphasis on the "consumption" rather than the "creation" side of content.

Differential evaluation is, at least on the surface, less forgivable than differential emphasis since we should be able to expect a more measured, balanced, and multiperspective consideration of the topic(s) by a historian. However, it should never be forgotten that "history" and "story" (both derived from the Latin root *historia*) share the same meaning. Thus, even a well-intended historian may provide differential evaluation as a result of the desire to entertain or to persuade their audience. By persuade, we mean to use logos, ethos, and/or pathos to influence the way a reader feels whilst reading. No one writes in a void; that is, every writer has in mind a group that they wish to influence and an agenda that they want to push. Taking this to its logical – perhaps illogical – extreme, even a historian who is motivated to influence their readers to have a so-called measured, balanced, and multiperspective consideration of the material may inadvertently steer their readers away from the more extreme elements of the history, and in doing so, perform a form of "low pass filtering" of the content, preferentially preserving the prosaic over the peculiar and in doing so, both providing a faulty *history*, not to mention a potentially less compelling *story*. The large, yet historically accurate, deviations from the norm are precisely what makes history worth studying and worth learning from. Hadrian's wall, built mainly to keep away a group of people (the Picts) the Romans simply could not get their heads around, was not built solely to protect Rome's northernmost expansion. Any discussion of Hadrian's wall that glosses over the tremendous behavioral and cultural barriers that led to the construction of an actual stone barrier misses out on both nuance and flavor that, if maintained, make the telling of the history more accurate, interesting, and understandable to readers of today. Yet, many historians gloss over such singletons of fact and in doing so, rub away those rough edges of history that are otherwise best able to penetrate the "fog" of normalcy and make a lasting impression on the reader.

Why do historians polish over their stories? There are many reasons, including limitations on the length of the writing and worries about providing details that are not of general interest. However, as we argue, even very well-intended historians are likely to perform such historical record "smoothing" simply out of fear of providing bias in a story. It is right at this point that you may be giving up hope for a true narrative.

Do not. Hope floats, and like wooden or air-filled flotsam, it can provide the means for the survival of historical truth. All writing, whether bodice-ripping romance or science-fiction enchantment at one end or historical reporting at the other, involves an engagement between the writer and their material. So, as a historian, go into it with eyes wide open, recognizing that you are likely to provide some form of differential emphasis and/or evaluation.

An important additional point to make here is that differential emphasis and evaluation are not necessarily associated with *differential coverage*. In other words, differential treatment can be the result even when the discussion seems balanced, and indeed, even when the historian is doing their best to make the discussion balanced. This makes differential emphasis and evaluation, and the unbalanced historical interpretation they can lead to, all the more insidious. If the historian is more familiar with one side of a historical interpretation, then by that simple fact they are more likely to provide a more nuanced discussion for the side of familiarity. Think of the Picts and Romans. Because of the copious literary records handed down by the Romans, and the virtual lack of any such record provided by the Picts, there is likely to be increased nuance when telling the Roman side of the story. Worse, an attempt to increase the nuance about the Pict side of the story (adding on plausible but also specious details about blue body paint and fighting naked, among other characterizations) is dependent on Roman narratives for its content, meaning that *it actually results in providing more Roman nuance*!

The overall effect is to provide selective complexity to a historical account (or person, or event, etc.). This is a familiar process for books, plays, movies, and other media. The "hero" or "heroine" of so many stories is afforded *selective complexity*, while other characters are much more simply portrayed. We know far more about King Lear than we do about the equally (perhaps even more) admirable Gloucester. We know far more about Hamlet (thankfully!) than the admittedly less interesting Rosencrantz and Guildenstern – or is it Rosenstern and Guildencrantz? See, who cares? Dickens takes this to an extreme, with his obviously dynamic characters (e.g., David Copperfield, eponymous with the major novel) contrasting sharply with his intentionally static characters (e.g., Dora Spenlow in the same *David Copperfield*). There are a virtually unlimited number of similar examples, again structurally imposed because of length requirements (for everyone except Proust, that is). The point is that the writer contrives to have us see a particular person (or more generally, a particular idea, group of people, etc.) as more worthy of emphasis and evaluation.

Yes, these are literary examples – stories as it were, not histories – but as with so much of history, the facts and the stories are intertwined. For example, there was a historical Amleth, described in the *Saxo Grammaticus* of circa 1200 AD, who if he moved the last letter in his name to the front became the more famous Hamlet, and has a name virtually identical to Shakespeare's own precious son, Hamnet, who died just a few years before Shakespeare wrote the play. History and story are related, and sometimes stories (the sailing directions in the Odyssey) are more accurate than histories, from Herodotus' accounts of giant ants, flying snakes, and sheep with tails so long a cart was needed to support them (remember, no one had defined history yet for Herodotus!) to contentious recent histories such as *1421: The Year China Discovered the World*. So, our need to uncover – and where possible remediate – mistruths in history means that we also need to uncover mistruths in stories that contain or are based upon historical events. This is a heavy responsibility, but it is the goal of this book.

Remediation is the biggest burden of that responsibility. It is one (relatively easy, in fact) thing to identify the existence of mistruths in historical documents. It is a little more challenging to classify, or create patterns for, these mistruths. Each chapter in this book covers one such pattern for mistruth, so obviously it is not *that* difficult. However, it is much more difficult to define and outline the means to remediate the mistruths that, according to the analysis here, are more or less guaranteed to arise in a historical account. We propose a six-step program as outlined here not as a foolproof means of remediating all of the mistruth, but as a means of identifying where it is more likely. In doing so, the most probable mistruths will be pointed out, even if they are not correctable.

Step 1: Acknowledge the selective complexity. Rather than claiming to have a fully balanced account of a historical item, it may make more sense to simply admit the selective complexity and try to characterize it so the reader can more informatively come to their own conclusion. Especially, if it is structural; that is, due to an innate differential availability of information favoring one interpretation over another. This issue is almost certain, for reasons as simple as the fact that usually there is a disparity in the popularity of opinion and as complex as the fact that transitive trust (how well the readers trust the different contributors to the discussion) is notoriously difficult to measure.

Acknowledging the selective complexity goes beyond simply stating that it exists. Its extent, by which it means the absolute value of the differential emphasis and/or evaluation, also needs to be estimated. If you cannot, or prefer not to, assess this, then there are natural language processing (NLP) tools that you can use to do so. Signs that one topic is being covered with greater emphasis or evaluation include simply the greater occurrence of the topic being named, but subtler (and more advanced) methods include determining that a broader vocabulary is being employed for one topic versus the other. Another elegant way of determining differential emphasis is to use summarization to reduce the content to its "essence" and then compare how much of the summary is about each of the topics.

Step 2: Argue against your point. Perhaps the easiest way to argue against your own point may be to start an argument about the point at stake, and then really listen to the person you are arguing with. It is easy, just invoke your inner Monty Python and state "I would like to have an argument, please." Then, instead of simply nay-saying what your opponent in argumentation declares, really listen. Even if you are not persuaded to change your stance (let us face it, it is highly likely that you will not be), you are likely to find out at least one good reason why your opponent thinks differently. Remember from the field of debate, your true talent in argument comes from being able to overcome your opponent's *best arguments*, not their weakest.

Step 3: Thesis, antithesis, and synthesis. Georg Hegel, a famous German philosopher often understood through his refutations of (also German philosopher) Immanuel Kant, especially countering Kant's placement of duty as central to moral behavior, brought his own powerful mechanism for fruitful argument to the forefront. Importantly, Hegel's "dialectic" provides a productive process for arguing with *yourself*. The dialectic consists of three sequential steps, which themselves can be quite elaborate. These steps are (1) thesis, (2) antithesis, and (3) synthesis, and are highly recommended for the uncovering of differential emphasis and elaboration. We explore the three parts in order.

The *thesis* portion is the easiest to understand. It is your claim, your proposition, your point to make, and your side to choose. Assert your interpretation of a historical event, and then support it with evidence such as peer-reviewed references and quotations. Opinions are valuable here, as are analogs, but the closer that you can tie them to the references (and presumably the facts), the less the chance for inadvertent mistruth.

The *antithesis* is also relatively easy to understand, but perhaps far more difficult to honestly implement. Unlike arguing against your point, as covered in the previous Step 2, the antithesis is intended to argue a point opposed to your own. This avoids differential emphasis and evaluation in at least two ways. First, having an anti to the thesis forces the writer to give equal time, space, and word coverage to the contrasting idea rather than simply giving additional time to the same idea, presumably in arguing against it, but still giving it far more coverage and thus more nuance and more complexity (think about this along the lines of "no press is bad press"). Secondly, by forcing an antithesis to be discussed in the affirmative, the overall polarity and sentiment of the verbiage will be similar; that is, supportive rather than contradicting. The antithesis, then, is not (though it can be, of course, but usually only in relatively simple cases) a simple 180-degree reversal of the thesis. Instead, the antithesis offers a different view of the world at the time of the historical event, and as such needs to incorporate a different perspective, a different "persona," and often even a different narrative process. The broader the combination of the two perspectives, the broader the fertile ground for the subsequent synthesis.

Speaking of which, the *synthesis* is where the skills of the narrator must come to the forefront. How are these two (hopefully) disparate viewpoints – the thesis and the antithesis – resolved with the goal of minimizing historical mistruth? Many times, the antithesis and thesis combine to create a much deeper understanding of the history – if your thesis is that Manzikert (a Seljuk Turk victory over the Byzantine army in 1071) led to the fall of the Byzantine Empire in Asia Minor, then the logical antithesis is that something else led to the fall of the Empire. Suppose your antithesis is, then, that the subsequent civil war within Byzantium led to its fall in Asia Minor. The synthesis of these two is not a simple combination of the two; rather, it is an elaboration of how the two elements worked together. The seeds of the civil war were already germinating at Manzikert, evidenced by the treacherous disengagement of Andronikos Doukas during the battle, and his swift return to Constantinople and leading role in the usurpation of the captured Romanos IV Diogenes (who was brutally blinded and fatally infected in 1072). Thus, the civil war and usurpation were simply conveniently possible with Romanos' capture, and the seeds for the civil war (not to mention the massive treachery at the battle of Manzikert) were already rooted in the rivalry and rot of the Byzantine court. As a synthesis, the civil war and Manzikert were simply symptoms of a more profound disease eating away the Empire from the inside.

Step 4: Separate opinion from fact. This is easier said than done, of course (or at least that's our *opinion*!). There is a certain tendency for a professional writer to assume that they are somehow less biased, less opinionated, and less capable of producing a narrative with differential emphasis than their peers. But, to our knowledge, there is no specific study that supports that assumption. It is, therefore, probably a better idea to just assume ubiquity and uniformity of susceptibility to differential emphasis, and in doing so, be extra wary of asserting opinions. Fortunately, separating opinion and fact starts with asking yourself where you got each element of information and then verifying the sources. It is ok to have opinions, it is just that you have to admit that they are just that.

Step 5: Plausibility and parsimony. Occam's razor, or the law of parsimony, states that in many cases, the simplest explanation is the most accurate. This is a long-view proposition, of course, since effectively the law of parsimony is meant to avoid "overfitting" an interpretation with a paucity of information. The simplest law that will match historical data yet to come is, of course, hard to predict. However, as a historical evaluator, this rule "simply" asks you to consider whether you are inferring evaluative information from your experiences in other situations, or freshly analyzing the situation at hand. Hand in hand with parsimony is plausibility: is your interpretation even plausible? In many instances, projecting technologies, processes, and modes of thinking from a later time back into a historical event – the wide range of anachronisms – creates fictional plausibility. An often-used expression is "Well, human nature has not changed, so..." but in reality, the way humans think is driven by their cultural processes and institutions as much as by their technologies. If you know better than to show Abraham Lincoln calling Frederick Douglass on a cell phone, then you should also know they were not going to be discussing the subconscious reasons that Northerners would not sign up for service in the civil war, either. The term "subconscious," after all, did not appear until 1889. It is, therefore, necessary, but not sufficient, to ensure that you make no technological anachronisms in your historical writings. You must be careful to do the same for other processes, practices, social structures, and even human behaviors. Yes, humans were essentially the same as today hundreds and even thousands of years ago, but the manner in which their brains navigated, formed words, interacted with other brains, and virtually every other aspect of context was different, and perhaps, very, very different. Assume plausibility at the risk of mistruth and remember that the simpler the assumptions of shared human experience, the less likely you are to commit presentism. Presentism, plausibility, and parsimony, therefore, are highly interrelated and must be considered simultaneously.

Step 6: Accept the miraculous...within reason. The last step in the process is taking a breath and trying to appreciate the idiosyncrasies of the particular historical event that you are evaluating. In some important ways, we can say that the universe is either miraculous or mechanical. That is, either the universe is so amazing, so profound, and so full of yet-to-be-discovered processes, that one can regard it as miraculous; or so mundane, predictable, and repetitive that one can regard it as solely mechanical. Since new discoveries continue to outrun our ability to predict them, we prefer to live life as if it were miraculous, and in doing so, the prosaic mechanics tend to disappear into the background. Also, in finding the miraculous in each historical event, you are more likely to find the key element of that historical event that allows it to be described and made useful to your readers. This prevents you from prepigeonholing the event.

With this, we have outlined our six-step program to address, and as possible remediate, mistruth. In some ways, this is the central chapter of the book, and these steps are central to our attempt to remediate mistruth. Once you realize that even well-intended historians are likely to provide differential evaluation, you accept the fact that there is no perfect narrative, and perhaps no unbiased history. Just as Hegel rejected the formalism of Kant's Categorical Imperative in favor of an innately conversational dialectic, historians may have to reject any notion of a historical account freed of differential evaluation and learn to frame history around the relative likelihoods. This is healthy for truth, to be sure, but also healthy for history as a liberal art, because it creates greater engagement, more discussion points, and clearer points for contribution to the readers. With this in mind, we move to the analogy between history with selective complexity and the visual artistry of Caravaggio.

5.2 Chiaroscuro of History

In art, chiaroscuro is the employment of contrasted light and shadow created by light falling unevenly or from a particular direction onto something (usually a person, persons, or a part of a larger scene). In other words, *chiaroscuro is differential emphasis* by the brightness, or luminance, of the different parts of an image. Originally made famous by Caravaggio (who is famous for a lot worse than historical mistruth, including brawling, murders, and of course the mistruth of defamation – you see he fits this section in so many ways!) as a "dramatic illumination" called *tenebrism*, chiaroscuro draws the viewer's attention to a specific aspect of a painting, much as differential emphasis draws a reader's attention to a specific aspect of the narrative.

Chiaroscuro is, therefore, a form of mistruth, providing intentional selective complexity. The difference between chiaroscuro and much historical differential emphasis is that Caravaggio is honest since he is clearly indicating what he means to differentially emphasize. Historians need to do the same with their "chiaroscuro of history," and do their best to at least identify the light source that provides the dramatic illumination.

As an example of how a chiaroscuro of history can arise, we consider the book "The Last of the Incas, the Rise and Fall of an American Empire," written in 1963. Originally identified as a useful reference for other aspects of Inca history, some interesting variants on chiaroscuro became evident upon reading the book from start to finish. Several of these will be elaborated here as they provide good context for how differential emphasis can arise unintentionally.

One of the most important special cases for differential emphasis is one arising from scientific or technological naivete, or to say it less kindly ignorance. In Inca history, leadership succession is shown to be the formula: brother + sister = next Sapa (supreme) Inca. The authors note, "Manco Capac…married his sister, and so did other, and possibly all, of the succeeding Sapa Incas" [Hyam63, p. 53]. They then proceed to imply that this recursive incest might be why the Inca leaders were so good: "Supposing their genes to be free from blemish, as it were, the result would have been to 'fix' the family genius for government" [Ibid.]. This is a family where your wife is your sister, your mom is your aunt, and your dad is your uncle. If there were a family tree here, it would have to be a Joshua tree for all the twisting and rejoining branches. The authors continue: "Certain modern experiments…show that acquired characteristics are heritable, [making] it easier for each succeeding Sapa Inca to learn the trade of kingship" [Ibid.]. Citing the "Egyptian Pharaohs who maintained the longest-lived and most stable empire in history," (a claim the Empire of Japan, among others, might contest) the authors "suggest, albeit tentatively, that systematic incest in the royal Inca line led to the line-breeding of men for kingship as Jersey cows are line-bred for butterfat" [Ibid.]. This was written in 1963, not 963, and yet the authors seem to be unaware of the actual genetic consequences of incest [Bair82]: the magnification of deleterious recessive genes, leading to malformations, blindness and deafness, schizophrenia, cystic fibrosis, heart problems, increased neonatal mortality, increased mental retardation, decreased IQ, and like in several European royal families, hemophilia. Their differential emphasis on the supposed value of inbreeding is, at least on the surface, a consequence of their lack of understanding of the science of genetics.

Another form of differential emphasis comes shortly thereafter in this book when Incan architecture is discussed. "Like the Romans, the Incas took their building style with them wherever they went" [Hyam63, p.57]. The Romans, according to the authors, built "circus buildings…[that are]… monuments to Roman architectural ineptitude and dullness [with]…nothing to recommend them but size and their unfortunate resistance to the insults of time" [Ibid.]. Never mind that structural integrity and resilience are a good – maybe the best – design consideration for building, but the authors then go much further: "If one sought a justification for the Spanish conquest it would be possible to find it in the beauty of the South American baroque, which the Spaniards introduced and which is such startling contrast to Inca megalithic building" [Ibid.]. At this point, we find the authors equating in severity (1) the difference in architectural style between Inca and Spanish with (2) the subjugation of an empire of 12 million people and larger than Texas and New Mexico combined. Presumably, obliviously, these authors have equated a possible (though I find the mortarless construction of, e.g., Sacsayhuaman, comparable in beauty to Spanish baroque) esthetic discomfort with the end of a civilization and the deaths of millions through disease and other disruptions. This seems, to us at least, orders of magnitude of differential emphasis.

Another few pages further on, and another factual error leads to differential emphasis – here on the role of surfeit members of one sex in Inca society. The authors claim that there are societally beneficial roles for extra women to play, particularly as concubines for the Inca (male) leaders. Such concubinage was possible, since "as in all societies which are adequately fed, clothed and housed – that is, in which health and plenty prevail – more females than males were born every year" [Hyam63, pp. 72-73]. This is not, however, true. Scientific studies have shown that, at conception, there is a 50/50 ratio of male/female, but that more female than male embryos die thereafter [Orza15]. In fact, males are usually born in excess and stress decreases the ratio while well-being and good health tend to increase it [Grec14], precisely opposite to the claims of [Hyam63]. Here, the authors have provided differential emphasis on the importance of excess females in contradiction to science and also to a far simpler explanation: that due to wars, accidents, and early deaths, all of which lead to a selective attrition of men, there will ultimately be an excess of women (as there are in the United States today) in the population, even though the majority of births are male.

One final example is given from the same book on the rise and fall of the Inca Empire, where the authors remark that the Inca state (known as Tahuantinsuyu) was, in 1530, aware of the coming Spaniards and likely aware of the other peoples, nations, and empires extending up the Pacific coast and maybe even to the Aztecs. The authors comment, "It is at least possible that the Tahuantinsuyu might have become coextensive with all Central as well as Andean America; and, under rulers line-bred for the work, they might have presented too powerful a front for any European conquest" [Hyam63, pp.109-110]. Ignoring the repeat of the "line bred" incest, do the authors really think that the Aztec, Tlaxcalans, Mayans, and others would just let him take over their kingdoms and territories, and so, present a united front that indeed would be daunting to the Spaniards (if not to smallpox, influenza, typhus, and the plague!)? For comparison, Kuwait, a nation for less than 80 years, nevertheless did not want to be subsumed by Iraq in some pan-Arabic state when Iraq took over their territory in 1990. Here, the differential emphasis is based on being able to see how, for the peoples of Mesoamerica and the Andes, the Spaniards were a far graver existential threat than the Inca. It is certain that the Aztecs and their antagonists (Chibcha, Mayan, Tlaxcalan, etc.) would not have been able to appreciate this, and would not have casually accepted a Tahuantinsuyan overlordship.

The differential emphasis here, therefore, is a form of presentism commonly referred to as 20/20 hindsight.

This section is not meant to be a "critical" review of this book on the Inca. Other parts of it, in particular the fast-moving, geographically anchored description of the civil war between Atahualpa and Huáscar, are both compelling and insightful. The authors also accurately portray the brutality, ignorance, and hypocrisy of the majority of Pizarro's men (there is certainly no differential emphasis here on the goodness of the Spaniards, among whom only Hernando de Soto comes across as respectable), and even admit Huáscar was a failure in "the quality of the long line of the able men whose heir he was" [Hyam63, p. 129]. Additionally, they later point out the massive impact that Eurasian diseases had on the people: "By 1523 [10 years before the murder of Atahualpa], smallpox had become epidemic, raging in many cities of the empire" [Hyam63, p. 123]. The critique here, then, is that the narrative inconsistently integrates the various factors and facts that led to the rise and horrific fall of the Tahuantinsuyu. As a historian, you are expected to keep multiple ideas in your head at the same time, and not to differentially omit them at critical times in the narrative.

5.3 Sagas of the Icelanders

From the Inca of Peru, we travel backward a few hundred years to a marvelously preserved set of tales that themselves project backward yet another few hundred years. Yes, we are talking about the Icelandic sagas, largely written in the 1200s and conveying a differentially emphasized history that covers the early years in Iceland (settled in the year 870, and more or less ending in 1056 when the first bishopric of Iceland was established a little north of present-day Selfoss, Iceland).

In these sagas, there is a treasure trove of historical records of remarkable accuracy which are used to establish family histories. Many in Iceland today can trace their roots, stems, and branches back to these early settlers, providing a rare comprehensiveness to a nation's genealogical record that has of course benefitted from a relatively short settlement era, a small population, and geographical isolation. As with other works of historical recording and fictionalized storytelling, there is a (sometimes shocking) amount of verifiable factual content. There is also a lot of myth-building. The difficulty in separating the fact from the myth-building is discussed in Chapter 4 (see the discussions on *Susanna* and Jesus' parables there). For the purposes of the mistruth created by differential emphasis, however, we are primarily concerned with the content of the sagas, and we will use a "commonality implies veracity" approach to separate the events that likely occurred from those that most likely were fabricated as part of the story-as-saga.

In order to apply this principle, we will first establish its merit by consideration of the field of historical analysis. As discussed previously, it is important to separate out what "is misleading by accident from that which is the result of personal bias; and to distinguish personal bias from cultural bias and general cultural relativity" [McCu00]. Performing this assessment is always probabilistic. Fortunately, the long history of historical analysis has led to some helpful guidelines, including the following seven compiled by [Thur97], which all other factors being equal, provide rules for relatively ranking historical sources:

1. Human sources include relics like a fingerprint; or narratives such as a letter or quoted statement. In general, relics are more credible and reliable than narratives.

2. Any source may have been forged or altered intentionally (or unintentionally). The stronger the indication of originality of the source (e.g., matched carbon dating), the greater its reliability.

3. The closer in time a source is to the event it reports upon, the more likely it is to be accurate.

4. Primary sources are more reliable than secondary sources, which are more reliable than tertiary sources, etc.

5. The credibility of a message is greatly increased by multiple independent sources providing the same message. A good example is the so-called "triple tradition" of events occurring in the three synoptic gospels, including the calling of Matthew the tax collector to be a disciple and the hometown (presumably Nazareth) lack of belief in Jesus' powers. More on the latter in (7.) to follow.

6. The likelihood of some bias is based on the motivations of the source (writer). Tendencies toward self-interest bias, as noted previously, should be minimized and/or complemented with accounts by sources with differing (preferably opposing) motivations.

7. If the source of the account can be established to have no direct interest in creating the apparent "bias" in the message, then the message is deemed more credible. The lack of hometown belief in Jesus, incorporated into the Gospels by his followers, certainly passes this credibility test since it does not support a universal belief in his powers.

Combined, these rules provide a good relative, if not absolute, means of assessing truth in historical reporting.

Langlois and Seignobos [Lang98] digested these input and others to create their own, quite useful set of seven considerations for source mistruth assessment in history, which they assert as an absolute means of assessing truth in several circumstances:

1. If all known (multiple) sources are in agreement about a historical event, it is considered proven.
2. If there are source disagreements, there is no automatic acceptance of the majority view, and it is quite possible every view may be biased, and therefore, stray from the truth. Critical text analysis is required to come to a conclusion here, not voting.
3. The source(s) whose explanation(s) are confirmable by outside authorities in some of its parts may be viewed as trustworthy overall if no discrepancies with outside authorities are proven – this is the "everything that can be verified is true, so the rest is likely true" clause.
4. When two sources disagree, the historian generally accepts the source created by the writer with more expertise or with eyewitnesses. This can be considered a "transitive trust" clause.
5. Eyewitness accounts are preferred when events that are reported on could have been accurately interpreted by most contemporary bystanders to the event. For example, someone today opening a pull tab can be recognized as doing so by virtually anyone alive; however, someone opening a pull tab can in the time of Muhammad might be viewed very differently – particularly if the can had been shaken beforehand.
6. If two independent sources agree, each of their reliabilities is enhanced. Note this is somewhat contradictory to the no-majority comment in (1.)
7. This is the wetted finger in the wind consideration: if two sources disagree and there is no other tiebreaker, then the source that seems better aligned with common sense is accepted. It is more likely a person was blown off the cliff by wind than that they learned to fly, for example.

With all of these rules in mind, then, we are equipped to begin our analysis of truth and mistruth in the Sagas of the Icelanders. A great place to start this complex set of dozens of tales combining history with hyperbole is the collection, "The Sagas of Icelanders," along with its comprehensive introduction by Jane Smiley [Smil01]. As noted in the introduction, the sagas are filled with descriptions of the back-breaking, never-ending work of these pioneers who populated Iceland over the roughly 200 years of the settlement era. Slaves (Irish captives comprising a large percentage thereof) provide shepherding and animal protection, often sleeping with the animals (in the fields or tiny sheds) throughout the frost-free seasons of the year, and then sleeping on the floor, or worse, the rest of the year {Smil01, p. xi]. It becomes clear that reading the sagas is akin to a deck-building game, like *Dominion*, in that the more you read, the more effectively they work together. Smiley points out that reading multiple sagas generally gives greater context to the others in a way not experienced by reading multiple Shakespeare plays (*Julius Caesar* has no impact on *Hamlet*), multiple Dickens novels (*David Copperfield* has no impact on *Great Expectations*), or multiple Mozart pieces (*Symphony 25* has no impact on the *Requiem*) [Smil01, p. xii]. For example, in *Egil's Saga*, "many of the characters of *The Saga of Gunnlaug Serpent-tongue*" [Smil01, p. xxxvi] are mentioned. An early pioneer marriage, Unn the Deep-minded and Olaf the White, are ancestors of characters in *Njal's Saga*, *Eirik the Red's Saga*, and the Eyri and Laxardal sagas [Ibid.]. Thus, the more sagas you read, the more each of the ones you have read makes sense. In addition, because of the high level of overlap between the sagas, commonalities of genealogy, events, event sequencing, and even arguments relating to why certain events occurred can be gleaned in a manner not possible for many other bodies of historical literature. As such, the sagas provide a tremendous case study for historical analysis in general.

The first item that becomes clear due to its consistent overlap in the various sagas is that "While women are more prominent and interesting characters in the sagas than in Homeric epic or *Beowulf* or the *Song of Roland*, the world of the sagas is still a man's world" [Smil01, p. xviii]. The sagas focus on horse gambling, honor violence, law and governance (local leaders are known as godords), and perhaps most significantly, the transformative voyage (usually to Norway) which is a hallmark of early adulthood: all of these being the province of men. Women in the sagas must work through men, which implies they have little agency in greater society and allows many to be portrayed as both shrewish and provincial.

A second item emerging from the consistent overlap of the multiple sagas is how everyday life in settlement-era Iceland was experienced. The sagas are lousy with descriptions of the architectural, civic, agricultural, and domestic manufacturing practices of the people [Smil01, p. xxxix]. What really differentiates the sagas – and in our opinion, adds increased likelihood of veracity – is that unlike the other 19th century realistic novelists for example, the Icelandic saga writers are very specific about the people, places, and relationships involved [Smil01, p. l]. The people mentioned can be traced to people alive today; the places mentioned can be readily visited today; and the relationships can be "proven" by genealogy charts. In addition, the larger world is accurately portrayed, with the same accuracy for places in Iceland applied to Norway, Greenland, and points further afield [Smil01, p. liv].

Moving to a few specific sagas, we start with *Egil's Saga*. The "hero" of this saga is both hero and antihero, or even villain, and from his childhood onward sets the stage for heroic ambiguity throughout this saga (and recurrent theme for all of the major sagas, and even some of the minor ones). Egil is both a genius and a monster, mixing top-tier skaldic poetry with puerile rage (some of it, no doubt, brought on by his osteopetrosis), skill in battle with dead drunkenness, and crafty linguistics in life-threatening conversations with pecuniary pettiness. As Pálsson and Edwards note in their introduction to *Egil's Saga*, there is a "dialectic nature [to] the saga – the light and dark sons, the Viking turned father – which brings out the complexity both of the individual character and of society" [Pals76, p. 13]. The dialectics that are incorporated do, in some measure, prevent the saga from having excessive differential emphasis. It is already so "male," with Egil rage-killing for events as trivial as loss at sports or having the best brew withheld until royalty arrives, with the narrative driven by male quests in travel and acclaim, and with a relentless emphasis on revenge and killing tied to the Norse concept of honor. As we see, then, there is a "close relationship between historical fact and the author's own creative purposes" [Pals76, p. 16]. The author makes the testosterone-shellacked world of Egil more palatable to a wider audience by incorporating poetry, chivalry (Egil, while violent and murderous, is not a chronic bully and in fact, takes the place of the bullied and overmatched Fridgeir in a duel forced upon him by a berserker rejected by Fridgeir's sister), and other acts of mercy and intelligence by Egil.

The dialectic used by the author (who is almost certainly Snorri Sturluson), therefore, matches the oscillation of the main character between goodness and evil, appeal and disgust, and honor and disgrace. It is a masterful work, written by an author with a wealth of story-telling experience. Our interest in *Egil's Saga*, though, germane to the theme of this chapter, is how this dialectic prevents differential emphasis. In the end, we are not sure what to make of him. Even in his last days, as a blind and elderly man mocked by the servants, our empathy and pity are offset by his hiding all of his gold from the family and killing off the servants who helped him cache the gold somewhere in the moors outside his home. We never really can like Egil, just as we never really can write him off completely. His ambiguity, then, prevents us from trying to take too much "history" from his story. It is a brilliant way to prevent historical bias, by preventing any net positive or negative emphasis on the main character.

Another saga of interest from the standpoint of differential emphasis is one that almost certainly overemphasizes the creativity and resourcefulness of its eponymous hero, Ref. In fact, the name *Saga of Ref the Sly* clearly outlines the emphasis the saga will take throughout. Ref is shown to be a superlative craftsperson, able to build the best Viking ships and the best-defended villages, each of which allows him to escape violence at the hands of his overtly jealous adversaries. This makes for compelling reading but stretches credibility in a way that *Egil's Saga* and the other major sagas do not. When Ref (the name means "fox," thus doubling down on the slyness in his moniker) was pursued to Greenland, he built a fort capable of releasing massive streams of water to prevent its burning by his enemies. They returned in greater force and were eventually able to start the fort on fire, but when they did, "quite unexpectedly the part of the wall facing the water fell into the ditch…The wall was as smooth as a single plank. And just when the wall fell, a ship on wheels ran along it and down to the water," [Smil01, p. 617] enabling his family's and his escape. Captivating reading, no doubt there, but also certainly fabricated. One notes that, unlike *Egil's Saga* and *Njal's Saga*, discussed next, the title of *Ref the Sly* is not neutral. Thus, there appears to be a signal in the very naming of the sagas regarding their differential emphasis: prosaic names like *Gisli Sursson's Saga* and *The Saga of the Greenlanders* are more likely to indicate balanced tales, while more colorful (and adjective-laden) names like *The Saga of Gunnlaug Serpent-tongue* and *The Tale of Sarcastic Halli* are more likely to indicate tales with differential emphasis (and in the latter example, the ability of Halli to instantly compose bawdy and skewering skaldic poetry is certainly hard to believe). Thus, the names of the sagas of the Icelanders are consistent with the general wishes of their authors to signal veracity versus mythology: differential emphasis (adjectives like "sarcastic" and "serpent-tongue") in the title signal greater differential emphasis in the saga.

Finally, we turn to the saga of all sagas. The saga so sweeping in narrative, so comprehensive in describing the lives of all elements of settlement-era Icelandic society, and so full of unexpected twists and turns that it could readily be milked into a trilogy of Hollywood blockbusters. We are talking about *Njal's Saga*, or more viscerally, *The Saga of Burnt Njal*. Where to start with this one? It is a central character (among many "central" characters) who dies with roughly 30 chapters left in the tale. Despite being the "hero," he is not "heroic" [Cook97, p. xv], and in fact, the saga is rife with cowardly acts – it is not just a saga about bravery and the Norse ideal. Its great length (roughly

96,000 words, and thus, substantially more than Jane Austen's *Persuasion*, with roughly 84,000 words) and the intentional ties to real people and places means *Njal's Saga* is central to the overall encyclopedia of sagas, with other works "proving" a historical Njal and Gunnar (Njal's closest friend and another hero of the saga) [Cook97, p. viii], even though in reality, they were most likely unacquainted. Gunnar, as ideal a hero as the sagas offer (athleticism, strong warrior skills, patience, and stoicism), is referenced in several other sagas [Cook97, pp. viii-ix], making him a saga "meta-hero" with cross-saga differential emphasis. Gunnar stands for the Germanic ethic of courage, honor, and blood feuding [Cook97, p. xxxiii], and so those who attack him and eventually overwhelm him due to numbers and the (not credible) betrayal of his wife are by the intention of the writer differentially identified as cowardly, dishonorable, and ultimately deserving of the blood revenge they will suffer.

Njal's Saga provides a cleverly woven combination of balance and imbalance. Unlike some of the brawnier sagas – such as the outlaw sagas of Gisli, Grettir, and Hord – *Njal's Saga* challenges traditional male and female roles [Cook97, p. xx], including through the depiction of Njal as beardless, pensive, and favoring negotiation to action. It also shows powerful and decisive women, including the wives of both Njal and Gunnar; the latter, Hallgerd, even being the agent of her husband's doom. However, excessive male chauvinism still occurs, with Flosi "wife-shaming" his friend to action [Cook97, p. 235] and with numerous episodes of male "effeminacy" being highlighted in order to goad men into action traditionally associated with Norse men of the era. Honor, especially male honor, permeates the saga. Clearly, *Njal's* author struck the right balance between differential emphasis and even-handedness, as the sagas were considered literally true by generations of Icelanders [Cook97, p. xxxiii]. It works as verisimilitude as a package because while there is emphasis on the male in *Njal's Saga*, there is enough emphasis on female empowerment to speak to the (relatively more) modern audience of the 13th century for which the saga was written.

One final note on differential emphasis in this most important of sagas. Because the emphasis in *Njal's Saga*, as with the Icelandic sagas as a rule, is on the so-called masculine virtues, the author is over the top with these decorations of the narrative. Perhaps, the most prominent example is Skarphedin's famous slaying of the instigating Thrain Sigfusson: "The ice slab was very smooth, and Skarphedin went along as fast as a bird in flight... Skarphedin...swung his axe at him and hit him on his head and split it down to the jaw, so that the molars fell out on the ice" [Cook97, pp. 159-160]. If that is hard to believe, the next sentence really drives home the black comedy of the event: “This happened in such rapid sequence that no one could land a blow on Skarphedin; he went gliding away at furious speed” [Cook97, p.160]. This goes against the laws of physics and is clearly embellished if not outright fabrication. But its fantastic nature works to differentiate it from the more credible parts of the narrative, and so, we can declare it “honest exaggeration” in synchrony with the “honest naming” of sagas meant to be taken less on face value (such as *The Saga of Gunnlaug Serpent-tongue* and *The Tale of Sarcastic Halli*) as noted above. All of this means that the saga writers understood that if you were going to mix truth with mistruth based on differential emphasis, you owe it to your readers to signal when you are doing each.

5.4 Assault on Tulsa

The Tulsa Race Massacre (May 31st to June 1st of 1921) consisted of a series of violent assaults upon Black Americans by White Americans resulting from the incarceration of a Black man who was imprisoned for an alleged interaction he had with a White woman (a 19-year old Black shoeshiner was accused of assaulting a 17-year old White elevator operator). In the resulting standoff, an unknown number of Americans were murdered or killed (most likely in the hundreds), and hundreds of homes were destroyed in the historically Black Greenwood District of Tulsa.

Tulsa was at the time of sort of economic Harlem, with the Greenwood District being referred to as a “Black Wall Street.” In continuity with the second coming of the KKK [Gord17], the racialized violence that erupted in Tulsa was in part due to economic stresses wrought by overall poor governmental systems. Racial fear and envy were part of the pervasiveness of White supremacy in the United States directly after World War I, and racial violence was a tool for enforcing the economic and political “status quo.”

Tulsa in 1921 saw the prosperity of the Greenwood District arise as a place of hope for Blacks. Prosperity was also enjoyed by Whites in Tulsa but seeing the “rise” of Blacks in such a racially charged atmosphere no doubt created defensiveness and tension. While capitalism promised prosperity to both sides, Whites in Tulsa (and elsewhere in the United States) viewed capitalism as another means of ensuring White advantage. When the “Dick Rowland Incident” allegedly occurred (the most likely explanation is that he slipped in the elevator and grabbed the 17-year-old White girl’s arm to keep from falling), no evidence was required for it to scale into an uncontrolled riot. In the first foray, Blacks defended themselves from the White mob admirably, but soon, the overwhelming number of Whites –reportedly aided by gunfire from airplanes! – led to the destruction of the district and 75 years of silence on the subject.

The Tulsa Race Massacre ended up becoming one of the most contentious and intentionally misremembered events in American history. The name of the event itself is rife with controversy as it was formerly known as the Tulsa Race Riots, a classification that removes the weight from the intentional destruction of Black Wall Street, the systematic White supremacist-motivated murders of upwards of 300 Black Americans, and the subsequent coverup and 100-year long struggle for the truth. Construing the massacre as a riot empowers a false middle-ground narrative, with a differential emphasis on "all sides mattering" in the incitement of the events. One anecdote reports a Black man firing the first shot, for example, as if to insinuate that both sides were equally responsible. This is tantamount to explaining that the assassination of Archduke Franz Ferdinand inevitably led to the hundreds of millions of rounds fired during World War I.

Such narratives only assist the offending parties and the parties with enfranchised power. The motivations for hiding the true nature of what happened in Tulsa seem easily identifiable, as it was segregation-era America and the institutionalized crimes of an abusive government and a plethora of White citizens were covered up to preserve White supremacy. However, the Tulsa Race Massacre is even more complicated than a simple act of racism. One additional compounding factor, which often "hides" behind racism, was classism. From this perspective, the destruction of a wealthy, growing area for the advancement of Black Americans was meant to limit the self-agency and self-advocacy of a historically underprivileged group. Specious legal follow-up to the event meant that funds were never raised or allocated to rebuild the community. In the years after the event, the truth was carefully kept from public view. Modern memorials and more balanced coverage have finally happened (especially around the 100-year anniversary of the event), but to date, no reparations have been made (with reparations being turned down by Oklahoma judges as recently as 2023).

With the Tulsa Race Massacre, we have an event in which differential emphasis is both inevitable and in one sense, appropriate. Initially, emphasis was wrongly placed on the shared culpability of both Black and White Tulsa residents. More modernly, emphasis for interpreting this historical event has been placed on the racism of White Americans as it should be. However, in focusing on racism, without complementary discussions of classism and self-determination, the historical narrative still runs the risk of oversimplification. The event was racist, indeed, but by failing to properly emphasize its economic and classist origins as well may be undermining economic reparations.

A full story, one integrating the racist, classist, and self-deterministic elements of the event, is more likely to lead to appropriate closure.

5.5 Cyber Salon – Red, Blue, Purple, Can't We All Just Get Along?

As we have seen from the "deeper dives" in this chapter – Inca, Saga, and Tulsa – it is important to account for the motivations of the narrator in the narrative. If we want to use what we have learned and apply it to cybersecurity, then an appropriate area is in adversarial attack and defense – the so-called "red teams" attacking and trying to penetrate a system and the "blue teams" defending the systems from the attack. In this section, we argue for the use of the red team/blue team approach rather than the so-called "purple team" approach in order to avoid "self-fulfilling security sign-off," using the principles of differential emphasis and evaluation to justify this stance.

The red and blue team approach not only makes a lot of sense but it is preadapted to some of the most powerful modern artificial intelligence (AI). Having a red team attempt to "learn" how to break into a system, while the blue team continues to relearn how to stop the red team from being successful is an "arms race" where the distinction between success and failure gets smaller each iteration. This is directly in keeping with generative adversarial networks (GANs) employment as one of the major elements of the generative AI (GAI) family of algorithms. In the classic GAN, introduced in the 2014 timeframe [Good14], there are two "teams" (in the form of a "team" or collection of nodes and edges called a neural network) in a so-called "zero sum" game where one team's gain is the other team's loss. That is, if the blue team finds a way to better differentiate authentic activity from adversarial activity (and thus keep the network safe), its gain, G_1, is equal in magnitude but opposite in polarity from the red team's loss, L_1. That is, $G_1 = -L_1$. Similarly, if the red team figures out a new manner to hide their adversarial activity by making it look legitimate, their gain, G_2, is also equal in magnitude but opposite in polarity from the blue team's loss of ability to detect this attacking activity, L_2. A familiar equation, $G_2 = -L_2$.

An important aspect of the GAN approach is that the red and blue teams work from an identical training set. In other words, the adversary (called the "generator" in GAN lingo and functioning as the equivalent of the red team) has access to public information and tries to create a situation that can pass for "indistinguishable" from the training set (but still be capable of exploiting the system). The system protector (called the "discriminator" in GAN lingo and functioning as the equivalent of the blue team) continues to learn to discriminate between the {legitimate} content and the {legitimate + exploit} content. This battle continues throughout the lifetime of the system.

A "purple team," as you might suspect based on your memories of fourth-grade art class, is a combination of red and blue. In fact, in security penetration testing, or "pentesting," the concept of purple teaming is that of bringing the red and blue teams together to test, and where needed, improve the system's security. The claim behind purple teaming is that it maximizes the contribution of each set of skills; that is, all of those on attack and all of those on defense. But it goes beyond the sharing of the same set of training data, and can quickly lead to an echo chamber effect where both teams are more concerned with showing off their areas of brilliance (not that it is a bad thing, per se), such that a sense of familiarity, premature complacency, or even "self-fulfilling sign off" of the pentest occurs. The problem is that once either team introduces their chosen topics, a sort of collective familiarity bias sets in, consistent with differential emphasis, and the conversation is more focused on the "knowns" of the two teams than on the unknowns. The advantage of the antagonistic red/blue approach is that neither side can "get comfortable" with what to expect the other side to have in terms of proficiencies, focus areas, and capabilities. This prevents the bias of differential emphasis and requires a broader preparedness by the blue team, as well as inviting a broader set of penetration attempts by the red team. This "fuzzing" of the red team's attacks and the blue team's capabilities keeps both teams on their toes, and as such, typically leads to a more secure overall system after the red/blue team exercise.

5.6 Summary

Differential emphasis and evaluation are the focus of this chapter and provide a pattern for mistruths based on *selective complexity*, in which one person, interpretation, or event is covered in much greater depth and/or nuance than another person, interpretation, or event in a historical narrative. The disproportionate nuance provided to the Spaniards over the Inca whose civilization they destroyed means that their history is more fully understood and elaborated than that of the Inca. That is, differential coverage, irrespective of polarity (positive or negative coverage), requires an attempt by the writer to address it. The six-step program outlined here requires (1) acknowledging the selective complexity, (2) arguing against your own point, (3) using the Hegelian dialectic to provide a richer overall synthesis of the historical reporting, (4) separating opinion from fact, (5) employing plausibility and parsimony, and (6) accepting the miraculous only within reason. After addressing the fall of the Inca, an analysis of truth and differential emphasis in the sagas of the Icelandic settlers was provided. In this analysis, the means that the saga writers signaled more or less differential emphasis is shown. A discussion of how differential emphasis has been applied to the Tulsa Race Riot of 1921 finished off the case studies for this chapter. The chapter concluded with the application of differential emphasis and evaluation lessons learned to the structuring of cybersecurity penetration tests, or pentests. By applying the recommendations, you as a cybersecurity professional may prevent "self-fulfilling sign-off" which might otherwise make you think your system is more secure than it actually is.

References

[Bair82] Baird PA and McGillivray B, "Children of incest," The Journal of Pediatrics 101, no. 5, 854–857, 1982.

[Cook97] Cook R, translator, "Njal's Saga," Penguin Books, 384 pp., 1997.

[Good14] Goodfellow I, Pouget-Abadie J, Mirza M, Xu B, Warde-Farley D, Ozair S, Courville A, and Bengio Y, "Generative adversarial nets," Advances in neural information processing systems 27, 2014.

[Gord17] Gordon L, "The second coming of the KKK: The Ku Klux Klan of the 1920s and the American political tradition," Liveright Publishing, 2017.

[Grec14] Grech VE and Mamo J, "The male to female ratio at birth," 2014.

[Hyam63] Hyams E and Ordish G, "The last of the Incas, the Rise and Fall of an American Empire," Barnes and Noble Books, 295 pp., 1963.

[Lang98] Langlois CV and Seignobos C, "Introduction aux études historiques, 1 vol.," 1898.

[Mala08] Malaga RA, "Worst practices in search engine optimization," Communications of the ACM 51, no. 12: 147–150, 2008.

[McCu00] McCullagh CB, "Bias in historical description, interpretation, and explanation," History and Theory 39, no. 1: 39–66, 2000.

[Orza15] Orzack SH, Stubblefield JW, Akmaev VR, Colls P, Munné S, Scholl T, Steinsaltz D, and Zuckerman JE, "The human sex ratio from conception to birth," Proceedings of the National Academy of Sciences 112, no. 16: E2102–E2111, 2015.

[Pals76] Pálsson H and Edwards P, translators, "Egil's Saga," Penguin Books, 256 pp., 1976.

[Rose18] Rosenshield G, "Tolstoi, Napoleon, and hero-worship: the paths of Pierre Bezukhov and Andrei Bolkonskii," The Slavic and East European Journal, 359–381, 2018.

[Smil01] Smiley J, editor, "The Sagas of Icelanders," Penguin Books, 848 pp., 2001.

[Thur97] Thurén T, "Källkritik," Stockholm: Almqvist & Wiksell, 1997.

6

Omniscient Historian

Reason should investigate its own parameters before declaring its omniscience

– Immanuel Kant

It's easy to be omniscient when you've done it all before

– Audrey Niffenegger

Abstract

The concept of an omniscient historian is, of course, an oxymoron. No historian can take into account the full context of any historical event and relies on the knowledge, opinion, and reporting of others for their own historical analysis. What is meant by "omniscient historian" in this chapter is a historian who acts as if they know everything. The omniscient historian projects their own interpretations, beliefs, and possibly words into the minds and mouths of historical figures. As many historians do, we could blame Herodotus, who projected thoughts and even dreams onto his characters. Sure, Herodotus wrote before history became a "science," but those eager to forgive him may forget that the events of the Greco-Persian War, of which he wrote, were already "ancient history" to his audience at the time. Herodotus, just like us today, can be guilty of reinterpreting events in light of their own current events. Herodotus, of course, was unable to project himself into the time (the Persian invasion) of his characters; instead, they were projected forward into his time (the precipice of the Peloponnesian War). Both eras were under the sword of Damocles (the Persians or their Sparta/Athens-led opponents), but it should be remembered that Marathon occurred in 490 BC, and the plague (contemporaneous with Herodotus's history) in Athens in 430 BC. This is the same difference in years between the Great Depression and the explosion of the Internet in the 1990s.

DOI: 10.1201/9788770048347-6

More recent (and excellent – they were Presidential Medal of Freedom winners and did their best to place a reader in the entire context of their reported histories) historians, Will and Ariel Durant, are also guilty at times of being omniscient historians. However, their style is to use some omniscience in an obvious, narrative fashion. They comment up front that, in their opinion, Jane Austen was the best writer of prose of her time. However, it is clear to at least this reader that they are inserting this as their opinion. Perhaps the same would have been clear to Herodotus' readers, or it simply was not an issue then (after all, what "normalization" of history had occurred before Herodotus, who wrote at the same time as the authors of *1 and 2 Chronicles*, *Malachi*, and *Nehemiah*?). This is part of what makes it difficult to "harshly" judge Herodotus. Also, there is likely to always be some "omniscience" added to a historical document, if for no other reason than that of showing the interpretative skills of the writer. The pervasiveness and the difficulty of preventing the omniscient historian are the subject of this chapter.

6.1 Introduction

A particularly egregious form of doctoring documents is that of the omniscient historian, where of course the term "omniscient" is used ironically. Were there to be an actually omniscient historian available for any given historical event, we would all benefit, of course. However, that is simply not possible. For one thing, no historian can get inside the heads of all the people involved in a historical event. For another, no historian is usually predisposed to (or has access to materials in order to) represent multiple opinions on a historical event evenly. In this sense, then, the omniscient historian is by default an ironic name for a historian who appears comfortable putting their opinions and versions of how they think history should have occurred into the mouths of their historical figures.

As noted in the abstract of the chapter, this practice extends back at least as far as Herodotus, who seemed not only to know what everyone thought but also what everyone *dreamed*. This could be written off as an opinion, except that Herodotus was reporting on real events with real (world-forming, in fact) consequences. Herodotus' lack of attribution is particularly galling: he never tells us how he came upon these crucial conversations, thoughts, dreams, and aspirations. There is, from the (again, arguably unfair) perspective of our times, an almost shocking amount of presentism in the histories of Herodotus. The Greco-Persian War was "ancient history" to his audience at the time, extending back to the births of their eldest citizens. The "compression of ancient time" that we have mentioned earlier is just as big of a concern to Herodotus as it would be to, say, George Eliot. She wrote her masterwork, *Middlemarch*, about fictionalized events in the Midlands of England from 1829 to 1832, from the perspective of two generations later (1869–1871 are the years she spent writing *Middlemarch*). Forty years in the Industrial Revolution changed a lot, and so Eliot needed to "undo" 40 years' worth of progress in order to capture the context of living back in those earlier times. In our opinion, she was more successful than Herodotus, who in writing roughly 2500 years ago can still be considered guilty of reinterpreting events in light of his own (then) current events. Herodotus is particularly culpable for judging the actions of those involved in his history while already knowing how it turned out. He found it difficult, if not impossible, to take this "future foreknowledge" out of his writing. That is, Herodotus was not able to project himself into the moment of his characters; instead, they were projected forward into his moment. Herodotus' characters were "modern" to his audience; that is, they were more like Greeks on the precipice of the Peloponnesian War than Greeks under the Sword of Damocles which was the Persian invasion. We can say, then, that Herodotus did not necessarily write bad history – it is that he did not separate history from his story.

More recent historians, Will and Ariel Durant, are also guilty at times of being omniscient historians. Their "omniscience," though, is overlaid on 2400 years of advancement in historical narration, starting with Herodotus and extending to their contemporaries, such as Fernand Braudel (who, one might argue, benefitted more from the Durants than the reverse). The Durants do try to take the reader into the "complete context" of the times of which they write so that the omniscience (reinforced by their focus on "great people" of the times) comes across in a more obvious, narrative fashion. For example, two of their volumes are heavily centered on "great men" Julius Caesar and Napoleon Bonaparte. It is clearer to the reader of today than it was to their original audiences several generations ago that focus on "great men" is a form of omniscience in which great events are centered on great people in order to streamline the narrative.

6.2 Herodotus

In addition to history-specific accounts, this book focuses on myth and literary accounts. Why are mythology and literature so important to history? It is not just that they can, like the Old Testament and Herodotus, contain a high proportion of factual history. It is instead that *even their nonfactual history*, as it were, is the *history of culture*, and thus is *actual history*. All mythology and literature, therefore, is a varying degree of factual (specific persons, places, and things) and actual (contextual, social, and communal) history. We should use caution in discarding actual history to focus only on the factual since without the actual history, the context in which the facts occur is nearly impossible to recreate.

In this section, we argue for a third, mellifluously rhyming, type of history, which is *contractual history*. That is, history (such as Julius Caesar's history of the battles against the Gauls, *Commentarii de Bello Gallico*, or *The War for Gaul* in English) that is part of a social contract between historians and the society about which they write the history. Such contractual histories usually laud the author (in the case of Caesar), the rulers (in the case of certain contemporary histories of China written during Mao's rule or certain contemporary histories of Russia written during Stalin's rule), or the society itself (such as Milton's *Defensio pro Populo Anglicano*, written in support of the parliamentary movement under Cromwell). Contractual history can revolve around an actual paid contract or can simply come across – as in for example the case of Milton's *Defensio pro Populo Anglicano* and follow-on *Defensio Secunda* – as apologetics. It is our contention, however, that such contractual history (even when more or less complete fabrication or opinion) is still important to an understanding of the history of its period. A complete history reports the facts, the culture, and the sentiment of the history – the sentiments of those living in the time of the history are innately important. How else can the Salem Witch Trials, the rise of fascism, or the Red Scare of the 1950s be understood? While a small percentage of people in any population are truly (i.e., clinically) insane, including sociopathic and even less commonly psychopathic individuals, nevertheless many different societies have displayed functional insanity as a result of the factual, actual, and contractual histories interacting in some form of synergistic manner.

Many previous historians, social scientists, and analysts have remarked on the possibilities for societal "collective insanity" to occur in times of crisis. One of the more haunting of these histories is Daniel Goldhagen's *Hitler's Willing Executioners* [Gold96]. In this analysis of the power of the Nazi regime to induce and/or entice ordinary German citizens into committing unspeakable acts of betrayal, violence, and callousness, Goldhagen shows how fear of reprisal to person, family, and friends allowed a group that never received more than about a third of the popular vote in a fair election to bully the world's most powerful nation into starting a disastrous war and fueling a Hieronymus Bosch fever-dream of a machine for eradicating specific scapegoated peoples. Goldhagen's analysis deftly combines the factual, actual, and contractual history of the Nazi era to show how a society can be overawed by an ambitious, energetic, and often (as is certainly the case with the Nazis) evil minority.

One of the important contributions of Goldhagen's work is that it successfully contradicts previous mistruths in history. One common pattern of mistruth is when a particular interpretation becomes a standard interpretation through repetition, often simply because it creates a pithy, perhaps, convincing story. This is *narrative omniscience of convenience*, in a sense. For example, a standard rationale for how the Nazis maintained power in Germany is that they coerced citizens to follow the edicts of the Nazis by threatening their families if they did not comply. Surely, at some level, that was the case, particularly for those higher up in the Nazi hierarchy or for those having societal influence. But Goldhagen's book shows that German soldiers, and by extension German people, actually had substantial ability to push back on the Nazis. Goldhagen shows memos in which German soldiers openly disobeyed orders given them by their superiors: "Hoffman also understood his parent institution to be so tolerant that he was willing to refuse a direct order and even to record his brazen insubordination in writing" [Gold96, p.4]. Yet, these same soldiers signed up to hunt Jewish people hiding in nearby rural areas, and the very Hoffman mentioned, led his men in the murder of tens of thousands of Jews. They could push back, yet willingly chose to participate in genocide. Altogether, this observation shows that an omniscient historian, in projecting onto Nazi Germany the fears that other societies would reasonably have about coercion and threat, would err by projecting their own morals and expectations onto Nazi Germany. Instead, Germany of the Nazi era was a nation that had been carefully and even expertly groomed (in many cases, without specific threat or coercion) for the externalization of violence needed for a nation only slightly larger than California to take on most of the industrialized world in a pitched battle and to be steeled for the grim and grimy task of extermination.

The telling of history, then, is filled with unexpected exigencies. It is an irony of historical narration that in order to tell the truth, you have to include myths, lies, and other forms of falsehood. That is, histories that ignore the lies of the society upon which they report *are themselves mistruths*. This is a paradox along the lines of "I am a liar, that is the truth," which adds further complexity – and further responsibility to the historian – to truthfully report on lies. The lies under which historical societies were swayed, guided, or even controlled are *truths of history*. In the present era, when deepfakes are increasingly pervasive and convincing, an understanding of the content and evolution of societal lies is all the more important.

Given this discussion, please do not anticipate that, as we now turn to Herodotus, we are going to defend some of the most egregious elements of *Histories*. We will not. Recognizing that mistruth is a part of history does not change it into truth. A mistruth of history is still a falsehood. But falsehoods have consistently driven much of the narrative of history. So, it is important to remember that even if the Greek populace reading Herodotus did not themselves believe *Histories* as representing the events as they *factually* happened, they largely believed that *Histories* represented events as they *actually* and *contractually* happened; that is, Herodotus' telling conveyed the worldview around the events which united the Greeks in thought, resolve, and the *prioritization of meaning*. This latter element, prioritization of meaning, is a difficult one to assess in a culture of which you were not a part. Some cultures – say those of the Enlightenment – are driven by reason. Other cultures – too numerous to mention – are driven by faith. Still others are driven by cultural beliefs in superiority ranging from Manifest Destiny in the 19th century to *hakkō ichiu* and Fascism in the 20th century. Herodotus, in combining factual events such as Marathon and Salamis with actual events such as the invocation of Gods such as Ares and Athena and with contractual events such as his need to warn Athenians against the escalation of the Peloponnesian War, gives a history that allows one to better place oneself in his time than does a simple factual history – even though the actual and contractual events are mistruths. In other words, without his mistruths, we have less of the overall truth. Thus, we wish to avoid the omniscient historian who erases the "lies of history" and superimposes their own truths just as much as we wish to identify mistruths for what they are. They are two sides of the same coin, in some sense.

Now, on to the *Histories* themselves. The first thing to note, from a mistruth in history standpoint, is that Herodotus' books are meant for more than just history. They are meant to entertain. A good perspective on Herodotus is provided by Debra Hamel: "The prose masterpiece [Herodotus] composed [is] a mix of geography and ethnography, political and social history, mythology and propaganda" [Hame12, p. 2]. Herodotus cannot be faulted by later historians for failing "to adhere to historical standards that didn't exist yet when he was writing" [Ibid.]. In fact, Strassler argues that much of Herodotus' hyperbole stemmed from his "sustained and serious curiosity about non-Greek lands and peoples" [Stra07, p. xxxii]. Given his generally even-handed treatment of Greeks and Persians (perhaps due to his living in Halicarnassus, a western Anatolian location on the liminal space between the Greek and Persian worlds), it follows the principle of parsimony that Herodotus was more open-minded about including incredible (and from our perspective, impossible) reports from outside the Greek world. One might, from a generous perspective, accuse Herodotus of acting like an omniscient historian in such cases out of a desire to be more inclusive than other, much more provincial, Greek writers of his time.

Herodotus, however, mixes admiration of external cultures with tales that he has almost certainly not fact-checked and that are also meant to shock his audience. Herodotus recounted "the most disgusting of all Babylonian customs" [Stra07, p. 107] as the requirement for every Babylonian woman to prostitute herself at least once in the "sanctuary of Aphrodite" [Ibid.]. Herodotus notes that the Assyrians (actually a different people from hundreds of miles north of Babylon, but they ruled Babylon maybe a hundred years before Herodotus wrote) called Aphrodite by the name Mylitta, and he castigates the women who are obliged to go to the sanctuary to (by law) sell themselves to the first man who offers silver (of any amount): "the wealthier women, haughty in their pride, think they are too good to mingle with the rest and ride to the sanctuary in covered chariots" [Ibid.]. This fantastical story (assuredly untrue) is brought across with verisimilitude, with Herodotus even noting "women who are tall and beautiful leave quickly, but unattractive women may wait...for up to three or four years" [Ibid.]. Imagine the burden to society this would create! This is rightly one of the elements of *Histories* which leads many to write Herodotus off as a liar or fake. The fact that he describes Babylon as having walls 100 meters high, as mentioned in Chapter 2, only furthers our conviction that Herodotus never actually visited Babylon. But he states this lecherous tradition as an omniscient narrator, perhaps to justify Greek feelings of superiority over their "oriental" competitors.

Before moving to more credible Herodotus accounts, we will remark on two more of the most absurd. In Book 7 of *Histories*, Herodotus remarks on the Battle of Thermopylae that "Three million foes were once fought right here / By four thousand men from the Peloponnese" [Stra07, p. 593]. The logistics capabilities for moving more than perhaps 150,000 warriors, of course, did not exist in the time of the Achaemenid Persian Empire, and that was true until modern times (note that ancient cities generally could not exceed 250,000 citizens for purposes of food supply logistics – the same logic applies to a "moving city" called an army). The second of these examples, mentioned briefly in our earlier Chapter 2, is Herodotus' pronouncement of the existence of ants in the upper Indus region of modern-day Pakistan that were "a bit bigger than foxes" [Hame12, p. 122]. It may well be that Herodotus mistranslated the Persian word for "marmot" [Hame12, p.123], but Herodotus remarks on their size without equivocation and adds that they mounded up sand containing gold [Stra07, p. 257]. These examples are brought up not to ridicule Herodotus, but rather to show how "fact-checking" and "questioning your sources" were difficult, if not impossible, in his day. Keep in mind that one of the worst punishments in his time was banishment. Most people never moved from their village, town, etc., of birth. There were no Lonely Planets, Air BnBs, or ride shares back then. Herodotus may have visited Egypt, but he certainly never saw Babylon, let alone Pakistan. Yes, his narrative is just as confident about the whores of Babylon (as an aside, did Herodotus in part inspire the *Whore of Babylon* account much later in the New Testament *Book of Revelation 17*?) and the ant-agonists of Pakistan as he is about the (more credible) 192 Athenian deaths at Marathon. Omniscience, therefore, overrules nuance and credibility. To Herodotus, the history that made the story interesting was his goal. If it was verifiably true (like the 192 Athenian deaths, supported by their tumulus which is visible to this day), so much the better. But if it was not verifiable and still made for an interesting tale, Herodotus was likely to include it.

Turning to less obvious mistakes, we consider other examples of omniscience and related likely mistruths in Herodotus' narratives. Our next example is Herodotus' subtly omniscient connection between the crucial battles of Marathon and Thermopylae. In book 6, Herodotus covers the Battle of Marathon: "Herodotus reports that 6400 Persians were killed at Marathon… [and]…only 192 Athenians died" [Hame12, p. 199]. In an interesting anecdote, Herodotus follows up his discussion of the casualties by mentioning that the Spartans, arriving late, are eager to see the battlefield: "They went to Marathon and looked at the rotting corpses. They praised the Athenians for their accomplishment. And they went back home" [Ibid.]. This is an odd story in some light until we bring to bear some mathematics. 192 might seem like an arbitrary number at first, lending it some credibility. And perhaps it is the right number of Athenian deaths. However, 192 is also exactly 3 times 64; in other words, three groups of 64. The number of Persians killed at Marathon is cited as exactly 100 times 64. Those numbers, therefore, boil down to a ratio of Persian to Athenian deaths of 100 to 3. And the Spartans were witnesses to this.

We move forward a decade to the Battle of Thermopylae. In this battle, the 10,000 Persian "Immortals" [Stra07, p. 529] are presumably those who are killed by the famous Spartan "300" led by Leonidas and perishing to a man in a final wave of Persian missiles and misanthropy. Herodotus estimates that the 4000 Greeks who remained in and around Thermopylae for the final battle killed 20,000 Persians [Hame12, p. 238], and his readers likely readily identified the 10,000 Immortals as those slaughtered by Leonidas and followers. That is right, 10,000 dead Persians to 300 dead Spartans, a ratio of 100 to

3, forming a perfect book end (a decade later) to Marathon. The Athenians, in other words, *had* to have killed 6400 Persians at Marathon to set expectations for the 300: Leonidas and his fellow sons of lions must pile up 100 Persians for every three of them that fall at Thermopylae. And, thanks to Herodotus's omniscience, controlling the casualties across a decade, they *did*. Does this mean that Herodotus is providing a fictionalized account of either battle? Actually not, but he is using his position as a historian (a role some say he invented, remember) to neatly tie together two different, but related, events, ten years apart, with the type of omniscience that comes from looking back at both events at the same time. Regrettable, but probably close enough to the actual results to be forgivable.

Next on the list for Herodotus is a historical "flair" that you might more readily associate with omniscience than the previous example: that of breaking the "fourth wall." Imagine if Hamlet, the Prince of Denmark, suddenly faced the audience and asked, "What would you do in my place? Trust the ghost and kill the uncle? To be a murderer or not to be, that is the question." It certainly would not be as brilliant a soliloquy; in fact, it would no longer be a soliloquy (nor really an aside, for that matter). Hamlet breaking the fourth wall would, quite simply, ruin the play. But does the breaking of the fourth wall ruin *history*? Herodotus notes an act of betrayal during the Persian War immediately after the Marathon battle, in which a shield signal was sent, but Herodotus excludes the possibility that it was sent by the Alcmaeonidae "because they were such a distinguished family" [Hame12, p. 201]. This sort of comment leads the reader to consider that the Alcmaeonidae were patrons of Herodotus, but there is no record of that being the case. Instead, as leading members of Athenian society, the Alcmaeonidae were important to speak well of. Thus, Herodotus' knowledge of the present state of the family has little to no bearing on whether they signaled the Persians several generations earlier, and thus can be considered to constitute "fourth wall omniscience."

Another not-so-subtle instance of omniscience (through presentism) occurs when Herodotus relates a story about Sparta and Plataea that occurred sometime before Marathon. Herodotus notes that "The Lacedaemonians [Sparta] gave this advice [for the Plataeans to ask Athens for protection from their aggressor, Thebes] not so much out of goodwill toward the Plataeans as out of their wish to create trouble for the Athenians by provoking them into active hostilities against the Boeotians [Thebes]" [Stra07, p. 472]. This projects the intense rivalry of the Peloponnesian War back onto a pre-Marathon Greece, which may or may not be merited (Sparta had never appreciated the reforms of Cleisthenes, for example). Regardless, Herodotus states the motivations of the Spartans as if it is a fact, which truthful or not implies his ability to read minds.

Another case of presentism-as-omniscience occurs shortly after the shield signal narrative. Cleisthenes, the tyrant of Sicyon (near Corinth in the northeastern Peloponnese), was looking for a proper match for his daughter, Agariste. Apparently, he had created a tier list of suitors, with Hippoclides in the S tier and Megacles trailing slightly in the A tier. However, Herodotus, always good at recreating – or creating! – memorable anecdotes, coins the expression "Hippoclides doesn't care," who at the gala to select the groom essentially invents break dancing by, according to Herodotus, dancing on his head. After he is told that he has been rejected as a groom in favor of "Megacles, who had had the sense not to make an ass of himself so close to the finish line," [Hame12, p. 203] Hippoclides is reported to have made his iconic and insouciant remark. A fantastic story? Maybe, maybe not. But one thing is certain. Megacles is the great-grandfather of "Pericles son of Xanthippos" [Stra07, p. 483], the great Athenian general and statesman, and thus, a person of power, prestige, and possibly patronage. Was Herodotus above presentism to promote patronage? Again, maybe, maybe not.

The last case of presentism-as-omniscience we relate from *Histories* occurs later as the Greeks, led by Athens, are preparing to take on Mardonius and his Persian army near Plataea. Herodotus portrays Sparta as messing with the Athenian messengers in the last desperate days as the Greeks try to pull together for the battle. The Spartans, for 11 days, acted as if they would not send any troops so that the Athenians finally said that they "would have to ally with Persia" [Hame12, p. 273]. At this point, the Spartans revealed that they had already sent 40,000 troops to the theatre of action (which is ultimately the tipping point for Greek victory). The boiling hostilities between Sparta and Athens in the time that Herodotus was writing provided the context for his presentism. Half a century earlier, in the lead up to Plataea, the Spartans and Athenians were unlikely to be playing games like this since Sparta's "Isthmian wall could be outflanked by sea" [Ibid.]. In other words, Sparta knew that it needed Athens as part of the coalition and would not have intentionally jeopardized their own future just to create temporary anxiety for Athens in some childish game of ambassador chicken.

Finishing with Herodotus, then, we have come to admire his creative and interdisciplinary approach to history. The former, however, leads him into a few dark alleys of mistruth, undermining his overall credibility. A careful rereading of Herodotus, of which we have only scratched the surface here, is able to help shine a light on that dark alley, allowing truth to avoid a beating and escape into the well-lit street of modern standards for historical narration.

6.3 Will and Ariel Durant

More recent historians, Will and Ariel Durant, are also guilty at times of being omniscient historians. However, it is a much different approach than that taken by Herodotus, admittedly benefitting from intervening 24 centuries of advancement in historical narration. Will and Ariel Durant, in spite of obvious faults (e.g., they are occasionally dismissed as historical populists rather than historical scholars), are powerful and important historians. This is high praise, and to support it, we first consider some of the other histories (not already mentioned in this book) that are particularly striking and in which elements of the overall Durant style shine.

6.3.1 A not-so-great and not-so-noble scheme

The first of these histories capturing an aspect of the Durant approach is a captivating book about the Acadian diaspora of the second half of the 18th century, when French Acadians, roughly centered around the Bay of Fundy in what is now Eastern Canada, were forcibly expelled by New England (Nova Scotia and Massachusetts, which then included Maine) troops. Entitled *A Great and Noble Scheme* [Fara05], the title is taken from a communication sent from Nova Scotia that was reproduced in the *Pennsylvania Gazette* on September 4, 1755, in which a great and noble scheme to rid the territories (what is now Nova Scotia and southern New Brunswick) of the French-speaking Acadians was proposed. Thousands were killed, mainly by famine and other hardships. Many more underwent a diaspora to places as far afield as Quebec and Louisiana (where the word "Cajun" derives from the word "Acadian"). Faragher also provided an early use of "big data" in historical demographic analysis to estimate the actual impact of the forced removal on the Acadian population. Faragher used population statistics for the French-speaking Acadians and projected them forward, subtracting the survivors, to estimate the actual impact of the "great and noble scheme." In doing so, Faragher addressed a mistruth of history, particularly in the reporting of acts of ethnic cleansing and forced displacements of people: the reporting of the number of individuals killed is not the most truthful report to provide. Suppose that a population of 10,000 grows to 20,000 in a generation without disruption (3000 deaths and 13,000 births). Due to disruption, their numbers drop to 7000 with 4000 deaths and 1000 births in the next generation. The number often reported by historians is 4000 deaths. However, as Faragher intimates in his summary of the demographic impact of the Expulsion of the Acadians, the number that is most salient is the 1000 excess deaths (3000 would have been expected to die of natural causes in a generation) plus the 12,000 less births. The demographic effect of the diaspora is, thus, 1000 + 12,000, or 13,000, exactly the difference between the otherwise anticipated number of people (20,000) and the actual number of people (7000) a generation later. Note, however, that reporting 4000 deaths is disingenuous in both directions: it overestimates the number directly killed by not subtracting the natural deaths and it underestimates the overall impact of the forced displacements by not including reduced births due to the trauma and suffering.

Thus, Faragher provides an *acceptable* form of *omniscience-as-presentism* applied to historical analysis and interpretation: the application of data science to a macro-event in order to provide a more comprehensive, more inclusive, and more credible understanding of the scale of such an event. This approach fits well with the goals of the monumental Durant history: that of *providing insights into representative lives of the people and their culture.*

6.3.2 Thanks taken back

We now consider another so-called "macro-event" nearly a century earlier, also in New England, to highlight a second admirable technique of the Durants. In this case, it is the attempt to integrate all aspects of civilization together into the narrative. The book in question is Jill Lepore's *The Name of War: King Philip's War and the Origins of American Identity* [Lepo09], and as the title suggests, it addresses the watershed conflict (1675–1676) in New England that, two generations after the mythical friendship cemented at the first Thanksgiving (1621), changed the relationship to enmity and mutual attempted extermination. How did friendship turn into an existential war for survival within 55 years? As with other macro-events, there are multiple, interrelated causes. The decimation of the Native population through disease, preferential alliance with the Puritans by some groups of Natives, and a hurried trial that resulted in the summary hanging of three Wampanoags were long-term, medium-term, and short-term causes, among others. Regardless, the fighting quickly spread throughout New England, and Metacomet (with adopted English name King Philip) led up to several thousand natives at a time against the roughly 110 towns of New England.

Without aid from England or any other European power for that matter, the Puritans faced an existential crisis that nearly resulted in the complete failure of the New England "experiment." Within the space of a year, native civilizations such as the Wampanoag (40% loss of lives) and Narragansett (perhaps 60% loss of lives) were effectively destroyed, and the Puritans themselves may have lost as much as 25% of their population [Cray09, p. 107]. Lepore, in relating the events leading up to and comprising "King Philip's" War brings truth in history through the proper evaluation of a "burning the bridges" turning point in Native/Puritan relationships. Lepore shows, convincingly, that this conflict made previously fluid boundaries between cultures become rigid ones, with no real room for reconciliation. Gone forever were the possibilities for cautious but tangible respect such as the world portrayed in Lydia Maria Child's *Hobomok* (set in 1629–1632). Instead, a wary Puritan population was forever changed, with the regional mass hysteria brought on by the uncertainties and the horrors of war with the Natives likely contributing to the witch hunts (the Salem Witch Trials of 1692 being the most famous but by no means a solitary event) which soon followed. It is worth pointing out that the most famous witch hunt of the era began with a Native slave, Tituba, being accused first.

Thanks to King Philip's War, the wonder of Thanksgiving was replaced by the horror of its opposite, Thanks Taken Back, with the permanent segregation of Native and Puritan societies; that is, what was left of them. This brilliant book by Lepore, then, like the Durants, shows how to recognize and explore critical turning point events in history and analyze them. In spite of the sharp focus on the specific macro-event, the conflict, Lepore integrates all aspects of, in this case, two civilizations, together in a narrative in order to offset a potential posture of presentism. Like the Durants, Lepore provides a story of civilizations, not just a war story.

6.3.3 Framing a year in the life

The next history book to consider here is James Shapiro's *1599: A Year in the Life of William Shakespeare*, which (like the Durants often do) focuses on a turning point in the life of a great person. In fact, the Durants have been (perhaps rightly) criticized for their great personal focus, a historical narrative approach not currently in favor.

Why 1599? Well, for one thing, it was the turning point in Shakespeare's already successful career and one that arguably raised him from the best of his time to the best of *all* time. *Julius Caesar*, the first play shown at the Globe (premiering in Spring of 1599), was a public sensation, an Elizabethan blockbuster, and a nice distraction for Londoners from both Essex's disastrous campaign in Ireland and the inconclusive naval engagements with Spain (The sinking of Spanish Armada in 1588 is well-known, but a similarly disastrous fate awaited the English Armada sent against Spain the following year, 1589, essentially setting the naval power structure back to square one).

In addition to the great tragedy, *Julius Caesar*, Shakespeare wrote *Henry the Fifth* (maybe the most commonly performed history of the Bard's, at least circa 2020), *As You Like It* (maybe the most commonly performed comedy of the Bard's, at least circa 2020), and then, just to top off the year, *Hamlet*. Coming back to the well-named (world-class) Globe, it was a huge stimulus for a burst of creativity on Shakespeare's part that year. Shakespeare and his troupe were making the bold but almost necessary move to the south side of the Thames from the confines, and confining nature, of the Theatre north of the Thames, taking the posts from the old Theatre from which to establish the new open-air structure. It was both a symbolic and a real chance to reinvent himself, and Shakespeare did: "What the Chamberlain's men did to the wooden frame of the Theatre, Shakespeare did to the old play of Hamlet: he tore it from its familiar moorings, salvaged its structure, and reassembled something new." [Shap05, p. 288] A now-lost version of Hamlet had apparently been staged just a few years earlier, perhaps very closely to the time of the passing of Shakespeare's beloved son, Hamnet, in 1596.

The death of Hamnet no doubt weighed heavily on the Bard. It is hard to doubt that he felt his son's death, in the words of the Ghost, "most foul, strange, and unnatural" (I.5.34). What father wants to outlive his child? As such, Shakespeare found the change of one letter from Hamnet to Hamlet an easy leap to make, and the story of Hamlet perfect to express his sorrow, his new globe of operations, and his endless creativity. Although apocryphal, the claim that Shakespeare himself acted the role of the ghost in Hamlet is a possibility almost stronger than truth, along the lines of a so-called "infallible medieval belief" in which tenets of faith were regarded as truer than facts. We will explore this possibility further here in light of this being a chapter on the omniscient historian before returning to the relationship between *1599* and the Durants.

As for the origin of this claim, Outterson-Murphy notes that "Understanding the Ghost as both actor and playwright might have encouraged the early disseminators of the theatrical legend, first mentioned in Nicholas Rowe's 1709 biography, that Shakespeare himself performed the Ghost in *Hamlet*" [Outt16, p. 264]. This is an important connection, not just from a literary perspective, but also from a historical one. The Ghost transparently (it is a ghost, after all, transparency is expected) provides a dual role: that of the motivator of the action of the play and that of the playwright itself (since the Ghost is providing the history of Claudius, including the murdering of his brother and the "incestuous" marriage relatively shortly thereafter to his former sister-in-law, Gertrude). The Ghost also later reminds Hamlet of the "business" that they have agreed on (the three "Swear!" utterances near the close of Act I); that is, Hamlet's promise to avenge his murder. Thus, like Shakespeare himself, the Ghost is an actor, playwright, and businessman, taking on the "Globe" in his life after the Theatre of being the King of Denmark. For many rabid fans of Shakespeare, this is akin to an infallible medieval belief and is asserted as truthful just because it is such a good story. It is such a good story, it has to be true, right, the ontological proof of truthfulness by an omniscient historian?

Coming back to the play, then, let us see why it creates a faith more truthful than fact for many a fan of the Ghost-writer. After a long response to Hamlet, the Ghost famously tells Hamlet "Adieu, adieu, Hamlet! Remember me" (I.5.91). The ghost then leaves, and Hamlet tells himself "Remember thee, / Ay, thou poor ghost, whiles memory holds a seat / In this distracted globe" (I.5.95-97). Note that the "globe" here is another of Shakespeare's triple plays on words. The "distracted globe" is Hamlet's head and brain, the "globe" is also this earth (Hamlet being alive, the Ghost not), and the "Globe" is of course the theater itself. With that latter Globe, Shakespeare had the chance to have all his talents come to bear on his success because he finally had control over the writing, the acting, the business, the timing, and the nature of his plays. Just as the Ghost, in convincing Hamlet (partly through showing himself to Hamlet's most trusted friend, Horatio) to avenge him, now drives the writing, the acting, the business, the timing, and the nature of the rest of the play *Hamlet*. Sure, the role of the ghost is switched between William and his son, Hamnet, but the similarities are not coincidental. How could Shakespeare, in so masterfully crafting the rest of *Hamlet*, not also take on the role of Ghost, which would just further emphasize his brilliance? A possibility so perfect that it is stronger than the truth.

With a larger overall perspective, we see that in *1599*, Shapiro shows us a process that was also often adopted by the Durants; that is, a focus on great people and their turning point events. 1599 was a year of transformation for Shakespeare – by moving the posts from the Theatre to the Globe, a new beginning, and perhaps by writing *Hamlet*, a new acceptance of his own loss. Regardless of whether Shakespeare himself acted as the Ghost, some form of exorcism was likely provided by play. And like the Durants, Shapiro shows us a triple focus: (1) a critical individual in history during (2) a critical time in their life performing (3) a critical accomplishment that elevated them even further in the pantheon of historically interesting personages. Although the focus on "great people" is less in vogue today than it was during the time of the Durants' writing, their focus on the triad of critical factors {individual, time, accomplishment} is still valuable for helping create a context for the discussion of the key cultural elements of a time, place, and people.

6.3.4 Animal, vegetable, or mineral?

What if, instead of a critical individual, a history was written about a critical animal, vegetable, or mineral? For the animal, we can look back all the way to Alexander the Great's horse Bucephalus [Will16]. For the vegetable, such histories have been around for a long time [Rhin41]. Perhaps the most interesting theme for a historical narrative is a mineral, in this case, salt [Kurl11]. In Kurlansky's *Salt*, the mineral is shown to drive exploration, the fishing trade, and conquest over recorded human history. Two anecdotes show the way in which a mineral can effectively substitute for an omniscient narrator. Kurlansky shows how the cod industry required more than 10,000 tons (ten million kilograms) of salt annually [Kurl11, p. 198], and thus, the limiting factor on the British cod business "were the number of ships and fisherman, and the supply of salt" [Kurl11, p. 199]. Perhaps, the most engaging tale in the *Salt* repertoire, however, is that of the creation of the crest for the colony of Turks and Caicos. Kurlansky notes that "everything goes to and comes from the mother country" [Kurl11, p. 432] under the rules of colonialism. So, when Turks and Caicos were asked to send a crest to England for incorporation into a flag for the colony, a "Turks and Caicos designer drew a crest that included Salt Cay saltworks with salt rakers in the foreground and piles of salt" [Ibid.]. Being 1870, Arctic exploration was on everyone's mind, and the "English designer assumed the little white domes were igloos. And so he drew doors on each one" [Ibid.]. For 98 years, these tropical igloos remained on the official crest, until finally being replaced by a flamingo. Using salt as the narrator is thus a creative and relatively comprehensive way of showing the history of culture, not just its events. It is a skill the Durants continually employed in their "integral history." As they noted in their final volume, they wanted to see all elements of civilization "in one moving picture, and as interacting parts of a united whole" [Dura75, p. vii]. Salt is shown to be an integral part of the united whole of human history.

6.3.5 The fish and the fishers

Continuing with Mark Kurlansky [Kurl97], it so happens that he covered animals in addition to minerals. Specifically, in *Cod*, he covered 1000 years of the history of the North Atlantic from the perspective of the *Gadus morhua*, or North Atlantic cod. This focus on a single commodity (also an animal) is an excellent vehicle from which to drive toward an actual omniscient history; that is, one who incorporates as many different inputs into a history as possible. Kurlansky deftly explains the action of many of the Icelandic Sagas (see

Chapter 5) by noting that the "Basques were not the first to cure cod. Centuries earlier, the Vikings had traveled from Norway to Iceland to Greenland to Canada, and it is not a coincidence that this is the exact range of the Atlantic cod" [Kurl97, p.19]. For many people, this statement provides an "A-ha!" moment. Surely, the Vikings were not exploring simply to escape oppressive overlordship in Norway. They were following the food. In fact, had they not been following the routes of the *Gadus morhua*, they almost certainly would not have been able to make such a long journey in the first place. Kurlansky's narrative, therefore, does not provide us with omniscience, but in providing a different perspective on the Norse odysseys of discovery, leads us a step closer to a holistic history, heaving aside the almost hagiographic Viking narrative that is nevertheless inconsistent with the later retreat of the Norse from Eastern Canada, among other inconsistencies. The Norse who were the so-called "hammer of the gods" were actually fishers and farmers, first and foremost.

A separate anecdote in *Cod* is also inspiring for the way in which it undermines an accepted "truth" of history. After mentioning the so-called discovery of North America by Cabot in 1497, Kurlansky notes that "Thirty-seven years later [in 1534], Jacques Cartier arrived, was credited with 'discovering' the mouth of the St. Lawrence, planted a cross on the Gaspé Peninsula, and claimed it all for France. He also noted the presence of 1000 Basque fishing vessels" [Kurl97, p. 29]. In other words, Cartier only discovered the St. Lawrence because the Basque fishermen were eager to keep it to themselves and as such did not publicize their much earlier discovery (fish being more valuable to them than discovery cachet). Whether or not there were actually 1000 boats there, the point is that discovery is usually due both to exploration and to the motivation to make a discovery public. Leif Erikson (or, more accurately, if the *Saga of the Greenlanders* is to be believed, Bjarni Herjólfsson in AD 986) set foot on the North American mainland half a millennium before Portuguese explorer-for-hire Cabot did. Even if L'Anse aux Meadows in northern Newfoundland is not the celebrated "Leifsbudir" settlement of the same saga, it is evidence of an early European landing in North America. Without financial or other (e.g., friendly natives) encouragement to settle, the wave of Norse settlement retracted back to Greenland and eventually completely died out in Greenland roughly 500 years into the experiment there, leaving Iceland the western end of European settlement as the Little Ice Age started to wane and the centuries of European exploration began in earnest. Did Cabot know about Greenland? Due to earlier Icelandic visits by sailors from Bristol, England, the answer seems to be yes, at least at the oral traditional historical level. As we have seen in earlier chapters (e.g., Tim Severin and the *Odyssey* in Chapter 4 and the myriad Icelandic *Sagas* in

Chapter 5), however, these oral traditions hold a lot of veracity in addition to fantasy, and it is quite likely that Cabot drew encouragement from them.

Because of what he found in researching the history of the cod industry, Kurlansky was next motivated to provide an additional, if related, perspective, in the case of an often-marginalized group of Europeans occupying north-central Spain and the Western Pyrenees of France and Spain. They have brought us the Jesuit order (Loyola was Basque), the "fastest ball sport" (jai alai), and one of the greatest war protest art pieces (*Gernika*, by Picasso). They were also the most daring, dramatic, and successful of the mid-millennial cod fishers, with their boats preceding Cabot to the Grand Banks. Their success rankled the English for two centuries, resulting in the resolution to the War of Spanish Succession in the 1713 Treaty of Utrecht including the end of Spanish Basque fishing rights in Newfoundland and Nova Scotia (and only limited access for French Basques) [Kurl99, p. 120]. Moving forward 224 years to the bombing of Gernika (Guernica in Spanish), the mistruths of the Hitler, Mussolini, and especially, Franco governments, are corrected by taking the Basque perspective into account. While Franco's regime denied for decades that Gernika had been bombed from the air (by German and Italian pilots and planes), the Basque survivors refused to be silenced. It did not hurt that Picasso immediately "chose as his subject [for the 1937 Paris World's Fair] the horror of the Guernica bombing" [Kurl99, p.201].

The history of cod and the history of the Basque, comprising perhaps 0.1% of the population of Europe, is important not just to Kurlansky, but to all of us. Like the Durants, Kurlansky understands that without providing different approaches to historical narration, the overall story loses nuance, complexity, and richness that is due – if for no other reason than respect – to those whose lives were every bit as glorious, anxious, mercurial, and varied as ours. This brings us to a direct consideration of the Durants and their attempts to be omniscient historians.

6.3.6 The Durants and omniscience

At this point in the chapter, we have seen that there is both a good side and a bad side to historical omniscience. On the good side, when multiple, independent historical perspectives are credibly combined into the narrative, the narrative moves closer to a truly omniscient history. Since that reduces mistruth (often the sin of omission, in this case), we are of course for this type of omniscient historian. On the bad side, when a historian interjects their own perspective, often at the expense of others, and moves it to primacy in spite of logical alternatives, this is a falsely omniscient history, and as such, a pattern for mistruth.

Which type of omniscience do the Durants provide? It is safe to say that they aspire to an actual omniscient history since when they are strong advocates for a particular historical person, they are generally capable of conveying to the reader that they are inserting this as their opinion. Perhaps the same "personal preference in the narrative" would have been clear to Herodotus' readers, or else it simply was not an issue back in his time. Regardless, the histories of the Durants give evidence that there is likely to always be some "omniscience" added to a historical document, if for no other reason than that of showing the interpretative skills of the writer. Some "omniscience" was inevitable in the Durants' histories since they were such independent thinkers. In spite of writing during the middle decades of the 20th century, when so much writing was heavily affected by the big ideas of capitalism, fascism, and communism, the Durants refused to provide only a single perspective on history. Instead, like Kurlansky with the perspectives of animals, vegetables, and people, the Durants strove for totality. Because of this structural approach to their history writing, they may have ended up with the least biased major history ever written. Although they focused on great "men" and "women" at times, as noted above, they also brought in the arts, the sciences, the explorations, and the cultural movements to deftly provide multiple viewpoints to each major era and event.

Because of their ability to incorporate multiple threads together in their "integral" histories, "the legacy of the Durants has largely remained intact. The fact that the couple's books continue to be read by intellectuals on both sides of the political spectrum is a testament to their integrity as historians, writers, and human beings" [Brin21]. Perhaps more importantly, the Durants have opened up history to anyone and everyone, and such an approach is a strong bulwark against mistruth: the more familiar a population is with its history, the less likely it is to be duped about its present. Also, refreshingly, "Where other historians rush to defend themselves against external attacks, the Durants welcomed criticism as it made them conscious of their own biases and shortcomings" [Ibid.] As Brinkhof astutely notes, "Omniscience will always be unachievable, but the Durants showed that it can still be of use to academics as a guiding principle" [Ibid.]. Thus, the type of omniscient historian that the Durants attempt to be is the "good side" from above.

How did the Durants strive for this "good" omniscience? As Brinkhof notes, "The Durants took great pains to remove themselves from the equation. Will...wrote and studied not to find justifications for his personal beliefs but out of a genuine interest in the world around him. As a result, his work combines a mature sense of reservation with childlike wonder" [Ibid.].

In their 11 massive volumes, the Durants gave a broad brushstroke to the history of the world, and a primer and first coat to the history of Europe. Since Will and Ariel lived longer than they had planned, according to Will and his wry humor anyway, they added the last volume, *XI. The Age of Napoleon*, at relatively advanced ages (*Volume X, Rousseau and Revolution* was published in 1967 when Will was 82 and Ariel was 69 years young), Will being 90 and Ariel 77 when it hit the presses in 1975. If there is the "bad side" of omniscience in their writing, for *The Age of Napoleon*, it was subtle and was more about assigning attributes to Napoleon and trying to cut through all of the mistruths that had been accumulated regarding this pivotal character in European history. Did they succeed completely? Spending perhaps 200 pages on Napoleon himself, of course not. His intellect, life, and impact could not be captured fully in thousands of pages. However, the Durants, as usual, tried to use all of history to create the culture and the context surrounding Napoleon in the 27 years from 1789 to 1815; starting from this context, they then tried to project plausible explanations onto the people and events of those times. In order to provide a narrative both comprehensive and thought-provoking, their writing acts as if the narrator is omniscient. It is an omniscience for immersion, for verisimilitude, and for patching together the various perspectives (art, music, literature, science, philosophy, work, and military) so that the reader can integrate them rather than consider them separate views. Does it work? For someone whose primary concern is military history: no. The key battles of Napoleon's career, from Wagram to Leipzig, and from Austerlitz to Waterloo, are not described in depth, but only to provide a sense of the timing of the different coalitions and losses. For someone whose primary concern is literature: no. Jane Austen, who from my reading is the Durants' favorite writer of the time, rates only a few pages in the volume. The same for people whose primary concern is poetry, music, painting, philosophy, science, or technology: no. But, if you want to move from how the various French citizens lived to how the various French citizens died, it all comes together rather well. The Durants provide just enough of every major type of context for you to get a feel for what living under or adjacent to Napoleon's hegemony must have been like. In other words, you feel confident to project your own omniscience onto the period without feeling that it is a mistruth. That is magical, and the Durants are the wavers of the wand.

6.4 Knowing Your Audience and Accepting Lack of Omniscience

The Durants, therefore, are able to – with their approach to "integral history" – make the reader forget that all history is, ultimately, a mistruth. In moving us from the sense of mistruth to a sense of "credible narrative with inadvertent mistruth," a good historian engages the reader in the exploration and hopefully stimulates them to uncover further truths (and mistruths) themselves. In other words, to avoid the type of omniscient historian we do not want – one that projects their own time, beliefs, opinions, and even factual errors onto the historical narrative – one has to acknowledge that mistruth is inevitable and that the historian is trying to address that. An important set of admissions by the narrator can aid in the establishment of credibility. The first is *making your intended audience known*. This lets your readers know who the narrative is meant to speak to, and may help them identify, understand, and possibly even correct any implicit biases associated with trying to persuade, impress, or support that audience. The second admission is *providing a comprehensive list of sources and influences* that were used in the creation of the narrative. By attempting to be exhaustive, you will also (honestly) show the reader what you have (hopefully inadvertently) missed in your research and thus as input/influence. A third, but by no means last, admission is *identifying input that you disregarded or discarded*. Not only might this convince your readers that you were exhaustive in your research, but it will help them to hone in on the most contentious sources for the information. This puts additional responsibility on the narrator but also makes them think through their writing in a more comprehensive fashion.

All three of these admissions, if followed to the best of the narrator's abilities, make it easier for another historian or narrator to use a historical account later since the information disregarded or discarded becomes the main focus of the comparative analysis. In general, a mistruth based on a stated decision is more acceptable than a mistruth based on omission, and much more acceptable than a mistruth based on intentionally ignoring input. Also, in stating the sources you relied on and those you decided against relying on, you are forced to consider both sides of an argument (thesis and antithesis, if you will), which almost always results in a more mature synthesis of the historical narrative.

With our consideration of the omniscient historian, we end up perhaps putting you, our reader, in some discomfort. After all, the overarching goal of this book is to determine mistruths in history and in doing so, to correct them. Yet, here we essentially concede that all historical narratives contain mistruths. The consideration of the good and the bad omniscient historian is, however, logically consistent with this larger goal. In addressing mistruths and in striving for true omniscience rather than (sanctimoniously, complacently, or even intentionally) assuming we already know the truth, we open up our narratives to constructive, considered, and relevant argumentation – particularly since we feel it our responsibility to identify the best issues to argue. The best form of omniscience, then, is being fully aware of where our interpretation of history is most likely to need additional consideration. It is worth pointing out that some of the most cited individuals in history, whether or not they were historians, are influential precisely because they are open to criticism. The Durants are certainly one notable example.

6.5 Cyber Salon – Analogy to US Patent Laws

This chapter's cyber salon addresses an area in which an omniscient historian is expected. This is the social contract of intellectual property (IP) called a patent, for which in return for providing a preferred implementation of a useful device, process, or product, the inventor is given rights to prevent anyone else from making their device, process, or product for two decades (for the most common type of patent, the utility patent, that is). After 20 years, all of society benefits from the knowledge of the *preferred implementation*. The inventor, meanwhile, has 20 years to build their invention if there are no blocking patents: yes, you can get a patent on something that you are not allowed to make yourself. In fact, you are allowed to get a patent on something that is illegal since laws change (think of marijuana-related inventions granted before 2012, which then became legal as Colorado and Washington [and ultimately many other states] made toking, poking, and smoking of weed decreed indeed).

The problem with patents is that good patents seem obvious after the fact, but in order to evaluate whether a patent should be granted (often several years later in time), one has to project oneself back to the time the patent was written to see if it really was obvious in the context of its time. In other words, one has to be, in effect, *omniscient* about what was known and what was not known at the time that the invention was filed. This is usually accomplished by evaluating dated content whose timing was on or before the data that the patent was submitted. This works well for unequivocally dated material but is more challenging when one tries to recapture what people *skilled in the art* knew at that specific point in time (needed for the nonobviousness part of the patent requirements).

Projecting context back in time is difficult for a number of reasons, several of which have already been cited in this book. First, there is the effect of presentism, particularly when the patent is obviously a good invention. Once you have a bridge, the thought of crossing a river with a raft seems ridiculous, and it is far easier to imagine that the bridge was always there. Once you have a smartphone, with its combination of Internet connectivity, music, video, camera, texting, and phoning capabilities, it seems like the idea for it was obvious long ago. In addition, there is the so-called *Stranger Things* effect, introduced in Chapter 1, where the impact of such a powerful invention (or set of inventions) makes it difficult to remember what the world was like before it (or them). There was a time when no one had the Internet, let alone a smartphone, and communication was slower, less personal, but also, perhaps more robust: mail, television, radio, telegraphs, telephones, public announcements, and shipping all operated on separate networks, reducing the chance for simultaneous failure in all modes of communication.

Another difficulty in determining whether a patent was legitimately novel and nonobvious when it was filed is the rapid rate of change in technologies. Sure, movies, radio, and television came relatively rapidly one after the other, and to people living in the 1900s, 1920s, and 1950s, these changes seemed rapid and perhaps even hard to keep up with. Now there are three times as many people on the planet, and dozens of times as many people working on creating new technologies. It may be a cliché, but the rate of change is changing, and because of the interconnectedness of technologies (not just the merging of phone, movie, radio, television, newspaper, and mail onto handheld computers and smartphones), it is harder and harder to see when which technological advancement arose, let alone when it became "obvious" to one skilled in the art.

To invoke another cliché, the increased interconnectedness of technologies is said to "make the world smaller," and this means that content is increasingly translated between the many languages that inventors speak around this small world. Because there is always some alteration of meaning in translating between two or more languages, this further obfuscates the preciseness of "what was known" at any given time in the past.

Patent workshops, including people who put forth "rules" and "patterns" for creating inventions, are another complication for trying to understand what the "state of the art" in the past was. The use of patterns and specific processes for invention are also readily input to machine learning and artificial intelligence (ML/AI) systems. A main problem with this topic is that projecting a pattern back in time is an insidious form of presentism: if a past invention is shown to match the steps in the pattern, it might be thought of as less novel than it was at the time. Ironically, it might have been part of the training set for the very ML/AI pattern generation mentioned!

Intellectual property (IP) mining, generating, granting, and denial, then, are in continuum with the world of cybersecurity, especially since automated (cyber) methods of both creating and denying the novelty of IP are similar to methods used to both attack and defend cyber assets in general. Perhaps the most interesting connection between presentism applied to the novelty and nonobviousness of IP and cybersecurity, however, is that each of them is based on an innate mistruth. Just as we can never assume omniscience (that is, complete truth) in a historical narrative (including in this case, the historical narrative around the novel and nonobvious creation of IP), but only strive for it, we can also never assume truth in any cybersecurity measure. The innate mistruth of cybersecurity is that you *do not prove a cybersecurity approach is secure*, you only know that it has not yet been proven insecure! For the history of intellectual property – and any other historical narrative – we can also never prove that a history is truth, but instead can only strive to show that no mistruth that we are aware of has been put forth. Cybersecurity, like a historical narrative, is an unending cycle between trying to find any mistruths (in the form of exploitable vulnerabilities) and trying to correct any known mistruths when they arise.

6.6 Summary

While the concept of an omniscient historian is an oxymoron, it is not necessarily a poor aspirational goal. In later chapters, we will provide techniques to help a historian strive toward omniscience, fully knowing that they cannot account for the full context of any historical event. A historian who acts as if they know everything is the type of omniscient historian that we warn against here. From Herodotus to the Durants, historians may take on particular authoritative styles in an effort to give gravitas to their writing. It should never be forgotten that a "story" is 5/7 of the word history, and so, any historian adding their own flavor and panache is likely to encourage people to read and study more history. Herodotus meant to entertain, perhaps even more than to enlighten. From this perspective, a contractual history (such as Caesar's history of the Gallic Wars) is valuable because it so thoroughly represents one perspective of a historical event.

Many historical narrators have already understood the need to avoid appearing omniscient. In *A Great and Noble Scheme* [Fara05], for example, Faragher used facts, and in particular, the population statistics for the French-speaking Acadians, to project forward in time and estimate an accurate demographic impact of the Acadian diaspora. Jill Lepore, in *The Name of War: King Philip's War and the Origins of American Identity* [Lepo09], considers many different sources of information – disease, alliances, and controversial trials among them – to explain a relationship of mutual thanksgiving turned to enmity and attempted extermination in just two generations.

Another form of contractual history, from a certain perspective, is biography. James Shapiro's *1599: A Year in the Life of William Shakespeare*

[Shap05] provides as much context around this pivotal year in the Bard's career as possible. While not omniscient, Shapiro's attempt to create an omniscient narrative for the reader works rather well. Can a biographical approach be extended to an inanimate object? In Kurlansky's *Salt* [Kurl 11], the "biography" of salt emphasizes how this mineral was pivotal in the expansion of exploration, fishing, and conquest over the entire recorded history of humans. Kurlansky also adopted an omniscience-creating approach in *Cod* [Kurl97], which could be viewed as the collective biography of this marine species. As with salt, the cod drove exploration, fishing, and even conquest. Taken together, these two books provide an even greater path toward "omniscience" in the narrative of the North Atlantic.

Considering all of these narratives, we are able to make three recommendations for the would-be omniscient narrator. The first is to identify your target audience. This will help the reader calibrate your writing, perhaps even correcting for any of your implicit biases. The second is to provide a comprehensive bibliography, including those that influenced you even if not directly quoted. The reader may then augment their reading of your history with sources not cited, should they choose to. The third recommendation is to identify input that you disregarded and/or discarded. This helps the reader to understand how wide a net you cast (even if you are not Kurlansky) and helps them understand which sources are points of contention in the historical events that you are considering. Applying these three recommendations, you can move toward being omniscient without coming across as a know-it-all. The chapter concluded with the analogy between this careful narrative approach and the requirements for intellectual property development.

References

[Brin21] Brinkhof T, "Is it possible to write an unbiased history of human civilization?" The Past, October 27, 2021, https://bigthink.com/the-past/history-civilization-durants/, accessed 23 November 2023.

[Cray09] Cray R, "Weltering in Their Own Blood': Puritan Casualties in King Philip's War," Historical Journal of Massachusetts 37, no. 2 (2009): 106–124.

[Dura75] Durant WJ and Durant A, "The age of Napoleon: A history of European civilization from 1789 to 1815," 1975.

[Fara05] Faragher, JM, "A great and noble scheme: The tragic story of the expulsion of the French Acadians from their American homeland," WW Norton & Company, 592 pp., 2005.

[Gold07] Goldhagen DJ, "Hitler's willing executioners: Ordinary Germans and the Holocaust," Alfred A. Knopf, 622 pp., 1996.

[Hame12] Hamel D, "Reading Herodotus: A Guided Tour through the Wild Boars, Dancing Suitors, and Crazy Tyrants of *The History*," Baltimore: The Johns Hopkins University Press, 334 pp., 2012.

[Kurl97] Kurlansky M, "Cod: A Biography of the Fish that Changed the World," Penguin Books, 1997.

[Kurl99] Kurlansky M, "The Basque History of the World," Penguin Books, 1999.

[Kurl11] Kurlansky M, "Salt," Random House, 2011.

[Lepo09] Lepore J, "The name of war: King Philip's War and the origins of American identity," 368 pp., Vintage, 2009.

[Outt16] Outterson-Murphy S, "'Remember me' The Ghost and its spectators in Hamlet," Shakespeare Bulletin 34, no. 2 (2016): 253–275.

[Rhin41] Rhind W, "A history of the vegetable Kingdom," 1841.

[Shap05] Shapiro James, "1599: A Year in the Life of William Shakespeare," Faber & Faber, 440 pp., 2005.

[Stra07] Strassler RB, "The Landmark Herodotus: The Histories," New York: Anchor Press, 960 pp., 2009.

[Will16] Willekes C, "The horse in the ancient world: from Bucephalus to the Hippodrome." Bloomsbury Publishing, 2016.

7

Anachronism

Whatever, in fact, is modern in our life we owe to the Greeks. Whatever is an anachronism is due to mediaevalism

– Oscar Wilde

Dignity is an anachronism

– Ellen Glasgow

Abstract

Anachronism comes from the Greek for "backward time," and the usual association of anachronism is presenting something in the past that could not have been (at least without aliens, time travel, or both). Mozart emailing Salieri his improvements for the overture of his latest opera or Julius Caesar getting a few grenades delivered by FedEx at Alesia are two egregious examples. But, other forms of anachronism, while perhaps less opprobrious, maybe even more damaging since they may be more likely to escape notice. One often subtle form of anachronism is the tendency of someone writing now to compress eras in the past. This is not exemplified by representing the Hundred Years' War, which ran from 1337 to 1453, as 16% less time than it was (after all, 100 is a pretty good rounding of 116). Rather, it is about representing longer periods of time as if they were closer together. For Example, Homer's *Odyssey* and *Iliad* were as far apart in time from the Peloponnesian War as the Thirty Years' War is from today, yet, many historians portray them as if they were much more contemporaneous. This is likely due to its relationship to another subtle form of anachronism, that of modern writers feeling that they are living in a time of maximum change. If indeed society, culture, technology, economics, etc., are changing faster now, it is easier to think of many successive past generations as being effectively simultaneous. However, both the compression of time and the bias toward increased dynamism of the

DOI: 10.1201/9788770048347-7

present can lead to a misrepresentation of the temporal relationship between past events, and thus, it can lead to historical mistruth. In this chapter, the manners in which anachronism can lead to – often severe – historical mistruths are described and discussed, along with relevant examples. The chapter concludes with a section on how to counteract anachronisms in your historical narratives and a cyber salon on the arms race between cyber attackers and cyber defenders.

7.1 Introduction

Twenty years' time 2000 years ago was still a long time, a generation or so in fact. Yet, it is natural for us to compress time in the past, probably in proportion to how long ago it was. This muddling of events as they extend back in time is inevitable. But just because 20 years is a small time compared to 2000 years, this does not allow us to compress years in the past if we wish to present a truthful narrative. This is a different, more subtle form of anachronism than an article depicting Julius Caesar calling Vercingetorix on a telephone. It is the distortion of linear time as we extend back in the past. The conflation of time between Marathon and the Peloponnesian War, and between the Plague of Athens and Alexander's Empire, is a natural means of "chunking" so many centuries of history. However, it leads to mistruths of historical representation.

The "traditional" or at least common anachronism is the one placing more modern technologies and even processes in the hands of earlier people. In earlier chapters, we used the Netflix series *Stranger Things* as the exemplar for this. Set in the 1980s and presenting verisimilitude to that period (disregarding the supernatural elements that drive the action, of course), its writers either could no longer place themselves or their viewers in a time where instant communication between multiple parties was not possible, or they simply chose not to. They anachronistically place smartphone technology into the show using infinite battery, infinite distance, and infinite depth-penetrating walkie-talkies, a technology that most assuredly did not exist in the 1980s. Obviously, the show was intended for a younger audience than people who experienced the 1980s first-hand; however, why strive for the other verisimilitude when the massive elephant of mistruth was right there on the table?

Another form of anachronism is worth introducing here: the commonplace perspective of a person thinking that they are living in a time of maximum change. Even though our great-grandparents might have started life rarely (or never, if we accept the combined wisdom of Fernand Braudel and

Samwise Gamgee) being more than five miles from their homes, they nevertheless saw trains, buses, automobiles, and eventually planes completely transform their transportation possibilities. Unable to communicate over long distances except by letter or telegram, they saw the advent of radio and telephone. A person living in the 1920s likely viewed the 1890s as foreign and inchoate as the youth of today do the pre-Internet world of the early 1990s. The fact is people have lived under conditions of rapid change throughout time. The law of parsimony, or shall we coin *the law of equitable cultural contribution*, argues for the amount of change in society being proportional to the size of society. In other words, we make no differential assumptions about the ability of an individual person to contribute to cultural change. "But wait," you may protest, "there are a lot more people alive today than in the time of my great-grandparents, so we are in fact at a time of maximum change." To which, our reply is that the sum of change arguably continues to increase, but it is spread over a larger number of people. Thus, major cultural changes (the Internet, satellite-enabled connectivity, smartphones, etc.) are experienced by vast numbers of people, but many other changes are confined to their niches in society, and with a much larger overall society, these niches are a relatively smaller percentage of humankind than in the past. A common but ultimately meritless trope of history is that there is a "last person to know everything," for which Aristotle, the two Bacons (Roger and Francis), John Milton, Gottfried Leibniz, and perhaps most contemporary, Thomas Young [Robi23], have been postulated as the embodiment thereof. Certainly, none of these folks knew everything: Aristotle, for example, did not bother to test his quite erroneous hypothesis that heavier objects fall faster than lighter objects. Was Aristotle "well-read" enough to be able to converse with anyone in any field of knowledge? Based on his "understanding" of gravity, one doubts he could have conversed intelligently with Archimedes (born 35 years after Aristotle's death) on engineering or mathematics. The point is, regardless of whether there was ever a person who knew "everything," it is without question that no one would postulate such a person, or even a supercomputer, could embody such a skillset in today's world. Thus, the "higher rate of change" of today's world is spread out over many more people, and the human brain, essentially unchanged in structure since the time of the Ancients, when actively engaged likely is capable of the same rate of change today as in the time of Taputti or Anaximander.

This form of anachronism, the belief in greater rates of change in the modern era than in the past – together with the assumption that we are more capable because of living in such a time – is perhaps the most powerful, or dangerous, form of anachronism, precisely because it is subtle enough to become the background, the canvas, or the assumption of present-day readers of a historical narrative. This is a form of presentism that is flavored by narcissism and serves to promote bias reinforcement, laziness, complacency, and perhaps even smugness, all in one. Carrying your bias back to the past is perhaps the greatest possible bias you can carry because tending to be dismissive of the past prevents you from learning from it.

Other approaches to categorizing anachronisms have been described. In [Mast22], for example, three different types of anachronism are defined and shown to have a different purpose as follows:

1. Behavioral or cultural anachronism
2. Parachronism
3. Prochronism

The first of these, behavioral/cultural anachronism, is an intentional choice to bring ideas, practices, or even items of the past into the present. Such an "intentional atavism" may provide a stylistic flair that is appealing to an intended audience. One example of applying this anachronism is to bring preindustrial approaches to food preparation forward as a means to engage a hipster audience; for example, using a mortar and pestle to grind bean powder rather than using a food processor. The second of these, parachronism, is the use of archaic processes, expressions, and/or equipment in today's world that are temporally out of place. An example of this might be using an 8-track system to perform espionage. The third, prochronism, is the more familiar "impossible anachronism," in which equipment, concepts, language, or practices are incorporated into a historical narrative transpiring well before the equipment, concepts, language, or practices were actually invented.

Moving to a wider perspective as we close out this introductory section, it is worth considering the quotes at the beginning of the chapter. With his traditional mix of irony and insight, Oscar Wilde notes that the modern application of Greek art, architecture, and culture is, for him, not anachronistic (thus it is a behavioral/cultural anachronism, and intentional), while the application of Medieval art, architecture, and culture is definitely anachronistic (i.e., parachronism). In this quote, Wilde shows us that the difference between behavioral/cultural anachronism and parachronism is itself a reflection of our own culture. Greek architecture was and is considered "cool" by Wilde and many others (think of the Federal Hall in New York City and the Quincy Market in Boston as two examples), while Medieval architecture is subject to amusement and/or ridicule (think of *Monty Python and the Holy Grail*). The second quote, from Ellen Glasgow, is a simple, elegant way of ruing the loss of past mores and morals; in other words, a much better way to say, "Kids these days!" or "People used to be judged by their character, not by how loudly they draw attention to themselves." With this introduction completed, we next draw your attention to a deeper consideration of how the "nonlinearity of time" anachronism can lead to mistruths in history that are perhaps disproportionate to what you might expect from it.

7.2 Nonlinearity of Time

Time is innately contextual, and in that sense, it is nonlinear. When you are in the "flow" of things, time may disappear altogether, with the body and mind more focused on the task at hand than, for example, a consideration of how a minute compares to ten minutes. When you are in a crisis situation, a second may seem to have more happening in it than a second does during "normal time." The simple observation that time seems to pass more or less quickly based on what is happening during that time is actually an important part of anachronism. As mentioned above, one form of anachronism we are particularly concerned with in historical narratives is the "distortion" of linear time as we extend back in the past. The less we know about a particular historical setting – its people, cultures, practices, technologies, innovations, and creations – the more likely we are to assign a longer "effective time" to a particular cultural practice, and the less creativity and technological innovation we are likely to give the people. In other words, a subtle progression that actually occurred is blurred together and reported as effectively a status quo.

Some historians have been guilty of equating the attributes of a historical *record* with those of the historical *era*. In other words, underrepresented people in history have been, unintentionally or not, represented as having lived lives that are less dynamic, less nuanced, and less interesting simply as a consequence of there being less "material" available to their historians. This also means, from the other perspective, that people whose historical record is richer are presented as having more dynamic, more nuanced, and more interesting lives. Such an imbalance takes away the flow, the flavor, and the flair of the past.

That being said, what sort of approach or approaches can be taken to correct this? After all, the historical record will always be imbalanced. As mentioned before, history is not always written by the victors, but it is always written by historians, in other words, literate people. A nonliterate society is not somehow "lesser" than a literate one: it simply cannot preserve its history in the same way. So, it is up to the same literate historians to correct this imbalance. One means of doing so is *using the narrative that you do have* – that is, the historical record of the group that has the more complete historical record – and applying it as a mirror for those groups for which the historical record is sparser.

For simplicity of description, the group whose account is well-covered will be referred to as the "remembered" group, while the group whose account is not well-covered will be referred to as the "forgotten" group. The main question to ask is what a society would otherwise have been without the forgotten group actually being present during the era. It is not just about demographics, although that is certainly a consideration (for more on that topic, see Chapter 6 and the discussion on the Acadian diaspora from Nova Scotia and New Brunswick). The discussion can be far more specific; for example, "What did their society do that they might not, or at least likely would not, have done otherwise?" This question can be asked about cultural, economic, military, political, religious, and social changes in the remembered society that might not be explained by an "independent trajectory" for this group alone, but instead require the presence of a forgotten society. A simple example will help. In the United States, the New Age movement, which first came to prominence in the 1970s, brought a tremendous influence of Native American spiritualism into the overall spiritual sphere of the United States, disproportionate to the size of the Native American community. Were the history of spiritualism in the United States to be only presented from the perspective of the "remembered" non-Native cultural, religious, and social perspectives, it might be hard to discern from where this movement arose. Once the (underrepresented) historical narrative of the Native Americans is considered, this "deviation" from the otherwise predicted spiritual path makes more sense.

The nonlinearity of time perspective is an interesting one and opens this discussion up to a physical (i.e., physics-based) analogy to help explain how to correct a historical narrative when there is a forgotten element in it. The analogy is based on the *black hole*, which is proven to exist (Cygnus X-1 being the most famous, but not only, example). A black hole does not, in theory, let anything escape it (Hawking radiation left aside for now), and thus, it cannot be seen behind its event horizon by definition (this is a tautology since the event horizon is defined as the limit of the hole's "blackness"). Space and time are bent by the black hole, leading to the identification of its presence by the absence of predicted behavior of space and time (the latter assessed by the behavior of electromagnetic radiation such as microwave radiation, 1.3 mm wavelength, and 230 GHz frequency, used for the Event Horizon Telescope). The impact of the black hole, therefore, is observed by what *does not otherwise happen* in time and space. The black hole changes the expected trajectory of space and time, and although it has no recorded history of its own, it certainly affects the recorded history of time and space outside of its event horizon.

Is it easy to determine what the impact of a forgotten element in history is? Absolutely not. But it is important to strive to do so in order to move toward a history that will not only be equitable, but also sustainable. In other words, a history that will hold up to future scrutiny precisely because it strives to represent, with as much verisimilitude as possible, the past. It is likely that the long-term impact of a historical account that at least attempts to correct the narrative for the disparity in the historical record will be the one that suffers the least from anachronisms. One method of meshing the remembered history with that forgotten is to employ *paired dynamism*. By this concept, we mean that changes in the groups whose lives are remembered are affected by the people whose lives are forgotten in direct proportion to the magnitude of the difference between the expected and actual (measured) outcomes for the people remembered (the strength of the black hole, using the previous analogy, that is). If there is an anomaly in a historical record of a people, it is almost assuredly due to the impact of another people whose historical record may not have survived as intact.

In order to fill in a time record to provide the richness that its length merits, the historian can bring up questions that can be addressed, at least in part, by the record that has survived. The questions to ask are, superficially at least, relatively straightforward, but they lead to a different type of background and literature search than might occur otherwise. The questions, in aggregate form, are:

> *How is the {cultural, demographic, economic, military, political, religious, and social} record of remembered Element A different from what would have been expected without the presence of forgotten Element B?*

Good historians have intuitively used these questions since the days of Thucydides. Of course, given the disparity of historical records for Elements A and B, the questions asked in aggregate above may not be, ultimately, answerable. Missing data can be imputed, but interpolation rather than extrapolation is preferred, and also, not always possible. However, asking these questions is an experiment worth doing because it opens up the mind of the historian to other possibilities and to the responsibility of expanding a length of time in the past to be as richly investigated as an equivalent length of time in the present. This has as a goal the elimination of time compression anachronisms.

This *paired dynamism* approach is important not just for the history we can construct now, but also for preparing the present for the historians of the future. Contextualizing history has become much more difficult because of the digitization and electronification of culture. Who owns each person's digital footprint, and how can it actually be reconstructed? It will be increasingly difficult as AI is used to auto-generate so much content for almost all people. What really is each person doing in a given time period? Clearly, the manner in which history will be reported is changing as quickly as cultures do. In preparation for this continual change, it is good to make historical reporting preadapted to accepting the need for paired dynamism, and thus, for linearizing (usually expanding) the time period covered. At least, ask the aggregate questions above, and to the best of your ability, address them in your narrative.

We now turn to some causes for the nonlinearity of time, with its disproportionate compression of events the further back we go in time, to arise. First off, it is natural for there to be a tendency to compress the past because of the relative paucity of content that exists for each century we go back. Secondly, each additional century that we go back in time, the more indirect its influence on today's history, in general. These two reasons for curtailing the narrative the further we go back in time are sensical, and with limited time for the overall investment in historical narrative, it is inevitable and largely reasonable to say less about the past the farther back it goes since functionally, its impact will be felt in its future generations that are increasingly explored in depth (ending with the narrative of the most recent times).

Offsetting these two causes for a "nonlinearity in time" which supports a compression of information (and thus anachronism in this sense) is a third cause, which, opposingly, argues for an increased relative investment in the times further back. This third, and perhaps most important, cause is that the more generations that we go back, the more recursive the anachronisms become. That is, the anachronisms of each successively more ancient era pile on to those of their successors, meaning any historical interpretation has to account for different relative and absolute anachronisms in the histories accumulated between then and now. The greatest number of anachronisms are piled up, obviously, for the narratives furthest back in time, and so, coming to an understanding of those histories may require extra investment in order to brush off the multiple layers of anachronism. Without exploring the origin of the anachronisms and attempting to correct for them, one may end up misrepresenting them, which opens up the historical narrative to a so-called "butterfly effect" (thanks to Ray Bradbury and Edward Norton Lorenz for this vivid metaphor) in which that perhaps small misrepresentation is magnified manyfold until reaching today.

Using an analogy to support the argument once more, here, we use paleontology as our source. The Burgess Shale is a famous fossil-rich rock deposit discovered by Charles Walcott (in 1909, although it was not until decades later that the magnitude of the discovery was understood) in the mountains of eastern British Columbia, Canada. Formed 508 million years ago during the middle Cambrian Period, the Burgess Shale is famous, and rather unique, in preserving the fossilized structures of soft-bodied biota (through what are called "soft-body imprints"). Although there is controversy (Stephen Jay Gould on one extreme and Conway Morris on the other) over how many of these odd creatures survived into later fossil records, one thing is certain: the world of the Burgess Shale biota was much different from the world that succeeded it. Thus, knowing what came out of the Burgess Shale in later fossil records is not a good history of the Burgess Shale era since their context was by definition different. The Burgess Shale world was held together by all of its parts, not just those preadapted, differentiated, or otherwise naturally selected by the late Cambrian Period that followed. To know the Burgess Shale by its survivors is therefore an anachronism that compresses the story of the Burgess Shale to its output, rather than its inner workings. Obviously, this is a metaphor that readily applies to any investigation of a historical era. Just because you know what came out of an era (e.g., bilateral, spherical, radial, and biradial symmetry in the case of the Burgess Shale biota) does not mean that you know how these came to be the output (many of the unique lineages of the Burgess Shale were evolutionary experiments that became extinct or else were marginalized at the expense of other body designs). Interpreting sequential civilizations by what carried forward to the following civilization not only impoverishes our understanding of the civilization, but it ignores the important natural selection process that history, like paleontology, is so dependent upon. The evolution of civilizations must be understood both by what they carried forth from previous civilizations and by what they did not carry forward. The selection process is both *positive* (it worked then, it works now) and *negative* (it worked then, it does not work now). In understanding those two aspects simultaneously, the flow, flavor, and flair of both civilizations shine forth, as desired.

If the Burgess Shale species are lumped together with the underlying Precambrian and early Cambrian species, along with the following late Cambrian, Ordovician, etc., species, the special experimentation of the Burgess Shale era is obfuscated into a larger, perhaps blander narrative. This can happen when eras are "chunked" together based on a single common element (often ethnicity). For example, in many histories, the times between the Trojan War and Alexander the Great (and perhaps even later than him) are covered together as "Ancient Greece." The Trojan War likely occurred just after 1200 BC, nearly 900 years before Alexander the Great. No people, regardless of their ethnic cohesion, remain static from one generation to the next, let alone the three dozen or so generations between Hector and Hephaestion.

As mentioned, it is understandable that a relatively small amount of time can be spent on the Ancient Greeks in, for example, a single semester class on some topic such as "Western History." That is irrefutable – time is always limited in our finite lives and world. What is the more important question to ask is, "How should that time be spent?" In other words, what contribution to the curriculum should the earlier, anachronistic (by curricular constraints) time period be given? Should it be simply cataloging the contributions to future civilizations; for example, emphasizing the borrowing of sculpture, architecture, and mythology by the conquering Romans? The Romans, after all, brought their own contributions – engineering, operations, and logistics among them. If you assumed, based on the analogy of the Burgess Shale, that the answer here is no, you have been reading carefully. Indeed, it may well be that such an approach is more likely to anachronistically "pigeonhole" the previous civilization. Instead, a focus on what influences *did not* carry forward may lead to a richer overall history. In other words, the most interesting elements of Greek Civilization, like the strangest biota in the Burgess Shale, are the elements that did not survive. Focusing on those attributes lends an overall richer historical narrative than simply representing them in light of what came later. It is important to note that, obviously, the ancient Greeks did not view themselves as living in the later Roman Empire's past, and so their historical narrative merits its own independent coverage.

So, how does one determine potential features of the historical narrative to focus on? We will oversimplify here by necessity since curriculum development is a complicated, arcane science. From the standpoint of both breadth and depth, it is recommended that the curriculum for an earlier historical narrative may be optimally designed to include those major elements of its culture and practices that are not co-opted by the later historical narrative that shares the same people, places, and/or processes. So, in moving from Ancient Greece to the Roman Empire, for example, it makes sense in the context of this advice to include a relatively in-depth discussion of the Greek navy. This is a good focus if Rome is next in the curriculum since Rome took its navy from Carthage, as a desperate realization of its own shortcomings during the Punic Wars. Rome took much from Athens, Sparta, Thebes, and Pella, but not their naval prowess. As such, a description of how the Greek naval power arose, reaching its peak, perhaps, at the great Athenian victory at Salamis, is appropriate. Athens lost the Peloponnesian War in large part because the opposing Greek combatants, led by Sparta, were able to win a decisive naval victory over Athens at the Battle of Aegospotami (near Gallipoli) in 405 BC. When the creation of Rome's navy is described later in the curriculum, the differences in ship design can be described: Greek triremes, long and narrow, were highly maneuverable and suited to their commonplace "shallow water" battles along the coast of Attica, Thessaly, and other Greek shores. Roman warships, based on the reverse engineering of the vessels of the then most powerful navy, Carthage, were thus adapted for open sea combat (Phoenicia, after all, extended from modern-day Lebanon to the Strait of Gibraltar). After showing how the Romans created their navy with a different inspiration than Greece, the narrative can then explore those elements of the culture and society of Rome that did come from the Greeks: sculpture, architecture, theatre, etc. This two-sided coverage – showing what the Romans both did and did not inherit from the Greeks – can be used to emphasize the broader ability of Romans to adopt the best of those people they conquered: esthetics from the Greeks and engineering from the Phoenicians.

It is worth noting here that the Roman Empire, like the world of the Ancient Greek city-states from the time of the Trojan war to the time of Alexander the Great, tends to be anachronistically compressed in time relative to the complexity offered to later time periods (such as the 1900s, for example). As mentioned, this is a different issue from the "compression" of content necessary due to the finite number of words that can be committed to the Roman Empire in a curriculum. The latter type of compression is *summarization*, and it is expected in order to ensure that all eras of a curriculum are presented. But the compression in time that we classify as a *mistruth in history* is not summarization – it is the representation of the Roman Empire in such a way that its 500 years (western) and/or 1500 years (eastern, or Byzantine) seem to be shorter than they are (this is without adding on the 500 years, that is 509–27 BC, of the Roman Republic that came before the Empire!). The time from the expulsion of the last Roman monarch, 509 BC, to the fall of Constantinople, 1453 AD, is in fact, nearly as long as the time from the start of the Roman Empire, 27 BC, until today.

So how can one accommodate the necessary (summarization) without creating the unnecessary (nonlinearity of time)? One way is to use the space wisely and provide a "defining" feature that can therefore be used as a stimulus for discussion by the readers of the narrative. For example, in describing the progression of Rome from a regional power, just barely able to conquer the Etruscans over a period of more than 300 years, to a worldwide power, a historian can use the themes of urbanization and inclusivity to show the way in which the Roman sphere of influence, success, and ultimately control, extended from Lazio to Tuscany to Cisalpine Gaul to, eventually, the evolution of the Mediterranean Sea into a Roman lake. Rome's population exploded to more than one million people during the early Empire, and Rome, because of its well-engineered roads, administration, and management of logistics, could be effectively viewed as an ecumenopolis during its peak: all roads lead to Rome because Rome was all. After all, Isaac Asimov, who popularized the notion of the ecumenopolis through his depiction of Trantor in the original *Foundation* trilogy, based much of this trilogy on his knowledge of the Roman Empire. Asimov's Trantor, in turn, provided much of the mold for Coruscant (which means "flashing," apt for a planet of perhaps three trillion souls that is effectively entirely lit up at night) in the *Star Wars* galaxy. Themes like this that relate to other fields, such as literature and cinema, draw the student in and allow them to discuss more deeply topics like demographics: for example, the Roman "ecumenopolis" was perhaps 70 million people in 5 million square kilometers while Trantor was described as having 40 billion souls (later increased/retconned to 400 billion by the end of *Second Foundation*) and Coruscant packed in a whopping 75 times more at three trillion. Obviously, the meaning of ecumenopolis itself changes with the level of agricultural and urban technology.

Having engaged students in the broad change in the population of Rome and its Empire over time, the narrative can then turn to the perhaps defining feature of the (Western) Roman Empire: the differentiation by technology, specifically engineering and construction. For example, the Romans, no doubt through a combination of luck, empiricism, and innovation, ended up creating what is now regarded as a "super cement," containing pozzolan, which is volcanic ash and dust sourced from zeolitic tuff at a location called Pozzuoli (thus the name) surrounding Mount Vesuvius. One of the secret advantages of pozzolan is that it reacts with lime (calcium oxide) in the presence of water to produce cementitious hydrates. This makes pozzolan cement especially resistant to sulfate attack, a bane to many other concretes, and excellent for use in hydraulic applications. In fact, "concretes developed by Roman architects and engineers have unique material characteristics that have never, to date, been replicated. Roman volcanic rock hydrated lime concrete prototypes could potentially further reduce CO_2 emissions; enhance chemical and mechanical resilience and self-healing properties; conserve freshwater resources through the use of seawater (or brines); and greatly extend the service life of concrete structures in marine environments" [Jack18].

This engineering work, allowing the Romans to master roads, aqueducts, and other civil engineering infrastructure, can then be compared and contrasted to the great scientific advancements of the Greek civilization that the Romans conquered and integrated into their Republic in 146 BC.

An interesting approach to historical education can be to show the students how the accumulation of wisdom is preadapted for the opportunity to express itself in technology and engineering. For example, the ability for the Romans to have invented electrical circuit elements may rest at the bottom of the Mediterranean just like the Greek Antikythera, waiting to be discovered. Moving back from the Romans to the Greeks, the history curriculum can then acknowledge that Rome did not advance on the Greeks in some ways. The Antikythera, discovered in 1901 and dating back to Greece around the time they were absorbed by the Roman Republic (and likely a few decades earlier), is effectively the earliest "analog computer." It was a complicated mechanical device that was used to predict astronomical events, including lunar and solar eclipses and the location of "navigational beacons" such as the planets (which means "traveler" in Greek). The type of "closed loop" discussion, moving forward to Rome after covering the elements of the Ancient Greek world that were not carried forward, and then returning to the Greeks after showing the Roman Empire's differentiators, enhances long-term understanding by revisiting the Greeks and thus reinforcing understanding of their great, if more inchoate, culture. While supporting the curricular need for summarization, it continues to "protract" the Ancient Greek era by tying it in novel ways to subsequent historical eras, and in doing so, helps mitigate the "anachronism through nonlinearity of time."

7.3 Whatever You Grow Up with is Not Technology (Inurement to Your Own Era)

As mentioned in the abstract of this chapter, a more common form of anachronism places more modern technologies and even processes in the hands of earlier people. This is prochronism, or the (at least to us) most familiar form of "impossible anachronism" in which something occurs before its time ("pro" = before, "chronos" = time). Sometimes these are intentional, as in comedies or in movies using soundtracks and/or expressions clearly more modern than the time of the movie's action. The unintentional ones are also unintentionally funny, such as the digital wristwatch on a civil war soldier in *Glory* and the Scottish kilt, not invented for another 300 years, on Mel Gibson in *Braveheart*. Even if you do not chuckle over those, you likely lose the immersion intended for a period piece. More subtle are the prochronisms typical of Shakespeare's plays; for example, the clock striking in *Julius Caesar*. Did Shakespeare make a mistake, did he add it intentionally for audience comfort, or was it some sort of ironic commentary on Caesar (e.g., being ahead of his time)? I vote for the mistake in this case, but in many others, it can be argued that Shakespeare intentionally introduced anachronisms for reasons ranging from plot convenience to social commentary and criticism [Rack86].

Can we correct all of the anachronisms in past narratives? The answer is almost certainly "No." A more germane question, then, is "Should we?" Here again, the answer is almost certainly "No." One reason is that a historical narrative is almost always married to other aims by the author(s). As Rood et al. note, "to engage with the classical past at all is inescapably to become part of an anachronistic community" [Rood20, p. 7]. Among the goals of anachronisms in the narratives of antiquity are those of the historical survival of ethnicities, the use of narrative as exemplarity (e.g., morals and fables), and for stimulating discourse and constructive argumentation [Ibid.]. Given that, many historical accounts are "interdisciplinary" in the sense that they – rightly to their audiences – combine historical narrative with other fields, including theatre (e.g., Shakespeare), film (e.g., *Glory* and *Braveheart*), literature (e.g., Herodotus' *The Histories*), and debate (e.g., Plato's *The Last Days of Socrates*), among others.

An important point to remember is that the role historical narratives play in a society and its associated culture changes over time. Not to get too "meta" here, but actually trying to write a historical narrative differently from the way in which other historians of your era do can make your narrative an anachronism, even if you are more truthful, accurate, and thorough than your peers. Or, in Herodotus' case, your lack of peers. Given that, to our knowledge, Herodotus was writing history in a "vacuum," it was natural for him to write history the way the great playwrights of his time wrote. Herodotus lived in Halicarnassus, near to Ephesus, and part of a thriving community of philosophic, theatrical, architectural, and sculpting talent. Ancient Greek philosophers were literally polymaths ("philo" = loving, "sophia" = wisdom), and so, Herodotus has the cultural expectation of including ethnographical, geographical, and literary content in addition to the historical content. It is a common trope that any technology a person grows up with is viewed as infrastructure, not as technology. For Herodotus, the "infrastructure" that surrounded him was that of a philosopher, and so, integrating historical narrative into a broader scientific, cultural, and literary narrative (including fiction) was natural for him in his time. The history that a person grows up with is not technology.

In modern history, there is both specialization (social history, progressive history, and quantitative history) and generalization (consensus history, integrative history). There is a greater expectation to represent multiple perspectives on history than was the case in earlier historical narratives. This is both an opportunity and a risk to contemporary historians. The opportunity is that of being able to visualize multiple perspectives on a historical narrative, which opens up the history to greater equity (showing each perspective), inclusivity (even when data are missing, showing the likely impact another group had through the paired dynamism approach mentioned in the previous section: "*How is the historical record of remembered Element A different from what would have been expected without the presence of forgotten Element B?*"), and diversity (particularly ensuring opposing viewpoints are both explored). Each of these is surely a strong reason for a broader historical narrative, in addition to the fact that it broadens the overall historical view, and thus, welcomes increased discussion and (friendly) argumentation. Overall, more information is considered, and more "passes" through the historical accounts that exist are undertaken. This is an opportunity to provide a broader, more balanced, and even "fair," historical account.

That very broadening is, however, itself a risk. With every additional perspective that is added to the narrative, there is a greater risk of adding a historical mistruth. The "exposure surface" is greater the more perspectives that you include, especially when you have – as is often the case – a disparity of information on the two or more perspectives. An analogy here might help. Think of Heinrich Schliemann, the self-fancied historian/defrauder who "discovered" Troy of the *Iliad* through an *Iliad*-advised, ill-advised, ill-conceived, and ill-executed dig that tore up and mixed together many different eras of "Troy" (the Troy ruins comprise nine archeological layers, each representing a sequential "Troy" built atop the previous 0–8 "Troys" that have occupied a hilltop for over 4000 years) even while more or less substantiating that the site he was digging (now Hisarlik, Turkey) was, in fact, the basis for Ilium of the *Iliad* [Moor16]. The problem is, in digging for specific artifacts (including almost laughably the Mask of Agamemnon which he unearthed at another dig in Mycenae, Priam's Treasure Trove and Gold, and the Jewels of Helen), Heinrich used less than professional archaeological techniques, to put it mildly. The odds that the treasure trove, gold, and jewels came from the same "Troy," let alone the correct one, have been proven to be essentially zero. Schliemann, it turns out, should have been named *Weitmann*, as in "far man" instead of "close man," because as far as being able to dig to a specific layer of Troy and only that layer, he was not even *schließen* (close). Sure, Schliemann is an exceptionally poor archaeologist/historian by today's standards, but the point is that, in trying to represent multiple historical perspectives at the same time, it becomes more likely that you will, like Schliemann, combine the mask, the treasure trove, and the jewels of three different perspectives in a noncohesive and thus nontruthful manner.

However, the Schliemann analogy was not just brought in to savage an acceptedly poor archaeologist. Schliemann's other fanciful interpretations (let us just mention his claimed finding of Odysseus' bed in Ithaca here) show another aspect of the anachronism of *Inurement to Your Own Era*. Schliemann had the arrogance, the insouciance, the ignorance, and/or the incompetence of essentially assuming that he could project himself backward in time onto the ruins of Troy, and they would exactly map to their description in the *Iliad*. As if nothing had happened – reuse, repurposing, recycling, removing, etc. – in the interposed three millennia! Our interpretation of, for example, Stonehenge, might change if it were comprised of rocks exactly as it was when first laid out starting more than 5000 years ago. Surely, Troy, with nine successive walled cities on the same spot, left very little of each preceding layer intact. Not only can we be inured to our own technology but also to our own perspectives on the past. Every archaeological site is undoubtedly much changed, especially one in which continued habitation has occurred.

However, even a site like Vesuvius, buried for nearly 2000 years, has changed significantly! We can infer a lot more about the way people lived in Pompeii than they did in Troy because of the better preservation, but it is still akin to the Burgess Shale: we can infer more about the structure and culture of the society, but still cannot recreate the richness of its conversations, mores, and context. What the eruption of Vesuvius allows that Troy does not, however, is the archaeological equivalence to dendrochronology in the dating of wood-based products. Since Vesuvius provides an exact time stamp (August 24, 79 AD), it allows us to match individuals, objects, and designs to specific other records preserved from the same time period (the writings of Pliny the Younger, a witness to the volcanic disaster at Pompeii and Herculaneum, for example). This allows us to place a specific "ring" of history into a specific slot in time and thus anchors our understanding of that time period so much the better.

The inability to reach beyond our current technology is further analogous to dendrochronology when the events no longer have a living witness. If the oldest humans on the planet can remember events 110 years ago, then in 2025, there is no living witness to anything that happened before World War I. The human "tree ring" of historical context is further limited by the small number of people alive at the 110-, 100-, and 90-year-old stages (and perhaps, by the higher incidence of memory-affecting illnesses among the elderly, although emotionally significant childhood memories seem to persist relatively well [Pete14]). Irrespective of these caveats, the human tree ring extends back perhaps a century for every degree of separation from the original experience; that is, someone born 100 years ago might have heard, while still very young, a first-hand account from someone quite elderly, meaning a second-hand account may go back, in fortuitous circumstances, up to 200 years. Beyond that, though, all of history is to at least some degree a matter of extrapolation. Sure, it is easy for geneticists to note that humans in ancient Mesopotamia, forming some of the first permanent agriculturally based settlements, had essentially the same brains as we do. But we are also aware from modern neurology, including fascinating imaging that shows real-time activity in the brain (e.g., through the imaging of glucose reactions; remember, your brain runs on sugar!), that the brain is highly plastic, and thus, "flexible" in its environment. Given the greatly different means of sensing one's surroundings being a denizen of ancient Sumer compared to being a large-screen display desk jockey of today, the difference in how the human brain works may be quite different. Blind musicians are well-known to have higher levels of absolute pitch and other indicators of musical prowess [Hami04], and this is surely due to their musical brain being able to "co-opt" parts of the brain that would otherwise have been concerned with vision. If a brain is exposed to different inputs and gives different outputs, then it makes sense that its internals might be different, as well. To rule this out is, well, to actively demonstrate both inurement to your era and arrogance about your own era. Part of the wonder of history is to be receptive to the differences between eras, and in doing so, appreciate the wide varieties of ways in which the human mind can work on its environment, and in turn, its environment can work on it as well.

7.4 Brother, Can You Spare Some Change?

Another "form" of anachronism, or at least a source of further anachronisms like those described in prior sections of this chapter, comes from the natural – if usually erroneous – tendency of humans to think that they are living in the historical era having the maximum change. Sure, there are historians (Claude Braudel among them) who note that our ancestors rarely (except for some military, governing, and trades personnel) traveled more than a few (perhaps ten) kilometers from their place of birth, due to a wide range of reasons, including brigandry, lack of safe (not to mention hygienic) inns, poverty, and lack of transportation infrastructure. This would have been especially the case for women, as men could join the army or navy, be a tradesperson, or even be more visible members of the government than was usually the case for women. What the actual percentage of people so "birth-place-bound" precisely was is really beside the point: the simple fact that people, in general, traveled less – far less – than they do today is a primary reason that many people today think that this is an era of maximum change in human living.

But other than perception, there is really no objective way of establishing this as a "truth." Human existence is the interaction of changes in economics, culture, religion, agriculture, manufacturing, construction, communications, energy, supply chains, and governance, just as much as in transportation. A reasonable viewpoint may well be that when a certain aspect of human existence appears static (say, distance traveled from birthplace), something else may be rapidly changing in a way later generations will not appreciate because they will take it for granted. Governance and religion in the late Middle Ages of Europe, for example, changed considerably, ending up with the Church (i.e., the Vatican) mediating much of the economic decisions between a rising mercantile class and an entrenched feudal class. Changes in communications, especially the development of private postal systems during the Renaissance, created massive changes in information exchange without necessarily affecting the modal distance from one's birthplace one traveled through one's life.

What does this all mean? It means that, without a comprehensive consideration of what changes were occurring, the magnitude of disruption that these changes caused to the modal person, and how these changes led to further changes cannot really be arrogated. This is because the magnitude of the change may not be the *perceived* magnitude of the change, which likely correlates with the degree of "stress for change" it caused for its denizens. After all, even a minor change in transportation means a lot when your main means of travel is walking. The actual rate of change may be less important than the rate of change divided by the current status of a particular aspect of human life. Having lived through the early days of the Internet, one of us can tell you that the difference between having no Internet and having Internet that affords 100 kB/s speeds was far, far greater than the difference between that 100 kB/s speed and current speeds of, for example, 900 MB/s. On an absolute scale, the first change is only 1/9000th the second change, but it is the impact it has on its citizens that really matters. Truly, the difference between the pre-Internet days and the early Internet days was astonishing. So, before thinking our time has such a high "stress for change," one must always remember how changes that seem little, even mundane, today (adding a single telegraph line between Washington, D.C., and Baltimore in 1843, or adding the first radio broadcast by KDKA, Pittsburgh, in 1920, for two examples) were spectacular to those living when they occurred.

All of this brings us back to a topic broached in the previous chapter's cyber salon. If indeed the rate of change in an area is more rapid than previous, then issues such as establishing precedence in intellectual property such as copyright and patents must become more difficult. With the world having added another *net* four billion people to the planet in the last 50 years, and with the explosion of the technology sector of the world's economy, there are literally dozens of times as many people working on the invention and creation of new technologies. As noted in that cyber salon, it is getting more difficult to establish precedence and establish a specific timestamp for when a particular technological advancement became "obvious" to one skilled in the art. Does this mean technology itself is changing faster than ever? Absolutely – and that has particular implications for the technology community. But does it necessarily mean that the ability of people to live through this rapidly changing state of technology is also becoming increasingly more difficult, stressful, and/or unmanageable? The answer there is decidedly no. Because it turns out that the technology used to create this rapid change can also be used to protect people from being overly stressed out by the change. For example, while artificial intelligence (AI) can be used (it is not encouraged) by some to assist them with creating new intellectual property, the same AI can be used to assess whether an intellectual property was helped by AI. In the end, the tools for detecting precedence, copying, and nonnovelty change, but the basics of what these constitute and how hard they are to detect do not change nearly as rapidly. Technology is often adopted at nearly equal rates by any two "juxtaposed" elements of society. Thus, newspapers, telegraph operators, and messengers originally stunned by the rapid rise of radio in the Roaring Twenties would soon thereafter have found ways to make their business complement radio or would themselves have joined the (pardon the play on words) wave of radio adoption.

As Voltaire famously said, "Plus ça change, plus c'est la même chose," and the value of that statement to help a historian interpret the significance of an event has not, well, changed much in the more than two centuries since. The rate of change by itself does not represent the impact of a historical change, and it is – and will remain – an anachronism to overestimate the amount of change occurring in the present by forgetting what the baseline was in the past.

7.5 Counteracting Anachronism: Means for a More Temporally Truthful Narrative

One of the more subtle forms of anachronism is the "nonlinearity of time," wherein a historical narrative that occurred long ago is compressed in proportion to the amount of time you have to travel backward to reach it. This is not necessarily linear (i.e., Alexander the Great might not get "exactly" half the pages as Charlemagne), and not necessarily even monotonic (i.e., Alexander the Great might receive more pages than, e.g., Alfred the Great), but as a moving average, the farther back one goes, the less the more ancient of two comparably impactful people (or events, processes, governments, economies, etc.) gets of coverage. In historical accounts, there will perhaps inevitably be "spikes" of interest, depending on the preferences of the narrator (the Greeks of Periclean Athens, Alexander the Great, Jesus, Julius Caesar, Genghis Khan, and Napoleon among them), but even among these potential "peers," the further back their lives, the more compressed the narrative tends to be.

A means of countering this otherwise "inevitable" anachronism is, as noted above, to complement the understandably compressed narrative about the historical figure of interest with later revisiting of them. This second visit, tying it into specifics of the later era, establishes the long-term importance of the earlier era, and reinforces learning overall. Think of the earlier era as a springboard to jump off and recognize that for some truly impressive dives, the diver might wish to bounce on the springboard several times before taking "flight." Note also that this recommendation is hardly earth-shaking. Great historians, even when they move on quickly from an earlier narrative to a later one, have in mind incorporating that earlier era anyway (otherwise, they might simply have ignored it). For a good example of employing this counterbalance to the anachronism of nonlinearity of time, Eisler's *The Chalice and the Blade* [Eisl88] is a good place to start. In this book, Eisler reviewed a number of past societies with a combination of archaeological and sociological insights to describe the possibility of either a "dominator" or a "partnership" model for structuring of society over time. In each subsequent era, Eisler connects their approach to civilization to those discussed previously – Crete to Catal Huyuk, Athens to Crete, the rise of Jesus to Athens, Social Darwinism to the Enlightenment, etc. In fact, much of the power of Eisler's connected narrative comes from how she explains otherwise puzzling practices of a subsequent era (the early Catholic church barring women from the priesthood) as a response to the (perhaps equally puzzling) practices of the previous era (the equal treatment and narrative empowerment of men and women in the story of Jesus). Much, but not all of course, of the variation of society from era to era, then, can be viewed as a response to the previous era, and a built-in "oscillation" that can result (thus, the oscillation between "domination" and "partnership").

Summarization, then, is not an anachronism by itself. It is a *constraint*. Constraints exist in most fields: building the Golden Gate Bridge, for example, is subject to the constraints of geography, currents, winds, and soil properties in the mouth of the San Francisco Bay. These constraints remove many possibilities for bridge design, and in doing so, may well provide the "filtering" necessary to find a faster engineering optimization than would be possible otherwise; that is, with a much larger, unconstrained set of possibilities. This is similar to the constraints that a particular meter – ballad or iambic pentameter, as two examples – place on poetry, music, or other artistic creations. Constraints, in fact, can be viewed in some ways as the flip side of adding too many perspectives. When a historian (over)reaches to provide every possible perspective on an event, they are certainly addressing the admirable goals of equitability and inclusivity, but they are also more likely to induce errors since the number of error possibilities increases geometrically with the number of perspectives. As a pithy reminder, then, the goal of the historian is to balance the need to provide multiple perspectives (including those that show the impact of a group not well-represented in the historical record by the otherwise unexpected change on a group that is well-represented in the historical record) with the need to not project too much from the present onto the past. This extends beyond technologies to sociology, ethics, economics, and other elements of human culture. With this, we turn to the related cyber salon and its discussion of anachronism in the "arms race" between attacker and defender.

7.6 Cyber Salon – The Arms Race Between Cyber Attackers and Cyber Defenders

The term "arms race" is used to refer to any competitive situation existing between two or more powers in which each power responds to an improvement in the offensive capabilities of another power by working to improve their own offensive (or defensive) capabilities. Two notable historical examples of this were the build-up of battleships among major powers before WWI, and the build-up of nuclear armaments by the United States and the USSR after WWII. An "arms race," as mentioned, can also be defensive in nature if, for example, a major power builds up a capability of checking another power's otherwise counterbalancing offensive capability (think of an aircraft carrier for obviating an adversary's battleships or a missile defense "shield" for obviating an adversary's nuclear armament). Major powers of today are looking at cybersecurity offensive and defensive capabilities as an important part of their overall military stance since all modern warfare is highly computerized and highly networked, and so cybersecurity capabilities can be viewed as being a "new" arms race. The arms race in cybersecurity, at the most general level, is the build-up of vulnerability exploitation (offensive) and intrusion protection (defensive) capabilities for cybersecurity professionals on one side, and their antagonists (such as advanced persistent threats, hackers, terrorists, etc.) on the other.

In this cyber salon, we discuss ways that a security professional can prevent an unhealthy arms race between themselves and their adversaries. By unhealthy, we mean one in which the cybersecurity stance is "anachronistic" with respect to key changes in the "balance of power," and so is providing a cybersecurity defense that is not prepared to win an arms race with the capabilities of their adversary. Worse, the anachronism, whether due to ignorance or complacency, means that the cybersecurity defenders may not even be aware of their disadvantage. This is the cybernetic equivalent of the infamous Maginot Line, which France invested in after WWI to prevent any future German invasion. Just as with the Maginot Line, simply throwing money and effort after defense is not sufficient – it needs to be directed at the actual likely attack locations.

Many cybersecurity defense approaches incorporate benchmarks to assess the state of their defense. These benchmarks complement, or may even be part of, regularly scheduled pentest (penetration testing) activities including the familiar red team/blue team exercises. Benchmarks are quantifiable measurements and features that are used to establish, initially, a baseline level of security as assessed by accuracy, recall, performance, sensitivity, and other salient output measurements. They continue to be used in downstream activities to track changes in these measurements over time. One problem with benchmarks, however, is that in the fast-changing world of cybersecurity, benchmarks can quickly become anachronistic if any of the assumptions about system/network processing, memory, and/or bandwidth change appreciably. This concern is exacerbated when the benchmarks are tied to specific performance (timing) metrics on specific hardware configurations.

For cybersecurity concerns, the arms race is concerned with both the software and the hardware employed by both the defender and the attacker. For software, the concerns are perhaps more obvious: the defender must employ operating systems, applications, services, machine learning (ML), and artificial intelligence (AI) software to protect their assets that are at least as sophisticated as the software used by the attackers. Governance methods such as a rigid patch rollout and specific policies around multifactor authentication (MFA), de-escalation of privilege, and other methods generally provide a means for arms race parity on the software side, although many of the applications (especially the AI and ML) and some of the processes (independent processes for the multiple elements of the MFA) may be expensive. Often cost is, in fact, the limiting factor to software arms race parity. Regardless, the means for software arms race parity are in general understood, particularly as they are the focus of the highly visible antimalware community and the online postings of common vulnerabilities by organizations such as CISA, Mitre (CAPEC, CWE, etc.), and OWASP.

With the understandably heavy reliance and focus on software, often overlooked are hardware anachronisms that may undermine the security of a network. Again, the network administrators and their users may have a false sense of security, particularly if there is spending for sufficient software-based protection (e.g., intrusion detection and prevention systems). We will illustrate this "complacency kills" anachronism by briefly considering different subsystems in networked computer hardware and showing where the anachronisms might arise.

Integrated circuits (ICs), or "chips," have increased in complexity over the years, and many seemingly innocuous chips now include relatively sophisticated interfaces, on-chip memory and processing, and communications capabilities that earlier vulnerability models do not account for. Increasing complexity within each chip may help to simplify the overall electronics design (since each chip may "chunk" what was before several separate chips), but each element on this overall electronics circuit is more sophisticated than the vulnerability models assumed that they were based on their training on earlier chip designs.

Cache, or high-speed storage between other elements of computer storage and the computer's processor, is another element of hardware that can be modeled on anachronistic data. The cache was largely associated with optimized memory management for central processing units (CPUs), and so, benchmarking how many security algorithm instances can be accommodated by a given security algorithm over a given time period (algorithm throughput) may be based on the assumptions of CPU design and manufacture. However, during the 2010s, dramatic changes in computing – including the massive convolution-based analysis of images needed for image recognition and generative image production, and the need to compute cryptocurrency mining operations with higher throughput – led to the massive employment of graphics processing units (GPUs), and a very different set of architectural and processing assumptions [Tayl17]. Models based on CPUs, and not GPUs, may therefore be anachronistic.

Next, the massive recent increase in the availability of inexpensive memory, and in particular, random access memory (RAM), fueled in part by the movement to solid state memory, has greatly changed the architectural options of data scientists and thus would-be cryptographic algorithm attackers. Not only does the vast increase in RAM obviate the need for certain cache designs, but it also means that many assumptions about how long it takes a personal computer to cycle through enough passwords to find a matching hash value are no longer valid. Coupled with the vast recent availability of personal data on targeted individuals from their online footprint (in particular their social media interactions) and the substantial improvement in cryptographic algorithm-cracking hardware, including the move to GPU-based cracking as mentioned above, means that perhaps 20 bits worth of security have been peeled off a number of cryptographic algorithms in the past decade [Sims22].

Another hardware subsystem has changed appreciably in the past decade, and in doing so, has likely obviated some of the cybersecurity assumptions about its deployment. This is the redundant array of independent disks (RAID) system used for data back-up/replication. As its name indicates, RAID was formerly realized through the use of a (usually company-owned) data center. In the 2010s, there was a rush to make cloud service providers the "RAID" of choice. Data localization then became a concern, and legislation such as the General Data Protection Regulation (GDPR) in the EU and the California Consumer Privacy Act (CCPA) in the United States was written to reduce the privacy and integrity risks caused by the cross-border movement of data. Regardless, the distributed nature of "cloud" and even "edge" computing (which colocates the RAID data with the location at which is created, but is therefore just as distributed as an organization's data sourcing) means that the data threat surface is substantially higher than it was assumed to be in many existing cyber-protection models.

Communications hardware has, of course, become more sophisticated over the years. While certain security risks are innate to the protocols involved in Internet-based communication, the hardware itself addresses a greater security threat surface as firewalls and intrusion detection and prevention systems, including access control lists (ACLs), dynamic host configuration protocol (DHCP) snooping, and port sniffing are incorporated into the hardware. This should not fool the network administrators into thinking they can cut corners elsewhere, and in fact, they need to make sure that any rules followed by the communications hardware do not conflict with rules elsewhere in the system (along the lines of having two antimalware services that each think the other one is malware and so afford less protection that either would have provided by itself). Regardless, the incorporation of more security features into the communications hardware may make the security models based on earlier hardware designs anachronistic.

Hardware for supplying power to computing equipment may also have changed enough recently to make existing physical security assumptions anachronistic. As more means of powering up computing devices, including inductive power and other wireless power transmission methods (e.g., power beaming), are adopted, there is an increasing amount of system software employed, which may be exposed to cybersecurity threats with little or no representation in the system's cybersecurity training sets. Suddenly, power requires more than surge protection but requires cybersecurity protection in its own right.

Other hardware threats abound that may make a current security posture anachronistic. Basic Input/Output System (BIOS) and other system-controlling software might expose a system to cyber risk if the update site can be spoofed or redirected. The CPU and the computer's motherboard may contain "extra" chips used for ill purposes that are included specifically for unanticipated and illegal data collection, processing, and exfiltration. Without board layout inspection, your computer may contain extra hardware that you certainly are not getting for free. Finally, Input/Output (I/O) ports and peripherals continue to increase in bandwidth requirements and sophistication over time and need to be remodeled by the cybersecurity protection model to avoid cyber-anachronisms. One thing is certain: hardware, like software, leaves no room for complacency by the cybersecurity protection team.

7.7 Summary

In this chapter, we have explored how the broad category of mistruth in historical narratives collectively labeled "anachronisms" extends far beyond the obvious – and humorous – prochronisms such as Gary Larson showing two dinosaurs smoking in *The Far Side* or Mel Gibson showing off his thighs in a 14th-century kilt. More insidious, and therefore more dangerous, anachronisms in historical narratives include a nonlinear treatment of time in the past compared to the present, with times in the past seemingly much more compressed. Another anachronistic perspective is one that seems to imply that people today live in a time of maximum change (which also serves the added advantage of "excusing" the historian for taking a superficially broad sweep across the earlier eras). A final anachronism of historical narratives focuses on how our perspective on the past is distorted if we cannot leave aside today's technologies and the social and cultural processes that they help create. Not only can we not project technologies backward in time to before they were invented, but we cannot project the *modes of behavior that they also create*. The chapter concludes with how anachronistic assumptions about computer hardware (and not just the more obvious software ones) can undermine an otherwise solid security posture.

References

[Eisl88] Eisler R, "The Chalice and the Blade: Our History, Our Future," HarperOne, 1988.

[Hami04] Hamilton RH, Pascual-Leone A, and Schlaug G, "Absolute pitch in blind musicians," Neuroreport 15, no. 5 (2004): 803–806.

[Jack18] Jackson MD, Oleson JP, Moon J, Zhang Y, Chen H, and Gudmundsson MT, "Extreme durability in ancient Roman concretes," Am. Ceram. Soc. Bull 97, no. 5 (2018): 22–28.

[Mast22] MasterClass, "What is an Anachronism? 3 Uses of Anachronism," https://www.masterclass.com/articles/what-is-an-anachronism-learn-about-the-different-types-of-anachronism-in-literature-and-film-with-examples, accessed 22 December 2023, posted 21 September 2022.

[Moor16] Moorehead C, "Priam's Gold: Schliemann and the Lost Treasures of Troy," IB Tauris & Company Limited (UK), 2016.

[Pete14] Peterson C, Morris G, Baker-Ward L, and Flynn S, "Predicting which childhood memories persist: Contributions of memory characteristics," Developmental Psychology 50, no. 2 (2014): 439.

[Rack86] Rackin P, "Temporality, Anachronism, and Presence in Shakespeare's English Histories," Renaissance Drama 17 (1986): 101–123.

[Robi23] Robinson A, "The Last Man Who Knew Everything: Thomas Young, the Anonymous Polymath Who Proved Newton Wrong, Explained How We See, Cured the Sick, and Deciphered the Rosetta Stone, Among Other Feats of Genius" (Revised Edition), Open Book Publishers, 2023.

[Rood20] Rood T, Atack C, and Phillips T, "Anachronism and antiquity," Bloomsbury Academic, 2020.

[Sims22] Simske SJ, "Data Handling," Inkjet Printing in Industry: Materials, Technologies, Systems, and Applications 2 (2022): 1081–1085.

[Tayl17] Taylor MB, "The evolution of bitcoin hardware," Computer 50, no. 9 (2017): 58–66.

8

Romantic Nationalism, Favoritism, Provincialism, Racism, Ismism

Nationalism is an infantile disease. It is the measles of mankind
– Albert Einstein

The beginning of Canadian cultural nationalism was not 'Am I really that oppressed?' but 'Am I really that boring?'
– Margaret Atwood

It is never too late to give up your prejudices
– Henry David Thoreau

Abstract

In romances, even in more complicated and richly told ones such as the *Lais of Marie de France*, the central characters usually move through trial and tribulation to find their happy ending. What about the other characters in a romance? Often, romances focus on the fate of the central characters, leaving out the equally compelling stories of the rest of the cast. Similarly, romantic nationalism and its various (if more evil) related forms (Manifest Destiny, Fascism, Sovietism, Mercantilism, etc.) focus on the "winners" of history at the expense of those who did not (willingly, at least) participate in this system. In this chapter, we show how romantic nationalism is always (at best) a selectively pruned version of the reality of past times. Such selective pruning, in fact, creates a historical bonsai effect, in which past events are greatly reduced in scale because they are so oversimplified and lacking in nuance. In more insidious forms, branches that did not grow from the same seed are artificially added to this bonsai, creating a monstrous chimera of history we usually describe as "isms," including favoritism, provincialism, and racism.

DOI: 10.1201/9788770048347-8

Among the historical events covered in this chapter will be Flag Day, the Battle of the Little Bighorn, and the Mexican War. The latter is the main thrust of Manifest Destiny in the United States, which we will show was not universally accepted even by the European Americans of the time (prominently John Quincy Adams and others) because they rightly predicted the negative consequences of this romantic nationalism on the peace and prosperity of the Native Nations and the United States itself. In considering the goals of the historical narrator, we will uncover why some of the "isms" of mistruth in history arise. The chapter concludes with a cyber salon focused on the way in which "romantic red-teamism" may lead to ineffective system testing.

8.1 Introduction

What is romantic nationalism? *Nationalism* (any type of favoritism applied to a nation, usually the "home" of the narrator) can be problematic enough, but when you add *romance* (meaning here a "love" story that is idyllic or idealized) to it, the problems for keeping a historical narrative free of mistruth become almost too much to overcome. Every blowhard populist has learned the lesson of romantic nationalism well: a so-called "rosy retrospection" is a well-known and commonplace form of cognitive bias; that is, recalling the past more positively than the past that was actually experienced. Other, related, terms for this are "nostalgia" and "the good old days." Except they were not. Like today, there was good and bad, and selective (or romantic) filtering of the past (or even fabrication of the past) is a means for a populist to create a rallying cry for "us" versus "them." The populist is able to create a narrative in which the elite (i.e., those who oppose them) have led society from that idyll, that Eden before the serpent first argued for fruitarianism, to the mess that it now is. Can there be truth in what the populist says? Of course. However, it is almost always a very selective filtering and even reimagining of the past and present (and thus, the future).

Why does romantic nationalism work for so many people? In some ways, it is a touch with "perfection," and perhaps because of that, it has continued appeal. If there is an ideal, a perfect, or at least near-perfect state, and the current state is a fall from grace and expulsion from the Garden of Eden that society once was, then who would not sign up for a return to that blissfulness? The problem is, what was that perfect state? Who was it for? Who did it exclude, exploit, or even extirpate? The point is that each person's "perfect state" in the past will be different and will selectively ignore those for whom this perfection may not have been felt at all. Somehow, the (successful) romantic nationalist populist is able to take this collective and make it seem universal, or at least, universal to enough people to get them into office, after which the reality will differ greatly.

We have sufficiently noted in earlier sections that historical retcons such as romantic nationalism are innately flawed, mainly because of the inevitable and incessant changes in society: economic, religious/moral, cultural, political, technological, and even military. Because these changes cannot be suddenly dialed back, there is no way to return to a previous, let alone "idyllic," state of society. The context will always be different. You might infer from this that George Santayana was mistaken when he commented, "Those who cannot remember the past are condemned to repeat it" (in *The Life of Reason*, 1905). However, Santayana meant "repeat" at the more patterned, or macroscopic, level; for example, allowing tyranny to arise due to complacence. Certainly, that type of repetition, exemplified by the rise of nationalism in a time of economic crises, does reoccur over and over again in history. In other words, some form of romantic nationalism is very likely to occur under a wide variety of conditions. Each time it appears, it will have different extenuating circumstances and context, but one thing is certain: it will always require magical thinking, and it will always be impossible to define in a tangible, let alone meaningful way. This is not said lightly: romantic nationalism arguably accompanies some of the worst events, times, and practices of history. It is responsible in varying degrees for some of the most atrocious of conquests, crusades, invasions, and dehumanizing of victims in all of history.

Mentioned above is the observation that romantic nationalism often involves *magical thinking*. In the field of psychology, magical thinking is a person's conviction that their personal thoughts, words, actions, beliefs, and even symbols can control, or at least strongly influence, the sequence of events in the "real" world. This form of auto-exceptionalism is, arguably, natural in the human condition (as a part of narcissism, whether at a healthy or an unhealthy level), as it motivates a person to do more, to believe in themselves, and to take risks. However, it can be dangerous when the specific (personal) is projected onto the general. Magical thinking, of course, is a form of mistruth. It is a conflation of the specific with the general, the past with the future, and the ideal with the literal. It may be possible, on occasion, with the right caveats to formulate a narrative that combines one of these sets (specific and general, past and future, or ideal and literal), but being able to meaningfully conflate all three sets is not really feasible. One of the most straightforward ways to detect romantic nationalism, in fact, is to run the following checklist:

1. Are the past, present, and future often combined into a directional narrative?

2. Does the narrative jump from the specific to the general and the converse?
3. Is the ideal portrayed as having been, at some point in the past, the literal?

If the answer to two or more of these questions is yes, then you are likely to be reading a narrative suffused with romantic nationalism. A first suggestion is to input the narrative into one or more fake news detection engines [Khan21], which will cover the "generic" aspects of uncovering a romantic narrative. A second suggestion, which will allow you to bring specific historical facts into the analysis, is to research multiple sources of information for every specific date, claim, or other fact in a narrative, with a special focus on the *precedence claims* in the article. A good example of this is the clearly nationalistically-driven claim, or reinterpretation, by (some of the populace of) Indonesia about the "megalithic site of Gunung Padang in Western Java, Indonesia ... [which] offers an opportunity to observe how national myths are both constructed and contested in recent times" [Suli21]. One of the hallmarks of romantic nationalism is the claim of precedence. Others include the vast (over)expansion of folklore and folk culture and a national epic or national narrative. Darker elements, of course, often accompany such romantic nationalism: the concept of a homeland or "fatherland," the belief in national/ethnic superiority, and the suppression of contradicting or even mildly altered narratives. Some other clues for detecting romantic nationalism in your reading, then, include:

4. Is one nation, ethnicity, or "people," portrayed as a "chosen people?"
5. Is one or more (dubious) claims of precedence made?
6. Is a different group's precedence rationalized or otherwise trivialized?
7. Are "universal stories" claimed as part of a national folklore, folk culture, national narrative, or national epic?

Here once again, two or more yes answers indicate a likelihood of a romantic nationalistic narrative.

With these tools at your disposal, you are ready to sniff out romantic nationalism. Based on the quote by Albert Einstein, *Nationalism is an infantile disease. It is the measles of mankind*, you might suspect that puerility is another indicator of romantic nationalism. But that is not necessarily the case. Plenty of romantic nationalism can be presented as serious literature, with science or more commonly pseudoscience used to support the argument. After all, scientists since at least the time of Broca (i.e., the American Civil

War) have studied brain size in order to justify their innate biases about relative intelligence in comparing ethnic groups along with men and women [Rush09]. In fact, scientists have often pushed a questionable agenda (nationalism in addition to racism and sexism) by using selective science to support conclusions they came to before ever collecting any data. A great way to declare a Master Race or a "Thousand-Year Reich" (Tausendjähriges Reich) is to provide supposed scientific evidence for the predecided declaration of superiority. Never forget to go back to the primary data before accepting a "scientific-sounding" narrative that just does not seem right.

We finish this introduction with brief comments on the final two quotes at the beginning of the chapter. As Margaret Atwood notes, cultural nationalism can take on many forms. For her, the romantic nationalism of Canada is ostensibly that of being oppressed. In other words, Canadians may wish to project a sense of victimization onto the rest of the world (presumably because of their bordering the powerful and oppressive United States). However, she hints that being boring is closer to the actual nationalism the country has (as perceived by non-Canadians). This is a clever way of letting people know that the nationalism a nation wishes to project may not be the one the world actually perceives. Finally, Henry David Thoreau notes that *It is never too late to give up your prejudices,* of which one would certainly be the prejudice toward viewing your own nation romantically. We hope that this chapter will help you, if that help is needed, to give up your romantic nationalistic prejudices.

8.2 What Really Is a Flag?

A flag is a tangible symbol, or emblem, that represents a country, state, or other institution. Most of us are quite familiar with flags from their ubiquitous display at the various holidays or other festivities that they are associated with. There is a wide range of importance placed on flags by the people they represent and by groups outside of the jurisdiction that they represent. The flag stands for something, and it follows that disrespecting a flag is a proxy for disrespecting the people that the flag represents.

There is now a flag for every nationality on earth, and it is reasonable to assert that a flag is a tangible incarnation of the romanticism felt by the nation represented. As such, we will review a few of these flags and from that get a sense of how deep romantic nationalism has embedded itself in modern consciousness.

A good starting point is the flag of Nepal. It is "the only national flag with a nonquadrilateral shape, with two triangular pennants stacked atop one another" [Klei24], which may speak to a romantic nationalism of trying to stand out, but is also purported to represent both its "roof of the world" mountain peaks and the nation's primary religions of Buddhism and Hinduism [Ibid.]. The rays emitting from the sun and moon connect the present to past Nepalese dynasties and suggest a long-lasting state.

Moving to Brazil's flag, its prominent green and yellow colors represent the historical dynasties of the "House of Bragança, which ruled over Brazil from 1822 to 1889" [Ibid.], and the House of Hapsburg (a long-lasting European dynasty that ruled Portugal, the "motherland" of Brazil, from 1580 to 1640). The latter is an interesting element of romantic nationalism since many of the migrants to Brazil during the 60 years of Hapsburg rule in Portugal were so-called New Christians, recently converted from Jewry due to the intolerance of the *auto-da-fé* in the "unified" Iberian Peninsula of that time. Why would a regime forcing conversions and then economically and culturally inducing emigration be incorporated into the flag? Obviously, this was done by "transplanted" Hapsburg power, with "Brazilian emperor Pedro I's wife – a descendant of the Habsburgs – suggest[ing] the yellow color to honor her heritage" [Ibid.]. The 27 stars connect constellations viewable from the historical capital, Rio de Janeiro, with Brazil's 27 states, and the incarnation of nationalism is completed with the slogan *Ordem e Progresso*, advertising Brazil as a nation of order and progress [Ibid.].

Sometimes romantic nationalism extends to multiple narratives. The United Kingdom's flag, the so-called "Union Jack," features "three heraldic crosses overlaid atop one another" [Ibid.], intended to convey the union of three nations into one kingdom (which, being crosses, immediately conveys the sense of the Trinity, or three-in-one, of Christian beliefs). The red cross (St. George, England and Wales) combines with the blue background and white "X" (St. Andrew, Scotland) and the red "X" (St. Patrick, Ireland). The flag ends up being more harmonious, perhaps, than the relationships between the three nations, especially those represented by red over the years. Such is the nature of romantic (vs. literal) nationalism, in many cases.

A final flag to mention here is that of Greece. It is simple enough, half-white and half-blue, but its white cross symbolizes both Greek Eastern Orthodoxy and the purity of modern Greek independence movements. The blue represents the sunny Greek skies, and the "nine alternating blue and white stripes represent the total number of syllables in the country's national motto, 'Freedom or Death,' as written in the Greek language;" [Ibid.] that is, *Eleftheria i thanatos*.

These four examples cover a lot of symbolic ground. That is to be expected since most flags have been designed to capture at least some aspect of the narrative of the represented region's nationalism: they are, after all, symbolic of a *nation*. Viewed less generously, however, a flag is the poster child for mistruth in history: as a boiled-down version of the national myth, the flag may be used to rehearse and thereafter institutionalize biased or even fabricated versions of history. This is especially problematic since the flag, in having the prominence of place in so many highly visible events, will be able to advance its narrative at the expense of any competing narrative. The ultimate, ironic reinforcement of this is, perhaps Flag Day. June 14 in the United States is a holiday celebrating the United States adopting the flag in much of its current incarnation way back in 1777. Many other countries have flag days, as well, and clearly celebrating the flag is yet another log on the fire of whatever myths it represents. Overall, a flag day seems in some ways fundamentally flawed since it may encourage celebrating the symbol rather than the reality.

In addition to flags, nations have other symbols to represent (and misrepresent) them. The United States has Uncle Sam, the bald eagle, the Statue of Liberty, the Liberty Bell, and other emblems, logos, slogans, and the like. One of the most ubiquitous is "*e pluribus unum*," meaning "out of many, one," to highlight the heterogeneity of US citizenry. If you really want a message to be internalized, put it on the currency, right?

This brings us back to a symbol so full of mistruths that we already included it in Chapter 6, under the omniscient historian. The crest for the UK colony, Turks and Caicos, was for nearly 100 years "a crest that included Salt Cay saltworks with salt rakers in the foreground and piles of salt" [Kurl11, p. 432]. However, the way colonies usually work is that the decisions are made back at the "home" nation, and so an "English designer assumed the little white domes were igloos. And so he drew doors on each one" [Ibid.]. This crest went directly onto the flag of Turks and Caicos, and there it stayed for more than 98 years. Proof, if needed, that flags can be symbols of mistruth.

8.3 Partitioning the Patriotism: The Battle of the Little Bighorn/Greasy Grass and the Battle of the Bucket

The Battle of the Little Bighorn (or if you prefer, the Battle of Greasy Grass) was discussed in Chapter 2 from the perspective of *omissions in history*. In the end, an argument was made for *adversarial accounts* in historical narratives potentially being better preadapted to historical accuracy than *collaborative accounts*, in which both sides of an issue in the narrative are motivated to provide the same (perhaps inaccurate) slant. In the context of Little Bighorn/Greasy Grass, the least trustworthy information is perhaps encountered when both sides are motivated to spin the same narrative, even if for entirely different reasons. There, we mentioned how both the Oglala Lakota and the US Army might have been motivated to spin the narrative that Crazy Horse killed Custer. The Oglala Lakota people may have wished to heap more glory on their already glorious warrior, while the US Army might have wanted to demonize Crazy Horse as a thinly veiled means of enhancing recruitment. Never mind the more recent motivation of the Crazy Horse Memorial Foundation! Such a "collaborative" account, it can be argued, is part of the larger "great person" narrative in many histories, wherein so much of the dynamism in historical events is attributed to the well-known individuals involved. Thus, even though the two most likely people to have killed Custer are the Sioux warrior known as White Cow Bull, followed by George Armstrong Custer himself, those narratives do not provide the same rallying cry for either side that the Crazy Horse narrative does. Never mind that a White Cow Bull might be just as crazy as any horse, he is just a lot less famous than Sitting Bull. And, for the Custer apologists out there (more on that shortly), is someone so famous for bravery if not reckless bravery really going to have been finished off by White Cow Bull? It just does not have the same romantic nationalism as Crazy Horse.

As mentioned, there were Custer apologists. Plenty, in fact. Among the reasons Custer lost the battle, so the "romantic" narrative goes, was betrayal by Benteen and Reno (they did disobey orders, after all, but then there were more than twice as many Native braves than estimated ready to run through the greasy grass); the failure to accept the use of Gatling guns; and the supposed better rifles employed by the Natives. All of which might, in some part, be relevant. However, Occam's razor (not used for the scalping of the US Army dead after the battle – this is a metaphorical razor) argues for the fact that the Natives comprised a "dream team" of the best warriors from a pool of some of the greatest athletes that the world might ever have seen: braves strong enough to hold onto a horse's side with their legs while deploying weapons with their free arms. Almost like an NBA team coming to take on your local high school squad. It is far more likely that Custer and his regiment's companies were simply overmatched, athletically and perhaps even skill-wise, by Sitting Bull, Crazy Horse, Chief Gall, and the other warriors amassed as part of the "Nations of the plains."

Moving from the Battle of the Little Bighorn, we come to the Battle of the Bucket. This is actually called the War of the Bucket, and Modena won its single-pitched conflict, the Battle of Zappolino. A battle that was the war, in other words. Battle of the Bucket has an alliterative quality, though, consistent with the romantic nationalism theme, and so that is what we will use. This battle occurred in 1325 AD as part of a much longer series of wars, conflicts, and hissy fits between the leaders of Modena and those of Bologna. The Modenese won the battle, capturing and destroying a number of Bolognese outposts, and ended by surrounding Bologna. Rather than siege the city, they performed a part-mock, part-meaningful ceremony outside the gates, then took the water bucket from the well outside one of the gates, Porta San Felice (in English, Gate of Saint Happy), and with the bucket and over two dozen captured Bolognese potentates, returned to Modena. The potentates were released from incarceration 11 weeks later, but the bucket is today still in Modena's *Camerino dei Confirmati*, safe even from public view (the public can see a copy that is shown in Modena's *Torre della Ghirlandina*). You would think this bucket would be forgotten, but its romantic value was crystallized by the mock-heroic poem *La Secchia Rapita* (The kidnapped bucket), published by Alessandro Tassoni in 1622 (note that was already almost three centuries after the battle). This poem includes instantly forgettable lines such as "the Bucket was soon to be locked away, in the tallest tower it remains to this day, up on high the trophy hangs bound, by a great chain nailed far off the ground" [Pala24]. Clearly, this is not Keats or Dickinson, but it has the same type of ease of repetition seen in the verses coming from other episodes of romantic nationalism (like the American Revolution, for example). The bucket, of course, is more than a means of bringing water to the surface in Emilia-Romagna; it is a symbol of Modenese overcoming odds and vanquishing those threatening their sovereignty. The public still goes to view a *copy of a bucket* that was in a well in one of the gateways to a city that they decided not to siege. And it is still a source of romantic nationalism *700 years later*. When in Modena, then, mock the bucket and you might, well, kick the bucket.

8.4 Manifest Destiny in the United States; Caesar in Gaul; Roland; Sagas

Romantic nationalism does not solely lead to the elevation of coopered condensation collectors to the status of relics. It also leads to the elevation of one group of people at the expense of another. A group on top often seeks to justify its elevation with a formal theory, such as Social Darwinism, Fundamentalism, or Supremacism, which is usually relatively easy to discredit but much less readily dislodged. Occasionally, the trendlines in history intersect in such a way as to bring several of these theories together at the same time and place. One such collection of romantic nationalism is "manifest destiny," a term that is essentially a euphemism for the imperialism of the (overwhelmingly of European descent) settlers and colonizers of the North American West in the 19th century, which reached its acme in the 1840s thus culminating in the United States taking advantage of the chaos and possible secession of major territories from the central government of Mexico to transduce hundreds of thousands of square miles of land from being part of Mexico (albeit for roughly 25 years since Mexico itself gained independence from Spain in 1821) into being part of the United States. Manifest destiny relates to American exceptionalism, which is a "preferred embodiment" of romantic nationalism in which a nation justifies direct or indirect control of another territory because of a greater moral purpose. Moral purpose, however, is nearly impossible to validate since, of course, morality and the means to disseminate that morality greatly differ based on a large number of factors, including everything from existing cultural practices to the existing level of poverty in the cultures involved.

Surely, the arbitrariness of relative moral purposes had something to do with intellectuals, such as former US President John Quincy Adams, turning away from earlier support for manifest destiny. By the early 1840s, it was clear that manifest destiny was being used to justify the westward expansion of slavery (meaning to Texas in 1836), and by 1843 Quincy Adams repudiated expansionism and manifest destiny. Again, a major problem with manifest destiny is the competing moral purposes of those expounding it. Manifest destiny supposedly was destined to promulgate the expansion of White American settlers from sea to shining sea. However, those in the North might have viewed this differently from those in the South, not to mention that abolitionists surely viewed it differently than segregation-preferring Whites in the North. As an abolitionist, then, Quincy Adams' view of romantic nationalism might have been for the creation of a Western land in which White, Black, and Brown people shared a particular set of morals. But segregation, let alone slavery, was not his moral view. Given the large percentage of Black and Hispanic cowboys that were part of the Wild West experience between the civil war and World War I, it is clear that Quincy Adams was not alone in this view.

Manifest destiny might have been specifically coined for the (by today's standards) illegal seizure of land by the United States in the mid-1800s, but the existence of its analog extends back throughout history. There is even an element of (fatalistic) manifest destiny in *The Iliad*, but it is more overt in three examples we will mention briefly here: (1) Caesar in Gaul, (2) Roland, and (3) the Icelandic Sagas.

In Caesar's *Commentarii de Bello Gallico* (*Commentary on the Gallic Wars* in English), Caesar cleverly weaves between fact (locations, dates,

Gallic customs) and fiction (430,000 Gallic warriors at the siege of Alesia!) in an effort to build a romantic nationalism that both represented Rome as more noble and indomitable to its adversaries and represented Caesar more as a man of the people (Caesar knew assassination was always a possibility in the hornet's nest of Roman politics, and so, this was a sort of insurance policy). Rest assured that when Caesar crossed the Rubicon, his marketing agent was there to record the moment. For Caesar, romantic nationalism was, first and foremost, a Caesar salad.

The *Song of Roland* is also a mixture of fact and fiction, intended to create a romantic nationalism using the Battle of Roncevaux Pass in 778 as the rallying cry. In reality, the Basques (responding to significant destruction of their territory, including the looting of the Basque capital, Pamplona, by Charlemagne's forces as they prepared to return to France across the Pyrenees) attacked the rearguard of Charlemagne's forces and wiped out a contingent of several thousand. The *Song of Roland*, a *chanson de geste* poem (i.e., epic poem), was written in 1080 AD plus or minus 40 years, more or less contemporaneous with the First Crusade (1096–1099) and certainly acting as a coreactant with that crusade to stimulate anti-Moorish romantic nationalism. The fact that the Basques are replaced with the Moors of Spain as combatants only emphasizes that ambition.

Then there are the Icelandic Sagas. Set at the turn of the (earlier) millennium, they portray the roughly 200 years of settlement and eventual conversion to Christianity of the largely Norse and Irish peoples that willingly or unwillingly arrived at those northern chores from roughly 870 AD (first settlers) to 1056 AD (first bishopric in Iceland). As romantic narratives go, perhaps the sagas do less to romanticize the early settlers than we might otherwise expect. In comparison to Roland, for example, they do not generally fight against overwhelming odds, selling their lives dearly in a battle conflating culture, religion, and morals. The sagas do make mention of the major battles of the time, in particular the battles of Hafrsfjord and Clontarf, but most of the action – including the violence – in the sagas is neighbor against neighbor. It is personal, local, and vindictive. Interestingly enough, however, this fits nicely with the romantic nationalism of a place such as Iceland. Isolated, icy, and independent, Icelanders created a national mythos focused on self-reliance, so why should not their narratives also be so? In many ways, living in Iceland is a bit like traveling into space – one must have everything one needs along with oneself because in a crisis, resupply is not likely to be expedient enough. This would have especially been the case during the Little Ice Age (roughly 1303–1850 AD), which was just around the corner when the most sweeping of the sagas (e.g., *Njal's Saga*) were first written down in the late 1200s. The Little Ice Age created greater isolation and may have helped congeal the strong part that the Sagas play in the Icelandic national narrative. Romantic nationalism based on a culture of isolation, self-reliance, and competition over sparse resources (so many sagas include violence erupting over the use of pastures and the collection of materials washed up on beaches) is directly in line with the reality of early Iceland. It may not be manifest destiny, but it is certainly a form of romantic nationalism: it is the image that a nation, in this case, a nearly treeless island hugging the Arctic Circle, wishes to project to the world.

8.5 What is the Goal of the Historical Narrator?

What drives a narrative toward romantic nationalism? In other words, what is the motivation of the narrator? When thinking of motivation as persuasion, often motivation is framed around logos, ethos, or pathos. Briefly, this is logic, ethics, and feelings used to sway a reader or listener. There are other potential motivations for the writer, of course, with one additional one being esthetics. In romantic nationalism, this one cannot be easily dismissed: a tale told the way *it should have happened* is highly amenable to Flag Day, Independence Day, or any other patriotic celebration that a nation might wish to advance.

The motivation of the narrator is important for the reader so that she can calibrate the narrative as she "digests" it. Is the narrative filled with syllogisms? Then, the reader is likely to see logos drive the narrative. Is the narrative filled with assertions of contrasting virtuous and immoral behavior? If so, then the reader can rest secure that ethos is a driving persuasive element in the narrative. If emotional reactions are routinely cajoled, then pathos is an important persuader in the narrative. Finally, if the story seems to tightly fit an advantageous romantic nationalism, then esthetics is part of the persuasiveness in the narrative. The reader, in the search for mistruth, might be well-served by looking for the relative amounts of each persuasion type. In romantic narratives, esthetics and ethos are especially likely.

Another sign of romantic nationalism can come directly from the identity of the author. If the author appears to be narrating some type of nationalistic message, the reader should research the author. Where are they from? Who do they identify with? What have their past writings focused on? If an article is worth reading, it is also worth understanding the context around it. The seven questions to ask about a potentially romantic narrative from above are a good place to start.

This brings us back to a couple of topics mentioned earlier in this chapter. The "Indonesian pyramid scheme," in which romantic nationalist

Indonesians falsely assert that pyramids in Indonesia are the oldest in the world is flawed not just because of the mendacity of precedence claimed. It is false because it incorporates a narrative concerned with celebrating the specific rather than tying it to the more universal, or at least to the more general, and thus celebrating a larger historical narrative. A narrative in which comparing and combining the great pyramids of the world – whether in Indonesia, Egypt, Iraq, Guatemala, Peru, Sudan, or elsewhere – is more important than asserting precedence. As mentioned above, narratives focused on precedence rather than continuity are often ones expounding romantic nationalism.

A second topic mentioned earlier is the fact that history is (and will continue to be) increasingly written by artificial intelligence (AI). The creation of fake news by massively parallel and massively trained AI systems has created an arms race between the formation of mistruth and the olfaction of mistruth; that is, sniffing it out. The history of technology has been defined by tradeoffs like the formation-olfaction one. Another common motif of technological history is that once a technology has been created, it is virtually impossible to keep it from spreading. From the chariots of the Hyksos [Carn05] to the atomic weapons of the United States, military advantages, once appreciated, are quickly reverse-engineered and then spread to all major powers. Today, military advantages are gained in more sophisticated ways (such as the possible advantages of CRISPR-Cas mechanisms for biological warfare and the use of AI for cyber warfare), but they are, like the proverbial genie, not to be put back into a bottle. With AI capable of writing narratives, even if far clunkier than those of humans skilled in the particular arts, a battle for the narrative of history has begun. Romantic narratives, then, can be *programmed* by individuals and made to look like they represent consensus views of history. Ironically, as it has become easier for AI to create content, there has never been a greater need for skilled historians. They are needed for more than simply countering the mistruths created by AI: they are also needed to incorporate the rationale behind why AI is being used to create fallacious narratives as part of the historians' ongoing creation of the narrative of history that each moment in the present represents. The best time to archive history, arguably, is while it is happening. As such, historians are needed for its stewardship and not just its curatorship. The arms race for the prevention of mistruths from the narrative of history, in other words, has been changed and the window between events occurring and the history of the same events being written has narrowed.

We finish this section with a reconsideration of relevant aspects of manifest destiny. Manifest is to make something real, certain, or embodied. So, manifest destiny is not only romantic nationalism but it is redundant (since destiny is something that will be real, certain, and embodied). A better term for it might be *manifest density* because it is decidedly dull-witted, unimaginative, and lacking subtlety. In fact, differential density is a hallmark of the sort of biased accounts consistent with romantic nationalism. Differential emphasis and evaluation, studied in-depth in Chapter 5, are often associated with romantic nationalism. This is because nationalism, in sanctifying the nation, tends to dehumanize its opponents. There is a manifest density of the narrative on the preferred people.

Having considered the origin, the detection, and the threats of romantic nationalism, we next turn to an illustration of how an understanding of this pattern of mistruth in history can be used in system-level cybersecurity. The particular application considered is pentesting, which is the topic of this chapter's cyber salon.

8.6 Cyber Salon – Pentesting

Vulnerability penetration testing (or "pentesting," mentioned in Chapters 5 and 7) of systems can suffer from a form of *romantic red-teamism* if cybersecurity professionals are not wary. Cybersecurity professionals reading this might think a mistake was made there: surely, romantic *blue-teamism* is what was meant. However, consider the role that each of these two teams play. The blue team is meant to respond to the attacks made by the red team. If the blue team is ill-equipped to fend off one of the red team attacks, then the system will fail in the exercise; however, the failure will be a *known outcome* of the exercise, and so, the system cybersecurity experts will know that a fix is required. This is a desired consequence of a red-team/blue-team exercise, and so, from the pentest goals standpoint, it is a success. On the other hand, if the red team fails to attempt to exploit a vulnerability, then the blue team may not even be aware of the danger. Which is worse, a known threat or an unknown threat? Unless the known threat is impossible to resolve (even with an "air gap" of the system), most would agree that it is better to know the threat. That is, in fact, why pentests are performed.

In order to see the insights that an understanding of romantic nationalism provides for pentesting, a quick review of what pentesting entails is merited. Pentesting is effectively a series of tests employed to reveal exploitable vulnerabilities. As mentioned above, a pentest (some write it *pen test*, especially those trying to increase their word count) is a form of red team attack, in that it is a simulated attack authorized by the system admins and other stakeholders. Penetration testers use the same processes, technologies, and analytics that unfriendly attackers do to identify and evaluate the vulnerabilities and threat surfaces in a system. Pentests can take on many forms, including the running of scripts, wardriving (used to test Wi-Fi network vulnerabilities among other location-specific vulnerabilities), and social engineering.

Each of these approaches has a wide array of possibilities, and a pentest based on a prespecified set of them is unlikely to fully explore the rapidly evolving threat surface of cybersecurity. Instead, the concept of fuzzing might be merged with these prespecified tests in order to provide a more representative and comprehensive sampling of the full threat surface in cybersecurity. Fuzzing is a term used to describe an automated testing process that inputs stochastic, nonvalid, and/or unanticipated data as inputs to a test script (or another program, more generally). To the scripts and other processes carried out by the red team, the addition of randomness, out-of-range inputs, and other fuzzing elements is likely to more fully stress test a system and is often a way to ensure that the outcomes of the pentest are not known beforehand. Of all the times to be complacent in your cybersecurity processes, the pentest may well be the least opportune.

By applying the concept of "fuzzing" to the pentest, one can avoid the cybersecurity equivalent of manifest destiny that might otherwise cause complacency and the *structural compromise* of networked systems. By structural compromise is meant a system compromise that is built into it by a failure of design. Just as manifest destiny is an approach to organizing society that is likely to fail by design since it creates and/or emphasizes an "us" versus "them" narrative, running a pentest whose basis is a familiar set of approaches may be manifestly destined to fail.

8.7 Summary

In this chapter, some of the worst "isms" of history, and in particular romantic nationalism, were considered as a commonplace, but avoidable, source of mistruth in historical narratives. The view of some previous historical time and place being ideal, idyllic, or ideologically superior to the present is an attractive narrative and one that will continue to arise in the present and future. In order to overcome this attractively false narrative, the historian needs to make sure that they are, first of all, able to discover when it is being employed. Seven questions were provided to help the reader address whether the text they are reading is romantic nationalism:

1. Are the past, present, and future often combined into a directional narrative?

2. Does the narrative jump from the specific to the general and the converse?
3. Is the ideal portrayed as having been, at some point in the past, the literal?
4. Is one nation, ethnicity, or "people," portrayed as a "chosen people?"
5. Is one or more (dubious) claims of precedence made?
6. Is a different group's precedence rationalized or otherwise trivialized?
7. Are "universal stories" claimed as part of a national folklore, folk culture, national narrative, or national epic?

Any one of these can be enough to identify romantic nationalism, although it is certainly true that the more one can answer "yes" to, the more romantically nationalistic a narrative is likely to be. Especially dangerous is when the narrative is connected to magical thinking. In these days where a continually larger percentage of the adult population has grown up as Internet, social media, and AI natives, the danger of romantic nationalism also increases with each passing year since the Internet provides a handy "echo chamber" for any belief system, no matter how unsupported it might be by the general public. Such echo chambers reinforce – and perhaps create outright – magical thinking.

The roles that flags can play in reinforcing a romantic nationalism were next discussed. Flags are not innately evil or sources of mistruth but can be used to support divisive and revisory historical fiction as if it were fact. Flags may help advance tribalism, and an "us" versus "them" narrative that is usually not worth revisiting, let alone propagating. When a bucket captured in a battle 700 years ago is still preserved in a museum, you might figure out that romantic nationalism helps explain this otherwise puzzling spite. Beware the symbols of romantic nationalism, especially where they help extend the narrative of mistruth.

Next, the relative ubiquity of manifest destiny-like ideologies in history was exemplified in the mid-19th century United States, Caesar's conquering of Gaul, the *Song of Roland*, and the Icelandic Sagas. After a discussion of how to discover the motivation for romantic nationalistic narratives, the chapter concluded with a cyber salon describing how complacency similar to that of romantic nationalism can lead to failure in penetration tests, or pentests, in cybersecurity vulnerability assessments.

References

[Carn05] Carney R, "The Chariot: A Weapon that Revolutionized Egyptian Warfare," History Matters, II (2005): 1–10.

[Khan21] Khan JY, Khondaker MTI, Afroz S, Uddin G, and Iqbal A, "A benchmark study of machine learning models for online fake news detection," Machine Learning with Applications 4 (2021): 100032.

[Klei24] Kleinman B, "Do You Know the Hidden Meanings Behind These National Flags?", DailyPassport, https://dailypassport.com/national-flag-hidden-meanings/, accessed 24 January 2024.

[Kurl11] Kurlansky M, "Salt," Random House, 2011.

[Pala24] Palazzo Comunale, Comune di Modena, https://salestoriche.unesco.modena.it/en/camerino-dei-confirmati/the-stolen-bucket/, accessed 10 February, 2024.

[Rush09] Rushton JP and Ankney CD, "Whole brain size and general mental ability: a review," International Journal of Neuroscience 119, no. 5 (2009): 692–732.

[Suli21] Sulistyowati D and Foe AW, "Indonesia's Own 'Pyramid': the Imagined Past and Nationalism of Gunung Padang," International Review of Humanities Studies 6, no. 1 (2021): 10.

9

Emboldening Situations

Do not wait for a coronation; the greatest emperors crown themselves
– Robert Greene

Fortune befriends the bold
– Emily Dickinson

Abstract

John Milton, the genius behind the epic poem *Paradise Lost*, became a cringeworthy, apologist sycophant to Cromwell under the emboldening situation of the Protectorate. Not able to see the Restoration in his near future, Milton said enough to land himself a cozy prison cell after that future arrived. It is trite, and as noted earlier incorrect, to say that history is written by the victors. Actually, Victor Hugo was more of a dramatist than a historian. The point is, when this expression is used, it is implied that the history the victors write about contains mistruth. History is more commonly written by people who are emboldened sufficiently by the current situation to justify placing it in the historical record. This is an untruthful way of justifying the current situation in preference to its alternatives. And yes, the victors will be emboldened to justify not only their current situation but also imagined situations to come. For this reason, the doctoring of documents during such times commands the attention of everyone.

Examples of emboldened chronicling include the manner in which the US Civil War is presented, the manner in which Adam Smith presented the free market economy, and the chartering of the Magna Carta in 1215. For many years, the Civil War was presented as being focused on the issue of "secession" rather than the more obvious (and more correct) focus on the issue of slavery. Adam Smith was emboldened to define and champion the free market economy in part because of the victory of the United Kingdom

DOI: 10.1201/9788770048347-9

in the Seven Years' War. The incompetence and unpopularity of King John emboldened the barons to draft and obtain approval of the Magna Carta, but the importance of the Magna Carta in history was itself the beneficiary of later emboldening by subjects of the English crown.

The chapter continues with a discussion of how emboldening arises, and how the age of the Internet helps it to arise and thrive. The chapter concludes with a cyber salon addressing human trafficking and how its purveyors are emboldened by technologies that also threaten legitimate networks.

9.1 Introduction

This chapter addresses the role of emboldening in the creation of mistruths in historical narratives. At the superficial level, this is perhaps the most straightforward of the mistruths to define. Emboldening is, after all, simply taking advantage of a situation. But, beneath the surface lies a complex and even bewildering list of factors that might encourage one to spout mistruth. If mistruth is universal, then these factors, following the *unity of opposites* dating back at least as far as Heraclitus, simultaneously exist in both of their opposing forms. Although there are surely far more, we will describe four such pairs of opposites here to see how they might arise under emboldening circumstances. The four pairs (or perhaps they can/should be considered axes) are (1) privilege versus penury, (2) justification versus judication, (3) empowerment versus subjugation, and (4) evanescence versus permanence.

Having advanced the usefulness of the concept of unity of opposites, it is perhaps easiest to illustrate this by considering the relationship between *privilege and penury*. The greater the distance between the privileged and the penurious (reaching out to the endpoints of the privilege-penury axis, as one way of viewing this), the greater the opportunity for the emboldening of both groups. For the privileged, emboldening is easy to understand. They have money, they have the ability to project themselves into the public spotlight, and they often have the need to justify their differential privilege. This is not a new concept. Andrew Carnegie in 1889 argued, in justification of his great wealth, that rich men are critical for society to advance in that they must use their great wealth to improve lives for the poor. He claimed, "Individualism will continue, but the millionaire will be but a trustee for the poor, entrusted for a season with a great part of the increased wealth of the community, but administering it for the community far better than it could or would have done for itself" [Carn89, p. 169]. In other words, Carnegie believed that the rich were "supermen" who amassed their wealth because they alone had the talent to do so, and without them, all of society might be poor. So adamant was Carnegie about the differential economic talents of the rich and the poor that he claimed, "It was better for mankind that the millions of the rich were thrown into the sea than so spent as to encourage the slothful, the drunken, the unworthy" [Carn89, p. 169]. In other words, the differential wealth in society was due to differential talent in creating (and amassing) wealth, and the wealthy were therefore overwhelmingly the proper stewards of all society's economics. This is an emboldening based on empowerment and can thus be viewed as a *reinforcing* emboldening.

In the many decades since Carnegie's claims were made, a significant shift has occurred in how the megarich are viewed. While still often admired and treated with deference, the general public does not anticipate them redistributing their wealth. As a consequence, there is a multifaceted emboldening of the poor to be expected. One facet is the false claim that less money is spent on antipoverty programs. For example, "Throughout Reagan's eight years as president, antipoverty spending grew, and it continued to grow after he left office" [Desm23]. In fact, "There is no evidence that the United States has become stingier over time. The opposite is true … Decade after decade, the poverty rate has remained flat even as federal relief has surged" [Ibid.]. The other emboldening of the poor, however, is well-supported factually. When the poor claim that they are being exploited, for example, by penalties placed on monetary overdrafts and by disproportionately high rents for low-quality living conditions, they are correct [Ibid.]. In other words, it is exploitation (low wages, high cost of banking, etc.) and "the condition of not having enough choice and being taken advantage of because of that" [Ibid.] that can be seen as emboldening the poor. When the poor can see that the policies and governance of their localities are not aligned with the ending of their poverty, their emboldening is one of despair, and thus, directly opposed to the emboldening of the privileged. In other words, rather than being a *reinforcing* emboldening, it is an *iconoclastic* emboldening. Reinforcing emboldening is Calvinistic, in the sense that those enjoying privilege are empowered to claim that they do so because of their disproportionate talents, tenacity, and temperament; while iconoclastic emboldening is associated with a penurious group viewing their situation being due to a combination of randomness, regulation, and rationalization. Both of these viewpoints – regardless of their quite different ethical bases – are likely to embolden their proponents to misrepresent history. For the privileged, the narrative may be focused on leadership and philanthropy, while for the penurious, the narrative may be focused on inequities inherent in a society in which the "trickling down" from above is the economic modus operandi. Regardless of whether there is an eventual trickle-down, the time delay between wealth creation and wealth distribution is almost certain to create a narrative schism.

A second pair of opposing factors to consider for the emboldening of a mistruthful historical narrative are the endpoints of the axis of *justification versus judication*. Here, the first extreme (justification) is a tactic needed by a person or process whose position in society does not bear the support of the laws of the land; in contrast, the second (judication) is a person or process whose position is supported by the laws, rules, regulations, and mores of its society. Justification can come from the privileged or the poor, and judication can also favor either group. For example, a privileged person might justify some type of societal control (from territorial hegemony to economic hegemony) based on their assertion of differential talent and organizational abilities of themselves and their colleagues. Judication, however, may require a specific percentage of those hired into a company to be locals or even require training and education of locals in order to justify the arrangement. These opposing viewpoints are almost inevitably to echo in the historical narratives. For example, justification may be used to portray a penurious group that operates outside the law as a liberator (think of the narrative of many a Communist "revolution"), while a privileged group that operates within the law but restricts the rights of other groups may use judication to defend their actions (think of the narrative of many a "conservative" dictator). Alternatively, justification may be used by a group of privileged people to promote a narrative of uninvited hegemony as an improvement in the standard of living for those conquered (including justification based on bringing a new religion to the natives), while judication may be used by the impoverished of one nation to nationalize foreign assets within their jurisdiction *carte blanche*, regardless of the integrity and the polarity (positivity or negativity) of the impact of each of the assets seized.

A third pair of opposing factors is *empowerment versus subjugation*. The relative empowerment of a group does not always track with their wealth (privilege vs. penury) or the laws of the locale (justification vs. judication). For example, the Jewish population in Germany during the Nazi takeover of 1933 was well less than 1% of the population [Gold07] and was neither penurious nor unprotected by laws. However, the violent racial nature of the Nazi regime made it readily apparent that Jews would not be empowered under the jackboot of Hitler. Empowerment is different from emboldening; for example, one can be empowered and not exercise that power, while one emboldened is exercising that boldness. Subjugation is, for most people anyway, a more forgivable reason for providing a biased, or mistruthful, narrative. A large part of the reason for modern-day "forgiveness" of subjugation-based narrative slant is the *legitimization of feelings*, which is perhaps much more of a modern phenomenon than one might expect. In other words, in many past societies, feelings themselves were subjugated to the mores of society. Medieval Europe is an example, though it is hardly the only one. In Europe from about 600 to 1400 AD, the combined hierarchical nature of feudalism and the legitimization of suffering through the Life of Christ helped create a society in which the historical narrative was written by those empowered, rather than those subjugated. Of course, low literacy rates and the correlation between literacy and empowerment had much to say about this, as well.

One additional pairing of opposing factors to consider here are those defining the axis of *evanescence versus permanence*. Short-term opportunities (such as John Milton's window of opportunity during Cromwell's reign, highlighted by his insouciant-to-regicide *The Tenure of Kings and Magistrates*) may unleash long-shuttered emboldening, especially from folks who might otherwise have been too cowed to speak up. Such emboldening is precarious in addition to evanescent, and Milton during the restoration enjoyed neither the restoration of his sight nor the restoration of his emboldening, focusing his admirable literary talents on such instant nonclassics as his *History of Britain* and *Art of Logic*. Not quite *Paradise Lost* or *Samson Agonistes*, to be sure. Perhaps Milton confused the success of Cromwell on the battlefield with success in changing a culture. Regardless, his emboldening provides a largely forgotten view of history, with his pro-Cromwell propaganda remembered only in the context of his life's story arc, and not for its content.

More permanent changes in history are, arguably, rarer, and therefore, perhaps more difficult to recognize as they unfold. Fast forwarding 200 years from Cromwell and migrating 15 miles southeast of London, we observe the emboldening of Charles Darwin as a consequence of the permanent change in society, culture, and history that evolutionary biology would bring. Darwin cut his intellectual teeth on a half-decade voyage aboard the *Beagle*, during which his attention to detail led him to ponder if one species can change into another (despite no knowledge whatsoever of genetics, let alone microbiology). This proved to be a universal acid, and Darwin could see natural selection at work in the selective breeding of stock and the differential survival of species after natural catastrophes occurred. Darwin was further emboldened by Alfred Russel Wallace's publication on speciation and encouragement by friends such as Lyell to publish his own, more fleshed-out, theory of speciation through natural selection. *On the Origin of Species* was published in 1859, and within just over a decade, the theory of evolution was accepted as fact by the overwhelming majority of the scientific community, as it has since.

Without blushing, one can say that Wallace's paper emboldened Darwin, helping him to recognize the permanence of evolution (the permanence of change, as it were). Darwin undoubtedly would not have been emboldened, as was Milton, by more evanescent factors.

We complete this section by considering the wisdom of the two quotes included in this chapter. Robert Greene, in his millennial-era masterwork, *The 48 Laws of Power*, advised: *Do not wait for a coronation; the greatest emperors crown themselves.* In other words, boldness begets success or fortune. Emily Dickinson, the virtuoso of verse, turned this around 180 degrees, saying *Fortune befriends the bold.* Is this a chicken or egg discussion (a discussion resolved, by the way, by Darwin's theories since eggs existed long before the speciation of the chicken!)? Hardly. Between these two quotes, it is an equality. Fortune and emboldening go together, and that is why at either extreme of each of the four axes we describe here (privilege vs. penury, justification vs. judication, empowerment vs. subjugation, and evanescence vs. permanence), emboldening can occur. To be bold is, in historical narratives, to be part of history itself. With this in mind, we turn to a few examples of boldness in action in the process of the creation and narration of the historical record.

9.2 The US Civil War

The US Civil War, which ran from 1861 to 1865 and killed a higher percentage of American citizens than the rest of its wars combined, was surely about slavery, was it not? After all, the Emancipation Proclamation was the output of Abraham Lincoln's emboldening from the encouraging fact that his army held the field at the end of the bloodiest single day of combat in US history (Antietam, September 17, 1862). Just five days after the battle, when it became clear that the Confederate Army had returned to Virginia and the offensive was defeated, in the third paragraph of the preliminary Emancipation Proclamation, Lincoln noted that "all persons held as slaves within any State or designated part of a State, the people whereof shall then be in rebellion against the United States, shall be then, thenceforward, and forever free." Lincoln was emboldened to free the slaves in all Confederate states – but not in Kentucky, Missouri, Delaware, and Maryland (and technically, not in its still limited existence in New Jersey). It took three more years of uncivil war and the death of Lincoln for the rest of the nation to catch up and end slavery as an institution in both rebelling and nonrebelling states.

A key question worth asking is, "What really was the nature of the emboldening garnered by Lincoln?" To answer this question, it is worth remembering that Lincoln did not meet Frederick Douglass until almost a year later (August of 1863), a full month after the North simultaneously won the battles at Gettysburg and Vicksburg, and thus, made all but inevitable a Northern victory. So, not Douglass, and perhaps not even the abolitionists, were the likely emboldening factors for Lincoln, at least initially.

Part of the difficulty with identifying historical emboldening is the difficulty of reconstructing the entire context around the individual or group when they became emboldened. The further we are from the actual events, the more difficult it becomes to distinguish what were real influences and what were perceived influences; in other words, distinguishing between what actually happened and what people thought might happen. More problematically, the historical record for that time in the past is highly unlikely to accurately represent the actual context. Emboldening, after all, means that the historical narratives reflect the emboldening of their writers. Fortunately, however, in the case of the Civil War, enough historical narrative has survived on each side to enable one to determine with some confidence the emboldening events.

The fact that diametrically opposed narratives have survived is a benefit to the modern historian because truth in general shines more brightly when the dark of mistruth is contrasted with it. That is, if only a single narrative survives, then with the passing of time, what was once understood in that narrative as opinion, irony, and even sarcasm, comes to be misunderstood as fact. The paradox of the truthful narrative, then, is that it contains within itself mistruths that are not mistruthful because they are understood to be mistruths by their contextually informed readership. Suppose, for example, that a factual Civil War "letter home" included the comment, "Gee willickers, Mom, I hope to be as good a general as McClellan someday," and the historian was not aware of the irony in this sentence. In this circumstance, the historian (and particularly, if the historian is an artificial intelligence) might view this as a positive reflection on McClellan.

As with much in historical narration, the reasons for the Civil War have been boiled down, or at least oversimplified, since its occurrence. For many years, the Civil War was presented as being focused on the issue of "secession," especially by those in the South, where the war has been called the War of Northern Aggression. It is not particularly surprising to find out that this naming for the Civil War became popular in the United States South of the 1950s when the battle to end segregation was being fought in earnest. It is more obvious (and more correct) to assert that the Civil War was fought over the issue of slavery, and this has certainly been the rationale championed by the North. However, just because this is a better explanation does not mean that it is the right, or at least only right, explanation. In this section, additional explanations for the Civil War will be advanced. They are meant not to show that secession and slavery were not causes of the Civil War, but that they were intertwined with a number of other issues that might have been emboldening to the Americans of 1861 in a way that they are not today.

The first, and perhaps most defensible, additional main cause of the Civil War was the fear by the North that the South would be able to rearchitect their supply chains to completely leave out the North and to do business directly with the thriving economies in Europe. The fact that Winfield Scott immediately called for a naval blockade of the south (including the Gulf and Atlantic coasts along with the Mississippi River), a strategy known as the "Anaconda plan" for the snakelike boundary around the south that the blockade resembled, is testament to this reality. The North responded to the Fort Sumter slap in the face by pulling off its scarf and wrapping it around the neck of the South. With the North squeezing the South's supply chains and the quick seizure of Memphis and New Orleans, the South's two major cotton exporting ports, the North could continue to supply some of the European demand during the Civil War [Hart15]. That is right, the North bought cotton from the South during the Civil War, which presumably helped some Southern plantations but did not amount overall to aiding and abetting the enemy. England turned to Brazil, Egypt, and India for some of their cotton during the Civil War, but the North continuing to export Southern cotton during the Civil War allowed the United States to reestablish much of its trade after the war ended.

Further support for the importance of cotton supply chain control in the Civil War is what happened after the Civil War; that is, the Reconstruction. The Reconstruction, viewed as the attack of carpetbaggers by the South, was implemented by the US Congress and lasted from 1866 to 1877. Presumably aimed at reorganizing the South and thus providing a pathway for them to reenter the Union, Reconstruction was supposed to define a society in which Whites and Blacks could live together. It is easy to forget that Reconstruction lasted three times as long as the Civil War itself. More than a decade was required, not to prevent segregation and Jim Crow laws, but rather to manipulate the Southern economy so that the North would be as prosperous as it was before the war broke out. Reconstruction, if one views it cynically, turned the slave into the sharecropper and Scipio Smith into Jim Crow.

When one considers the simultaneous economic and hegemonic goals of the North – prevention of Southern supply chain autonomy, economic hegemony through the use of New England as the primary importer of Southern cotton, control of export and import trade with Europe through Northern corporations, continued reinforcement of Yankee naval strength, and continual modernization and expansion of Northern manufacturing – enough context is provided to the more simplistic "secession versus slavery" debate over the causes and goals of the Civil War to realize that such a binarization is also a colossal oversimplification. As with most wars that both sides are willing to fight, the Civil War – given enough understanding of the overall cultural and social issues contemporaneous with it – was largely caused, maintained, and resolved by economic concerns.

Given this larger and more complex set of causes, sustaining factors, and resolving factors for the Civil War, we now interpret how the emboldening of oversimplified narratives arises using the four pairs of factors following the concept of *unity of opposites* as described in the previous section. The first of these is privilege versus penury. For privilege, it is clear that the wealthy in the South used their privilege to assert that the war was fought to counter Northern aggression, and so the Civil War was about secession, not slavery. The opposite is true for penury: the poor in the North were emboldened to claim that the war was about slavery by the fact that secession did not mean as much to them and that they genuinely wanted moral rectitude and/or superiority over their Southern counterparts. Fighting to end slavery ennobled them in a way that fighting to keep the nation together, or simply to defend an economy that was not making them rich anyway, would not have.

Next, turning to justification versus judication, it is arguable that justification also contributed to the South naming the conflict the War of Northern Aggression. After all, their ports and shorelines were under enemy control, and it was they, not the North, who faced starvation, humiliation, and the end of their antebellum culture. It is easy to look back on slaveowners and a much broader society largely comfortable with the owning of human beings as evil, and so, dismiss their justification. But to do so entirely would be to miss out on the continued slavery in Missouri, Kentucky, Delaware, Maryland, and (to a tiny extent) New Jersey throughout the war. As illustrated above, the North benefitted economically from slavery just as did the South. For judication, there was a very mixed bag north of the Mason–Dixon line before the Civil War. Slavery was not banned, judicially, in New Hampshire until the 13th Amendment to the US Constitution was ratified in 1865. Part of the brilliance of Lincoln's Emancipation Proclamation was to find the most likely means to have judication created that would inevitably lead to the complete banning of slavery throughout the United States. By pushing the Emancipation Proclamation, Lincoln had judication "signed off" since it was doubly advantageous to the North, both for its moral reassurance to anyone fighting the South and for the potential chaos it might cause in at least some emboldened locales in the South.

Additional advantages arose from Lincoln's judicial emboldening. The Emancipation Proclamation essentially signaled that, when the war was over, slavery would also be over. There would be no middle ground possible as the eight states with the largest slave populations (Virginia, Georgia, Mississippi, Alabama, South Carolina, Louisiana, North Carolina, and Tennessee) were all in the Confederacy. Kentucky, at number nine, and Missouri, at number eleven, combined with Maryland and a few other states that had just a small number of slaves had only approximately 10% as many slaves as the Confederacy, and so were not going to be viable as slave states thereafter. The genie was out of the bottle, and Lincoln broke the bottle to boot. In addition, the Emancipation Proclamation provided for the admittance of Black men into the Union Armed Forces, enabling the occurrence of the positive feedback of those freed to free others.

Turning next to empowerment versus subjugation, the Battle of Antietam can be seen as empowering the North, but winning the Civil War was the most empowering factor of all. With the war won, the North seized the opportunity to rearchitect the economy of the South, and in a way that favored the North. Reconstruction was as much about Northern economic hegemony as about preventing a Jim Crow South from arising. To be fair, the end of Reconstruction coincided with a massive wave of immigration into the United States, predominantly from Southern and Eastern Europe, and so, it is hard to disambiguate the economic advantages of Reconstruction from the even larger advantages brought to Northern industry by the wave of hard-working and often skilled immigrants. Regardless, the North clearly did not become emboldened enough to prevent a Jim Crow South, and so, the end of segregation as a major, perhaps *the* major, force in the Southern economy took another hundred years to happen.

For those subjugated, the slaves (of which 90% were in the Confederacy and nearly 100% of the remainder in the border states that did not join the Confederacy) were the obvious choice. Initially emboldened to join the Union army, their continued emboldening came after realizing that Reconstruction was not going to make life appreciably better for them if they stayed in the South as sharecroppers. There was a delay in the Black movement to the North until the so-called Great Migration of the first 2/3 of the 20th century resulted in six million Blacks moving across the Mason–Dixon line, but migrate they did because of the seemingly inescapable racial violence, depressed economic opportunities, and subjugation of the Jim Crow South. Emboldening moved from joining the armies of the North to becoming part of the North.

The last *unity of opposites* pairings to consider here is that of evanescence versus permanence. It is clear that Antietam, mentioned above, provided an evanescent emboldening. Compared to the two days of Shiloh, the three days of Gettysburg, and the 48 days of Vicksburg, Antietam is just a day. But it was the bloodiest single day of the Civil War, and the Northern victory (meaning that they held the field at the end of the day) gave Lincoln the chance to see an evanescent emboldening of the North that had not been possible in previous victories. The brilliance of Lincoln was in recognizing how this evanescent emboldening could be made permanent, and so he took the outcome of that horrible day and turned it into a permanent emboldening of the North, of the abolitionists, and of all of those looking to justify the continuation of the bloodshed for some reason more noble, more visceral, and more everlasting than the simple prevention of secession. Lincoln took an evanescent emboldening and scaled it up considerably, using it to virtually ensure the eventual ratification of the 13th Amendment at a time when McClellan and the other Union generals were not able to follow up instances of battlefield success with more success. Lincoln's transduction of the temporary into the enduring also made forthcoming battlefield losses easier to explain to a North that was hemorrhaging its youth: each setback was a step backward for the inevitable giant leap forward.

9.3 Adam Smith

Adam Smith (lived 1723–1790) certainly had a generic name, but his impact on economics and philosophy was specific and profound. For Smith, the intersection of economics and philosophy led to the creation of capitalism. Smith saw what Mercantilism was doing to the economy of England with its protection of national markets and its merchants: by strangling imports and building a strong export economy, Mercantilism was producing anything but a free market economy, and it served to make the countries with strong exporting capabilities (such as England) largely unable to benefit from the flow of goods since more was sent out of the nation than was brought in. In his masterwork, *The Wealth of Nations*, Smith outlined what was to become the now well-respected academic discipline called economics. But his approach started with philosophy first and foremost. He introduced the concept of the division of labor, which by itself contained the kernel processes involved in Henry Ford's later production lines and outlined an intelligence-respecting process for "rational self-interest" and competition that he saw leading to both national and vast personal prosperity.

Smith was not given a free pass by any means (he received plenty of criticism, especially from those with a vested interest in Mercantilism), but it is safe to say that he felt emboldened by many of the events of his time.

The manner in which Smith presented the free market economy, for example, would have been understood by his peers as a negative statement on France, England's great rival. France, in its attempt to maximize exports and minimize imports, honed, and therefore, relied upon its triangular Atlantic route: France to Africa to the Americas and back to France. In its attempt to prevent reliance on imports, France left itself exposed to poverty and resentment in France, which helped lead to the French Revolution and the beheading of its King and Queen. It was also exposed to the sin and risk of slavery, which resulted in the violent and successful overthrow of the French authority in Haiti. France abolished the slave trade from 1794 to 1802, and again permanently in 1818 after it had been temporarily reestablished by Napoleon in his global conflict with England and its allies. Thus, all elements of its Mercantilist triangle eventually failed, but Smith could see its end as early as 1776 when he published *The Wealth of Nations*.

Smith's view of capitalism as the offspring of both Anti-Mercantilism and the Philosophy of Rational Self-Interest relied on what he termed the "invisible hand" of self-interest, competition, and the principle of supply and demand which incented those who produced to provide better goods and services in return for being able to command a higher price for the improved products. Adam Smith was emboldened by at least three major world events of his time in order to champion his triad of self-interest, competition, and supply and demand. First, Smith noticed the increased self-interest coincident with the Enlightenment. As the Medieval years and their focus on religion came to a close, to use a cliché, man became interested in man again. Adam Smith rightly saw the rise of humanism, secularism, and eventually even narcissism as emboldening of a political system more focused on the here and now; in other words, one that *capitalizes* on events as they occur rather than on events as they should occur. Secondly, Smith was emboldened by the law of competition (perhaps even helping lay the groundwork for Darwin's theory of natural selection a century later) that was a key part of the commerce in England's never-sunsetting Empire. After all, does Mercantilism really matter if your empire is a "world onto itself"? The unraveling of Mercantilism was, structurally, sewn into its very fabric. When all trade is internalized, then imports and exports by mathematical definition become equal. The path from Mercantilism to an economy entirely bound by the frontiers of the empire was, in hindsight, a well-marked one. Smith's emboldening was simply to note this perhaps obvious progression. A third cause for emboldening was perhaps less obvious: Smith recognized how the laws of supply and demand would govern the economy of the homeland and the colonies. This emboldening derived from Smith's early understanding of the creation of wealth through productive labor. In Smith's view, enlightened self-interest could be counted on to induce society to optimize its use of its resources. He was further emboldened by the amassing of extra capital as the financial strength of the empire increased. In *Wealth of Nations*, Adam Smith further anticipated how enlightened self-interest would result in enlightened taxation, wherein the amount of taxes an individual would be assessed is proportional to the taxpayer's return benefits from the state. Clearly, he did not anticipate tax sheltering, but he certainly anticipated capital-based investment and the now-obvious idea that those with capital would optimize their investments to create more capital.

How can oversimplified narratives arise when considering the concept of *unity of opposites* as applied to Adam Smith and the birth of capitalism? For the axis of privilege versus penury, the contrast between capitalism and socialism aligns with privilege (the "winners" of the capitalistic system, emboldened by success to argue for the historical veracity of capitalism) and penury (the "losers" of the capitalistic system, emboldened by the success of perceived less-talented people under capitalism to declare the historical veracity of socialism) rather neatly. Interestingly, both arguments contain within their core a flaw. For the privileged argument, looking at the historical origin of capitalism as a progression from Mercantilism, one notices that the tenets of capitalism require trading economies to be mutually open in order to avoid the same trap of Mercantilism (where it is mathematically impossible for every nation to export more than it imports). Capitalism is, therefore, structurally incompatible with other systems, and in order for it to be adopted, practices more insidious than the invisible hand of capitalism's self-interest, competition, and supply and demand would be needed. For the penury argument, the contradiction is perhaps more forgivable, but nevertheless, equally structural: in order to ensure fair distribution, not only would an omniscient third party be needed to ensure this distribution, but an *incentive* would be needed to convince the third party to impose this fairness. How would the incentive be determined? As you might have guessed, it would be through some combination of self-interest (incented, of course), competition (to be the third party), and even supply and demand (of relevant information so as to determine what is "fair"). These structural flaws in the comparison of capitalism and socialism act in a manner similar to the Hegelian dialectic of thesis (capitalism) – antithesis (socialism) – synthesis (socialistic capitalism), which is the synthesis figured out in some manner by every successful economy that history has ever seen. Neither extreme is fair, and neither is consistent with human ethics, practices, or majority preferences, and so, when a society succeeds, it does so by incorporating some combination of the "best" of both capitalism and socialism. This means that the emboldening of capitalism and the emboldening of socialism are equally mistruthful.

Turning to the axis of justification versus judication, each extreme illustrates an emboldening from the type of economics introduced by Adam Smith. Capitalists are emboldened by the creation of untold wealth during the time since capitalism was adopted. After all, even the penurious in today's world have access to cell phone data and services and transportation possibilities, among others, not even possible for the very richest people of Adam Smith's day. Emboldened by increased median life spans, improved vaccinations, and other medical inventions, improved infrastructure (water, appliances, travel), vastly improved opportunities for women (child care, equal opportunity in the workforce, birth control, etc.), and many other advancements of the Industrial Revolution, proponents of capitalism are emboldened to claim these advancements are due to Adam Smith's economic process. Others, however, will point to the consequences, including drastic impacts on the environment, natural resources, and the climate, and assign these to capitalism and its emboldened proponents and practitioners.

On the judication side, then, are the responses to these presumed excesses of capitalism. Emboldened by the accumulation of wealth in the hands of individuals and powerful industries, fines for pollution, greenhouse gas (GHG) emissions, and lack of proper worker safety (e.g., OSHA, or Occupational Safety and Health Administration, violations) have become part of the judication against capitalism. This is an interesting emboldening since it is the supply side (the producers) being fined and not the demand side (the consumers). From a broader view of capitalism and its "invisible hand," it can be argued that the supply and demand share equally in the culpability; however, no need to feel sorry for the supply side, as their fines are perhaps not so "invisibly" passed on the demand side in the form of increased prices thereafter (think of greenwashing, pinkwashing, and social washing as three such cynical mechanisms for "sharing the costs" for everything from GHG emissions to providing a more inclusive set of products). A more straightforward judication, from the perspective of capitalistic emboldening, is judication against monopolies. While monopolies naturally arise due to efficiencies of scale, they nevertheless obviate the invisible hand of supply and demand by placing the pricing decision in the hands of the suppliers benefiting from the scale. Some might argue that the tendency for monopolies to arise undermines the entire concept of capitalism. We will simply note that it emboldens judication and does not necessarily have a surfeit of truth or mistruth over the emboldened justification arguments throughout the quarter-millennium of capitalism.

Each reader is likely to have, at this point, a "favorite" combination of points on these axes. If you are a proponent of free market capitalism, for example, you might find yourself emboldened by the arguments of privilege and justification. If you are a socially conscious capitalist, perhaps the privilege and judication arguments strike the right balance. If you are in favor of massively increased minimum wages, then perhaps the penury and judication arguments embolden you the most. The point is, none of them has a monopoly on the truth, and that is not because of Teddy Roosevelt!

The third axis to consider is that of empowerment versus subjugation. For empowerment, one need look no further than the so-called "one percent"; that is, the wealthiest 1% of the population. This expression was the name of a well-known documentary in 2006, "The One Percent," and gained further fame (or notoriety, at least) in 2011 when the Occupy movement declared, "We are the 99%." On the opposite end of this axis is subjugation, which, as an antithesis to the one percent, is the working poor. These are folks whose working days are comparable in length and stress to the one percent but with orders of magnitude less remuneration. In between these two extremes are the lower middle class, the middle class, the upper middle class, and the lower upper class, if you see things hierarchically.

From a historical reporting perspective concerned with truth, it has to be established that there is a problem. This is complicated by a number of factors, including the fact that history does not repeat itself, by the change in modes of production and consumption of goods and services, and by the changes in what wealth comprises over time. Certainly, "wealth inequality has been sharply rising in the United States and across many other high-income countries." [Suss24]. Currently, less than 10% of the families in the United States possess 70% of the national wealth, meaning they have a mean of more than 20 times the wealth of the other 90% of the population. The changes are regional; for example, "the South persists as a region that broadly exhibits high inequality, [while] central and formerly manufacturing-dependent Midwestern regions have seen a substantial worsening of inequality over this period" [Ibid.]. At the surface level, this is proof of the increasing empowerment of the wealthy and increased subjugation of the rest of the population. However, relative wealth is only part of the story. The wealthy would argue that such disparity is inevitable as part of a society that incentivizes inventiveness and the accumulation of wealth by those who provide significant societal advancements. Thus, disparity (relative wealth) might increase as a consequence of absolute wealth increasing for the vast majority of people. However, there are plenty of rebuttals to this viewpoint, including the counterargument that life expectancy disparity is also increasing in the United

States [Chet14]. Further emboldening of the 90% or 99% (or even 99.9%, if you agree with Paul Krugman [Krug11]) comes from historical analogy, with one narrative being that the United States is approaching a wealth disparity similar to that in France before the Revolution. Piketty notes, however, that in "France just before the Revolution of 1789, the proportion of national wealth held by the top 10 percent was about 90 percent, and the fraction possessed by the top 1 percent was as much as 60 percent" [Pike14, p. 544]. This is a greater than 80 to 1 ratio of wealth, many times higher than that in the United States in 2024. The less wealthy, however, are convincingly argued to be suffering from continually reduced social mobility since World War II [Song20], correlated with the increased wealth disparity. Unsurprisingly, then, the historical narrative here relating to the societal impact of capitalism is nuanced and more complicated than either extreme of the empowerment-subjugation axis of emboldening. The truth falls somewhere in between, although the preponderance of data over the last 40–50 years increasingly does support the emboldening story of the subjugated.

The final axis to be considered in this section is that of evanescence versus permanence. In a capitalistic society, the stock market is a principal evanescent element, while real estate and gold can be viewed as more permanent elements. In many situations, volatility in evanescent elements of a capitalistic society results in a move to the more permanent elements. However, from a financial standpoint, there is a significantly higher degree of flexibility for the wealthy since they can afford to think more with a more "long-term" perspective if it is financially warranted. In other words, they can set aside a considerable (and much higher) percentage of their income to be capital; that is, to be long-term invested. As Piketty notes [Pike14], this is the true sign of wealth. Income is ephemeral and capital is more "permanent." Any historical narrative in which wealth is indicated to be synonymous with income is rather untrustworthy. It is the excess above what is needed to live day to day that determines wealth. With that in mind, what is the real ratio of wealth in the United States today, or in France in the days leading to the Revolution? Far more than the 20:1 and 80:1 ratios, respectively, cited above, that is for sure. As we have seen, mistruth in historical narratives is often very difficult to determine, but perhaps never more so than with economics.

9.4 The Magna Carta

From economics, we now turn to the world of politics and governance. For some folks, the Magna Carta ("great charter" in Latin) is a pivotal moment in the development of representative governance. It may not have been so at the time, and surely most of the people ruled by King John were unaffected by, if not entirely unaware of, the signing of the Magna Carta. Hardly a volcanic historical event, and so, you can see why it was not called the *Magma* Carta.

A quick review of what the Magna Carta comprises is in order. According to the UK Parliament, "Magna Carta was issued in June 1215 and was the first document to put into writing the principle that the king and his government was not above the law. It sought to prevent the king from exploiting his power, and placed limits of royal authority by establishing law as a power in itself" [UKPa24]. In other words, there was separation of king and state to the extent that the laws could be determined independently of the king's preferences. Up until that point in time, there was very little resembling a Parliament in any part of Europe, or the rest of the world for that matter. Perhaps the closest "thing" to it (pun intended) was the Althing, a legislative body created circa AD 930 in Iceland. However, Iceland was definitely on the boundaries of civilization, and the entire large island had an estimated 30,000–40,000 settlers at the time. There was communication between Iceland and England, of course, between 930 and 1215, with such major events as the Battle of Clontarf (April 23, 1014) and the Battle of Stamford Bridge (September 25, 1066) in Ireland and England, respectively, involving large percentages of Norse participants. The Battle of Clontarf plays a prominent role in the later chapters of the arguable masterpiece of Icelandic Sagas, *Njal's Saga*, and emphasizes the effective communication between the various lands bordering the North Atlantic and the North Sea during the three centuries from the establishment of the Althing to the Magna Carta. The separate saga of *Haralds saga Sigurðarsonar* (*Harald's Saga* in English) relates the Icelandic contribution to the forces at Stamford Bridge. So, in short, there was communication between England and the closest "thing" to a Parliament in the North Atlantic long before 1215.

So, why did it take until 1215? Why did not the emboldening come earlier? After all, it is not like King John was the first bad king that England ever had. In the same time period, for example, Stephen (ruled 1135–1154) brought forth a period so bad it was named "the Anarchy." Also, with three kings fighting for, and only one surviving, the battles of 1066, why did not the nobles demand their rights then? The answer is, there is not one simple answer. Rather, in the case of denying the rights of kings, several elements of emboldening are likely needed at once. Let us look at what they might be.

John, unlike his predecessor and brother, Richard I, was not popular. Whereas, Richard was viewed as an alpha male and awarded the nickname "Richard the Lionhearted," John was unprepossessing, uncharismatic, and unsuccessful and so earned the nicknames "Lackland" and "Softsword."

These were not only references to his loss of land in France (Normandy was lost to King Philip of France in 1204) and his lack of martial prowess but also likely a direct mockery of his manhood. After 1204, John had essentially no credibility with the English barons. Losing Normandy to France was bad enough, but John also massively raised the tax rates in order to pay for his disastrous war, and just to add insult to injury, he took over investiture in the Church, appointing his own people to powerful positions such as Archbishop (the Pope actually excommunicated him from 1209 to 1213). He also imprisoned people and seized the lands of nobles without trial. All of these comprise disrespect and abuse of royal power, and thus, there were indeed several elements of emboldening. Together with the rise of the Icelandic *Sagas*, we term this *coemboldening* and view it as a special case of emboldening in which a number of factors not generally associated with each other contribute to emboldening. We next describe how coemboldening is related to confounding and why it can lead to historical mistruth.

Confounding is an event that can occur in statistical evaluations of causal inference. It arises in several situations, but for our purposes here, it arises when a spurious association is inferred because two factors that each correlate with a (hidden) third factor are misinterpreted to be casually related. An example will be helpful. The number of *Spongebob Squarepants* episodes streamed in a locale is directly correlated with the amount of squirrel food purchased in the same locale. To our knowledge, these two items have nothing to do with each other, unless people purchasing the squirrel food are somehow mistaking their little grey yard denizen for Sandy Cheeks. Much more likely, however, the streaming of these episodes and the purchasing of squirrel food are instead correlated with a third factor; namely, the population of the locale. Both streaming and food purchasing increase as the population increases, and so are related to (and caused by) the population increase. More people, more squirrel food sold, and more underwater cartoons watched. Coming back to the Magna Carta, in the case of King John and the emboldening of his nobility so as to force him to sign, the confounding factor for both the *Sagas* (which were being written as early as 1190) and for all of King John's mistakes may well have been a general *push for democracy* in the later High Middle Ages exemplified by the conflict of church and state (the Investiture Controversy), the Crusades, the Norman Invasion, and even the Reconquista. The *Sagas*, in other words, would be wrongly interpreted as emboldening the nobles, and so, too may have been King John's own egregious (but perhaps not unprecedented – remember King Stephen) miscues. After so many centuries of medievalism, perhaps both the *Sagas* and the Magna Carta were correlated with King John's disasters because of the confounding factor, or for this specific section the *coemboldening* which is the perhaps inevitable turning of the societal tide toward greater freedom.

The Magna Carta was a set of demands placed on John, which he resisted. As a result, the nobles withdrew their allegiance and marched against John in May 1215, taking London shortly after. John signed the charter, which granted rights and freedoms to various people and groups in English society, but continued to work against it, even communicating secretly with the Pope (after all he had been through with the Vatican, no less!) in an effort to gain Papal cancellation. John died a year and a half later, and the charter was ratified with his young son, the new king, Henry III. This last point is important as we turn to an analysis of the emboldening of the purveyors of the Magna Carta.

The emboldening elements necessary to make the Magna Carta happen are complex and can once again be viewed along the four axes of *unity of opposites* introduced earlier. Privileged emboldening is assignable to the barons, who were able to pin their troubles on King John even though they had been perhaps similarly responsible for the failures in Normandy (after all, John was hardly an army of one, not to mention there were baronial uprisings that contributed to the defeat). The penurious, meanwhile, were emboldened by King John's high taxation rate to paint him, possibly, worse than he actually was. For justification, John's detractors were emboldened by the sense of futility in both losing the war and having to pay more taxes: in effect, paying more for less. Judication was the entire purpose of the Magna Carta, and thus, John was so reticent to see it approved and so sought a "higher" judication in the Pope. On the third axis, the nobles were empowered to put the Magna Carta forth, while the subjugated peasantry who comprised roughly 4/5 of the population were not affected by it at all since they were not free men. Only centuries later were the subjugated to be emboldened to use the Magna Carta as a rallying point under Charles I, thanks largely to the efforts of Edward Coke. When the *Bill of Rights* was finally approved in 1689, the emboldening of the subjugated finally saw light. Thus, there may have been nearly half a millennium delay, but the emboldening eventually came for the subjugated as they started to gain more rights. Finally, the evanescence versus permanence axis can be addressed for the Magna Carta in harmony with those already described. The evanescent emboldening was that of the nobles realizing John's immense unpopularity in light of the loss of Normandy and his raising of taxes. The permanent emboldening was that of the increasing percentage of the English population who were allowed to participate in its political and social life as the centuries after the Magna Carta transpired.

Emboldening, then, is a source of mistruth in historical narratives, even when the narrative is pleasing. This is, for most people, the case for the Magna Carta, where the narrative is one of people rising up against an arrogant and undeserving monarch for the betterment of society. It is a powerful narrative, and with more than 800 years of social, governmental, and occupational progress since its original signing, it is facile to ascribe a more powerful influence to the Magna Carta than was actually part of the 13th-century world in which it arose. Why is that? Because, in this case, we see that – unlike the more balanced pros and cons of the four axes of *unity of opposites* observed for the United States Civil War and for Adam Smith and capitalism – both extremes of all four axes are *against* King John. This means that pursuers of mistruths in historical narratives cannot simply rely on the axes to provide balance. King John is not defended by either extreme for a number of reasons, including the fact that he died soon thereafter and so was unable to defend himself to posterity, as well as the fact that more powerful historical factors, such as the impetus for increased freedoms and democracy for a larger proportion of European society, worked against a more balanced legacy in which John's less reprehensible qualities – his assiduousness and bravery, for example – are used to contextualize his failures. Capable historians do provide nuance around King John and his reign, but the fact that the narrative for both extremes of each of the four axes of the unity of opposites is aligned against him means that the historical narrative about him, no matter how "fair" it may appear, almost certainly errs in terms of truthfulness against him.

9.5 What Emboldens Emboldening?

Having provided a few examples to illustrate some of the breadth of historical emboldening, it is now important to address how emboldening arises, and how the age of the Internet has helped it to survive, thrive, and in many cases, obfuscate the truth. Essentially, human nature being what it is, emboldening arises under a number of circumstances. In many cases – perhaps the majority of cases – it is associated with the emboldened party seeing future rewards arise from their acting upon the emboldening. This, of course, leads to escalation of the emboldening, or in other words, a chain reaction of motivation for mistruth.

An example of historical emboldening is the Phoebus Cartel and planned obsolescence [Kraj14]. During the height of the post-World War I stock market boom, the small group of manufacturers who essentially controlled the lightbulb market got together and planned how to make their products *worse*. In fact, by "early 1925, this became codified at 1000 hours for a pear-shaped household bulb, a marked reduction from the 1500 to 2000 hours that had previously been common" [Ibid.]. The reason for this was a calculated return on investment (ROI) in which accounting had shown that a lifespan of 1000 hours was viewed as "good enough" by the consumers, and so, making a lightbulb last 50% or 100% longer was an ROI of –25% or –50% that really was not noticed, and thus, valued by the customer. Through this realization, accounting created the "industrial strategy now known as planned obsolescence" [Ibid.]. The emboldening came from the recognition that no additional advantage to the brand was created if quality increased, and a huge advantage to the ROI of the company (and presumably to accounting's end-of-the-year bonus) was garnered by keeping the quality only as good as necessary. The best way to counteract this emboldening? The lack of consumer complacency.

We do not have to go back far in history to find examples of emboldening, of course. The echo chamber of the Internet is an emboldening situation. With the Internet and its support of individual selective exposure to content, no matter how ludicrous one's beliefs are, one can find an online group to agree. Worse, in many online environments or ecosystems, the participant is often able to find their beliefs reinforced, repeated, and unchallenged by rebuttal. One's beliefs, instead, are echoed, and so, the alternatives are not aired. For this reason, as a historian, one must always strive to present the historical narrative in such a way that all parties in a culture or environment would be able to accept the narrative. They may not like what had actually happened, but they would agree that the narrative was consistent with what actually did happen. As mentioned previously, one way to allow options to be aired is to use a dialectical method, in which the narrator respectfully considers the "antithesis" to each thesis. This is one of the reasons for employing the *unity of opposites* – that is, privilege versus penury, justification versus judication, empowerment versus subjugation, and evanescence versus permanence. In employing these, four thesis/antithesis-like pairings must be considered.

However, employing dialectical approaches is not, by itself, sufficient. This chapter, and in particular, the section addressing the mistruth in the Magna Carta narrative, illustrates that emboldening is often asymmetric. Under asymmetric emboldening, both ends of a continuum may be motivated to provide a similar bias to the overall narrative. This was shown to be the case for King John of England, who was unarguably not England's finest ruler, but also was unarguably not given a fair report by the privileged nor the penurious, the justified versus the judicated, the empowered nor the subjugated, and neither in the short-term nor the long-term. Arguing for fairness in the narrative of King John may seem a luxury rather than a necessity since he was undoubtedly responsible to a large extent for making the Magna Carta happen. However, it is important to defend even King John in order to ensure that proper evaluation of historical narratives under conditions of emboldening are not "given a free pass."

After all, an egregious and preventable form of emboldening is just that provided by a historian *unwilling to recognize differential emboldening* in historical narratives. Once a narrative is established and supported in a ubiquitous manner, it largely goes unquestioned since the emboldening required to challenge the consensus narrative may be onerous. This type of unchallenged consensus leads to concepts as different in nature as the Jesus of Suburbia (the prosperity gospel) and the ability of people to recover quickly from the loss of consciousness (how many dozens of people have you seen in real life get clonked on the head and jump right back into things after regaining consciousness?). Emboldening, in other words, quickly becomes a positive feedback cycle, wherein each emboldening is a multiplicative factor until the emboldening becomes (usually temporarily) the de facto belief. From Dutch tulips in 1636 to cryptocurrencies and sports gambling in the 2020s, emboldening is a *societal ouroboros*, feeding on itself and somehow becoming larger as a consequence. Not only does growth through auto-cannibalism defy the laws of thermodynamics (specifically, the third law) but it also ignores the pain and opportunity costs involved. In the case of sports gambling, for example, the ROI for the modal gambler is far less than other investment strategies.

An example from the field of science is worth considering for highlighting the difficulty in providing a narrative that is truthful through time. Bisphosphonates (aka diphosphonates) are a class of chemicals that have been used for decades to treat osteoporosis and other bone disorders, especially postmenopausal osteoporosis in women. These chemicals work by targeting osteoclasts. Osteoclasts, as the name implies, are "bone breakers," meaning that they are cells that digest human bone. This is not usually a problem, because osteoclasts remove older bone that most likely had developed microfractures due to fatigue after being used millions of times since it was originally deposited. More importantly, once the osteoclasts finish digesting a portion of bone, the process flips and osteoblasts are brought in to deposit new, crack-free, and unfatigued bone. It is a renewal process, formally referred to as bone remodeling. But, for it to work properly, osteoclasts – bone iconoclasts, if you like! – have to do their destruction before the good, new bone can be constructed.

Into this situation comes the treatment for osteoporosis that are the bisphosphonates. They shut down bone remodeling by reducing osteoclast activity. There are several effects, but the most important are reducing the development of the precursor cells to osteoclasts (called osteoclast progenitors) and by increasing osteoclast apoptosis, which is a process by which osteoclasts commit cell suicide. With reduced osteoclast activity, then, bone turnover slows. This leads to more bone over the short term, and increased bone mineralization over the medium term since the bone that is already there continues to mineralize (mainly through the increased deposition of calcium and phosphorus-containing ions, if you are a chemistry fan). So, bisphosphonates lead to increased bone density, mineralization, and in the short-term, increased bone compressive strength because of this. Sounds good, right? The problem is that over the medium to long term, bisphosphonates oversuppress bone turnover, and so micro-cracks in the bone are formed that do not heal. Eventually, these micro-cracks find each other, and so synergistically, combine and propagate. Atypical fractures which tend to heal defectively are often the result.

So, are bisphosphonates a true or false treatment for osteoporosis? Based on the admittedly highly compressed story given here, the answer is still "it depends." Short-term, there is likely an advantage gained for otherwise compromised bone because the increased mineralization at least temporarily may provide increased compressive strength, minimizing the risk of new fracture. Medium to long-term, however, the answer is that bisphosphonates have a significant deleterious effect on bone health, strength, and resistance to fracturing and other impact-driven damage. So, if they are to be used at all, it is only short-term to prevent pending fractures and to give the patient and their health care provider a chance to provide other, longer-term remediation.

The bisphosphonate story highlights what is an important component of truth and mistruth in historical documents; that is, the temporal dependency of truth. A pithy way of summing this up is to say, "What was true then is not necessarily true now," and technology is a principal means of obviating former truths, from Copernicus and heliocentricity to Pasteur and spontaneous generation and miasma. But technology is not the only way to convert what was once generally accepted as truth into what is generally accepted as mistruth. The next example covers a very different process for transforming truth into triteness, if not outright mendacity.

What happens when a real-life "Emperor's New Clothes" occurs? Let us face it, the "Emperor's New Clothes" is a timeless tale precisely because of its universality. In a situation where someone with power, prestige, or public support spews pure nonsense, they often thrive, or at least get away with it, precisely because of one or more of those attributes of privilege. Their position in society, in other words, emboldens them to behavior unthinkable for someone not so emboldened. On the margins of such privilege are the charlatans who have taken advantage of the gullibility of the masses throughout history. From the fictional King and Duke of Mark Twain's *Huckleberry Finn* to the nonfictional George Gurdjieff, P.D. Ouspensky, and Helena Petrovna Blavatsky, there have likely always been "snake oil salesmen" taking the pulse of society and profiting from the fears, anxieties, and nihilisms of its individuals. Esotericism, of course, cannot be discarded in its entirety, but even the esoteric teachers who chose not to incorporate magical elements into their schools of thought, such as Gurdjieff and Ouspensky, ran the risk of creating systems based on their own personalities and were often dismissive of the "normal lives" of those in the societies in which they hoped to, and to some extent did, flourish. Esoteric teachers have found self-emboldening catchphrases, such as Blavatsky's "There is no religion higher than truth," to provide their would-be followers an explanation for any criticism directed at them. In other words, emboldened esoteric teachers have always known that to succeed, the best way to divert people from mistruths is to claim a market on truth. One must always beware of the deflection mechanism for someone's own faults through projecting them onto others, from Ouspensky's "Do not expect to hear the truth from others, nor to see it, nor to read it in books. Look for the truth within yourself, not without yourself," to a more recent person's claim that any criticism directly at him is "fake news." In each case, it may only take an innocent child to point out the emptiness – and nakedness – of the emperor whose new clothes actually do not amount to much of anything at all.

9.6 Cyber Salon – Human Trafficking

In this chapter's cyber salon, we consider human trafficking and how its purveyors are emboldened by technologies that also threaten legitimate networks. Human trafficking is, from one perspective, an example of an emboldening situation in which its purveyors abrogate the personal physical security of their victims. The "cyber-physical" security of the victims is compromised, often with no access to advocacy groups and of course often highly correlated with a lack of citizenship (and lack of command of the local language) in the jurisdictions where they are trafficked. The emboldening on the side of the perpetrators, or "practitioners," of human trafficking, derives from the powerlessness of the victims (lacking language, citizenship, and other rights in their environment) and the increased power of the traffickers that comes from such technologies as the Dark Web and anonymized/deidentified financial transactions.

From this perspective, an effective means of countering human trafficking is to limit, or better yet remove, the emboldening factors. In many cases, the emboldening factors for human traffickers include some combination of policy, governance, risk, and compliance. If a jurisdiction does not prescribe policies holistically designed to reduce human trafficking, then the governance of human trafficking will also have missing elements. Policy, therefore, has to be more proactive than reactive, or else the time delay between the practice of trafficking and its discovery will allow the perpetrators to more successfully cover their tracks. This means that human trafficking needs to undergo a change similar to that of cybersecurity in general; that is, to move from a situation in which reactive efforts are replaced with proactivity.

This change in cybersecurity posture (i.e., policy, governance, and operations) dates back to 2009 when Forrester's John Kindervag coined the expression "Zero Trust Model." The Zero Trust Model (ZTM) embodies an assumption that every extant network already has been penetrated by a threat actor, or "rogue agent." This means that nothing – no agent, no network, no device, no transaction, etc. – can be assumed to be secure, and all resources associated with the network must be accessed securely regardless of the person, place, or thing accessed and/or accessing. The same model can be applied to the processes and structural mechanisms that may be useful to reduce trafficking. That is, hiring, payrolling, application of statutory deductions, garnishments, health care, severance, and overtime wage assessments are among the many "checkpoints" that can provide the sort of transparency needed to apply the ZTM to all employment. In making each of these processes *transparent and universal*, human trafficking will be much less likely to be committed, and even less likely to be disguisable. To that end, standardized reporting on all aspects of employment, including independent matching of employee rolls by the hiring entities with reported employers by those hired, is a move toward transparency. Annual, or even semiannual, interviews of all personnel working for a business may need to be required in order to address deviances in these two reporting structures. Perhaps interviews should be both transparent and universal in order to prevent the greater relative ease with which trafficked personnel can be prevented from reporting their situations. In spite of instantaneous communication capabilities unthinkable a generation or two ago, most communication now is via the Internet. The loss of separate critical infrastructures – for radio, phone, television, telegraph, mail, and newspaper, as examples, all of which are now handled by the Internet – may make it easier for the traffickers to impose "parental controls" on those trafficked. Emboldened by this loss of parallel reporting structures, then, human traffickers may find it easier to silence those who they traffic. Taking away this emboldening by adding non-Internet-based means of identifying trafficked individuals is certainly one recommendation: thus, the call for independent ledgering by employers and employees and periodic interviews. Using more secure, ubiquitous Internet-based means of corroborating reported working hours and conditions is, of course, a complementary pathway to eliminating such emboldening. Keep in mind that traffickers may be emboldened, but there is nothing "bold" about what they do.

9.7 Summary

In describing how emboldening can result in historical mistruth, four axes of evaluation were advanced: (1) privilege versus penury, (2) justification versus judication, (3) empowerment versus subjugation, and (4) evanescence versus permanence. Using a little self-reflection here, are we the writers emboldened to write this chapter because of the tremendous prevalence of fake news in our time? No doubt we are. Thus, a fifth axis to consider might be pervasive deception versus prevailing truth.

Regardless, as was made clear by the explanation of the effects of bisphosphonates on bones, mistruth often has a temporal nature and is more or less truthful depending on the time scale over which it unfolds. If we lived in Cromwell's England, for example, perhaps some of the apologist vernacular used by Milton to support Cromwell would seem more truthful than it does looking back over 350 years. Overall, this chapter intended to illustrate how history is a set of truths and mistruths waiting for the right incentives to be "told," rather than ever really being objective. Emboldening simply means that many who can benefit from falsehood will gladly promulgate falsehood if they feel the risk is low or at least the benefits outweigh the risks. Your goal as a purveyor of objectivity is to be bold enough to confront the emboldening, and in doing so, perform the role of the child in Hans Christian Andersen's *The Emperor's New Clothes* by allowing the naked truth to be seen for what it is.

References

[Carn23] Carnegie A, "The Gospel of Wealth, 1889," Foundations of Business Thought (2023): 165–170.

[Chet16] Chetty R, Stepner M, Abraham S, Lin S, Scuderi B, Turner N, Bergeron A, and Cutler D, "The association between income and life expectancy in the United States, 2001–2014," Jama 315, no. 16 (2016): 1750–1766.

[Desm23] Desmond M, "Why Poverty Persists in America," The New York Times Magazine, posted at https://www.nytimes.com/2023/03/09/

magazine/poverty-by-america-matthew-desmond.html, 9 March 2023, updated 3 April 2023, accessed 2 March 2024.

[Gold07] Goldhagen DJ, "Hitler's willing executioners: Ordinary Germans and the Holocaust," Vintage, 2007.

[Hart15] Hurt RD, "Agriculture and the Confederacy: Policy, Productivity and Power in the Civil War South," Chapel Hill: University of North Carolina Press, 2015.

[Kraj14] Krajewski M, "The great lightbulb conspiracy," IEEE spectrum 51, no. 10 (2014): 56–61.

[Krug11] Krugman P, "We are the 99.9%," New York Times 24 (2011): A35.

[Pike14] Piketty T, "Capital in the 21st Century," 2014.

[Song20] Song X, Massey CG, Rolf KA, Ferrie JP, Rothbaum JL, and Xie Y, "Long-term decline in intergenerational mobility in the United States since the 1850s," Proceedings of the National Academy of Sciences 117, no. 1 (2020): 251–258.

[Suss24] Suss J, Kemeny T, and Connor DS, "GEOWEALTH-US: Spatial wealth inequality data for the United States, 1960–2020," Scientific Data 11, no. 1 (2024): 253.

[UKPa24] UK Parliament, "Magna Carta, When was Magna Carta first issued?" https://www.parliament.uk/magnacarta/#:~:text=Magna%20Carta%20was%20issued%20in,as%20a%20power%20in%20itself., accessed 7 April 2024.

10

Valence and Arousal, Kronos, Timing in a Document

Arousal leaves us mind-blind

– Malcolm Gladwell

Timing is everything

– Molly Sims

Abstract

Up to this point, our approaches to document mistruth have been largely qualitative and/or anecdotal in nature. In this chapter, we progress into a collection of related mistruth patterns that are readily amenable to quantitative measures for document doctoring. Natural language processing, or NLP, is an increasingly complex set of approaches, extending to advanced artificial intelligence processes, that provide document doctoring detection new means to uncover document valence, arousal, kronos, and timing, each of which may be associated with intentional "slant" of a document by its author. Sometimes, without proper context, it may be quite difficult to distinguish slant. Not only are many accounts rife with irony, sarcasm, and various figures of speech which complicate the automated means of assessing valence, arousal, kronos, and timing but there are also often elements missing from documents that would otherwise help to anchor a reader seeking the truth to understand better the environment. When a writer knows their audience, the writer is often able to omit certain information due to audience familiarity or a shared cultural, moral, religious, and/or social background and understanding. In this chapter, we show how both inclusions and omissions can lead to misinterpretations of texts through the lens of valence, arousal, kronos, and timing.

DOI: 10.1201/9788770048347-10

10.1 Introduction

Quantitative analysis of text has been around for a long time. As an example, consider the Caesarian cipher, which is named after Julius Caesar who used a shift of three forward to encode each letter (in modern English, this would make "JULIUS" become "MXOLXV," for example), but likely borrowed the approach from earlier (perhaps far earlier) inventors. It is highly likely that the recipients of such an encoded message noticed the nonrandom distribution in Latin and used this to speed their decoding.

In modern English, the most common letters, more or less in order, are E, T, A, O, N, I, and S. If you quantitatively analyze a Caesarian cipher, then, you realize that these letters occur, now ordered alphabetically, with the following relative prevalence in a chunk of text (the longer the chunk, the closer the distribution will be to this), called Distribution A:

3 * * * 1 * * * 6 * * * * 5 4 * * * 7 2 * * * * * *

Distribution A

Here, 3 corresponds to "A" being the third most used letter, 1 to "E" being the most used letter, 6 to "I" being the sixth most used letter, etc. Suppose we then get a chunk of gibberish letters with the following distribution of the seven most common letters, called Distribution B, which has been Caesarian cipher encoded:

* * * * * 2 * * * 1 * * 5 * * * * * 6 7 * * * 4 3 *

Distribution B

This looks a lot different from the first Distribution, but if we shift it left one space (with wrap around), we get Distribution C:

* * * * 2 * * * 1 * * 5 * * * * * 6 7 * * * 4 3 * *

Distribution C

Comparing this with Distribution A, we see that there are now some top seven occurrence letters aligned:

3 * * * 1 * * * 6 * * * * 5 4 * * * 7 2 * * * * * *

Distribution A

* * * * 2 * * * 1 * * 5 * * * * * 6 7 * * * 4 3 * *

Distribution C

Namely, the "1" and "2"; the "6" and "1"; and the "7" and "7" align. However, if we shift Distribution B left five places, we get Distribution D:

2 * * * 1 * * 5 * * * * * 6 7 * * * 4 3 * * * * * *

Distribution D

Now comparing Distributions A and D side by side, we get:

3 * * * 1 * * * 6 * * * * 5 4 * * * 7 2 * * * * * *

Distribution A

2 * * * 1 * * 5 * * * * * 6 7 * * * 4 3 * * * * * *

Distribution D

Here, the "3" and "2" align; the "1" and "1" align; the "5" and "6" align; the "4" and "7" align, the "7" and "4" align; and the "2" and 3" align. We could quantify the degree of match by summing up the products of matches as shown in eqn 10.1:

$$\text{Matching} = \Sigma_{\text{matching}}\ (8 - \text{value}[1])\ \ (8 - \text{value}[2]). \tag{10.1}$$

Here, value[1] is the rank of occurrence for the matching place in Distribution 1, and value[2] is the rank of the occurrence for the matching place in Distribution 2. We subtract from 8 so that all ranks 1 to 7 result in a positive value (from 1 to 7) and so that the higher prevalence rankings count more. For the comparison of Distributions A and C, then:

$$\text{Matching} = (8{-}1)(8{-}2) + (8{-}6)(8{-}1) + (8{-}7)(8{-}7) = 57$$

For comparing Distributions A and D, the matching value is:

$$\begin{aligned}\text{Matching} = {} & (8{-}3)(8{-}2) + (8{-}1)(8{-}1) + (8{-}5)(8{-}6) + (8{-}4)(8{-}7) \\ & + (8{-}7)(8{-}4) + (8{-}2)(8{-}3) = 123\end{aligned}$$

Clearly, Distributions A and D are the better match, and in fact are the best possible match for any shift of 1 to 25 (a shift of 26 results in no change, or what is called plaintext). So, we know that the Caesarian cipher was a shift right of 5 (encoding) since the decoding works best with a shift left of 5 (to return to the original letters). Why are the top seven letters not in the exact same order, and in fact, why is "H" and not "I" one of the most common seven letters in the encoded Distributions (B, C, and D)? It is because the encoded text in Distributions B, C, and D does not have the same order of prevalence as the "ideal" (or predicted) Distribution A. Instead of {E, T, A, O, N, I, S}, the ranked order of occurrence in Distributions B, C, and D is {E, A, T, S, H, N, O}, but the order is similar enough that the Caesarian cipher shift used is relatively easy to determine.

This straightforward example, then, shows how quantitative methods can be used to analyze text. In this case, the "truth" is the text decoded by shifting the right number of spaces so that the original text is readily decoded. In more complicated cases, like valence, arousal, kronos, and timing, more powerful analysis techniques such as sentiment analysis will be used. But the principle is the same – the text is the input to an algorithm, and some type of quantitative output, capable of being compared to other quantitative output, will be garnered. In this way, different hypotheses about the text content can be relatively evaluated and some type of "best" interpretation may be possible from the quantitative output. With that in mind, we turn first to document valence.

10.2 Valence

Valence is a term familiar to anyone who has taken Chemistry 101. The valence of an atom is the number of electrons in its outermost orbital, or shell, and determines its reactivity, or ability to combine with other atoms. So, in chemistry, valence is the number of ionic or covalent bonds an atom can form with other atoms. In documents, valence is the positivity or negativity of the document, which is more akin to the chemical term of ionic charge. For our purposes, the feeling of a "positive" or "negative" charge is a good analogy to document valence.

In the previous section, we introduced quantitative approaches to text analytics based on the Caesarian cipher since it provides a gentle introduction to an increasingly (due to new artificial intelligence and machine learning approaches) complex field of natural language processing (NLP). NLP can be used for such advanced topics as sentiment analysis, which needs to take into account whether or not polarizing words suitable for assigning valence are being used iconically or ironically, enthusiastically, or sarcastically. Advanced NLP, therefore, is dependent on the timing of judgmental, opinionated, or specifically emotional words or phrases in a document. We can use the presence of valence and its timing in a document to categorize documents as one of four types, as illustrated in Table 10.1.

In Table 10.1, four "extremes" of the use of valence in a document are introduced. These are simplified forms, and in most cases, documents will change their valence multiple times, instead of not changing at all or only making a single change as in Table 10.1. However, such complex valence documents are a sequence of the four patterns for valency in Table 10.1, so understanding these four simple patterns will help you understand the motivation of the writer in each valence change or continuation.

Table 10.1 Four different (simplified) approaches to the use of valence in a document, and the intended effects on the readership (active, diminuendo, crescendo, and passive). Please see the text for details.

Case	Introduction	Conclusion	Type	Description
1	−Valence	−Valence	Active	Triggering and motivating, engages immediately, causing anger/arousal, ends with emotion
2	−Valence	+Valence	Diminuendo	Triggering then resolving, starts strongly and then provides peaceful conclusion
3	+Valence	−Valence	Crescendo	Starts peacefully, builds to a highly aroused negative valence at the end
4	+Valence	+Valence	Passive	Peaceful, accommodating, nonanger, nonarousal throughout

In Case 1, negative valence is maintained throughout, and this "negative" tone can be used to trigger or motivate readers. The advantage of this "active" approach is immediate engagement of readers for whom the topic is a concern, with likely arousal motivating them to continue reading the information. The document also ends strongly, with reinforcement of the emotion that it started with. This may not lead to arousal for a change in behavior and instead, is often used to reinforce what the reader already believes.

In Case 2, a negative valence is eventually replaced with a positive valence, an approach labeled *diminuendo*. This is a "triggering" event followed by resolution, starting "strongly" and then providing a peaceful conclusion. This approach to valence is time-tested to provide motivation: the "negative" front end unveils the problem, motivates the reader to desire problem resolution, and then provides a solution (usually in a positive light). Because of leading the reader from darkness to light and from negative to positive, there is an emotional appeal to this approach in which it is possible for a skilled narrator to hide mistruths under the guise of positive emotions.

In Case 3 of Table 10.1, a document starts on a positive note and ends on a negative note. As the opposite of diminuendo, this form is dubbed *crescendo*, and indeed it builds to the need for action. Often, the positive valence illustrates a desired state, perhaps even the status quo, and the transition to a negative valence highlights a danger for the current state, with the reader perhaps being motivated to take action.

In Case 4, a positive valence is used throughout. This is dubbed "passive" because out of the four "models" for dynamic valence overviewed in Table 10.1, it is arguably the most neutral in approach. Generally upbeat, with no change in valence, this is an excellent approach to conveying information without trying to bias the reader. From a historical standpoint, continued positive valence is especially important if two or more perspectives on a historical event or time are used; for example, the stories of an explorer people and a Native people. By presenting the narrative neutrally, the writer is then able to use more emotional valence patterns later to highlight their perspective.

These four cases are "extremes" and in most cases, oversimplifications, as many documents employ valence that changes polarity several times, with negative and positive valence used to evoke different reader reactions. However, that does not change the importance of valence as a tool for a writer wishing to influence their audience (and what else is writing but an attempt to influence?). A writer may have a different intent than the simplified active, diminuendo, crescendo, and passive templates cited (which will be referred to as "primitive" patterns for valence henceforth), and as such may decide to sequence different primitives in specific orders in order to draw the most engagement from their readers.

Suppose that the four primitives are associated with letters, with active being "A," diminuendo being "B," "crescendo" being "C," and passive being "D." Then, a longer body of work can be "tessellated" into a sequence of these patterns, effectively using them as a quaternary code like the nucleotide sequences that are used to characterize genetic information in deoxyribonucleic acid (DNA) and ribonucleic acid (RNA) which is the basis for life on earth. Suppose, for example, that a book employed the diminuendo valence for the first nine chapters, and then provided a positive path forward in the tenth and last chapter using a crescendo valence. Such a book could be characterized as "BBBBBBBBBC." If another book used the same method, except for fully negative third and seventh chapters, it could be characterized as "BBABBBABBC," and the two books would be considered relatively similar, sharing 80% of the same letters in the same place; that is, both are "BBXBBBXBBC" where "X" implies there is nonagreement.

A more direct quantitative approach can be used by replacing the primitives A, B, C, and D with their binary equivalents. If "positive" is assigned binary "1," then negative is assigned a binary "0" and so active (A) is represented by the binary string "00." Following this reasoning, diminuendo (B), crescendo (C), and passive (D) are represented by the binary strings "01," "10," and "11," respectively. Using this binary string representation, the two strings mentioned in the previous paragraph ("BBBBBBBBBC" and "BBABBBABBC") instead become "01010101010101010110" and "01011101010111010110," respectively. Note that these two strings now only differ in two places (the 5th and 13th locations in the strings, which are "0" in the first string and "1" in the second string). The difference between the two strings is 2, and this is out of 20 possible differences. Thus, the normalized Hamming distance, a measure of dissimilarity between two binary strings (used for computing string similarity in many applications, not just text analytics) which is always in the range of 0 to 1, is 2/20 = 0.1. This is well below the value of 0.5 which is the expected difference between two unrelated strings, and so, we can declare these two strings to be similar (90% similar, in fact). This normalized Hamming distance can be used to compare any two documents, so long as the documents are described by the same number of primitives (here, 10). Of course, simpler means of comparing documents (such as comparing the percentage of primitives that are A, B, C, and D) exist, but this normalized approach allows a quantitative measurement of similarity to be calculated. Note that these strings represent a "valence strategy" for a document, and if any two documents, even if rather dissimilar in overall length, are divided into the same number of consecutive segments, then they can be compared using the normalized Hamming distance measurement described here.

Classification of documents by valence is, not surprisingly, dependent on the proper assessment of negativity and positivity in an article/document. Fortunately, in these days of machine learning and AI, NLP and sentiment analysis tools exist to allow these approaches. An increasingly broad set of tools are available for the calculation of valence. Databases of salient relative valence (and arousal), for example, have existed for years. The EMOTE database [Grüh16], for example, provides "researchers with a corresponding word pool, the database of English EMOtional TErms (EMOTE) [and thus] provides subjective ratings for 1287 nouns and 985 adjectives. Nouns and adjectives [a]re rated on valence, arousal, emotionality, concreteness, imagery, familiarity, and clarity of meaning." Importantly, the output of EMOTE is numeric (in this case, decimal) in nature, allowing for ready quantitative analysis. For the valence of nouns, EMOTE provides scores ranging from killer (1.15), devil (1.19), and terrorist (1.24) on the negative end of the range to peace (6.52), heaven (6.55), and paradise (6.68) on the positive end of the range. For the valence of adjectives, EMOTE provides scores ranging from abusing (1.03), deceitful (1.08), and ungrateful (1.13) as the most negative to alive (6.69), respectful (6.70), and respectable (6.92) as the most positive. The range of values is from 1.0 to 7.0 since a 7-point scale (with 1 being the most negative, 4 being neutral, and 7 being the most positive) was used to collect user input in a survey. From this, scores below four are associated with negative valence, and scores above 4.0 are associated with positive valence. The same is true for sections of text, where the sums of all the valence scores for all the nouns and adjectives, divided by the total number of nouns and adjectives scored, gives a mean valence consistent with those in Table 10.1.

Having discussed some of the mechanics around the assessment and assignment of valence, we can now turn to how valence is used by writers, and particularly, those of historical narratives. If, as a writer, you allow the reader to formulate their own judgment first, you are less likely to be attempting to persuade the reader through your argument. Documents with mistruths often start with a negative valence and (as we will see) a negative arousal in an effort to engage the reader's emotions. However, more subtle writers can lull the reader into agreement with them through the use of positive (or neutral) valence, and so be able to induce a stronger response when the narrative shifts to negative valence.

One presumably historical narrative worth discussing for its valence is Julius Caesar's *Commentarii de Bello Gallico* (*The Conquest of Gaul*, in English) [Gard83]. Although the book is presented as factual, the modern consensus is certainly that the work is a propaganda piece written and/or dictated by Caesar as a means of building his image and justifying his crossing of the Rubicon. Since the books are generally believed to have been composed and made public in 50 BC, and the Rubicon crossing was the next year (49 BC), this interpretation makes sense. Regardless of the exact timing, it is clear from the nature of some of the book's most preposterous claims that it contained significant amounts of historical mistruth.

The *Commentarii* provide a relatively neutral valence throughout, presumably in an effort to lend credence through the seeming impartiality of the narrative. Occasionally, however, the narrative slips into more polarized valence, and these excerpts seem intended to call attention to what Caesar is hoping his audience will most remember. Relatively early in the account, for example, Caesar responds to his army's panic regarding recent tales they had been told of the "enormous stature, incredible courage, and splendid military training of the Germans" [Ibid., p. 47]. Caesar's account notes that "Caesar summoned the centurions of every grade to a council, and began by severely reprimanding them" [Ibid., p. 47], thereby establishing simultaneously Caesar's authority, bravery, and keen understanding of his army. In a supposedly historical account, then, it may surprise you to find out that Caesar's speech "had a dramatic effect on *all* ranks, and inspired them with the *utmost* enthusiasm and *eagerness* for action" [Ibid., p. 50, the emphasis is ours]. One final example from the *Commentarii* will suffice. At the end of the first part of the account, when the Romans were expulsing the Gaul intruders, Valerius Procillus was rescued by "Caesar himself, who was with the pursuing cavalry…[which]… pleased Caesar as much as the actual victory, for the man whom it rescued from the enemy's clutches and restored to him was the worthiest in the whole Province" [Ibid., pp. 56–57]. Caesar himself, in other words, rescued the most important person captured by the Gauls. In a neutral narrative such as this one, the hyperbole, Caesar-positive valence, and frankly fictional nature of the account is rather obvious.

Valence, it should be noted, can change not only in polarity but also in magnitude. This gives the narrator multiple options for using valence to draw attention to particular elements of the narrative. If, for example, the narrator switches from a mildly polarized narrative of one valence (e.g., positive) to a mildly polarized narrative of the opposite valence (here, negative), then the reader may not immediately recognize the change. This is a good strategy when the author wishes to be subtle in leading the reader to draw particular conclusions, or at least feel a particular way about the narrative. The author may or may not decide to spend some time in neutral valence as a transition here, depending on how slowly and perhaps subtly they want the valence to transition.

In addition to the "pattern" above (changing a mild polarity to its mild opposite polarity), there are at least five other primitive patterns of valence change worth listing.

1. From neutral to strong valence. This can be used in an attempt to actively engage the reader. A good historical writer may use this to change from a descriptive narrative to an opinion and make it clear that their own opinion, interpretation, or even slant is now being given.

2. From strong valence to neutral. As opposed to the previous pattern, this approach may be used to signal to the reader that the narrative is returning to an impartial account. It can also be used like a painter uses white highlighting to signify the border of one idea or section.

3. From strong valence to mild valence, both with the same polarity (i.e., both positive or both negative). This pattern can be used to prevent "burn out" by reducing the magnitude of the polarity, but without changing the "slant" of the narrative. It is often used in polemics, with Thomas Paine's *Common Sense* and other writings of the so-called "founding fathers" of the United States being good examples. Here, the narrator does not wish to provide an alternative valence, but they will

differentially emphasize the elements of their criticism. Polemics are usually associated with a consistent negative valence, but positive forms of this pattern exist, with odes and apologias being two forms.

4. From strong valence to mild valence of the opposite polarity. Here, the writer goes from strongly negative to mildly positive, or strongly positive to mildly negative. This approach gives the appearance of balance or even impartiality, but the valence of the words is usually stronger for the interpretation that the writer actually favors. Its inverse, from mild valence to strong valence of the opposite polarity, only differs by which "side" of a narrative the writer wishes to introduce first. Musically, this pattern is comparable to the dynamics of bands like the Pixies or Nirvana, which quickly switch from quiet and peaceful to loud and dissonant.

5. From strong valence to opposing strong valence. This pattern is perhaps the hardest to read for any extended length of time. It is the most polarized of polemics and usually comes across as unfocused and biased since it has the wildest possible swing in valence. Not to play the Hitler card here, but the propaganda of Fascist dictators certainly can be studied to see this pattern in action. Yes, the word for it is certainly polarizing.

With these patterns and with the type of quantitative valence scoring that is possible using databases such as EMOTE [Grüh16], one can now assess both the magnitude and type of valence being used in a narrative. For example, using EMOTE, mild valence might be between 3.0 and 5.0, and strong valence below 3.0 or above 5.0. It is worth noting that valence changes are inevitable in writing, and in literature are more or less essential, but they are especially important to outline in a historical narrative. The distance between opinion and mistruth is never great.

10.3 Arousal

Arousal, the practice of using emotion-eliciting language in an effort to get the audience more engaged in the narrative, can be thought of as a special case of valence. However, arousal can be elicited without significant or specific valence. In fact, as the EMOTE database shows, the nouns most associated with positive arousal are bliss (1.30), calm (1.31), and breeze (1.32); while the nouns most associated with negative arousal are terror (6.37), rape (6.42), and suicide (6.63). For adjectives, those most associated with positive arousal are easy (1.19), thankful (1.25), and calm (1.29); while those most associated with negative arousal are violent (6.31), abusive (6.72), and abusing (6.91). Is there a correlation between valence and arousal? Absolutely. Interestingly, however, less than half the variability in arousal is accounted for by valence [Yik23]. Also, there is a strong cultural dependency on whatever relationship there is between these two "factors" for engaging the readers; for example, valance only accounts for 5% of the variance in arousal in Finland (the lowest of any country studied), but it accounts for nearly half (43%) of the variance in arousal in China [Yik23]. These cultural factors cannot be ignored, and they certainly at least partially explain why influential speakers in one culture may have less impact when translated into another culture and/or language.

Perhaps such cultural factors account for at least part of the relative amount of valence and arousal (not to mention kronos and timing, or "kairos," which are covered later in this chapter) that occurs in a historical narrative. A good historical narrative to consider for its way of providing valence and arousal is Peter Green's highly regarded history of Alexander "the Great" of Macedon [Gree91]. This text is selected not because it conveys mistruth in history; rather, it is of note here because Green uses valence and arousal effectively to draw differential attention to different aspects of the narrative. This, in turn, draws the reader's attention to the points the writer wants to make. Is this a mistruth? No, but it is preferential attention to certain details, and when used by a writer with less integrity (or even just less skill) than Green, it can be used to provide a form of mistruth.

In *Alexander of Macedon*, valence and arousal are skillfully used throughout. As a starting point, we consider Green's narration of the famous meeting between Diogenes and Alexander in 336 BC in Corinth (in which Diogenes essentially tells Alexander to move aside since he is blocking the sun Diogenes wishes to continue bathing in). Known to many as "the cynic," this epithet gives you a good view of how Diogenes went through life. In addition to insulting Alexander, Diogenes famously criticized and interrupted Plato while arguing that he (Diogenes) was a better heir to the teachings and practices of Socrates. Diogenes also showed no respect for Alexander the Great; of course, this was before Alexander set out from Greece to create his world empire, but his accomplishments to that point in "uniting" Greece should have at least made him *Alexander the Intimidating*. For example, Green makes it clear how Alexander and his army had coopted the rest of the peninsular Greeks into subjugation, from Laconia to Illyria. Nevertheless, Diogenes was not overawed. In fact, he was "conspicuous by his absence" [Gree91, p. 123] during Alexander's visit, and only got the opportunity to insult him because Alexander actually *came to see him*. In a delightful paragraph, Green provides a host of arousing terms, at least according to several arousal databases [Brad99] [Grüh16] [Scot18], including "embarrassed" and "elaborate formality" on the part of Alexander [Ibid.]; "jeering" and "belittling" on the part of Alexander's followers; and "stubborn" and "alienated intransigence" on the part of Diogenes. Green completes his account of this famous anecdote by noting that "[i]t is not surprising, in the circumstances, that their encounter should have been so abrasive" [Ibid.]. Are the arousing terms needed to draw our interest to the story of Diogenes, or are they needed to draw us to Green's own telling of it?

Further on, Green describes Alexander's anticipation of the Thracian plans at the Battle of the Carts in 335 BC. How could a sentence like this not pull you into the narrative: "One of the qualities which most clearly distinguishes Alexander from the common run of competent field commanders is his almost uncanny ability to divine enemy tactics in advance" [Ibid., p. 125]? Here, the juxtaposition of arousal for Alexander ("qualities," "distinguishes," "uncanny," and "divine," the latter having the additional association with a god) with the much more prosaic description of other talented field-commanders ("common," "competent") is both highly noticeable and no doubt intentional. Green then describes how Alexander planned two levels of response to the anticipated tactics, with his troops parting where possible to allow the carts to pass by or covering themselves with shields to let the carts pass over [Ibid., p. 126]. He culminates with "[e]ven allowing for partisan exaggeration, this is a remarkable tribute to Macedonian drill and discipline" [Ibid.]. In other words, Green himself recognizes, and even admits, his use of arousal while cleverly employing it further ("partisan exaggeration," "remarkable," "tribute").

The next example of arousal worth noting is how Green describes the campaign against Cleitus and the Illyrians. This was also before Alexander led the Macedonians into the Persian Empire when he was newly king and during the time when the resentment of the Peninsular Greek states and their allies combined to keep Alexander in a "whack-a-mole" situation of trying to keep rebellions in check. In describing how Alexander recovers from putting himself and his vanguard in a tenuous situation, Green notes "If the young king was to blame for letting himself be cut off in this fashion, the ruse by which he extricated himself must stand as one of the most eccentrically brilliant stratagems in the whole history of warfare" [Ibid., p. 132]. If these words – "young," "blame," "letting," to place you in his predicament, followed by "extricated," "eccentrically brilliant," "whole history" – do not arouse you, well then you probably just do not like reading. When Alexander finishes his recovery, he invents the use of catapults as field artillery, inspiring

Green to state that "Once again he had concluded a complex and hazardous operation without losing a single man" [Ibid., p. 134]. It is "complex" and "hazardous," and yet, one simply could not have less casualties!

A final example from Green's book (at least for this section) helps to illustrate the difference between valence and arousal. When Alexander put down rebellions, he left no question as to his authority. Green makes this clear with Alexander's response to the most powerful of the peninsular Greek city-states, Thebes (which had "surpassed" Sparta at Leuctra in 371 BC): "No previous disaster of this sort had ever struck the Greek world with quite such horror and amazement as the annihilation of Thebes" [Ibid., p. 149]. If you have ever wondered why the name of the Acropolis is so much better known than the name of the Cadmea, Green has settled that for you with the strong arousal of "disaster," "horror," "amazement," and "annihilation." He adds "totally destroyed," "wholesale deportation," and "enslavement" shortly thereafter. It works. We can infer from this narrative about an event 2400 years ago why Attica today has 3.8 million people and Boeotia 100,000, and why Athens is a world city and Thebes a local one. Arousal, then, works whether its valence is positive or negative, to drive home what the writer feels are the most important points to make in the narrative. Arousal, used properly, can be the crucible in which history is ground to create learning.

Arousal, of course, is often intentionally employed in order to engage the reader. There is nothing wrong with using arousal per se, although it can cause – intentionally or unintentionally – the reader to mistake emotion for veracity. We see that with arousal, the difference between a gifted narrative (Green) and mistruth (use of arousal terms in unsubstantiated, opinionated, or otherwise specious support of a historical figure, event, people, etc.) can be difficult to assess in a "pass/fail" fashion. Instead, statistics (such as those provided by NLP or the survey results of arousal databases [Brad99] [Grüh16] [Scot18]) are needed, and varying degrees of arousal can be reported, leaving the reader to draw their own conclusion. This is why the arousal databases discussed here are so important. When analyzing a narrative, feel free to assess the relative arousal of what you are reading with a narrative that you are more convinced does not employ excess arousal. This is a historical narrative technique that argues for simultaneous quantitative and qualitative evaluation.

10.4 Kronos

Turning to kronos, we are concerned with the sequencing of the various elements of the narrative. In most historical accounts, including the two main foci of this chapter (*Commentarii de Bello Gallico* and *Alexander of Macedon*), the narrative starts with the oldest material and works forward to the most recent (or at least, the least ancient in the case of these two narratives) events. Surely, mistruth cannot be conveyed simply by the order in which events are portrayed? For example, is a progressive-in-time narrative any more or less truthful than a narrative rife with flashbacks? It seems that either can be used truthfully, and the temporal relationship between the elements of the narrative is likely to be aligned with the goals of the writer. Which means that the more interesting question to ask about kronos is how uniformly is the range of time covered by the narrative represented in the overall account?

History is often represented as having a set of turning points, and there is some merit to this perspective. Like evolution, which can – to perhaps force an analogy – be considered the broader "history of life," the history of earth's civilizations may well undergo a combination of gradualism mixed with punctuated equilibrium, the great ideas of Charles Darwin and Stephen Jay Gould working together to create a realistic narrative with just the right emphasis. The problem then becomes, who decides what the right emphasis is? Is the slowly-moving "baseline" culture, tied to current states of technology, sociology, governance, and economics, among other factors, more important than the so-called punctuations, like the French Revolution or various major wars? Even without considering the subjectivity of whether to include an event as punctuation (e.g., the Gutenberg Press since various forms of repeated printing existed before it), there is still the tradeoff between an invention being made and a civilization being receptive to it once invented. This means that kronos cannot usually be separated from kairos, but it also means that the ability of the historian to evaluate punctuated events is difficult, if not impossible, to separate from the definition of punctuation based on its later – perhaps much later – impact. In other words, is a turning point in history actually a turning point if the people at the time of the so-called turning point did not recognize it as so? Or does that mean that other, later events were actually necessary for it to become a turning point? And, if so, are those later events just as important? These are hard questions, and rather than answer them, we propose a way to at least measure them as a tool for the interpretation by qualified historians of the era or eras.

This decision reduces the more complex questions of the previous paragraph to a single, somewhat more straightforward question: How can one quantitatively assess the degree of punctuated equilibrium versus gradualism used by a historian? If a single comparative value could be used to characterize the amount of "punctuation" used in a narrative, then readers would be able to know beforehand one measure of the likely "kronos" bias the narrative will have. Fortunately, such a characterization is possible, and we provide the process to derive this value, named the "percent punctuation" in a narrative. The steps in the process are as follows (Algorithm 10.1):

Algorithm 10.1 Steps in computing percent punctuation in a narrative.

1. The narratives to compare should span roughly the same time period.

2. The time period spanning these narratives should be broken into a plurality of equal-length time periods. For example, if it is the history of Nazi Germany, then a year might be the right level of discretization (e.g., 13 years from 1933 to 1945); whereas if it is the history of the Roman Empire (say, 625 BC to AD 476), then a century works out well (11 units of 100 years and the extra 2 years added to the first or last, for example). In the example for this section (Table 10.2 and Figure 10.1), the time period is broken into 10 units of equal length in time.

3. The amount of text (in words, pages, etc.) devoted to each of these equal-length discrete time units is then assessed. In the cases where events fall into two or more of the units of time, an appropriate sharing can be assessed based on the relative time in each unit, etc. Increasingly, this can be done with AI, although expert human oversight, at minimum, is suggested. In many cases, chapters in a narrative will denote the years covered.

4. The percent of text in the narrative devoted to each unit of time is assessed. In the example, if a completed "gradualism-inspired" narrative is written, each unit is expected to have a similar amount of text coverage. This is shown by the rightmost column in Table 10.2 and the third curve in Figure 10.1. Once the percentage of text coverage in each unit is assessed, the units are then (usually) rearranged in time so that the unit with the most text coverage is listed first, and the unit with the least text coverage last, etc. This is a ranked order, as shown in columns 2 and 3 of Table 10.2. Here, Curve 1 has 40% in one unit, 18% in another, followed by 11%, 8%, 8%, 5%, 4%, 3%, 2%, and 1% in order (thus, the sums of 40%, 58%, 69%, ..., 99%, 100% in column 2). Curve 2 has less imbalance, with ranked percentages of 25%, 21%, etc. Note that the mean is 10% for this example, and 10% for each unit is exactly what is met by the data in column 4 (full gradualism).

5. Next, the area under the curve but above the "ideal" curve of uniform coverage (the full gradualism model) is calculated. This is similar to a Reimann sum in calculus, but do not be thrown off, it is just

Table 10.2 Three different curves (see Figure 10.1) displaying different levels of punctuated equilibrium and gradualism in a narrative, computed per Algorithm 10.1. Text 1 spends a maximum of 40% of its length discussing 1/10 of the narrative's time period, while Text 2 peaks at 25%. The ideal "gradualism" narrative of the last column spends exactly 10% of the narrative in each 1/10 of the overall time period.

Tenths	Text 1 (high punctuation)	Text 2 (moderate punctuation)	100% gradualism
0	0.0	0.0	0.0
1	0.4	0.25	0.1
2	0.58	0.46	0.2
3	0.69	0.61	0.3
4	0.77	0.71	0.4
5	0.85	0.79	0.5
6	0.9	0.85	0.6
7	0.94	0.89	0.7
8	0.97	0.93	0.8
9	0.99	0.97	0.9
10	1	1	1.0
Residual (above 0.5)	**0.249**	**0.196**	**0.0**
Percent punctuation	**0.498**	**0.392**	**0.0**

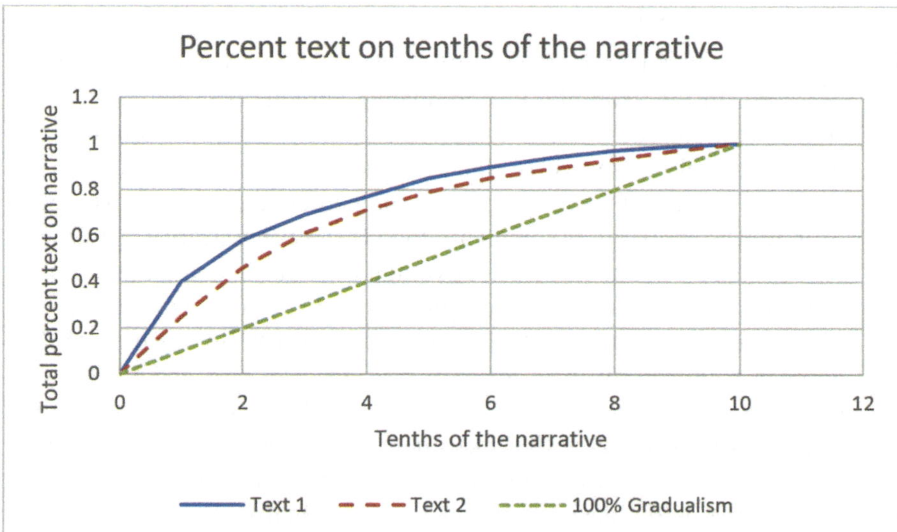

Figure 10.1 Three different curves from Table 10.2, as computed using Algorithm 10.1, are shown graphically. The area under Text 1 or Text 2 and above the "100% Gradualism" curve, divided by the maximum value of 0.5, yields the percent punctuation metric.

the difference between the real curve and the ideal curve, multiplied by the width of the bins and summed for all differences. This is thus (0.40–0.10) × 0.1 + (0.58–0.20) × 0.1 + ... + (1.00–1.00) × 0.1 for the column 2 data, which sums to 0.249. Since the most this difference can be is 0.5 (if 100% of the narrative is about only one of the units, and the other units never discussed), this 0.249 is 49.8% of the maximum punctuation.

6. By the same approach, curve 2 has 39.2% punctuation. Any two narratives can be relatively compared simply by comparing their percent punctuations. Note that the column 4 area "above" uniform is 0.0 since it is uniform, and so, it is 0% punctuated (and 100% gradualistic).

While the algorithm to compute the percent punctuation (Algorithm 10.1) is relatively straightforward, it is not always easy to assess the timing of each event in a narrative. However, some attempts at assessment will help give you an idea of whether the narrative propounds a "critical event" (punctuated) view of history or a slow and steady (gradualism) view of history. If the former, it may be very helpful to compare the relative similarity of any two narratives. This is readily accomplished by aligning the time periods exactly in time (not rank-ordering them as in Table 10.2) and then computing the similarity of the two narratives, which is just the sum of the minimums of the two narratives in each time unit. This is shown in Table 10.3 for the data from Table 10.2, where it is worth noting that the order of the tenths here is not ordered as in Table 10.2 (where they were rearranged from largest to smallest percentage), but instead is the actual linear time (kronos) order so that the two narratives are exactly aligned in time. The overall similarity is 0.67 (that is, 67%), which means that the two narratives differ by 33% in their relative emphases on the overall narrative.

Of course, the example shown here is intentionally somewhat simplified in order to illustrate the approach in a digestible fashion. But its value is clear. The type (punctuated equilibrium vs. gradualism) of each narrative can be computed for comparison, and the narratives can also be relatively compared for how they cover the overall time period. Two narratives with very similar percent punctuation (Table 10.2) and with a similarity (Table 10.3) close to 1.0 are likely to be also similar in trustability.

Returning to *Alexander of Macedon*, then, if the quantitative approach outlined by Algorithm 10.1 is employed, the punctuations in the narrative are certain to be associated with the great battles of his campaign – Thebes, Granicus, Issus, Gaugamela, and Hydaspes among them. This is because Green's narrative, not unlike the modal narratives of great leader-generals of

Table 10.3 Similarity of Text 1 and Text 2. Note that the order of the tenths here is not rank-ordered as in Table 10.2, but instead is the actual linear time (kronos) order so that the two narratives are exactly aligned in time. The overall similarity is 0.67 (i.e., 67%).

Tenths (in order)	Text 1	Text 2	Similarity = min(1, 2)
1	0.18	0.21	0.18
2	0.03	0.10	0.03
3	0.04	0.06	0.04
4	0.08	0.04	0.04
5	0.40	0.15	0.15
6	0.11	0.25	0.11
7	0.01	0.04	0.01
8	0.02	0.03	0.02
9	0.05	0.08	0.05
10	0.08	0.04	0.04
Overall similarity	--	--	**0.67**

history such as Napoleon, Alexander, Caesar, and Genghis Khan, has a strong narrative in which the perspectives of each side of their conflicts have survived in the historical record and are thus represented. Most of Alexander's battles punctuate a long period of marching and preparations, not to mention administrative processes, but take up a disproportionate percentage of the narrative. Wars and battles of history, like it or not, are examples of punctuated equilibrium in action. But the degree of punctuation is different for, say, *The Story of Civilization* by the Durants (at least within each volume – they of course wrote many more pages on the age of Napoleon than on France in, say, 830–860 AD) than it is for the narratives of Caesar and Alexander described in this chapter.

This section shows that kronos, or linear timing, can be quantitatively assessed using percent punctuation. Other methods, including entropy methods, sentiment analysis, and artificial intelligence approaches, are increasingly used to automate some if not all of the steps in Algorithm 10.1, but starting with that algorithm you can already begin to compare different narratives for their relative focus on "turning points" in history versus a more uniform or "gradualism" narrative.

10.5 Timing

Kairos is a term often used for timing, as in "the right timing," and the alliteration of kronos and kairos is indeed tempting. However, we wish to refer to an even broader sense of timing here, including not just a "gestalt" or convergence of time events such as one might employ with "kairos," but also including the timing of knowing one's reading audience well enough to know when to best introduce a topic, idea, or opinion in order to influence them in a desired way. After all, the goal of writing – and maybe particularly writing mistruth – is to convince the reader to believe your message. We are employing timing here, believing that valence and arousal need to be covered before timing in order for you, our reader, to more fully engage in the topic of timing.

Writing the right things at the right time, like being in the right place at the right time, is important. Many of the more famous people in history are so because of this form of timing. For example, among all the great philosophers in history, Immanuel Kant (1724–1804) stands out as one of the greats. To be sure, his work on ethics (including the Categorical Imperative), epistemology, and esthetics are top-notch and continue to be influential, but would Kant be as influential as he is if he had been born at a different time? To consider this, one must keep in mind that Kant's avid philosophical writing did not begin until approximately 1770, after David Hume (1711–1776) had stripped the certainty of knowledge to that of observation only (and, to extend his own skepticism, maybe not even that). Hume asserted that reason is only capable of interpretation based on what humans have experienced, a system called *empiricism*. Such a system leads naturally to skepticism, and Hume followed through on that by insisting that innate ideas do not exist, and that causation could not be established, but only observed with no guarantee that a "conjunction" (a bit like weak correlation) would continue.

This undermining of the existence of innate and even abstract ideas awoke Kant, famously, from his "dogmatic slumber" and motivated him to put together his system, which unsurprisingly is based on the assertion that far more than empirical knowledge is possible. Without Hume, and without the attention Hume and other empiricists of the time received, Kant might have been a respected footnote in the history of philosophy. Instead, he became arguably the pivotal philosopher of the late Enlightenment, and his work on the motive rather than the terminology of ethics guides much of criminal justice to this day. Kant's mettle (or metal?) was forged in the furnace of Hume's positivism, and no matter which of the two great philosophers you admire more, follow, or build your own Weltanschauung around, it is safe to say that the timing of Hume's system greatly impacted the timing and impact of Kant's. Kant knew what to write at the precise time that writing it could help counter the epistemological and ethical void created by Hume. Framing his innate truths around ethics also allowed his system to reach farther than those of Socrates, Plato, or Aristotle, and return metaphysics to a fruitful intersection of ethics and science. By embracing both, Kant may not have brought any more truth to philosophy (philosophy, after all, exists because truth in some matters is essentially impossible to establish!), but he almost assuredly eliminated some mistruths of omission.

Turning back to Alexander, we see in his actions the flip side of the coin of Kant – the man of action versus the man of academics; the man who leads from the front with a spear in hand versus the man who leads from his desk with a quill in hand; the man who changes his battle plans on the fly based on reality on the ground versus the man who other people set their watches on by where he is on the ground. Nevertheless, the two very different great people have timing in common. In each of his major battles, Alexander showed an unprecedented (and perhaps never since equaled) combination of strategy and tactics. At Granicus, for example, Alexander wanted, originally, to attack in the afternoon in order to shorten the amount of daylight available for the battle. Ignoring the advice of Parmenio, Alexander prepared for an attack against a well-fortified enemy. Whether or not there was an unsuccessful attack that afternoon, Alexander pulled back and waited until the cover of darkness to outflank the Persians with a dawn crossing. This movement was doubly advantageous – it allowed the Macedonians enough time to cross a sufficient body of phalanx troops to hold off a Persian attack, and it afforded them an entire day for battle under new circumstances in which a whole day would be required [Gree91, pp. 174–177]. Timing about time was Alexander's tactical insight here. He also showed mastery of defense and offense, perceiving a downstream fording of the Granicus would allow him to benefit from the defensively superior positioning he had seen the Persians employ the afternoon before. Knowing the disparity in defensive versus offensive capabilities of all his troops – from peltasts to hypaspists to skirmishers to infantry phalanxes to light and heavy cavalry – in real-time was a timing skill Alexander displayed in each of his major actions.

Turning to Gaugamela, Green highlights Alexander's timing to put his generalship in a favorable light: "Alone in his lamplit tent, by sheer inventive genius, he had invented a tactical plan that was to be imitated, centuries afterwards, by Marlborough at Blenheim and Napoleon at Austerlitz" [Ibid., p.290] Alexander was going to draw as much of the Persian cavalry away from the center as possible, and then with what "was going to need the most delicate timing" [Ibid.] he would strike hard at the now-undermanned center. Green's recognition of Alexander's timing itself is timed to be central to his narrative of Alexander at Gaugamela, which is arguably his most important victory. Note the context he uses: "Alone in his lamplit tent," which Green has no way of verifying, gives us the feeling of calm before the battle. Alexander plans while others are anxious; Alexander is an inventive genius while Darius is his unwitting dupe; and Alexander – not Marlborough or Napoleon – is also the mastermind behind Blenheim and Austerlitz, two of the more decisive battles of European history.

One further battle illustrates the timing of how Alexander's timing is celebrated in Green's account. In Alexander's last epic battle, at the Hydaspes River in Punjab, India, Alexander had "learnt that Abisares, the rajah of Kashmir, was on his way south ... To let them join forces was out of the question. Porus, then, must be dealt with in the next forty-eight hours" [Ibid., p. 392]. Because Porus and his army occupied a strong defensive position on the other side of the Jhelum River, this involved a river fording disguised to look like a smaller contingent than the main army in order to avoid Porus guessing "where the main blow would fall" [Ibid.]. This crossing was complicated by heavy rainfall, multiple islands mistaken for the opposite shore, and the possibility of Porus sending sufficient forces. Once across, however, Alexander had his best troops in position to outflank Porus, who was still facing a seemingly massive Macedonian force under Craterus just across the river downstream of the ford. As Green notes right after the success of the ford, "This was a brilliant plan, and the dilemma in which it placed Porus has become something of a classic for military historians" [Ibid., p. 393]. His timing of when to celebrate Alexander's timing is key to the narrative.

Interestingly, Green's narrative explains one final perfection of timing in Alexander's career: knowing when to die. Since Alexander was almost assuredly incapable of running a mature, sprawling empire, Alexander's death was timed perfectly for him to leave on the high note of having conquered much of the known world. Green notes that "for Alexander conquest and *areté* were all. The dull but essential routine of administration held no charms for him" [Ibid., p. 473]. If Alexander had lived past the not-so-ripe old age of 33, would he be remembered more like Queen Zenobia (of the short-lived Palmyrene Empire) than as Alexander the Great? It is all in the timing.

10.6 Bringing Them All Together

This chapter has shown that not all mistruth in historical narratives comes from the misreporting of facts. It may come from the valence (positive or negative tone of reporting), arousal (what aspects of the narrative use the more exciting words), kronos (how evenly discussed all of the time periods in a narrative are), and/or timing (when the narrator chooses to use valence, arousal, and other "slant"). In modern journalism, enabling language is often employed in an attempt to hide the slant of the narrator under the camouflage of legitimate reporting. One such mechanism is to use third-person, unnamed sources with ambiguous expressions such as "People have commented..." or "It has been reported on the scene..." This undermines narrative integrity, to say the least.

Arguably, it was not that long ago when journalistic integrity was paramount. Walter Cronkite, for example, was identified as "the most trusted man in America" in a US poll during the tumultuous years of him being the CBS Evening News anchor (1962–1981). Is it the 24-hour news stations, social media, or intentional purveyors of misinformation that are to blame for the loss of integrity? Likely the combination, of course, but the common factor is that news providers feel the need to provide provocative content in order to stand out. Influence, irrespective of the polarity of the valence, the type of arousal it causes, and the nature of bias in kronos and timing, is what gets readers (and listeners) in today's diverse, rapidly-changing, and feverish world of journalism. In other words, to get readers, you are very likely to use some combination of the four methods described in this chapter. After all, in fairness, we just did.

10.7 Cyber Salon – Document Valence

Under the modal conditions of a would-be cyberpunk attempting to socially engineer a recipient, the cyberpunk is encouraged to provide the "reveal" up front. How many emails have you received along the lines of "Our poor little backwater government has millions of dollars to give you if you can just help us hide the money in an offshore bank account"? The reveal must be upfront, or the reader is likely to simply delete and move on to yet another of the hundreds of unsolicited communications they receive each week. The "hook" in social engineering, in order to land the would-be victim anyway, needs to be compelling, personal, or relevant – and better yet, all three. The best socially engineered fishing attempts (actually, they are named "phishing" attacks) involve personalized information, especially personalized vernacular.

Of course, we happen to live in a world that is rather perfectly designed to automate the creation of just such personalized information and vernacular, not to mention personalized style, conversation, and modes of interaction. As if it were not bad enough that your browser, your cell phone, and your app providers are collecting any and all information on you, your devices are also listening to you and worse still aggregating all of that information to provide a model for your preferences, behaviors, and at some level, your personality. Once that information is accumulated, it can be sifted to find out things about you that you might not even know yourself, through correlation of your attributes with those of other people. This is particularly dangerous because your lack of introspection may well mean that you are more vulnerable to social engineering. For example, if you have no idea that you love smartwatches with certain branded characters on them, when these machine learning algorithms figure it out, they can comfortably target you with advertisements for these devices, knowing from your online history that you have not previously purchased them. Let us face it, you get a lot of advertisements that seem eerily related to conversations you have had earlier in the same day. Those are creepy enough. But imagine if the algorithms uncover some personal preference of yours that you have not told anyone – in-person or online – before. That is not only eerie, but it is also paranoia-inducing. But, used "effectively," it can be a very dangerous phishing attack, because you may not even be aware it is happening.

Worried? Well, do not be (yet), because actually, it is far worse than what has been depicted so far. Next, imagine that you are using some form of single sign-on, where you log on to multiple resources simultaneously. This is sort of the spiritual opposite of multifactor authentication, where multiple authentication steps are required for authorization of access to a single resource. With single sign-on, you have simultaneously increased the vulnerability surface, logged on to multiple devices and/or services, and potentially allowed someone else access to resources you have forgotten you are even signed onto. Worse, this means that all of the interactions on all of these devices, services, and applications can by definition be aggregated. This aggregation increases the statistical power of the training data for the social engineering algorithms, making them more effective at getting you to do what they want. Which might be just to increase the breadth of what you sign onto!

Regardless of how worried you are about the previous two paragraphs, it is likely obvious to you at this point that the efficacy of phishing is related to the valence, arousal, kronos, and timing of the phishing messages. One should be especially wary of the diminuendo approach, where something negative is presented, along with a magical solution that will restore you to a positive. One should also be concerned with the timing: if the message content seems too relevant to be a coincidence, then it likely is not a coincidence. Remember that each of us has our own influences, including which combinations of valence work. Are you a cynic? Then flowery, upbeat messages are both less likely to influence you and less likely to be socially engineered. In the age of artificial intelligence, the mantra may well be that the more compelling a message is to you, the more likely it is to be engineered specifically for you. In other words, if something appeals to you, it was probably meant to. This situation will only get worse as more and more is known about what "works" to get your attention – what valence, arousal, kronos, kairos, and timing affect you the most. Interesting times to be sure, and as Edward Verrall Lucas noted, "Suspicion of happiness is in our blood," especially if we are to be cybersecurity professionals. For such a person, happiness is assumed to be a socially engineered situation until proven otherwise.

10.8 Summary

In this chapter, we have introduced methods for quantifying certain persuasive elements in texts, including valence, arousal, kronos, and timing. Each of these potential vehicles for mistruth is amenable to quantitative measures. Generative methods, primarily via generative AI and generative machine learning, can thus be used to both create and assess these linguistic methods. This creates an arms race between the production of socially engineered reactions to a text on one hand, and the ability to discover social engineering on the other. In this chapter, we have shown how both inclusions and omissions of the positive and negative, incitement and prosaicness, and sequential and nonsequential timing can lead to, or at least hide, mistruth in a narrative. The mistruth may be unintentional. For example, audiences of texts differ in sophistication, and in their familiarity, with the content around the words over time. In Shakespeare's *Hamlet*, there are implied stage actions, and the reader must have contextual knowledge of the Elizabethan stage to understand the implied directions and actions [Shak12, pp. xxiii–xxiv]. If a future explorer uncovers an 8-track tape, for example, they will be unlikely to also uncover a working 8-track tape player, and so the infrastructure, or context, for the content on the 8-track tape will not exist. Similarly, early cuneiform writings have been considered to be prosaic accounts of granaries and other food stocks, but later discoveries of "Rosetta Stone" like trilingual inscriptions have revealed cuneiform to include planetary calculations far more advanced than previously considered [Neug13]. No writer can reasonably include all of the context required to fully interpret a text generations later, and thus, some mistruth about a narrative is almost assured for any reader. The role of the historian may well be to assess the degree of context that is left out. This is indeed a daunting task.

References

[Brad99] Bradley MM and Lang PJ, "Affective norms for English words (ANEW): Instruction manual and affective ratings," Vol. 30, no. 1. Technical report C-1, the center for research in psychophysiology, University of Florida, 1999.

[Gard83] Gardner PJ, "The Conquest of Gaul," Penguin Classics, London, 1983.

[Gree91] Green P, "Alexander of Macedon, 356-323 B.C.: A Historical Biography," University of California Press, 1991.

[Grüh16] Grühn D, "An English word database of emotional terms (EMOTE)," Psychological reports 119, no. 1 (2016): 290–308.

[Neug13] Neugebauer O, ed., "Astronomical cuneiform texts: Babylonian ephemerides of the Seleucid period for the motion of the sun, the moon, and the planets," Vol. 5. Springer Science & Business Media, 2013.

[Scot18] Scott GG, Keitel A, Becirspahic M, Yao B, and Sereno SC, "The Glasgow Norms: Ratings of 5,500 words on nine scales," Behavior research methods 51 (2019): 1258–1270.

[Shak12] Shakespeare W, "Hamlet," edited by Mowat BA and Werstine P, Folger Shakespeare Library, Simon and Schuster, 2012.

[Yik23] Yik M, Mues C, Sze INL, Kuppens P, Tuerlinckx F, De Roover K, Kwok FHC, et al., "On the relationship between valence and arousal in samples across the globe," Emotion 23, no. 2 (2023): 332.

11

Hyperbole

Will all great Neptune's ocean wash this blood clean from my hands?
– Shakespeare's *Macbeth*

I live in a constant state of hyperbole
– Eden Sher

Abstract

If hyperbole is a child of history, then its father is Herodotus. But it would be hyperbole to blame Herodotus for this form of mistruth. Exaggeration is a natural progression from the mythical to the tangible, with "god-like" being the most genuinely hyperbolic term of all (think of Heracles and his hyperbolic transformation from man to god). An earlier historian may have needed to inject storytelling into their history since the motivation of many listeners was that of hearing a tale rather than the truth. Such motivation and persuasion were observed in different forms in other early traditions, including the Judeo-Christian and Confucian-Taoist traditions. Hyperbole remains a part of writing to this day, and in this chapter, we will highlight some of the hyperbole used to justify the British Empire and the revolution that launched the United States. Text analysis means of assessing the relative level of hyperbole (from stating one's opinion on one end of the scale to making outlandish, unsupportable claims on the other) will also be provided in the cyber salon.

11.1 Introduction

Following a chapter in which quantitative evaluation of text was featured (Chapter 10), the reader might be in the mood for less "technically challenging" material. If so, it is convenient that the topic of this chapter, hyperbole, is

DOI: 10.1201/9788770048347-11

in many ways the most straightforward "pattern" for mistruth. Exaggeration – whether simple overstatement or the harder-to-tolerate braggadocio – is what we mean by hyperbole. When we say everyone understands hyperbole, then, we are using hyperbole, but we are also relatively close to the truth. Almost all humans are capable of understanding when exaggeration is occurring. If this is so, then why do purveyors of braggadocio, from politicians to professional athletes, seem to get away with hyperbole? The answer, in at least a significant number of situations, is that we want the offender of the hyperbole to be correct. Perhaps the hyperbole strikes a chord that we want to hear. Whether you call this magical thinking, blind faith, or simply the willing suspension of disbelief, narrators, orators, and writers have historically taken advantage of their hyperbole being able to appeal to the preconceived biases and beliefs of their audiences. It is, after all, much easier to convincingly promulgate a mistruth when your audience hopes, wants, and even believes the mistruth you are generating.

Because of the widespread use of hyperbole, examples will not be difficult to find. However, in providing our examples, we are concerned with three major rationales for hyperbole: conversion, undermining, and reinforcement. As such, from the effective infinity of examples that hyperbole (without exaggeration!) can provide, we will focus on specific documents to illustrate both their depth and breadth. Such a triad of rationales is embodied in the American Revolution. This is a structural embodiment since in the 13 British colonies that declared independence in 1776, as John Adams with his usual acuity noted, there were roughly equal numbers of colonists who wanted to become independent (the Patriots), who wished to remain in Britain (the Loyalists), and who really did not care to support either side (the neutral). In this situation, hyperbole was used to reinforce the Patriot message, undermine the Loyalists, and convert the neutral. But, before building to this complex, three-pronged manipulation of hyperbole, we will explore situations in which only one or two of these motivations are employed. For that, we will provide hyperbole examples in Judeo-Christian and Taoist traditions before moving on to the British Empire. With that, we can bring the point home with hyperbole around the American Declaration of Independence.

This approach sets us up for the nuances of this chapter's cyber salon, in which the topic is hyperbole in cybersecurity assessment and prevention. This hyperbole will be shown applicable to reinforce those advocating stronger security postures, to convert those who are ambivalent about the state of their systems' cybersecurity, and to undermine those who are overconfident about their systems' cybersecurity status.

11.2 Judeo-Christian and Confucian/Taoist Traditions

If you want hyperbole, a good place to start is religion. This is not a knock on religious people; rather, it is a comment that hyperbole is *structural* in religion. Religion by definition simply is hyperbolic, being the belief in, worship of, and/or relating of humanity to spiritual, supernatural, and transcendental aspects of some type of "superhuman" power(s), particularly in most cases, God(s). If you invoke the supernatural, you have hyperbole compared to the just natural, right? That is an oversimplification, focused on the use of hyperbole to convert people to a particular religion.

Of course, almost all religious and spiritual practices incorporate hyperbole, and much of it is focused on conversion to one belief system or the undermining of another belief system. Our goal here is decidedly *not* to perform a comparative analysis across religions. That would require an encyclopedia, not a mere chapter of information. Instead, we will use two religious traditions to show how pervasive hyperbole, perhaps inevitably, is in religion.

We begin this discussion with the Judeo-Christian tradition, meaning the *Old Testament* and *New Testament*. In *Joshua 11:4*, the Canaanites are described as having "a great army, in number like the sand on the seashore" [Bibl24]. As noted in [Ibid.], "pretty much no one on earth would take that description at face value...Even if we restrict ourselves to just the beaches of Canaan, taking that phrase at face value would demand a Canaanite army of billions upon billions... Not even the most boneheaded literalist would think to take '*in number like the sand on the seashore*' at face value" [Ibid.]. Aside from mentioning that almost every literalist is boneheaded (it is called the cranium, maxilla, and mandible) and thus being one, it is worth noting that Joshua is rife with what might be considered hyperbole from our perspective; for example, in *Joshua 10:37*, Joshua is effectively accused (or lauded) for genocide: He "took [Hebron], and struck it with edge of the sword...and its towns, and every person in it; he left no one remaining."

As [Ibid.] notes, "ancient conquest accounts are filled with hyperbole. They describe huge armies, complete conquests, quick travel over impossibly long distances, annihilation of enemies, and instantaneous victories...being ancient conquest accounts they are no different – they claim the same improbable things." The author goes on to explain that these historical accounts (and Joshua is indeed some form of historical account) are not narrative histories such as we might expect from an impartial narrator. Instead, they are written in the genre of their day, and that the "audience they were written for was so foreign to us that they may as well be aliens. To expect their conquest accounts to look like *our* narrative histories seems mighty odd" [Ibid.].

Regardless of whether one is the strictest of atheists, an agnostic, or a "true believer" as it were, one should not let religion become a barrier to interpretation of a historical narrative. Whether you feel that the Bible is the word of God or the purely speculative creation of a variety of issue-motivated ancient writers, you are likely to appreciate that the writer or writers were concerned with keeping their readers (or listeners) interested. Whether veracity or mendacity, it is written to engage. It is nothing remarkable to note that ancient historians were often only partially – even triflingly – concerned with conveying the truth in their narrative. If a writer's goal is not verisimilitude, the tarpaulin is then pulled off that powerful vehicle for audience investment, hyperbole.

The use of hyperbole does not always engage the entire audience, of course. Often, the writer is intentionally speaking to a particular audience, and other readers and listeners may mistake the hyperbole for some other type of narrative. Returning to the Judeo-Christian tradition, hyperbole is often used to emphasize points that are specific "coded messages" to followers but may be misinterpreted, even mocked, by nonfollowers. In *Luke 14:26*, for example, Jesus is quoted as saying "If anyone comes to me and does not hate father and mother, wife and children, brothers and sisters – yes, even their own life – such a person cannot be my disciple." Nonfollowers might see this as hate speech against family and friends, and maybe even a call to cultish mass suicide. A secular person friendly to the *Gospel of Luke* might, however, interpret it as a message against complacency, with the "hate" meaning "recognize their comfort and complacency in their relationship with." But Christ was not Jim Jones, nor was he Winston Churchill (whose tautological expressions include "This is no time for ease and comfort. It is time to dare and endure."). Instead, he was a leader who led through parables, poetry, proverbs, and of course, hyperbole. By "hate," he no doubt meant "show willingness, as necessary, to break with their." Christ was, above all, controversial and willing to stick his neck out for his beliefs. Hyperbole in his words was backed by exaggerated courage in his actions. Without his exaggeration, Christ might have been less effective in his ministry. If his hyperbole is a mistruth, then it is a mistruth to break up the complacent truth of his times.

Turning to the Confucian and Taoist traditions, we see hyperbole used not by Confucius and Lao Tzu but instead by their so-called followers who attributed fantastic quotes to them. This can be viewed as a hyperbole of undermining, where hyperbole is added afterward.

We start with Confucius. Confucius' Analects 9.29 can be translated literally as "The Master said/Wise person not doubt/Benevolent person not worry/Courageous person not fear," which is consistent with the interpretation

"The Master said, The wise are not confused, the Good do not worry, and the courageous do not fear" [Conf03]. However, four years later, the translation "The Master said, The wise are never perplexed; the humane, never anxious; the brave, never afraid" [Conf07] appears. Where did the three "never" come from? A recommendation for practice becomes an absolute. Surprise at such a change in how Confucius has been viewed over time is nothing new; for example, Julia Ching mused, "[Confucius] was surely no deity figure, but a humanist and a scholar...It is interesting that later generations nearly made him a god, but actually made him a king...to highlight his wisdom [and] his moral claims to rulership" [Chin91]. Geir further notes that "The deification of Jesus and Gautama happened fairly soon after their deaths, but the glorification of Confucius by Chinese culture did not happen for 500 years" [Geir93]. The successful deification of a person previously thought merely wise or even brilliant is going to take some retrofit hyperbole.

Turning to Lao Tzu, so many quotes have been retroactively attributed to him that entire books have been written in an attempt to clear the air. One means of uncovering quotes fraudulently assigned to Lao Tzu, in fact, is in detecting hyperbole in the quotes [Sten20]. Take, for example, the quote "As soon as you have made a thought, laugh at it" [Ibid., p. 35]. Either you are going to have to blank your mind in a way possible only for Patrick Star, or you are going to spend every waking (and sleeping) minute laughing. Next, Lao Tzu supposedly said, "Care about what other people think and you will always be their prisoner" [Ibid., p. 61]. Always? That is both a depressing and a puzzlingly predictable world. Another quote stands out not just for hyperbole, but also for its surrealness: "Emptiness appears barren, yet is infinite fullness" [Ibid., p. 77]. Full is 100%, right, so what is infinite fullness? Emptiness is fuller than fullness? That is not Lao Tzu, that is a lie, too.

Hyperbole is not just about exaggeration. It can also be about attributing modes of thought or behavior to someone that are entirely inconsistent with their behavior. For example, the quote "Highly evolved people have their own conscience as pure law" [Ibid., p. 100]. Yikes, there is both a hint of social Darwinism (2000 years too early) and some type of horrible "ism" with the allusion to purity. Lao Tzu followed this up with solipsism, claiming "Music in the soul can be heard by the universe" [Ibid., p. 170]. Never mind that "music" and "soul" are odd vocabulary for him – the universe? Hard to have higher hyperbole than that! This is echoed in another speciously attributed quote: "To a mind that is still the whole universe surrenders" [Ibid., 255]. You are at war with the universe? And you won? Gilgamesh and Prometheus, you are hacks compared to my still mind. It gets worse. When Lao Tzu supposedly says, "The moment truth is asserted it becomes false" [Ibid., p. 222], are we supposed to believe him? In that case, at that moment, we are supposed to not believe him. It hurts my brain to even write this.

These are among the worst examples of hyperbole, and because of that are helpful for us in discerning factual from fictional Lao Tzu quotes. They are useful here as they illustrate for us the power of identifying hyperbole. Identifying hyperbole is, like it or not, a life skill for us all. One must triage hyperbole the way one does their snail mail or email. Some of this mail is intended to get your attention, some to distract, some to inform, and some even to convert you to the sender's cause. Never think it is uniformly intended or valuable: hyperbole has a wide range of purposes, and here we have shown the employment of hyperbole for the conversion of the religious neutral.

11.3 The Sun Never Sets on the British Empire

Having, at least in part, addressed hyperbole in conversion, we now turn to hyperbole in reinforcement. Nationalism is a natural vehicle for hyperbole. How else can you get a sprawling, heterogeneous population to buy into something so much bigger than any individual in it? Rather than trying to discuss every empire from the Akkadian to the American, we will focus on what is arguably the largest in recorded history, the British Empire in the 100 years from the fall of Napoleon to the fall of Franz Ferdinand, and explore some of the mechanisms for hyperbole in reinforcing this unwieldy, unprecedented, and ultimately untenable construct.

At its peak, the British Empire was advertised as "the empire on which the sun never sets." On the surface, this is fact. Excluding rare and hair-splitting contradictions such as the darkened skies associated with two Indonesian eruptions (Mount Tambora in 1816 and Krakatoa in 1883), the comment seems a relatively innocuous statement that it was always daytime in some part of the British Empire. But there is a problem with this metaphor: the sun sets on every part of the British Empire every day (again, with the hair-splitting exception of Northern Canada during the summer months in the Northern Hemisphere). A less hyperbolic expression would be instead the assertion that "the sun is always shining on the empire." A subtle point? Perhaps, but consider that saying the sun never sets is an implication of permanence while saying that the sun is always shining implies a changing perspective. Empires project themselves as permanent, inevitable, and reassuring. The minor hyperbole here is consistent with *reinforcing* the idea of empire with its inhabitants.

The Pax Britannica (itself a term reinforcing the concept of empire, since the Pax Romana of 27 BCE–180 CE is the expression adopted and modified here) saw Britain not only control its sprawling territories but also bottleneck world trade with its powerful navy. Only Britain had access to all the different raw materials of importance to that era, which spread from Latin America to Africa, and from the Middle East to East Asia. In many ways, modern propaganda was formulated during the British Empire's peak. For the colonies with White settlers, propaganda focused on a delicate balance of autonomy and the advantages (trade, protection, etc.) of remaining part of the empire. For the rest of the colonies, stability and trade were a main part of the hyperbole of the propaganda. Propaganda will be covered in greater depth in Chapter 14, but for now, it is sufficient to recognize that hyperbole is often a part of propaganda, although it does not have to be.

Interestingly, the hyperbole around the empire was itself undermined from within. Adam Smith, in that fateful year 1776 (more on that in the next section), published *Wealth of Nations*, and essentially argued against the need for the empire [Smit76]. Long before the globalism and neocapitalism of the post-World War II era, Smith argued for free trade (replacing mercantilism), arguing in effect that greater circulation of goods would provide the best means of improving lifestyles in the areas under British investment and protection [Ibid.]. Despite the Revolutionary War, which lasted until 1783, trade between the nonempire United States and the British Empire thereafter increased, supporting Smith's argument that political hegemony was not necessary for economic success – less clear is whether economic hegemony, which Britain certainly enjoyed, was necessary for this increasing trade [Ibid.].

The point about economic hegemony is important for understanding the need for British propaganda. During the Pax, Britain ruled the seas and thus could (and did) act as a "global policeman" and brag about its "splendid isolation." Both terms have subtle hyperbole of reinforcement. The term "policeman" implied a willingness to put oneself at risk to provide a better world for others, and the "splendid isolation" implied a distancing of Britain from the wars and other negatives in Europe. In effect, Britain was washing its hands of problems in Europe (which it effectively blockaded economically) and portraying itself as a force of good in the world. This while controlling the economies of its own empire (roughly one-fourth of the land and the people on Earth) and effectively, due to blockade power, controlling other economies from China and Thailand to Argentina, Uruguay, and Chile.

Britain, a relatively small nation, was a demographic powerhouse, having perhaps the sixth-largest national population and the largest empire population (above China) at the time. Its population explosion may be due in large part to the serendipitous surfeit of surface coal in England [Free16], which also allowed them to build out a nationwide industrial base long before any other country. This industrial advantage (and in particular, their communication advantage) allowed them to come out on top in the rebellion of 1857–1858 and make India "the Jewel in the Crown" in yet another hyperbolic expression.

Perhaps one reason hyperbole was so important for the British Empire was because of "how minimal the cultural impact of the empire was" [Port06]. As Porter notes:

> "The flood of imperial propaganda in Britain during this period suggests two further conclusions, which unfortunately are mutually incompatible. The first is that people must have been convinced by it, simply because it was so ubiquitous. That is certainly the impression given by taking just one side of the picture. The other possible inference, however, is that it cannot have been as effective as this, or imperialists would not have felt the need to continue propagandizing as they did" [Ibid.].

Given the nuanced reasons for hyperbole here – reinforcing of the empire, undermining of competitors to the empire, and conversion of those in Britain's "informal empire" (such as China and Argentina) to full supporters of the empire – we would argue, instead, that these two conclusions are actually mutually compatible. The propaganda did convince some people through reinforcement and conversion, but where it did not, it helped to undermine the empire's competitors and so, reduce the number of Sepoy-level rebellions to just the one during the so-called Pax Britannica. To be alliterative, hyperbole helped hinder high levels of upheaval by reinforcing the loyalty of those in the empire, converting new peoples to see the empire as valuable, and undermining those who would rather see the empire exist only in the past.

11.4 The American Revolution

Having now seen how hyperbole can be brought to bear for people receptive, nonreceptive, or skeptical of its message, we now discuss how all three came to bear on the hyperbole-laden propaganda associated with the (United States) American Revolution of 1776–1783. We mentioned above that in many ways, modern propaganda was formulated during the British Empire's peak. However, the hyperbole associated with the 1776 Declaration of Independence certainly provided a good template.

In several ways, the years around and including the Declaration of Independence were a "perfect storm" for hyperbole. John Adams famously noted that about one-third of the colonists were in favor of independence (Patriots), another third was in favor of staying with Britain (Loyalists), and the final third was neutral. With no consensus, hyperbole was encouraged. With the rapidly increasing stakes involved (treason was, after all, punishable by hanging, drawing, and quartering), the revolutionary leaders were motivated by more than financial reasons to recruit new rebels. Once again, hyperbole was encouraged. These are structural reasons; in other words, unlike the propaganda involved in, for example, the hyperbole of marketing campaigns, this was hyperbole essentially necessary for survival.

After the battles of 1775 (Lexington and Concord, Bunker Hill, and the siege of Boston as the major ones), the English-speaking colonies from New Hampshire to Georgia needed to assess their odds for success if they united to break the tie to Mother England. Paul Revere had already ridden, and even though it had to wait until 1861 for Henry Wadsworth Longfellow to swath this ride in hyperbole ("the fate of a nation was riding that night" and "a word that shall echo forevermore!" being but two examples), the ride was already subject to hyperbole and Paul Revere was a major in the infantry. Thomas Paine's *Common Sense* (see below) came out in January, and its vitriol and hyperbole provided a strong argument for reinforcement of the rebels, not to mention a rationale for the neutral to join the revolutionary cause. In this circumstance, the leaders of the revolution put together a tiger team of textual talent, led by the uneven brilliance of Thomas Jefferson, to craft a document capable of engaging all three of Adams' segments of society, from the seditious to the steadfast.

The process of making the Declaration of Independence is described in even-handed detail in Pauline Maier's *American Scripture* [Maie12], from which we take examples of hyperbole addressing each of the three sectors of society. Starting with reinforcement, it is clear that the Declaration is the logical next step for the revolutionary cause. The Declaration must come across as reasonable, rational, and righteous to rally the rebels whose support is paramount to revolutionary success. Maier does this by stitching together the threads in American thought that have led to the call for independence, noting Paine's hyperbole that "Americans could 'form the noblest, purest constitution on the face of the earth'" [Ibid., p. 32] and that the rebellion has the "power to begin the world over again" [Ibid.]. Paine, in some ways, embodies the perhaps necessary hyperbole of a rebellious cause. As a thought experiment, though, suppose that all that the leaders of the American Revolution really wanted was to remove a layer from the top of society in order to reinvest that overhead (in the familiar form of taxation without representation) in themselves. Suppose in other words, that the Revolution was really just about money. That is not a particularly difficult stretch of the imagination. If so, the leaders of the Revolution would still need the same hyperbole that they employed for the more noble purposes of providing freedom, self-governance, and the removal of *tyranno rex*.

Partly because of the success of this hyperbole (note that the lack of equal rights for women and the continuance of slavery after the Declaration of Independence indeed argue for a more economic and less noble rationale for rebellion), Thomas Jefferson "became a Christlike figure whose 'disembodied spirit was…upborne by the blessings of ten millions of Freeman' in a fanciful Fourth of July ascension" [Ibid., p.190]. Such posthumous veneration was reinforced by the fact that the Revolution was successful. Suppose that Washington, after the disastrous battle of Long Island/Brooklyn in late August 1776, had not been able to extract the 80% of his forces that he was able to get to New Jersey, and so, the War was over just two months after the signing of the Declaration. Would Jefferson (and Adams, and so many others) be venerated, and made gods in the eyes of many modern patriots? It is safe to say that the answer is no.

Maier also shows how hyperbole was used to undermine the British. In fact, from the standpoint of extracting hyperbole from Maier's *American Scripture*, it is probably unsurprising that this was the easiest set to find. Early on, Maier notes that "Even Robert Morris, a 'conservative' Pennsylvanian of English birth, reported that the seizing of American ships and burning of colonial towns along 'with numerous acts of wanton barbarity & Cruelty perpetrated by the British Forces has prepared Men's minds for an Independency'" [Ibid., p.28]. John Dickinson was more succinct, saying that colonials "must bleed at every vein" [Ibid., p. 29]. Thomas Paine excelled in employing all three of our "types" of hyperbole, so he also contributed to the undermining of the British, excoriating the King with "I rejected the hardened, sullen-tempered Pharoah of England for ever; and disdain the wretch, that with the pretended title of FATHER OF HIS PEOPLE can unfeelingly hear of their slaughter, and composedly sleep with their blood upon his soul" [Ibid., p.33]. Such vituperation helped to season the Declaration, including the assertion in its preamble that George III was "trying to establish 'a detestable and insupportable Tyranny'" [Ibid., p. 48]. Hyperbole was used to accuse the British of intentional property destruction and the intentional incitement of Native Americans and slaves to rise up against the colonists [Ibid., p.79]. The use of the word slavery appeared to be a particularly powerful means of applying hyperbole in the time of Paine, with the Maryland delegation to the convention criticizing King George III for "his determined and inexorable resolution of reducing these Colonies to abject slavery" [Ibid., p. 81]. Upon reading the declaration, a New York City crowd pulled down a statue of a horse-mounted King George, with the comment "the IMAGE of the BEAST was thrown down" [Ibid., p. 157]. The head was then severed, and the lead portions were used to make bullets. Once you have played the Satan card, there is not much more to say about hyperbole.

Instead, we will move to the third motivator for hyperbole, that of converting the neutral. Maier also has plenty to show here, and that is understandable because whichever side (Patriot or Loyalist) was able to engage the hearts and minds of the neutral was going to command a majority. Carter Braxton of Virginia's delegation, for example, used hyperbole that was all-inclusive in language, saying that the colonists had always lived in a "restless state" under British rule [Ibid., p. 35]. Maryland's Declaration just two days later (July 6) claimed that "the 'Legislative and Executive powers' of the British state had 'invariably pursued for these ten years past a studied system of oppression'" [Ibid., p. 78]. The words "always," "studied," and "system" in these two quotes are carefully chosen to be inclusive, giving them a better chance to convert the neutral.

This inclusiveness was important because while the Patriots were trying to convert the neutral colonists, Loyalist elements in the colonies were also trying to convert them. In the *Scots Magazine*, for example, the Americans' attempt to separate "'themselves from G[reat] Britain' suffered for the lack of 'truth and sense' and so reflected 'no honor' on their 'erudition or their honesty'" [Ibid., p. 106]. Such accusations could hardly sway someone who bought into the polarizing rhetoric of Thomas Paine, but it may well have made sense to moderate elements, who were the elements most likely to be (currently) neutral. To offset this, it was important for Jefferson to take a much more measured, calm tone than Thomas Paine. This effort is clear when one compares the 12 tyranny charges against George III in the Declaration of Independence in comparison with the eight such charges in the earlier Virginia preamble. Specifically, there were four new charges [Ibid., pp. 108–109], each of which shows Jefferson reaching out to the neutral. The first new charge accused George III of calling "together legislative bodies at places unusual, uncomfortable, & distant...for the sole purpose of fatiguing [the public] into compliance" [Ibid., p. 108]. The second accuses George III of preventing "the administration of justice totally" [Ibid., pp. 108–109]. The third states that George III "has made our judges dependent on his will alone, for the tenure of their offices, and the amount and payment of their salaries" [Ibid., p. 109]. Finally, the fourth is even broader, claiming George III "has erected a multitude of new offices by a self-assumed power, & sent hither swarms of officers to harass our people, and eat out their substance" [Ibid.]. In each case, Jefferson shows that the Declaration is concerned with tyrannies applied to the entire colonist society. The language was even modeled on that of the English Declaration of Rights [Ibid.], likely to provide continuity of approach and thus some form of "comfort through familiarity."

Jefferson, further, combined language to convert the neutral with language that identified George III and by extension the Loyalists as the enemies of freedom: "'Future ages will scarce believe,' Jefferson wrote, 'that the hardiness of one man, adventured within the short compass of twelve years only, to build a foundation, so broad and undisguised for tyranny over a people fostered & fixed in principles of freedom'" [Ibid., p. 138]. But the delegates assigned to polish the Declaration (and thus, be at odds with the often-stubborn Jefferson) knew they needed to tone the language down a bit to ensure appeal to the neutrals: "Everywhere else they moderated Jefferson's claims. Where the draft declaration accused George III of dissolving houses of representatives 'repeatedly & continually,' the delegates crossed out '& continually,' which went too far" [Ibid., p. 145]. Thus, a more nuanced hyperbole was needed to reach out to the neutral. So nuanced, in fact, that it left off women's rights (let alone women's suffrage) and the issue of slavery out of the Declaration. Frederick Douglas was deadly accurate when he noted that the "Declaration had one purpose and one purpose only: to explain and justify American Independence from the British Crown" [Ibid., p. 204]. Had the Declaration tried to include the Emancipation Proclamation or the 19th Amendment, the neutrals, who were sadly but also certainly not clamoring for either of these two later independences, would have sided overwhelmingly with the Loyalists. The end effects of these noble inclusions would have been a certain loss in the ongoing War for Independence.

In a way, then, the Declaration of Independence, rather than being a radical document as it was portrayed by some of its enemies, was actually a compromise, with the delegates assigned to it tempering some of its more polarizing statements (i.e., the most strident of Jefferson's original rhetoric). After all, the Declaration did not need hyperbole for reinforcement. That type of exaggeration was already present in the writings of Thomas Paine. While Jefferson and Adams later bristled at how much credit Paine was given (and gladly claimed) for inciting American independence, his role in reinforcing the resolve of the rebels cannot be ignored. *Common Sense* was published half a year before the Declaration, and it was rife with righteous hyperbole:

> The sun never shined on a cause of greater worth. Tis not the affair of a city, a country, a province, or a kingdom, but of a continent – of at least one eighth part of the habitable globe. Tis not the concern of a day, a year, or an age; posterity are virtually involved in the contest and will be more or less affected, even to the end of time, by the proceedings now. Now is the seed time of continental [colonies'] union, faith, and honor. The

> least fracture now will be like a name engraved with the point of a pin on the tender rind of a young oak; the wound will enlarge with the tree, and posterity read it in full grown characters. [Pain84, Paragraph 58]

After Patrick Henry spurred delegates to support the revolution, Paine published his essays, collectively called *The Crisis*, in late 1776. Not only did he urge the colonists to support the troops but he referred to George III as "a common murderer, a highwayman, or a housebreaker." This *must* be hyperbole because there was nothing common about any murders George III may have condoned. Moreover, this rhetoric was unlikely to be broadly influential to the neutral colonists, to whom the writer of *Common Sense* and *The Crisis* was most likely viewed as a *Paine in the ass*. Instead, a more calculated hyperbole was used to persuade the neutral. And that calculated hyperbole is known as the Declaration of Independence.

11.5 Cyber Salon – Exaggeration

Cybersecurity pundits are, in general, a talented bunch. But, like any other group of people, they can exaggerate. Given how much of our infrastructure, culture, content, and economy has moved to widely accessible, widely distributed online access over just a few short years' time, it is understandable why they might use hyperbole to describe the huge vulnerability surface that this situation creates. Lose security on the Internet and we lose our economy, our culture, and our history.

As we have attempted to show in each chapter (and each cyber salon) to this point, veracity in history is certainly in jeopardy at the moment. But, if it helps with any anxiety this might cause, that has always been the case. If a certain power (the royalty, the priesthood, the illuminati, etc.) has control over some aspects of the truth (usually in terms of media, from what is seen on clay tablets at the beginning of history to slate tablets in today's world), then that power has, in some sense, a handle on the truth.

This is an important issue for cybersecurity since at least superficially, the need for online security is a universal concern. But like every system in which everyone is nominally equal (with a nod to Orwell's *Animal Farm*), some people are more equal than others. That is to say that some people have a much larger online vulnerability surface than others. This being so, these people have more to lose if authentication, authorization, access control, availability, and archiving (just to cite the entries under "A") are compromised. The more you have to lose online, then, the more concerns you might have about cybersecurity vulnerabilities overall, which may make you predisposed to falling for hyperbole about the risks you face.

The risks of cybersecurity are exaggerated, of course, under a number of important circumstances in addition to when one has a lot to lose. Vulnerability has a temporal aspect to it, and people feel more at risk right after a security breach has been publicized. Exaggeration also can occur when one stands to gain from people's anxiety; for example, when you are selling malware detection, pentesting, or intrusion detection software, you may wish to highlight recent risks or exaggerate the vulnerability of others based on real-time circumstances.

Of course, text analysis approaches can be used to assess the relative level of hyperbole. Increasingly, analytics can be used to characterize the *type* of hyperbole that is being employed [Burg18]. Without exaggeration, it is clear that hyperbole can come in many forms – from simply emphasizing one's own opinion on one end of the scale to making outlandish, unsupportable claims on the other. Hyperbole in cybersecurity claims is relatively easy to identify: it involves qualitative rather than quantitative evaluation of the cyber threats. When evaluating the veracity of a cybersecurity vendor's claims, look for quantitative statistics that can be verified by other reports, preferably in the form of technical publications such as might be accessed via professional digital libraries (such as IEEE and ACM). Of particular utility are data describing not just the percent of vulnerabilities that the software service will protect you from (after all, lengthy lists of known bugs are posted on sites such as MITRE's Common Vulnerabilities and Exposures, or CVE, list and Common Weakness Enumeration, or CWE, list), but the reduction in damage corresponding to exploitation of a vulnerability. The overall vulnerability is the number of exploits multiplied by the mean financial damage of an exploit. The best, and least hyperbolic, cybersecurity software propaganda will address the vulnerabilities, the odds of an exploit, and the mean costs of an exploit simultaneously.

On a related issue, any cybersecurity provider that does not admit there is no such thing as zero risk is guilty of mistruth. Not reporting the (nonzero) probabilities of an exploit is a warning sign. So, in addition to looking for specific quantitative support for their claims, you are looking to make sure that the reported risk levels are reliably estimated. Of course, some hyperbole is expected: security vendors are expected to provide some form of justification for their products. In alignment with the reinforce/convert/undermine reasoning for hyperbole described above, particularly for the United States Declaration of Independence, we expect security providers to provide propaganda that reinforces the beliefs of those championing stronger security postures, converts those who are unsure of the state of their systems' cybersecurity, and undermines those who are confident, complacent, and/or insouciant about their cybersecurity status. Perhaps, given the absolutely critical need for cybersecurity in today's world, this type of hyperbole is a little more tolerable than most.

11.6 Summary

Hyperbole is a common form of mistruth in documents. For many people, including us, this is somehow a more forgivable type of mistruth due to the fact that it is relatively easy to detect, is often intended for a different purpose than a factual narrative, and often adds a welcome touch of flavor to the writing. Moreover, skilled narrators know how to incorporate hyperbole in a way that makes us want to believe it, either as magical thinking, blind faith, or a more conscious willingness to suspend disbelief. Offsetting these, perhaps charming elements of hyperbole, however, there is a real danger when the narrator is able to synchronize the hyperbole with the preconceived biases and beliefs of their audiences. Not only is it easier to promulgate a mistruth when your audience hopes, wants, and even believes the mistruth you are generating but it is also easier to coerce your audience into beliefs and even actions that they might otherwise never have ventured.

In this chapter, from the effectively limitless possible set of examples of hyperbole, we narrowed our discussion down to four main topics in history: the Judeo-Christian and Confucius-Lao Tzu traditions as the first two, and the British Empire and the American Revolution as the latter two. With the Judeo-Christian tradition, we showed how hyperbole was used to add spice to the narrative consistent with its goal of converting nonbelievers and entertaining existing believers. With the Confucian and Taoist traditions, we showed how hyperbole was added by later narrators in order to reframe secular traditions as something more; in other words, an attempt at conversion. With the British Empire, hyperbole was used both to undermine detractors and to reinforce the belief system of members of the empire. Finally, with the hyperbole surrounding the creation of the American Declaration of Independence, we were able to show how each of the three principal rationales for hyperbole – conversion, undermining, and reinforcement – were used. We felt among so many other sources for hyperbole, the fact that the neutral, Loyalist, and Patriot elements were each roughly one-third of colonial society made this a rather ideal situation in which to describe those three motivations for hyperbole. Paine's rhetoric may resound through the ages, but Jefferson and the rest of those involved in the editing of the Declaration of Independence are the ones who won over those critical neutral colonists.

These sections naturally led to this chapter's cyber salon, in which the exaggerated claims of cybersecurity assessment and prevention were discussed, along with text analytical methods to evaluate these claims. As with the historical examples, cybersecurity hyperbole is used for a threefold purpose: (1) to reinforce those championing stronger security postures, (2) to convert those who are unsure of the state of their systems' cybersecurity, and (3) to undermine those who are confident, complacent, and/or insouciant about their cybersecurity status.

References

[Bibl24] Biblical Historical Context, Joshua 10 and 11: Genre and hyperbole, https://biblicalhistoricalcontext.com/conquest-of-canaan/joshua-10-and-11-genre-and-hyperbole/, accessed 26 July 2024.

[Burg18] Burgers C, Renardel de Lavalette KY, and Steen GJ, "Metaphor, hyperbole, and irony: Uses in isolation and in combination in written discourse," *Journal of Pragmatics* 127 (2018): 71–83.

[Chin91] Ching J, "Who Were the Ancient Sages?" in Ching J and Guisso RWL, eds., *Sages and Filial Sons* (Hong Kong: The Chinese University of Hong Kong Press, 1991), p. 17.

[Conf03] Confucius and Slingerland E, " Analects: With selections from traditional commentaries," Hackett Publishing, 2003.

[Conf07] Confucius and Watson B, "The Analects of Confucius," Columbia University Press, 2007.

[Free16] Freese B, "Coal: A human history," Basic Books, 2016.

[Gier93] Gier NF, "On the deification of Confucius," *Asian Philosophy* 3, no. 1 (1993): 43–54.

[Maie12] Maier P, "American scripture: making the Declaration of Independence," Vintage, 2012.

[Port06] Porter B, "Peril and Propaganda, *c*.1900", in *The Absent-Minded Imperialists: Empire, Society, and Culture in Britain*, Oxford, 2006.

[Smit76] Smith A, "The wealth of nations," 1776.

[Sten20] Stenudd S, "Fake Lao Tzu Quotes: Erroneous Tao Te Ching Citations Examined", Arriba, 2020.

12

Transitive Trust and Transitive "Sus"

Trust has to be earned, and should come only after the passage of time
– Arthur Ashe

It is not fair to ask of others what you are not willing to do yourself
– Eleanor Roosevelt

Abstract

Recommendations are powerful tools for conveying trust and mistrust. Applications for everything from admission to school to applying for jobs require transitive trust to provide authentication of the applicant. The rationale is that, if your recommender is trustworthy, so are you. Transitive "sus" (suspicion, that is) can, unfortunately, occur if your recommender is not viewed favorably by the admissions/hiring personnel. Just as Michael Pollan says, "You are what you eat eats," when it comes to transitive trust, "You are trusted as those you trust are trusted." The concept of transitive trust is initially fleshed out here with respect to the broad topics of individualism, capitalism, forced optimism, and toxic positivity.

Transitive trust and sus will be discussed in this section with a particular focus on how war is declared (including both World Wars and the more recent wars in Vietnam and the Middle East). An interesting additional form of transitive trust occurs in historical documents, however, which requires addressing here. This is temporal transitive trust, in which there is trust (or its opposite, suspicion or nontrust) that spans generations. Ancestral sin, for example, has a large presence in the Icelandic sagas. In this chapter, we will discuss Njal's Saga and Egil's Saga in light of this form of transitive sus.

In the cyber salon, transitive trust is explored as an important element in cybersecurity. Transitive trust relates to the potential of shared trust to deceive a party. If person X trusts person Y, and person Y trusts person Z, then

DOI: 10.1201/9788770048347-12

under transitive trust, person X will also trust person Z. Is this always a good thing? The answer, as you must be anticipating, is "not necessarily."

12.1 Introduction

Trust, as Arthur Ashe has noted, should have both magnitude and frequency; that is, it should build with repeated occurrence, and it should build over time. To this, Eleanor Roosevelt noted, must be added the exchange aspect of trust; that is, the fact that trust is circularly transitive. If A trusts B, B trusts C, C trusts D, and D trusts A, then all four of them should, in theory, trust each other. After all, it is not fair to ask someone to trust someone you trust unless you are willing to trust someone they trust. This transitive "chain" we denote as A→B→C→D→A.

Transitive trust, however, is not really that simple. This is due in part to the statistical concept called *interaction*. Interaction can develop when there are three or more factors or variables, and the effect of one causal variable on the measured output is conditionally dependent on the state of another causal variable. In other words, the effects of the two variables are not additive. Post hoc tests for analysis of variance (ANOVA) such as Tukey's Honestly Significant Difference are used to identify the specifics of interactions in a statistical test of multiple variables, but interaction can be more readily described by giving an example. For example, your Uncle Bob's driving behavior during heavy traffic changes significantly from his driving behavior under light traffic. His driving changes for the better when he is in a good mood – he is calm, drives more carefully, is more passive to aggressive drivers, and the like. His driving, however, changes for the worse when he is in a bad mood – he is irritable, impatient, and himself now the source of aggression in heavy traffic.

We have previously discussed confounding variables, and they are related to interaction. A humorous, or at least fascinating, example of confounding variables is the strong correlation between wearing sandals and the number of homicides in a given city. A sloppy analysis might suggest that wearing sandals causes people to commit homicide (or the converse, that committing homicide makes one want to wear sandals). A more careful analysis would determine that each of these variables is correlated with daily high temperature; that is, hotter days make some people want to wear open-toed shoes and other people want to commit murder. The caution here is that correlated variables are not necessarily transitive variables, and so, they can (in this case obviously) break the transitive chain A→B→C→A where A is hot weather, B is sandal-wearing, and C is committing homicide. Instead, two "trust" relationships exist, A→B and A→C, but the link of B→C (or C→B) is missing.

In general, transitive trust will behave like the hot weather, sandals, and homicide example, wherein some connections are legitimately made, some are not, and the overall connectivity is not (usually) determined beforehand, but must instead be explored empirically. Related to trust, of course, is influence, and this is a part of the effectiveness of propaganda (for more on that topic, please jump ahead two chapters). Influence is a transitive item, and the chain of trust can be "bought, bot, or bait." This is our mnemonic for someone paying to influence (think of commercials and other advertisements), automating the influence (think of chatbots), and/or someone performing a bait and switch wherein they look like they are giving you information, but what they are really trying to do is figure out what gets your attention and what you might be willing to pay for. With these approaches in mind, we now turn to a few powerful areas in which transitive trust must be considered – from the perspective of our freedom, our governance, our outlook on life, and our emotions.

12.2 Individualism, Capitalism, Forced Optimism, and Toxic Positivity

Self-diagnosis can be the first step in breaking transitive trust. Perhaps, that is because self-diagnosis is preadapted to mistruth. Without even having to invoke that lover of his own reflection, Narcissus, it is relatively safe to say that for most people, the modal person that they have trouble evaluating fairly is themself. So, what happens when a society emphasizes individualism above a wide variety of other possible factors? Self-actualization and all the other benefits of individualism aside, what we are concerned with is the question, "Does a focus on individualism help foster mistruth?"

We might rephrase this question as "If you emphasize your individualism, then how do you expect transitive trust to occur?" If A, B, C, and D are all individuals who have widely different behaviors with respect to a spectrum of different input conditions, the trust you might have for each individual is likely to be rather distinct for each of them. The more familiar you are with the particular personality peccadilloes of a person, then, the more likely you are to not simply automatically invoke transitive trust. That is, you may love your friend, but you may also be aware enough of their errors in judgment to not automatically trust everyone, and everything, that they trust.

Which brings us back to self-diagnosis. If the least trustworthy diagnosis one can make is the one about oneself – which is more difficult to show statistically than you might think but is innately reasonable – then, in an era in which the coopting of mental health conversations is rife, how do we determine when to apply transitive trust? Mentally diagnostic terms have become part of the mainstream conversation: "We diagnose and receive diagnoses: O.C.D., A.D.H.D., generalized anxiety disorder, depression. We're enmeshed, fragile. Our emotional labor is grinding us down" [Wald21]. There are some, on one side of the self-diagnosis continuum if such a thing exists, who view self-diagnosis derogatorily, viewing it as weakness, pretention, or even, clout-mining. And, according to some reports, there are definitely reasons for concern about the validity and reasons for self-diagnosis, specifically among social media-intensive teens [Yoon24]. There is even the concept of performative mental health problems as identity signifiers: "I argue that in user-generated ADHD TikTok videos, the performance strategies of creators and platform affordances of TikTok indicate these videos function as identity work rather than health information" [Leve24]. In other words, ADHD and other neurodivergent self-diagnoses exist to be worn as badges of honor by some: "These performances and understandings of ADHD demonstrate resistance against medicalized narratives of the disorder and introduce neurodivergence as an identity signifier with emerging group understandings" [Ibid.].

However, the relative amount of mistruth in self-diagnosis is highly contextual, and we "can put more faith into patient self-reports, including those in web-based experiments such as social media posts, when individuals report diagnoses of depression and anxiety disorders" [Rutt23]. That means when someone self-diagnoses as depressed or anxious, they really are depressed or anxious. For other self-diagnosis, however, the diagnosis is less credible. In addition to the problematic nature of neurodivergence self-diagnosis described above, for "mania and bipolar disorder, the questionnaire scores did not differentiate individuals who had been diagnosed from those who had not" [Ibid.]. In other words, this means that transitive trust is graded, with a range of trustworthiness running somewhere close to that of 0% (for mania) to 100% (for depression and anxiety) depending on the specific item to be trusted. Worse yet, in the case of self-diagnosis, the criteria for mental health are subjective and highly opinionated but are often treated as an exact science.

The DSM-5-TR, the Diagnostic and Statistical Manual of Mental Disorders, Fifth Edition, Revised, was published to "assist the 200,000 psychiatrists worldwide to better care for individuals with … life-altering and potentially destructive conditions, and advance a more synergistic and cumulative international research agenda to find the causes and cures for these disorders" [Regi13]. However, the DSM-5-TR must be understood and applied by the mental health professionals who themselves are guilty of unreliable self-evaluation: "Results indicated that 25% of mental health professionals viewed their skill to be at the 90th percentile when compared to their peers, and none viewed themselves as below average. Further, when compared to the published literature, clinicians tended to overestimate their rates of client improvement and underestimate their rates of client deterioration" [Walf12]. One thing is certain here. 25% of mental health professionals are not in the top 10%.

What all of these self-diagnosis articles illustrate is that transitive trust in another person is unpredictable, and the lack of reliability is exacerbated by the idiosyncrasies of each individual. Turning from the transitive "sus" of individualism as illustrated by self-diagnosis, we turn to another issue with tremendous gravity: governance. Communism will be discussed in the next chapter under the pattern for mistruth of versioning, but capitalism is appropriate to be addressed here.

Capitalism is a form of governance based on an economic system (also called capitalism) where goods, services, and other production are privately owned (by individuals, companies, consortia, etc.) rather than owned by the government. Because of this, products, prices, and other economic factors are "controlled" by competition in a so-called free market. It should be noted that mistruth is structurally built into this definition. There is no such thing as a free market, because in such a situation – human nature being what it is – slavery, monopoly, deception, fraud, and inequity would thrive, and ultimately, intervention would be necessary. It is an idea (not an ideal) that serves as an incentive for some as a system that rewards creativity and initiative. But it cannot actually exist. In this section, however, we are more concerned with a second structural mistruth that is indirectly associated with capitalism. This is a conflation, or at least near conflation, of the *red herring fallacy* and the *either-or fallacy*, the former being a process of getting people to argue about a topic ancillary to the main point, and the latter oversimplifying a nuanced topic to be a choice of A versus B only (such as capitalism vs. communism). For capitalism, getting people to argue about how well capitalism is serving them is a diversion from a deeper discussion about whether capitalism is actually a viable system. This issue has become increasingly important as over half the wealth (and capital) in countries such as the United States is owned by less than 10% of the population: "The share of overall wealth held by the top 1% has increased from around 25% in 1980 to more than 40% today; for the top 0.1%, it has increased from less than 10% to more than 20% over the same time period" [Hubm21]. The mistruth lies in the fact that people may not be depressed by the lack of success in capitalism as much as they are by capitalism itself. The either-or fallacy, part of a broader polarization of many modern societies, demonizes the so-called "alternative" to capitalism, which is communism, when, of course, a fairer discussion to have is the one around what options are between these two extremes. Here, the possibility of transitive trust in an economic system is oversimplified to a binary comparison, rather than a more nuanced combination of trust and suspicion which almost assuredly leads to a more pragmatic, realistic, and practicable governance such as social democracy. The key takehome from this section is that the overall trust that you have in society is transitive – it is a product of the trust you have in the systems of governance, economy, and culture multiplied by the trust you have in the way these systems are instantiated in your society. Higher confidence in the way capitalism is expressed in your society, then, can be obviated by your overall lack of trust in capitalism. This transitive trust helps explain, at least in part, the sometimes-poor communication between protestors and those happy with the status quo – not just in capitalism, but in any system in any society. The protestors often challenge the systems used, such as capitalism or communism, while the defenders of the status quo are only willing, or even capable, of trying to change the attributes of the systems without actually changing the systems themselves. This is to some extent analogous to the position of the Christian Church in European society during the Middle Ages. When horrors were perpetrated by the Church, they were interpreted by the Church as the faults of the persons in the offices, but not of the offices themselves. Meanwhile, the Medieval populace did not share this distinction and used transitiveness to simultaneously trust, or mistrust, both the Church and its representatives. This transitiveness explains in part why the Reformation, which effectively ended the Middle Ages, spread so quickly [Dugg78]. There was a disagreement on the nature of how transitive trust could be applied to the actions of the Church and its officers. Using our earlier diagrams, the people viewed transitive trust as A→B→C where "A" is the medieval secular populace, "B" is the representatives of the Church, and "C" is the Church. When "A" could no longer trust "B," the chain of transitive trust leading to the trust of "C" was broken. The Church argued instead for a chain of A→C→B, so that loss of trust in "B" did not break the chain between "A" and "C." The Reformation shows that the former chain was the one that mattered most.

This insight into transitive trust leads us to the topic of *forced optimism* and its correlate *toxic positivity*. Here again, the problem with transitive trust lies in the mismatch between how the people who are unwillingly made to experience forced optimism view the transitiveness compared to how the society expounding the forced optimism views this transitiveness. As Arthur Schopenhauer wrote in *The World as Will and Representation*, "There is only one inborn error, and that is the notion that we exist in order to be happy... So long as we persist in this inborn error... the world seems to us full of contradictions."

Schopenhauer has his supporters and certainly his detractors, as is expected of a philosopher whose overall outlook on life is nihilistic (at best). However, he is certainly right about happiness, and this can be extended to asserting that forced optimism is a form of peer pressure that, like many others, can do a lot of damage. In fact, "[f]orced optimism during sustained periods of trauma and grief can be counterproductive, and even harmful. Toxic positivity encourages us to deny dark emotions, even though they are proportionate to the times" [Lee21]. That is, not allowing a person to work through their unhappiness can "stunt the healing and recovery processes" [Ibid.]. In other words, forced optimism and toxic positivity are characterized by the avoidance, suppression, or rejection of "negative" emotions, and ultimately experiences. Not only is this a contradiction (most people, including Schopenhauer of course, along with most religions, believe that suffering is unavoidable) but it is more insidiously meant to be a way of shutting down dissent, discussion, and debate. If you live in a society in which you are depressed because of the system under which society works, normal mental health approaches (e.g., pharmacology) are not going to help, because you will still be in the system. The system needs to change, and your inability to be forced to be optimistic or to swallow the toxic positivity is arguably the fault of the system, not you.

Returning to the subject of capitalism, we conclude this section with a consideration of transitive trust in light of one of the landmark efforts in political philosophy of the 21st century. In *Capitalist Realism*, Mark Fisher addresses the underlying, intentionally and carefully hidden problem with capitalist society; namely, its ability to distract people from the real problems in society. As Alex Niven remarks in the introduction to the 2nd edition, *Capitalist Realism* brings home the fact that "mental suffering might have something to do with structural flaws in society as a whole" [Fish22, p. xiii]. Perhaps the key structural flaw is the assumption that the Berlin Wall brought the "end of history" in accord with Francis Fukuyama and others [Ibid., p. 6]. Fisher notes that while this thesis "may have been widely derided, ... it is accepted, even assumed, at the level of cultural unconscious" [Ibid.]. In terms of the topic of this chapter, then, capitalism now benefits from the transitive trust of most of human history over the past century, dating back at least to the Bolshevik Revolution of 1917. Centenarian anomalies aside, this is all of the lived history for the eight billion people alive, and it is a dangerous conflation. Similar "end of history" theses, including Thomas More's *Utopia* (which is astonishingly radical even to this day) or the natural drive toward rationality (embodied by many great thinkers in the Enlightenment), have not panned out, but had less potential for damage as do the assumptions underlying capitalism as the "end of history."

Part of what is different about capitalism compared to other utopias of the past is its ability to coopt other conversations, integrating even rebellion against capitalism as part of the fiber of the commodification culture: "'Alternative' and 'independent' don't designate something outside mainstream culture; rather, they are styles, in fact, *the* dominant styles, within the mainstream" [Ibid., p.9]. This is transitive trust in a dangerous, ahistorical history, wherein every aspect of society – including and perhaps even featuring – rebellion against society, is normalized. This illogicality induces torpor, hopelessness, and eventually, the craving for nonstop distraction. Thankfully, the Internet arrived just in time to satisfy that itch.

The combination of capitalism as the end of history and the Internet has helped induce what Fisher refers to as *reflexive impotence*, where youth "know things are bad, but more than that, they know they can't do anything about it" [Ibid., p. 21]. Part of the impotence comes from the State's ability to privatize the endemic depression and anxiety in late capitalist societies: these problems fundamental to unchallenged capitalism are treated "as if they were caused only by chemical imbalances in the individual's neurology and/or by their family background – any question of social systemic causation is ruled out" [Ibid.]. Thus, late-stage capitalism both benefits from its use of transitive trust to claim to be "the end of history," and its use of transitive "sus" to assign its most nightmarish elements to the individual rather than the social, economic, and cultural practices it requires.

The Internet helps to anesthetize the victims of reflexive impotence by moving them into a state Fisher calls *depressive hedonia* [Ibid.], in which individuals have "an inability to do anything else *except* pursue pleasure" [Ibid., p. 22]. This need for constant "dopamine fixes" itself can be addressed by other commodities, such as dopamine cycle-breaking books and therapies [Lemb21]. The need for instant gratification, regardless, may create a lassitude in which any realistic challenge to pervading capitalism is highly unlikely. Students "want Nietzsche in the same way they want a hamburger; they fail to grasp – and the logic of the consumer system encourages this misapprehension – that the indigestibility, the difficulty *is* Nietzsche" [Fish22, p. 24]. Capitalism has, uncoincidentally, brought us fast food: tasteless, predigested, unhealthy food that will surely kill us, but at least it does not challenge us.

Even Nietzsche, as contradictory and inflammatory as he was, can be coopted by capitalism, his rebellion against the status quo somehow normalized and thus the "transitive trust" of antiauthority endemic to Nietzsche somehow transferred to capitalism in spite of it being "the man."

As mentioned above, consumerist capitalism also "denies any possibility of a social causation of mental illness. The chemico-biologization of mental illness is of course strictly commensurate with its depoliticization. Considering mental illness an individual chemico-biological problem has enormous benefits for capitalism" [Ibid., p.37]. Mental illness can be profited from, in fact, reinforcing the capitalist "regime," and assigning this illness to idiosyncrasies of the individual further removes capitalism from being targeted as the root cause. The fact that capitalism both causes and profits from this mental illness is one of the more perverted transitive trust/sus combinations imaginable.

Ironically, capitalism has not led to the reduction in bureaucracy that was the promise of anticontrol society landmarks such as George Orwell's *1984*. The diversionary tactic of getting people who are victimized by capitalism's worst aspects to fight about the symptoms rather than the disease is a hallmark of Kafka's writings (*The Castle* even more so than *The Trial*). Bureaucracy can disavow itself of responsibility, using transitive sus to blame the requirements, regulations, and rules in a hazy web of institutional denial. As Fisher notes, "Kafka was the greatest writer on bureaucracy because he saw this structure of disavowal was inherent to bureaucracy" [Ibid., p. 47].

Fisher further illustrates how the chain of transitive sus, which should lead to mistrust of the system or at least the chief beneficiaries of the system, is instead assigned to minions of the system. He notes that "a direct experience of the centerlessness of capitalism is an encounter with the call center" [Ibid., p. 63]. This lack of a center is consistent with Kafka's castle: in the castle, "the center is missing, but we cannot stop searching for it or positing it. It is not that there is nothing there – it is that what *is* there is not capable of exercising responsibility" [Ibid., p. 65]. This is intentional – both capitalism and the castle obfuscate the chain of responsibility in order to break, or at least discourage, the chain of transitive sus between the consumer of capitalism and the K. of the castle. It is not capitalism that is failing me, it is that darned call center person. It is not the castle that is failing me, it is the bureaucrats who will not provide me with entrance. These diversionary tactics are not accidental – they help to break the transitive sus that might otherwise lead all the way to the root of the system.

Fisher's book and thesis culminate with the credit crisis of 2008. Here, the impact of late-stage capitalism being able to block transitive sus from percolating from its populace to the societal institution (i.e., capitalism) really shows. Had the same crisis occurred under a different form of government, would people have not questioned the government system? Instead, "It quickly became clear that, far from constituting the end of capitalism, the bank bail-outs were a massive reassertion of the capitalist realist insistence that there was no alternative" [Ibid., p. 78]. This is tantamount to assigning a 100% trust coefficient to capitalism and never allowing it to participate in creating mistrust, transitive or by itself!

Note that any system in power tries to break such a chain of transitive sus. After all, it helps keep the system in place and contains any changes necessary to stay in power to cosmetic ones. As promised, we will tackle communism from a different perspective in the next chapter, so do not feel that capitalism is getting an unfair bad rap. The key point here is that any system that is somehow absolved from a transitive mistrust, or "sus," situation is much more likely to remain in place whether it should or not. So, even if you do not agree with all the points made by Fisher, they are still useful to illustrate how social constructs, and in particular for Fisher's late-stage capitalism, benefit both from how transitive trust and transitive sus are and are not applied.

12.3 Now War is Declared and Battle Come Down

In a famous line from *London Calling*, the Clash states "War is declared and battle come down." Given the intensely destructive nature of war, one has to wonder what possible circumstances would motivate two parties to willingly declare war. We are not talking about theft here; for example, when a much more powerful state decides to simply overrun a smaller, weaker, or less organized state. We are talking about situations in which the two sides are powerful, motivated, and relatively evenly matched. In such a case, history has shown that the spoils for the victor are almost assuredly going to be far less than the losses the victor will suffer in the course of the fray.

In spite of people in the 1910s, 1930s, 1960s, and 2000s being as intelligent as people today, World War I, World War II, the Vietnam War, and the War in Afghanistan happened. Because these wars did not work out well for those who declared them, it is worth considering how transitive trust and sus combined to help the powers that (used to) declare them. The historical facts behind each of these declarations are the subjects of numerous books, and our point here is not to repeat those books or even to try to provide a comprehensive analysis, but rather to extend transitive trust and sus to their combination to show how powerfully they can be combined (and manipulated) to sway people to a cause – even a cause as questionable as war.

The cited cause of World War I was the assassination in Sarajevo, and certainly that was the flash point. But the events that led to World War I were the transitive trust and sus already locked in place long before the gun was in the hand of Gavrilo Princip. The transitive trust of Serbia for Russia meant that Austria needed to call in its trust in Germany before declaring war on Serbia. Moreover, the trust of Serbia in Russia was likely to involve transitive trust extending to France and Great Britain, the former in alliance with Russia and the latter in alliance with France. The link in the transitive trust chain was probably weakest to Great Britain, so the government there (presumably delighting at the opportunity to use France and Russia as a means of putting a quickly rising Germany in its place) used transitive sus, depicting Germans as Huns despite the centuries since Atilla. Great Britain also used transitive sus through practices such as handing out white feathers to men not wishing to enlist, marking them as cowardly. Overall, the transitive trust the Allies and Central Powers had for themselves and the transitive sus they had for the other alliance led to a situation in which the perceived threat felt by each side continued to rise. This combination of trust and suspicion, transitive across the two alliances, made Europe a powder keg, ready to explode, even with a trigger smaller than the assassinations in Bosnia.

What about the Second World War? In Europe in the 1930s (the war in the Far East started much earlier, with the Mukden Incident and the Japanese invasion of Northeast China occurring in 1931), war was expected. When trust broke down after the allowance of the Czech takeover, the United Kingdom and France vowed to support Poland should there be a German invasion. In addition, despite sociopolitical differences, France and Russia were allied since 1935 through the Franco-Soviet Treaty of Mutual Assistance. Thus, the United Kingdom, France, and Russia were a "Triple Entente," inevitably connected together should one be attacked, while the aggressive powers left out of early colonization, Germany, Italy, and Japan, created an "Axis" alliance. Transitive trust within the alliances (Entente and Axis) and transitive sus between the alliances thus meant that any declaration of hostilities between any two nations in these alliances would quickly escalate, like a chain reaction, to involve all powers in the two alliances. Which, of course, it did.

After World War II ended, the so-called "Cold War" between the Communist and Capitalist blocs was next on the agenda for world anxiety, paranoia, and transitive trust and sus. Another overreaction (in 1964, the Gulf of Tonkin incident led to the greatest escalation of this two-decade conflict) was inevitable because, in Vietnam, it became clear that while the main purpose of blocs was superficially mutual protection and assured mutual destruction, the real ramifications were actually to simultaneously reinforce transitive trust and sus, and so, created a greatly enhanced vulnerability surface and the increased likelihood of small scale hostilities to rapidly expand into large scale war. After 20 years and more than four million casualties, the cost of this "vulnerability exploit" became clear. Détente was necessary in order to avoid this type of transitive trust and sus in the future. Nixon's historic visit to China in late February 1972, is, therefore, tightly related to the US signing of the Paris Peace Accords (January 27, 1973). Nixon knew the role China was playing in the Vietnam conflict, and he and his advisors also knew that because of their location adjacent to Ho Chi Minh's fiefdom, time and supply chain efficiency were on their side. By early 1972, it was clear that the United States could not win the war, either in the field or in the press. The time was right to break up the transitive trust between Vietnam and China, and thus the humiliation brought on the United States by the Paris Peace Accords the next year was greatly reduced by the weakening of the tight connection between Vietnam and China. Did Nixon know this going to China? Almost assuredly, and the results are clear: the United States–Vietnam Bilateral Trade Agreement of 2001 and the favored nation status it brought to both nations in trade was less than three decades after the Paris Peace Accords.

Turning to a concluding conflict of interest here, the conflict in Afghanistan playing out over the first two decades of the 2000s, the Cold War was now a thing of the past, but transitive trust and sus still played a powerful role. After the 9/11 event of 2001, the US government and many US citizens felt that the Afghanistan conflict was a "necessary war of self-defense." This meant that without an invasion, they felt the terrorist attacks on US soil would continue. It did not take long to find out that the Taliban were ensconced in Afghanistan, effectively having a huge, mountainous territory in which to operate with relative impunity. The United States quickly manipulated, coerced, and/or convinced its allies, using the transitive trust between the United States and important nations such as the United Kingdom, Canada, France, Germany, and Italy to ensure that the Afghanistan conflict was not perceived as a unilateral US effort. The United States also took advantage of transitive sus by declaring, with then-President George W. Bush as the mouthpiece, that "Either you are with us, or you are with the terrorists" (September 20, 2001). In effect, other nations would either have transitive trust or transitive sus with respect to the United States, with no relevant middle ground.

It is worth noting that the War in Afghanistan, unlike the other three discussed, did not benefit from a nationwide draft to provide troops for combat. This meant that the proponents of the conflict were able to employ another transitive trust mechanism with the general public, getting them to trust the government not to extend the war to civilians. This requires a professional "standing" military, which has a heavy price for taxpayers. That investment, ironically, may further extend the transitive trust of the military through a situation akin to the sunk-cost fallacy. Regardless of the differences between how each of these conflicts was begun, one conclusion is obvious: transitive trust and transitive sus are powerful motivators for convincing a populace that the declaration of war is justified. In order to prevent such "chain reactions," mutual defense treaties need to be carefully reconsidered for how extensive the expected limits of transitive trust are expected to be under crisis situations.

12.4 Njal's Saga and Egil's Saga

Next, we return to the Icelandic sagas, one of our favorite topics in part because of their unique blending of history and creative writing (see Chapters 5, 6, and 8). The word "saga" means tale, but its origins are even more interesting for our purposes. In Old Norse, "saga" means narrative, but its relationship to the English word "saw" (as in "used to see") helps explain its adoption into English. So, essentially, a saga is a narrative that was seen, a creative reinterpretation of actual history. The truthfulness of sagas can be established in Iceland, Greenland, and even Newfoundland, where the place names are reflected in the scenery, such as *Þríhyrningur* (or the mountain with 3 peaks in English) in Njal's saga. However, many of the events in the sagas are incredible, such as Skarphedin's famous slide on the ice to kill Thrain or Gunnar's purported ability to jump to his own body height while fully armored.

Part of the reason that the Icelandic sagas are simultaneously so important and interesting stems from the idiosyncrasies of the history of Iceland. Because the characters in the sagas can be traced to modern times, there is a cultural investment in the sagas that is not visible or perhaps even possible for most other histories. This is an interesting "second form" of transitive trust that can be labeled *temporal transitive trust*, which is trust that spans generations. Even if the sagas are filled with verisimilitude, such as the Sagas of Erik the Red (*Eiríks Saga Rauða*, filled with plausible voyages and encounters with Skrælings) and Ref the Sly (*Króka-Refs Saga*, filled with elaborate but plausible engineered systems), there is certainly *a posteriori* narration occurring. With *Egil's Saga*, for example, the author is Snorri Sturluson, a descendent of Egil's, who is clearly motivated to write about Egil in a more positive fashion than he might otherwise. There is reinforcing transitive trust from Egil forward in time to Snorri, and from Snorri backward in time to Egil. Thus, it is no surprise that *Egil's Saga* ends with an explicit declaration of this connection across more than two centuries: "A great family line descends from Thorstein [Egil's son], including a large number of prominent men and poets" [Stur04, pp. 238–239].

The impact of such centuries-spanning transitive trust is not limited to the Sagas: one need look no further than *The Lord of the Rings* and other works of J.R.R. Tolkien, not to mention the contemporaneous works on *The Chronicles of Narnia* by C.S. Lewis, to see how far this transitive trust can be taken. Without the lineage and the transitive trust, admiration, and loyalty it is intended to provide, many of the Tolkien works (and in some cases, the Lewis tales as well) are a matter of the "best people" simply being the ones who have survived the amassed slaughter of these gripping but equally gory narratives.

Related to the transitive trust of the main characters of Njal's and Egil's saga – including such rich characters as Egil, Gunnar, Hoskuld, and perhaps the most archetypal Viking of all, Kári Sölmundarson – is the transitive sus of the characters whose lineage either ends in the Saga Age or who are not important in the times of the authors. This transitive sus can be viewed as a form of *ancestral* sin, the concept of inheriting a fated punishment for the sins of one's ancestors. Transitive sus in the sagas is tightly related to fate and is used to explain why misfortune occurs in multiple generations of the same family. The "sins of the father" is a common motif of the Old Testament, particularly the Pentateuch (Exodus, Numbers, and Deuteronomy to be more specific), and shows how the *kristnitaka* (taking of Christianity) in 1000 AD influenced the centuries-later writers of the sagas. Blood feuds and honor killings are mechanisms for the ancestral sin to propagate and/or be fulfilled, but often (as in the case of Hoskuld in *Njal's Saga*) the person paying the price for this transitive sus is as innocent as any character can be.

Transitive trust and transitive sus in the sagas are particularly poignant precisely because we can see these mechanisms at work even when we know that the narrative is (largely) fictional. This gives us pause because the same types of verbiage are visibly at work in supposedly factual narratives. Transitive mechanisms in history are therefore powerful underminers of the truth. As historians seeking truth, we must be careful to strike a balance between trying to understand more about the context around historical situations while trying not to overuse transitiveness. Both eternal recurrence (Nietzsche) and indeterminism (from Leucippus to Robert Kane) are possible in history, making transitiveness problematic in its very structure.

12.5 Cyber Salon – Transitive Trust

With this caveat in mind, we consider the role of transitive trust in cybersecurity. Transitive trust relationships in cybersecurity must be evaluated with respect to the potential of shared trust to deceive a party. We will start with what transitive trust means on an interpersonal level. If person X trusts person Y, and person Y trusts person Z, then under transitive trust, person X will also trust person Z. This is based simply on the fact that person Y trusts person Z, and in fact, person X may not even know or have any experience with person Z. Transitive trust is, from this perspective, the "vouching" for something or someone. Research on social networking demonstrates that relatively unconnected individuals with a mutual friend may link to each other out of an assumed social pressure to do so. Links, being relatively independent (from the statistical definition of independence), therefore, have variances that are additive. The odds of transitively trusting someone or something that is not trustworthy increase with both the number of connections and the length of the trust chains.

For cyber-physical security, additional odds may work against privacy, security, access control, and authorization based on the terms that you agree to for authentication. If, for example, you use a so-called "single sign-on" approach, then your authentication approach is a "one-to-many" authentication logging you onto multiple systems with a single sign-on. In a virtualized world where your credentials are passed from one system to another, single sign-on is particularly vulnerable to cyberattacks since it allows one to log in once and access potentially highly distributed services without re-entering any additional authentication information. Single sign-on can be viewed as an approach that "legitimizes" transitive sus. Suppose that logging onto a service, system, or software application is associated with a 0.1% probability (numerically, 0.001) of a successful information breach. Then, if your single sign-on simultaneously logs you onto 20 services, systems, and software (which is quite possible on modern systems featuring a wide variety of useful applications), the probability of a breach moves to $1.000 - (1.000 - 0.001)^{20}$, or 1.000 – 0.980, or 0.020. This means a 2% chance of a breach, which is one chance in 50 instead of the original one chance in a thousand. Under this situation, if you log in just over 25 times, assuming each situation is independent of the others, then you are just as likely to have a breach as to not have a breach. For this reason, information technology (IT) experts recommend not using single sign-on except where absolutely necessary, and if you must do so, they recommend limiting the number of services, systems, and software signed onto to the minimum necessary.

Of course, remote breaches are only one form of cyber-physical security breaches. Transitive trust in a family, office, or public Wi-Fi situation can lead to breaches simply because your trust in a network extends to trusting the behavior of all the people in the network, like it or not. One compromised device in a network may be all the attackers need to fully exploit the network because any "good" attacker is going to quickly scale up the breach and search for safe places to hide so that the attack is effectively permanent. In order to understand the severity of this threat, we will briefly discuss the main steps in a successful cyberattack. While we present a six-stage attack, there are variations in the number and content of each step, but these steps are comprehensive enough to help understand and prepare for most attacks.

First, the threat agents (or "attackers") perform intelligence gathering, which is the process of performing salient analytics on the system(s) they wish to breach. This gathering is usually meant to be comprehensive, but at a minimum includes network data; team, role, and department mapping; and software/operating system sniffing so that they can identify likely exploits.

The second stage is called "point(s) of entry," and this is where social engineering approaches such as spear phishing are employed. Spear phishing benefits from the team, role, and department mapping that was performed in the previous step since it involves crafting and sending personalized messages in order to trick the target (intended point of entry) into sharing information, installing software (i.e., malware), or giving access to a system. Artificial intelligence (AI), and in particular generative AI (GAI) is increasingly involved in all steps of this stage. With more and more of your preferences, personality quirks, and friendships now visible online (especially on social media), you run the risk of providing GAI with sufficient training data to do a really good job of impersonating someone you know or seeming to genuinely know you. Remember that not checking out URLs before clicking on them, not validating that your friend actually sent you such a request, and posting too much information about yourself online are all forms of inappropriate transitive trust in the link, the message content, and the entire world of cyberspace, respectively. Remember that anything you post on social media has to be assumed visible to the entire world, regardless of what the service provider tells you. Clearly, there is no vulnerability surface larger than that!

The third stage of the cyberattack is called "command and control," and this is where the point of entry has been breached and the attacker gains control of a system within their desired target network. Maybe the social engineering worked, or maybe the user simply made a mistake and clicked through on a seemingly anodyne pop-up ad. Either way, the attacker is now in the system and in charge.

From the perspective of the attacker, the fourth stage should occur immediately. This is the act of lateral movement, in which hacking activities are either hidden or at least made resilient by the movement of the necessary elements to fulfill the attack within the network. This may obfuscate the entry point or even successfully "cover the tracks" of the attacker. Once moved laterally, "easier" exploitation avenues may open up.

The fifth stage is called maintenance, and this is when the attacker officially becomes a squatter. The threat agent now creates a new backdoor. They can add malicious "patches" to target specific services, software, and data repositories. They can even, if sophisticated enough, create in situ servers that allow the attacker to act as a user in the network. The possibilities here are expanding with the increasing use of in-place AI systems. Untrained AI has huge swathes of unused memory that can be used to hide malicious code, sensitive data to be exfiltrated, and other software (such as in-place encryption) that is helpful to hide the tracks of the attacker. Encrypting malware, for example, prevents it from being detected by many commercial malware detection software systems since they are often using pattern matching to detect malicious code. This is another example of transitive trust gone awry – if you insist on using an AI-based operating system, you are going to need to trade off security (keeping the AI and its large untrained memory footprint at a remote location) with privacy (keeping the data local so it is not shared). One way or another, you have to trust the AI provider and either their memory or your own.

The sixth stage of the cyber-attack is when your private data becomes public or else ransomed. This "data exfiltration" stage involves information theft – note that the recent trend is to read the data in place (on your network), rather than transfer it out, which is an effective way to avoid detection. What is transferred out is the important information that can compromise your business, your privacy, your future, or any combination thereof.

Why does social engineering often factor into successful cyberattacks? One explanation is that influence is a transitive item, and the chain of trust, as mentioned earlier, can be "bought, bot, or bait." By bought, we mean that someone can pay to influence you, especially if they know enough about you to craft a compelling communication. By bot, we mean that AI can be used for these communications, and with the rapidly increasing ability of chatbots and other generative AI to create believable messaging, this task is only going to get easier for cybercriminals. Finally, by bait, we mean that someone can use any of a variety of "bait and switch" behaviors in which they look like they are giving you information but are actually performing data mining on you. Since transitive trust and sus are such powerful methods of steering human behavior, finding out what you trust and what you are suspicious about gives a social engineering-based attack much more powerful "buy in" from, sadly, you.

12.6 Summary

Society is both built on and threatened by transitive trust and sus. Without transitive trust, it would be very difficult to hire anyone since recommendations are a key element in the hiring process. Without transitive sus, it would be difficult to tackle negatives in society, from ecological threats to criminal behavior. When we truly trust someone, we also trust their judgment, and as a consequence, we often trust what they trust. When we do not trust someone, that often has a negative impact on our trust in anyone they recommend or "like" in social media parlance.

In this chapter, we tried to illustrate (without being exhaustive) how pervasive, persuasive, and provocative transitive trust and sus are in history and society in general. The amount of transitive trust versus transitive sus that should be used, for example, is dependent on context. We know, for example, that some forms of self-reporting (e.g., on anxiety or depression) are highly reliable, while others are much less so. We have also seen that most people (we cited mental health professionals, but this is consistent across career fields) rate themselves above average, even though the reality should be a mean of "average."

We followed with a discussion of how transitive trust can be used to divert discussion from addressing the actual underlying problems and instead focus on symptoms. While we provided this discussion around capitalism, we might have done so with any number of other topics. A misapplied transitive trust can lead to forced optimism and its counterpart, toxic positivity. Mark Fisher's work on *Capitalist Realism* was used to show how transitive trust in the way history has been reported can prevent a healthier discussion of how society should be continually reevaluated.

The subject of the declaration of war was next addressed, focusing here on the US involvement in the two World Wars, the Vietnam War, and the more recent War in Afghanistan. The overconnected nature of transitive trust and sus was shown to be a key factor in how World War I broke out from an assassination. A similar scenario in the 1930s (Entente and Axis treaties) all but guaranteed the outbreak of that horror. In Vietnam, the Cold War provided the requisite transitive trust and sus. Nixon craftily mollified the US loss by wedging transitive sus between China and Vietnam as the war came to an end. George W. Bush almost overtly stated that everyone would either have transitive trust in the US efforts in Afghanistan or be transitively sus if they did not sign up for the US agenda.

Next, the use of transitive trust and sus in the sagas of the Icelanders was discussed. The application of transitive trust and sus to both multigeneration success and failure was shown, along with its applicability to *The Lord of the Rings* and other works of J.R.R. Tolkien and blood feuds and honor killings in general. Transitive trust and transitive sus are thus powerful motifs in both actual and quasi-factual historical narratives.

The chapter concluded with a consideration of how transitive trust and sus can be used to both achieve success in a cyberattack and also to increase the verisimilitude of spear phishing and other means of initiating a successful attack. One of the biggest concerns about AI is not that it will replace humans, but that it will help untrustworthy humans to more readily craft believable narratives that aid them in initiating cyberattacks.

References

[Dugg78] Duggan LG, "The Unresponsiveness of the late medieval Church: A Reconsideration," *The sixteenth century journal* 9, no. 1 (1978): 3–26.

[Fish22] Fisher M, "Capitalist realism: Is there no alternative?" John Hunt Publishing, 2022 (2nd edition).

[Hubm21] Hubmer J, Krusell P, and Smith Jr., AA, "Sources of US wealth inequality: Past, present, and future," *NBER Macroeconomics Annual* 35, no. 1 (2021): 391–455.

[Lee21] Lee K, "The Difference Between Hopeful Optimism and Toxic Positivity," *Psychology Today*, 9 February 2021.

[Lemb21] Lembke A, "Dopamine nation: Finding balance in the age of indulgence," Penguin, 2021.

[Leve24] Leveille AD, "'Tell Me You Have ADHD Without Telling Me You Have ADHD': Neurodivergent Identity Performance on TikTok," *Social Media+ Society* 10, no. 3 (2024): 20563051241269260.

[Regi13] Regier DA, Kuhl EA, and Kupfer DJ, "The DSM-5: Classification and criteria changes," *World psychiatry* 12, no. 2 (2013): 92–98.

[Rutt23] Rutter LA, Howard J, Lakhan P, Valdez D, Bollen J, and Lorenzo-Luaces L, "'I haven't been diagnosed, but I should be'—insight into self-diagnoses of common mental health disorders: cross-sectional study," *JMIR Formative Research* 7, no. 1 (2023): e39206.

[Stur04] Sturluson S, "Egil's Saga," Penguin Classics. Penguin UK, 2004.

[Wald21] Waldman K, "The rise of therapy-speak," *The New Yorker*, Cultural Comment, March 26, 2021.

[Walf12] Walfish S, McAlister B, O'Donnell P, and Lambert MJ, "An investigation of self-assessment bias in mental health providers," *Psychological Reports* 110, no. 2 (2012): 639–644.

[Yoon24] Yoon D, Gil S, Trumbull J, and Lim S, "TikTok and the Prevalence of Self-Diagnoses and Psychological Disorders Among Teen Users," *Journal of Student Research* 13, no. 1 (2024).

13

Versioning

Always be a first-rate version of yourself, instead of a second-rate version of someone else

– Judy Garland

I think all good reporting is the same thing – the best attainable version of the truth

– Carl Bernstein

Abstract

History is innately versioned, and thus, one could cynically argue that at most, one history is truthful. In fact, however, there are multiple forms of truth along with multiple forms of mistruth. Adding to the mistruth of versioning is the relative time after the event, along with the context of the historian. Previous chapters have highlighted the contextual basis of mistruths. Here, the focus is on reinterpretation; that is, taking existing histories and updating them. This leads to hagiography and excoriation, along with everything in between.

Different versions of historical contexts also exist, driven by the context of the times. In this chapter, we will discuss versioning as applied to *The Communist Manifesto* and American Exceptionalism, followed by a section briefly addressing differences in racial violence over time, including overt, covert, and passive-aggressive forms suited to the allowances of their times. This chapter also addresses hagiographic construction, in which heroes can rise from the ashes of ruined reputations based on the selective filtering of a current version. The cyber salon for the chapter addresses versioning in cybersecurity applications, with a consideration of authentication and forensic validation being applied for different versions of content.

DOI: 10.1201/9788770048347-13

13.1 Introduction

Versioning is an important topic, not just because it is used to preserve multiple interpretations of history. The existence of multiple versions implies that more than one history may be truthful. Extended further, the need for versioning implies that there are multiple forms of truth along with multiple forms of mistruth. This is part of the reason why versioning had to wait almost until the end of the book to be introduced. If you have read through the book from its start to here, you are very likely convinced about the multiple forms of mistruth. Versioning will provide more fuel for that, but it will also provide a path to a truth in history, which is of course paramount. Versioning, in effect, is universal acid (no such thing exists, but if it did, it would act like the acid in the *Alien* movie series, one would think) that cuts through all writings about the past, undermining confidence in the veracity of any and all historical narratives yet also providing a path to the plurality of truths in a historical narrative.

Versioning as a source of mistruth naturally arises in some proportion to both the relative time after the event narrated and to the current concerns of the historian. Using historical events, real and/or imagined, to support any combination of policy, governance, or practice in today's world is rather easy to understand, if less so to appreciate. This can be viewed as "history as a weapon," and this weaponization of history has likely been part of every regime throughout history, especially aggressive, unpopular, and illegitimate regimes. It hardly seems fair to argue a "negative" point by using Mussolini, Hitler, and Stalin as examples, but we are going to do that anyway.

Starting with Mussolini, the "father" of fascism, we see him rather literally using history as a weapon. Mussolini fancied himself as a modern-day equivalent of an ancient Roman emperor (presumably not Caligula, Commodus, or Nero, that is). So, he borrowed the *fasces*, a symbol of the power of a magistrate in ancient Rome, as the mark of authority in his own dictatorship. What are these *fasces* of feral fascist fame? It is a wrapped bundle of rods with an axe blade on one side: in other words, a symbol of danger and perhaps also fragile masculinity. Mussolini sought to engage his citizenry in the mythos of his new Roman Empire by continually invoking symbolism from the earlier (and far longer-lasting) Roman Empire. Mussolini adopted the fasces in 1926, and it fronted a modern "empire" lasting 17 years (Italy surrendered to the Allies on September 9, 1943) rather than the 503 years of the "old" Roman Empire (27 BC–476 AD). Mussolini's version of the Roman Empire was a mistruth of both a structural and a functional nature. Structurally, Italy was not a leading power in the first half of the 20th century, in contrast to

Pax Romana which made Rome the center of power in the Mediterranean for centuries. Without Germany, Italy was not able to win in North Africa (without a modern Hannibal, no less) or Greece. Functionally, Italy was not an Empire, with Mussolini heading the Fascist Party after having turned from his earlier socialism. Communist partisans captured and killed him in 1945. His life may have ended with the words, "Aim at my heart." His dictatorship lasted less than a generation. Hardly a new Roman Empire.

Next, we consider briefly how Hitler used history as a weapon. Prussia's victories over Austria and France two-thirds of the way through the 19th century resulted in the creation of a nearly pan-German state, which was less than half a century old when World War I broke out. In Hitler's version of Germany's history, there were three kingdoms or Reichs: the first being the Holy Roman Empire which Napoleon dismantled in 1806, the second being the aforementioned one created by German (largely Prussian) battlefield victories (the German Empire of 1871 to 1918), and the third being the empire Hitler saw his rule establishing. Hitler looked back to the middle years of the Holy Roman Empire to use history as a weapon – and justification – for his actions. He felt Germany was the rightful dominant power in Europe, but circumstances – and French and British intentions – had kept this from occurring. The Thirty Years' War (1618–1648) had been neither holy, nor Roman, nor Imperial. Instead, non-German (and non-Roman) armies trampled over German soils for (secular) reasons largely unimportant to Germans and as a consequence Germany (the "Empire" remained) was ruined. Two hundred years were needed to repair the damage, with additional delay because of Napoleon. Then, in the First World War, England had the temerity to back France, and combined they were able to withstand Germany – with some help from Italy and America. What if Italy were an ally and America were kept out of the war? With the Anschluss, Germany already had Austria and thus with Italy, the odds looked much better than in 1914–1918, right? His version of the truth was that Germany had been kept from its rightful place in the hierarchy of national power; that is, at the top. Given the change in alignments, it is not difficult to see how Hitler sold this version to the German populace.

Finishing our triad of terrible tyrants, we describe Stalin's ability to weaponize history. Joseph Dzhugashvili may not come trippingly off the tongue, but his alias "Joseph Stalin" sure does. Another man with a mellifluous and well-known alias (Eric Arthur Blair, alias George Orwell), not to mention a lifetime of socialist support, pointed out Stalin's mistruths in *1984* and *Animal Farm*. The former book is of primary concern here, because in it, Orwell keenly points out that "He who controls the past controls the future. He who controls the present controls the past." Small wonder a socialist like Orwell (who fought against Franco's fascists in the Spanish Civil War) felt betrayed by Stalin. Rather than following the communist view that the mass of humanity – the "common people" as it were – drove history, Stalin advanced himself as a "great man" in order to justify his decidedly uncommunist actions. In doing so, he compared himself to Ivan the Terrible, Peter the Great, and other past Russian dictators, using them as justification for his own decidedly uncollective actions.

Versioning of history, therefore, is as Orwell suggested, the privilege of those in power. It is also the privilege – and the necessity – of those not in power to fight back against such mistruth. Such versioning did not end with Stalin, of course, and Putin has continued Dzhugashvili's approach to history in the war with Ukraine [Khis22]. As Khislavski has noted, "The annexation of Crimea was legitimized by the disputed 'Korsun Legend'. This firmly established narrative has made it possible to proclaim Crimea to be the cradle of the Russian nation and a sacred place." Putin, of course, also invokes World War II as much as possible, which is referred to by many other Russians and Putin as the Great Patriotic War. Wolfrum notes that history is weaponized when it is used to legitimize aggressive military and political decisions and when it is used to integrate majorities and exclude minorities [Wolf01]. In effect, this version of history is considered more important (and is more powerful) than the memories of survivors of the events weaponized [Ibid.].

These examples, from Mussolini to Putin, illustrate how the motivations, goals, and context of historical narrators can create mistruths in versioning. A major focus of versioning is to use, usually through repurposing, history to justify current policies, governance, and action. What type of repurposing could be more closely tied to history than *The Communist Manifesto*, which we consider next?

13.2 The Communist Manifesto

Originally published as a 23-page pamphlet, *The Communist Manifesto* is one of the most significant documents in the overall historical narrative. Karl Marx and his friend, coauthor (especially important for the eventual completion of *Das Kapital*), and champion, Friedrich Engels, saw England as the natural birthplace of their envisioned worldwide Communism. They also saw the revolutions in mid-19th century Europe as the midwife of this birth. However, as Martin Malia notes in the introduction to the version of the *Manifesto* we consider here, "the Communist failure stems from the perverse logic of Marx's project itself" [Marx11, p. 34]. The version of history that Marx and Engels predicted required coincidental "historical necessity and revolutionary worker consciousness" [Ibid.], which is flawed since other, less radical solutions to the worker issues associated with mid-19th century Europe can succeed – think of social democracy (such as Fabianism in Marx-contemporaneous London) and the New Deal in the Depression-era United States as two examples [Ibid., p. 35].

After a brief introduction, the *Manifesto* starts off with the famous statement, "The history of all hitherto existing society is the history of class struggles" [Ibid., p. 62]. This version of history is not necessarily a "mistruth" as much as it is a tautology (or at least a self-fulfilling prophecy), because Marx and Engels proceed to define all "oppressor and oppressed" combinations as sets of classes. For them, "in the Middle Ages, feudal lords, vassals, guild-masters, journeymen, apprentices, serfs" [Ibid., p. 63] are considered classes. While disparities in wealth and opportunities between these two groups exist, and are regrettable, the very nature of an apprenticeship is that it is a learning stage followed by another so-called class such as guildmaster or journeyman. Of course, Marx and Engels see history as moving toward less and less shades of gray: "Our epoch, the epoch of the bourgeoisie ... has simplified the class antagonisms. Society as a whole is more and more splitting up into two great hostile camps, into two great classes directly facing each other – bourgeoisie and proletariat" [Ibid.]. But later, they note that the "bourgeoisie itself, therefore, supplies the proletariat with its own elements of political and general education ... [furnishing] the proletariat with weapons for fighting the bourgeoisie" [Ibid., pp. 76–77]. This is a fundamental counter to the tenets of Marxism: the natural arising of hierarchy or what Marx calls "class." Marx sees class everywhere yet expects the end of history to do away with classes. Clearly, the manner in which communism rolled out in Russia – and everywhere else it has established itself – shows that "classes" in the broad sense defined in the *Manifesto* will arise in every society.

The *Manifesto* is also a good example of versioning in history because its original version was shortened due to the realities of history between the first publication in 1848 and the German edition of 1872. It was also translated into Russian and English, making those versions different pictures of the "truths" of communism. For our purposes in this chapter, however, it is the versioning of all of history that particularly strikes us in rereading the *Manifest*o in this post-Cold War era. Certainly, manufacturing was the dominant sphere for technology during the lives of Marx and Engels, and so, the evolution of economics to be based so much more on accessories, services, and all the intangibles around software applications was not anticipated – nor addressed, if even addressable – by Marx and Engels. With the vision of more than seven-quarters of a century since its writing, it is clear now that rather than striving for a classless society, the *Manifesto* might have better served its readership in striving for a class-fluid and class-evolving society. Especially given their rather broad definitions of class, Marx and Engels wrote themselves into an irresolvable contradiction (a point certainly not missed by George Orwell in *Animal Farm*, as mentioned above with regard to Stalin) by defining class so broadly on one end of their argument that the reader realized class hierarchy was inevitable as part of the human condition, and then on the other end of their argument trying to show how the collectivism and other aspects of communism could end class warfare. Even if communism has not led to quite as many as 100 million deaths [Rumm93], this contradiction about class hierarchy seems to be a large factor in the general consensus that communism has not worked. The danger of the *Manifesto* is not its intent: a reread of it shows the concern for the plight of those being crushed under the wheels of early capitalism. Rather, its danger lies in its manner of using historical versioning as a means of trying to retrofit history to the version of the future that the authors favored. One might term this in broad terms as a *structural mistruth*; certainly, it is a versioning mistruth.

Of course, we are not the first to recognize the flaws fundamental in the *Manifesto*. From the comfortable view of being able to look back half a dozen generations later, the fundamental flaws of communism are particularly easy to see. Stephen Kotkin, in his afterword to the *Manifesto*, notes that Marx failed to distinguish "the tyranny of imperialism … from capitalism" [Ibid., p. 124] and "Capitalism has thrived following global decolonization" [Ibid.] which emphasizes their differences. Kotkin also notes that the Manifesto was "influential but based on a dangerously flawed theory of history" [Ibid., p. 125]. Rather than perceiving history as the ever-changing mixture of cultures, creeds, and creativities that it is, Marx took Hegel too much to heart and viewed communism as the end goal, or telos, of history [Ibid.]. Because of that, "Marx erred even more grievously in forecasting the disappearance of the middle classes" [Ibid., p. 127] which of course was necessary for his polarizing narrative of bourgeoisie versus proletariat, but again contradicted his own view of the ubiquity of class by leaving out a (middle) class that would naturally have to arise in any nations not wishing to tear themselves apart.

13.3 American Exceptionalism

From communism, we turn to the state that perhaps best exemplifies the advantages, the mistakes, and the contradictions of its "opposite," if we – perhaps oversimplifying – call that capitalism. That state is actually several dozen states and is known as the United States. Its exceptionalism is right there in front of you just by considering its name. Many other nations have states, or *estados*, or états, in America. Moreover, there is a North and South America. This same state calls its citizens Americans, again emphasizing their exceptionalism in the Western Hemisphere.

Do not feel that the Eastern Hemisphere has escaped exceptionalism, however. The United States has toppled governments all around the globe. From Hawaii to the Philippines, from Nicaragua to Cuba, from Haiti to Honduras, from the Dominican Republic to Japan and Germany, and not to mention all the other interferences from Vietnam and Korea to Iraq and Afghanistan, the United States has kept busy deciding – for right or wrong – to be the global hegemony enforcer. In many cases (Iraq in 1953, Guatemala in 1954, Congo in 1960, Brazil in 1964, and Chile in 1973) the United States ousted (or significantly aided in the ousting of) democratically elected leaders. These five examples have in common that they are during the "Cold War" when any hint of socialism, let alone communism, in another country meant that a substantial percentage of the United States was willing to support the removal of a legally elected government. It is safe to say, therefore, that the United States has a "self-publication" that reads very differently from what other nations write about the United States. Did the United States end up saving lives by ousting these governments? Like so many other issues in history, there is no real way to know. It is likely that in some cases, lives were saved and misery was reduced overall. But the converse is also likely. Each situation is its own, and no two versions of actions such as coups against legally elected governments are likely to be the same, just as no two versions of how these coups are narrated are likely to be in agreement.

Do the victors write history? Yes, but unless destroyed so do the vanquished. There are almost always two, and usually more than two, versions of the truth. They all exist simultaneously, and none of them is likely to be without mistruth. Truth in history is probably only an idea, but it is also an ideal, and being able to appreciate the need to move a narrative as close to the ideal as possible is, well, the ideal idea. With that, we turn from how versioning affects external narratives of the United States to how versioning affects internal narratives of the United States. Since we do not shy away from controversy, we are going to dive right in and discuss racism and the three main incarnations of the KKK over the past century and a half.

13.4 Racial Violence over Time

To say that the United States has a history of racial issues is a bit like saying smoking four packs a day might be bad for your health. Encyclopedias, let alone books, can be written on this topic, but in this short section, we will be focused on specific historical versioning; that is, the three main versions of the well-known racial hate group, the Ku Klux Klan (KKK), and how they were tied to the larger societal mistruths in which they thrived and ultimately faded.

The first major incarnation of the KKK began right after the Civil War in the United States. The so-called "first Klan" was founded in Pulaski, Tennessee, on December 24, 1865, less than nine months after Appomattox Courthouse. The KKK was thus created in the shadow of the end of the Confederacy and the prohibition of slavery. The Klan started their operations during the Reconstruction of the South, and so, covert operations were the norm. Convenient for their agenda – set on ensuring that the South remained hierarchical with rich Whites at the top and all Whites above all Blacks – since their violence was unlawful and they did not know when the Reconstruction would conclude. The so-called "Jim Crow" laws were throughout much of America (not just the Confederacy) during the operating period of the first KKK, but the KKK itself did not achieve most of its heinous goals.

The second, and by far largest as a percentage of the US population, version of the KKK was the second version that saw its "heyday" in the 1920s. Founded in 1915, the second version of the KKK was different from its predecessor, as it operated not in the shadows, but in the open. "Far from appearing disreputable or extreme in its ideology, the 1920s Klan seemed ordinary and respectable to its contemporaries" [Gord17, p. 3]. The second Klan also targeted immigrants, Catholics, and other minority groups even while supporting rights for "White" women. The open nature and acceptance of the second Klan led to its status as a political movement and a force of social change, akin to fraternal orders such as the Masons. However, the Klan's resurgence in the 1920s was not without opposition, and the Klan would be reduced to "…a fraction of its peak strength by 1926" [Ibid., p. 7]. The KKK was reversioned, or resurrected in the 1920s, yet saw its demise soon after. The second Klan's rapid rise and fall are both due to the period of history in which it was born, internal factors of American society that allowed for the Klan's expansion, and the variety of missteps that led to its fall.

Several important historical trends converged to create a society susceptible to the second Klan. It is not a mistake that the second, and most prominent, era of the Klan arose in the aftermath of the Great War and the subsequent flu pandemic. Before World War I, the United States was self-focused, with its foreign policy best described as isolationism. Five million men served, over 115,000 died, and nearly half a million were casualties in World War I. More than 600,000 US citizens died of the Spanish flu in the year after the war, and so, Americans were feeling in large part burned by the end of their self-imposed isolationism. America's exposure to the world also included immigration, which was at a high enough level in the 1920s that the Klan was able to drive legislation for immigrant quotas in the Johnson–Reed Act of 1924 [Gord17, p. 195]. A return to "Americanism," then, was an easy framework from which to attract members and support. Americanism was closely tied to anti-intellectualism and disdain for the elite [Ibid., p. 42], and helped consolidate the second Klan with the burgeoning middle class. In addition to isolationism and Americanism, the 1920s was the era of Prohibition. The rhetoric around the now-illegal use of alcohol was easily adopted by the Klan to proscribe Catholics and Jews [Ibid., p. 96], who were caricatured as large-scale consumers of alcohol, inside and presumably outside of their services. Additionally, the Nineteenth Amendment was ratified at the start of the 1920s (August 18, 1920), giving women the right to vote. The Klan readily coopted this by pushing hard (relative to their times) for women's rights – so long as the women were White and Protestant. A final trend of the era beginning with US involvement in World War I was the migration of Blacks to industrial cities in the north. Even though the second Klan was strongest in regions like Indiana (which was 97% White Protestant in the 1920s), part of the draw was the fear that non-WASPs would soon be arriving and changing their way of life. All these factors – isolationism, immigration, prohibition, women's suffrage, and migration – led to a period of rapid change. Fear, prejudice, and the loss of middle-class status were the result of these aspects of American life in the 1920s, and they very readily drove Klan membership.

Several internal factors in American society in the 1920s contributed to the second Klan's meteoric rise. One factor, designated Brandolini's law, is known familiarly as the "bullshit asymmetry principle," and states that it is ten times more difficult to disprove nonsense than to create it [Ibid., p. 55]. The second Klan operated in an era before radio, let alone television and the Internet, and so used its influence to dictate much of the content in newspapers. This allowed them to create their version of the news and steer middle-class readers into their belief structure. The second Klan played on the strong need for social status in the 1920s by providing a hierarchical structure to their version of the fraternal order. Fraternal orders were an important internal factor in American society of the 1920s, and many of them were quite positive elements in society, "essentially insurance cooperatives providing for burials, medical expenses, and the support of widows" [Ibid., p. 30]. The Klan readily tapped into the positive associations of the fraternal orders, even though in many ways their hierarchy acted more like a pyramid scheme [Ibid., p. 65] than a fraternal order dedicated to specific acts of charity. The United States of the 1920s was undergoing multiple structural changes, particularly after the challenges to the precepts of Western society arose due to the fiasco of World War I. America's rising nativism was readily adopted into the second Klan's rhetoric because it meant that membership in the Klan automatically conveyed belongingness that was deeper than simple fraternal order membership: Klan membership meant authentic membership in the nation itself. With this as a central precept to the Klan's drive for members, it freed the Klan to decentralize, and thus adapt to the widely different states and regions of the United States. Decentralization was empowerment, and the "autonomy for local Klaverns" [Ibid., p. 67] meant that savvy Kligrapps (Klavern administrators) [Ibid., p. 212] could customize their recruitment and meeting strategies to fit the personalities of the locale. Note that there are even more bizarre titles in the second KKK; for example, the head of a Klavern was called an "Exalted Cyclops" [Ibid., p. 211]. These names no doubt conveyed "exceptionality" to the members. Another aspect of the United States of the 1920s, the relative paucity of information sources, allowed the Klan to exaggerate its membership without fear of the hyperbole being proven. The true scope and the even larger claimed/envisioned scope of the Klan was a magnet to new members, who joined both to belong, but also to simply avoid being left out. Together, these different attributes of life in the United States in the 1920s were readily incorporated as recruitment vehicles for the second Klan.

Fortunately, the second Klan – like the first – was not destined for a long life, as scandals and divisions within its own ranks led to its downfall. Not unexpectedly given the nature of its makeup and temperament, the Klan fell apart from the inside in a manner as meteoric as its rise. It is likely that the Klan's prominence would ebb naturally, along the lines of the Elks, the Shriners, or the Masons. However, several astonishing missteps accelerated the decline of the second Klan. First off, the Klan failed at keeping its monetary avarice hidden from its membership. Throughout the United States, second Klan members who originally groused at the cost of membership became aware of the profiteering due to the high costs of dues, the massive sales of Klan paraphernalia, the lifestyles of its leaders, and several high-profile cases of criminal embezzlement [Ibid., p. 191]. If that were not enough, the leadership of the Klan became engaged in several high-publicity scandals that sullied the Klan's already shaky reputation. In Oregon, Klan leader Ellis O. Willson raped and then killed his secretary in misperforming an abortion. Not content, he did it again to another secretary [Ibid.]. Philip Fox, editor of a prominent Klan journal, killed his rival [Ibid.]. High-profile Klansmen were just as felonious: Indiana Governor and Klansman Ed Jackson was found guilty of bribery and led an embezzlement ring [Ibid., p. 192]. By far the most sensational catastrophe was perpetrated by Indiana Grand Dragon Stephenson. He raped and tortured his secretary in a closed train car, mutilating her with bites which led her to poison herself. His callousness, his utter disdain for her, and his savagery were rightly viewed by Klanspeople as "sinful hypocrisy" [Ibid., p. 194]. This episode chased nonradical second Klan members from the organization in both shame and revulsion. The scandals turned the rationale for joining the Klan upside down. Rather than fearing to miss out on what the Klan had to offer for career advancement and socialization, Klan members now felt that belonging would be a liability. With the leaders of the Klan disgraced, the image of God-given dignity and moral superiority was erased, and the Klan's reputation crumbled. By 1927, Klan membership had "...shrunk from several million to about 350,000" [Ibid., p. 191]. The collapse of the Klan had less to do with a sudden American revulsion to its reported ideals and practices, sadly, but rather to the Klan's own failures and shortcomings.

The second Klan's rapid rise and fall is due to the period of history in which it arose, internal factors of American culture and society that aided the Klan's expansion and popularity, and the variety of missteps and internal mishaps that led to its demise. Post-WWI sentiment about America's role in foreign affairs led to the Klan's emergence as a strong political voice and social change, and the creation of the "melting pot" of 20th-century American life led to isolationist, racist, and xenophobic ideals in many Americans which aided the Klan's rise to prominence. The Klan's fall had less to do with a change of racial attitudes in America than with the blunders of the Klan's policies and leadership. Although the second Klan lasted only a few years, the sentiments of racism, xenophobia, and totalitarian ideals that came with it still linger in American society, waiting under the surface for a flotation device to appear.

In between the second and third Klans, Superman was introduced (1938) and World War II happened. One of the first things Superman did after the war ended was voice his antipathy toward the Klan in a radio serial running in the summer of 1946 [Bowe12]. In these episodes, "Superman exposed Ku Klux Klan codewords, rituals, and its bigotry – all based on intel collected by activist Stetson Kennedy – before a national audience. The show damaged the group's reputation and led to a steep decline in membership from which the KKK never recovered" [Fran20].

So, if the KKK never recovered, then what was the third Klan? Here, rather than being overt or covert, it was perhaps best described as being passive-aggressive and semicovert. The main focus of the third Klan of the 1950s and 1960s was in opposing desegregation and the entire Civil Rights

Movement. The passive aggressiveness came from their reduced power (due to the scandals of the 1920s, Superman, and other factors – hopefully including some reduction of racism in the United States), and so, the third Klan partnered with Southern police departments (think of MLK's famous *Letter from Birmingham Jail*) and even (in the case of George Wallace in the same state of Alabama) with at least one governor's office to try to amplify their reduced influence. Three versions of racism, from overt to covert to semicovert, all of them share the same perverse ideology. What these three versions of the Klan show is that different historical eras require different versions of the same organizations. While the KKK is a decidedly unpleasant organization, it is still accurate to say that even well-intended organizations will need different versions to thrive in different historical eras.

13.5 Hagiographic Construction

One of our favorite edifices on the planet is the Hagia Sophia, possibly the diamond among all the absolute gems of architecture that help make Istanbul one of the world's most stunning cities. Roughly 1500 years old and simultaneously beautiful, looming, and idiosyncratic, it would be hard not to be a fan of it. Meaning "Holy Wisdom" in Ancient Greek, its name is appropriately related to the topic of this section, hagiography. Hagiography has expanded in definition from meaning the recording of the life of a saint (hagio = saint, graphy = recording) to meaning any idolizing or romanticizing biography. With hagiography, a historical character can be washed clean of any of their dirt and placed on a pedestal of perfection that almost assuredly is insulting both to the readers and to the historical figure that they are reading about.

Nauseating as a hagiography might be, if the person is not known to have caused any serious harm to others – say, Shakespeare or Mozart or Jane Austen, for three examples – then we can probably read through the biography with a knowing smile and simply tell ourselves, "No harm done." However, when the person whom the biography is about has actually caused serious harm, we need to more carefully consider the version of the person in the biography in contrast to the version of the person who lived, breathed, and possibly propagated seriously damaging thoughts and/or actions in their lives. The versioning, as in so many cases above, may tell us a lot more about the author(s) and their times than about the historical figure in the hagiography.

We will start with the easy ones – positive biographies or biopics about really bad people. When it comes to really bad people, most people place Hitler at the top of the list, with an occasional sprinkling of Pol Pot or mention of Stalin. Saying Hitler is unusual is certainly not a risky viewpoint, but in his case, it is doubly unusual since the hagiography is written by Hitler himself. Yes, we are talking about *Mein Kampf*, which in German means (roughly) "my struggles." In reality, the book (insofar as we were able to stomach perusing it for content) is more about the struggles Hitler saw of the German people that he meant to convince to share his hatred of communists, Slavs, and especially Jews. In the book, Hitler self-identifies as Aryan (he was of middling height, Austrian and brunette, not the tall, German, blond you might think of when "Aryan" comes up in conversation – and if it does, you need better conversational topics), and so, when he distinguishes the so-called "genius" of the Aryan race from the so-called parasitic nature of the Jewish "race," Hitler is performing self and group hagiography.

Perhaps scarier than auto-hagiographies are the hagiographies of truly despicable people, particularly when created after their deaths. It is likely not the intent of such biographers, but in portraying truly evil people in a "sympathetic" way, a biographer always runs the risk of creating a "fan base" for such malevolence. Such an outcome was apparently part of the television series, *Dahmer – Monster: The Jeffrey Dahmer Story*, which starred an occasionally shirtless Evan Peters and generated a lot of "simp" reactions on TikTok and other social media platforms. As one of us (the older one, obviously) used to live on 21st and Wells in Milwaukee during Jeffrey Dahmer's time at the nearby Ambrosia Chocolate Factory, we can tell you – that guy deserves no hagiography. Nevertheless, Jeffrey Dahmer is hardly the only serial killer to benefit from hagiography. Many mass murderers, from Al Capone and Dillinger to Bonnie and Clyde, benefit from the fascination many biographers have for their temerity and their panache (real or imagined). The movie *Bonnie and Clyde* (1967), for example, may have projected some of the social protests of the 1960s back onto this hardly progressive couple of the early 1930s. These two were elevated from robbers of small-town stores to Robin Hoods, an interpretation without factual merit. Understandably, a large group of people could sympathize with bank robbers in the early 1930s since the Great Depression and its associated bankruptcies and foreclosures soured many people on the existing financial network, but 13 murders are still 13 murders.

Not every biography of truly awful people, however, has a hagiographic element to it. In *The Devil in the White City* [Lars03], for example, H. H. Holmes, often cited as America's first serial killer, is depicted as the sociopath that he clearly was. The author, Erik Larson, clearly is trying not to glorify Holmes, and his version of the serial killer is more critical than the versions of the serial killers (Bonnie and Clyde, Dahmer, and Hitler) mentioned above. However, does even this version of Holmes somehow lead to potential admiration, even adulation, of Holmes? The sad truth is, yes. But there is only so far that you can go in a version of history in an attempt to not encourage whack jobs – they exist, they are going to be motivated differently (meaning more irrationally) than other people, and it is simply not your fault if they are motivated to like someone you have clearly identified as unworthy of adulation. Holmes, for example, created a city block-sized building replete with torture chambers, hidden rooms, and even a furnace to ash the bodies of people he killed. If relating these facts in a narrative inspires a reader to admire Holmes, that is not the fault of the narrator. Of course, those who admire Holmes (do a web search on "admirers of HH Holmes" – this search comes back decidedly nonempty) may be drawn to his supposed charisma or "success" in tricking women into his chambers, but still, there is nothing in Larson's narrative that is going to make anyone normal admire him. There is, alas, perhaps no version of the story of Holmes that keeps someone irrational enough to admire him from doing so.

In an age increasingly driven by video, biopics have become of comparable prevalence and importance to biographies. The same problematic nature of inaccurate versions of biographies occurs in biopics. As one example, the movie *A Beautiful Mind* starring Russell Crowe and Jennifer Connelly made John Nash seem much better (especially toward his wife) than he actually was. The movie *300* turns the extermination of a Spartan force at Thermopylae into a puzzling hagiography of White nationalism, and *The Blind Side* has a White savior message hagiographic to Leigh Anne Tuohy (played by Sandra Bullock) and her family. Versioning Genghis Khan as John Wayne in *The Conqueror* is not only puzzling but also incomprehensible insofar as to what the hagiography is intended to convey – the glorification of Genghis Khan or through association with John Wayne glorification of the European subjugation of the American continent through analogy? In *Amadeus*, the hagiography of Mozart is at the expense of Salieri in a decidedly fictional account, here of a good person but still hagiographic. What do all five of these biopics have in common? The message is clear that the real history was a version not interesting enough to convey. In fairness, the opposite of hagiography also occurs in biopics; for example, the portrayal of Jim Morrison as a dropout who throws fits makes Oliver Stone's *The Doors* a version of history far removed from reality. However, that exception proves the rule that biopics are, in general, versions of history more akin to literature than truthful narratives.

One last specific hagiography needs to be mentioned, particularly since its subject was an object of admiration for one of us as a student of engineering, math, biochemistry, and physics. This is the autobiographical *Surely You're Joking, Mr. Feynman*. In an infamous chapter, Richard Feynman tries out methods of seducing women and refers to women who accepted drinks from him as "whores" or worse. He also asked a freshman student if he could draw her nude while he was a professor at Cal Tech. This is disturbing material now, but 40 years ago, one gets the feeling that Feynman was trying to come across as "cool" or "hip" in a way acceptable to his (overwhelmingly male) readership of the time. Is it worse that Feynman may have acted this way or that he felt he needed to message acting in this way? That is not clear, but it is certainly clear that what constitutes hagiography changes over time. A version of a historical narrative that may have been acceptable in one era is not in another. This adds even more variability and complexity to the versioning of history.

13.6 The Forensics of Narratives

At this point, we hope to have shown how historical narratives are never fully truthful from every relevant perspective. Moreover, they simply cannot be, because different perspectives bring different values, different emotions, different belief structures, and different experiences on the part of the narrator and all of the readers. Because of this, there cannot be a single truthful version. All narratives are probabilistic in the sense that an (honest) narrator must be carefully considering the relative importance of their sources, their eventual audience, and of course, all of the elements of their perspective (values, experiences, beliefs, and emotions) as they write.

In this section, however, we switch from the role of the narrator to that of the reader. We argue that it is precisely because of the ambiguity of truthfulness inherent in authoring a historical narrative that a reader must be ready to invest in their reading. Reading a historical narrative, that is, is not a passive event. Instead, each narrative requires the reader to both discover and discern the overt, covert, and semicovert content in the narrative. This requires hard work, not least because the nature of the interpretation necessarily changes over time. Forensics of the overt elements of the narrative is an analysis of the words themselves – meaning the content of the narrative. Forensics of the covert elements of the narrative, in contrast, require the context of the narrative to be analyzed. Of the two, it is likely that the covert elements are more problematic the further from the historical era the narrative gets. This is because of the selective filtration of context over time. Filtration does not simply mean that some materials from the past have disappeared; rather, it means that what was more relevant contextually when the history occurred is less relevant contextually today, and vice versa.

A simple anecdote illustrates this point. The online streaming of music allows new generations to hear the music of previous eras, with some exceptions, as simply as they can hear new music. However, the streaming behavior of modern listeners is unlikely to follow that of the original audiences. The most streamed Pixies song currently, for example, is *Where Is My Mind?*, even though this song – not released as a single in the late 1980s when the album it was part of, *Surfer Rosa*, came out – was overshadowed for young Gen X listeners at the time by *Surfer Rosa*'s one single *Gigantic* and shortly thereafter by the two popular singles on the Pixies album *Doolittle* (*Here Comes Your Man* and *Monkey Gone to Heaven*). The context in which *Where Is My Mind?* is the most listened to Pixies song, therefore, is a different context than when the song was originally released. The reasons for this require investigation, as the current generation of listeners is selecting based on the content of the songs and their new context (streaming was not part of the late 1980s music experience).

What about the concept of semicovertness? This is the middle ground between the content and the context. Continuing to use music streaming to illustrate this concept, when the Internet or other modern sources of information (e.g., movies) provide additional information or additional association of a previous song with today, the semicovert, or intangible, aspects of a musical piece can suddenly become a factor in the interpretation of the narrative. A good example of this is Queen's *Bohemian Rhapsody*, which benefitted from two movies (*Wayne's World* in 1992 and the Queen biopic *Bohemian Rhapsody* in 2018) to become one of the most streamed songs over half a century after its original release. The semicovert nature of the song is its importance to the overall evolution of rock opera, the band Queen, and the influence of Queen on later musicians.

Applying this more broadly to historical narration in general, the semicovert element of a historical person, place, or thing is its preadaptation ability to the time in which a narrative is written. There is a term for this concept: presentism. Presentism is when interpretations of the past are flavored by ideas of the present (which may not have existed in the historical era described). This has multiple facets to it: judging people – and in particular their overt actions – in the past from the lens of today (see the discussion of Richard Feynman in the previous section for one example), which while appropriate (because we are the living readers, after all) may also brush aside the covert elements of the past (like the expectations of behavior, which for example, may have influenced Feynman's rather misogynist chapter in *Surely You're Joking, Mr. Feynman*). All of this makes sense, but then there are other aspects to presentism as well, and these involve the semicovert forensics necessary for an active reader-as-interpreter of a historical narrative. Here, the reader is encouraged to realize what is advantageously coopted from the narrative to support a present narrative. Often, this involves selective filtering of the past; for example, deeming Abraham Lincoln as a hater of Native Americans for the 38 Dakota men hanged in Mankato, Minnesota in December of 1862 without considering that this was during the portion of the US Civil War when Lincoln needed more Minnesotans to join the Union army and that hundreds of Minnesotans had died in the so-called "US-Dakota War of 1862" such that settlers were calling for a far more dire response (over 300 Dakota men were sentenced to death, and Lincoln commuted all but 39 of them, those 39 being involved in the massacre of civilians). The semicovert nature of this narrative is to place the executions in the context of centuries of mistreatment of Native Americans by the US Government (and its precursors). The overt story clearly has multiple truths – one of Native Americans, who feel that those executed were prisoners of war; the one of the Minnesotans, who felt that nearly 300 more should have been executed; and the one of Lincoln, who felt that only those who had engaged in noncombat killings should be executed. The covert story is even more complicated, involving how the Dakota felt about the wave of immigrants moving into Minnesota, how the Minnesotans felt about the Dakota and the ongoing Civil War, and how Lincoln felt about the importance of Minnesota in his strategy for the Civil War and the railroads and northwestern expansion, among many other issues. The combination of overt, covert, and semicovert considerations here means that this historical event will continue to be interpreted and reinterpreted in eras to come, with no single consensus on absolute truth.

We thus see that history in which the reader invests will generally end up with a multiplicity of interpretations and with nuanced discussion leading to a narrative that allows for discussion, disagreement, and continual reinvestigation. What this means, then, is that history is not meant to be conveniently wrapped up and set aside: in the end, the goal of history is to be inclusive of multiple interpretations, and not reductionistic to one truth. Mistruth in history is inevitable, but the severity of the mistruth is almost certainly in most cases minimized when the multiple potential truthful versions of the narrative (as seen from the multiple perspectives of those involved) are acknowledged and reported upon. The "larger" the history, the less chance a truth has been left out, even if that means multiple, mutually incompatible truths must be considered simultaneously.

13.7 Cyber Salon – Versioning

The cyber salon for this chapter addresses versioning in cybersecurity and cyber-physical applications, with a brief consideration of authentication and forensic validation being applied for different versions of content. In order to explain the concept of overt, covert, and semicovert cybersecurity, we start with cyber-physical security since it is tangible (i.e., tied to real objects). We then move to cybersecurity proper. Finally, we discuss the analogy between the versioning of cybersecurity and with versioning of history.

Cyber-physical security is the security of physical objects through combined online (cyber) and in-hand (physical) processes. One particularly opportune location for such versioning is on the packaging of a good that commands a large enough price to make it worthwhile for fraudulent parties to counterfeit, repackage, resell, or otherwise tamper with the intended sales history of the good (e.g., by changing the expiration date). For packaging, there is a triad of cyber-physical mechanisms that, when used together, provide protection from fraudulent activity. The first is a unique ID, which is manufactured (printed or otherwise integrated into the packaging). The process of putting a unique identifier on each item is called *mass serialization*, and it allows each package to have a unique code, like a username, in the online database. Usually, the ID is stored in a bar code, an RFID chip, or some other mechanism on the packaging, although occasionally it is on the item inside the packaging. This ID is usually overt, and functions similarly to a username. The second mechanism is an anticopy mechanism, which keeps someone from simply copying the packaging and reusing it. This is often covert and can be used by investigators or even customers with specialized software to discern whether the label or other packaging is original. The third mechanism is antitampering, which shows that the package has not simply been opened before and is now being reused for illicit purposes. This is often semicovert, in that, the customers know where it is (like a tear strip) but are not sure what information may be associated with it. It should also be difficult to work around, so that tampering cannot be hidden from the next person to whom the used package is being passed off as original. Combined, these three mechanisms (mass serialization, anticopy, and antitamper) offer three different versions of security for physical items.

Many goods and (especially) services these days exist entirely in the cyber realm, of course. This includes among many other examples communications, video streaming, the social internet, web-based services, electronic games, and of course, artificial intelligence (AI). Here, different versions of authentication, authorization, and access control are required to ensure that fraudulent activity is not occurring, as well. The first, or overt, level of authentication is simply the content itself. You might remember *Star Wars* or *Break on Through* by *The Doors* a certain way, and then when watching or listening to the latest version of each on a streaming service immediately realize that they have been edited. The overt content has changed, and you can "validate" that with your memory. Encrypting these digital assets creates a covert version of them since without the proper decryption key, you cannot properly stream them. Another version of streaming content can be gained by "signing" them, for example, with a digital signature. A digital signature (or hash), as described in the first chapter, is a "one-way" function of a message m that creates $H(m)$, its hash, which is shorter than the original message, meaning it cannot simply be an encrypted version of the message m. It is long enough, however, to make the chances of a hash collision diminishingly low, so that there is a very low probability that anything resembling the signed information can be made to have the same hash. From this perspective, then, the original overt content is the unique ID, the encrypted version of it is the copy prevention approach (since copying the encrypted version as many times as you like will not compromise its content if you do not have the correct decryption key), and the hashed version provides antitampering protection (since if you tamper with the content in attempting to fraudulently reproduce it, you will not get the correct hash value).

In these cybersecurity approaches, we clearly see the analogies to the cyber-physical security mechanisms. Combined, these security approaches provide provenance (i.e., proving that the data has not been tampered with throughout the so-called "chain of custody" between its creation and where it is when you validate the encryption, hash, etc.), as well as "track and trace" (establishing where the good or service has been). The importance of versioning is illustrated in a wide array of cybersecurity applications, with each version of the content (overt, covert, and semicovert) being relevant as a different version of the truth (or "provenance"). Different versions of the same overall cybersecurity or cyber-physical security narrative allow all of the different participants (manufacturers, distributors, warehousers, retailers, resellers, and consumers) to participate, each of them with their own perspective on the "truth."From this versioning, it is clear that multiple parties often need to contribute to the validation of content. Distributed ledgers, including their more modern relatives, blockchains, provide a means for *collaborative* authentication and forensic validation. When you decrypt content with your own key, this is the equivalent of overt content since your key is enough to reveal the content. Other content can be encrypted with a key that you do not have authorization for, and so, this content is covert or invisible to you. Additionally, some content is shared and can be decrypted by a key that multiple parties have access to. This can be thought of as semicovert, but the basic idea is that the encryption key or keys are used to validate who signed the data at one point in time. In a blockchain or other distributed ledger, it is virtually impossible for someone to be able to modify the content and still have decryption work for everyone in the ledger since the odds of having content that is both readable and that will have a hash collision that makes sense for every key used is essentially zero to as many decimal points as you care to view.

Distributed ledgers are in some sense analogous to historical versions since content can be digitally signed at different times with the order of the signing important for context. A distributed ledger can be thought of as an "agreed-on truth" signed off on by many different parties – the closest we can get to a consensus that is truthful to many. Is there a way to take a distributed ledger approach to multiparty historical narratives? We think so, and perhaps, we can call it *distributed legacy*. With this, the role of the "chief narrator" is to seek out arguments for each perspective on history and allow all parties to "sign off" on the narrative as representing this multiplicity of views. Sometimes, simply acknowledging that there is another perspective will be sufficient; other times, inviting someone to expand on an alternative perspective will be necessary. It all depends on the nature of the narrative. Collaboration is not a bad thing; in fact, it can be argued to be that which makes us human [Meli10].

13.8 Summary and Conclusions

In this chapter, we considered how to interpret different versions of a historical narrative. In some cases, this means identifying versions that have not been reported. But, even when all versions are available, the more difficult question might be "What is the correct version?" In this case, our answer is perhaps surprising: this is not the right question.

Instead, looking back over this and the previous dozen chapters, we have learned that there are usually many forms of mistruth in a narrative. What we have hoped to show in this chapter is that there are also many forms of truth, and perhaps, above all else, that is what versioning really means. To say it alliteratively, every history hoping to be helpful needs multiple versions. As a narrator, you should trust your reader to be able to come to your opinion of truth even when you do not omit perspectives that are different from your own. The best way to version, it can be argued, is to include as many relevant versions as feasible. Such a "distributed legacy" will both serve your reader and whatever objective version of history is possible quite well. This means that the "right" question to ask as a historical narrator becomes the more interesting, and perhaps, more readily approachable one of "have I left out any reasonable perspectives from my narrative?" Even if you choose to be dismissive of other perspectives, by including them in your narrative, you make it easier for others to follow your work.

This chapter also was intended to make it clear that "end of history" narratives such as neoliberalism and earlier fascism, communism, and the Pax Romana are doomed to failure because history, quite simply, never ends. It is preadapted to continual reinterpretation, and we believe that one major reason history is so compelling is because of its effect on today and tomorrow. The cyber salon – in this chapter and the others – shows how relevant an understanding of truthfulness in history is to the very relevant and very modern field of cybersecurity. If the command of historical narrative interpretation is only in the hands of those who would use it to manipulate people, then history will enslave rather than free people. Being able to identify mistruths in a narrative is therefore paramount.

American Exceptionalism, as one example, is a false narrative that limits the possibilities both of Americans and non-Americans. Understanding how "isms" such as racism (discussed in this chapter) and classism are used to control narratives was illustrated through the three versions of the KKK in the United States. Hagiography, particularly those of despicable people, was also shown to be a method of versioning used to control the narrative not only of history but the present and future as well. One need not be an indiscriminate iconoclast to be a good student of history. Just remember that if the narrative sounds too good to be true, it most likely is.

Using a "forensic" approach to history, finally, was shown to be a good approach for analyzing the overt, covert, and semicovert elements of history (its content, context, and changes in context over time). It was also shown to have strong analogies to the use of mass serialization, anticopy, and antitamper approaches in cyber-physical security design. Even more direct analogies to the use of overt, covert, and semicovert protection of information in cybersecurity were shown, emphasizing once more the relevance of truthful historical narrative analysis to important cultural, social, and communication issues of today.

References

[Bowe12] Bowers R, and Bowers R, "Superman versus the Ku Klux Klan: the true story of how the iconic superhero battled the men of hate," National Geographic Books, 2012.

[Fran20] Francisco E, "Superman crushed the KKK in 1946. Here's why he's doing it again in 2020," Inverse, May 13, 2020.

[Gord17] Gordon L, "The Second Coming of the KKK: The Ku Klux Klan of the 1920s and the American Political Tradition," New York: Liveright Publishing Corporation, 2017.

[Khis22] Khislavski G, "Weaponizing History: Russia's War in Ukraine and the Role of Historical Narratives," Journal of Applied History, 4(1–2), 102–125, 2022.

[Lars03] Larson E, "The Devil in the White City." New York: Vintage (2003).

[Marx11] Marx K (Author), Engels F (Author), Malia M (Introduction), Kotkin S (Afterword), "The Communist Manifesto" (Signet Classics) Mass Market Paperback – May 3, 2011.

[Meli10] Melis AP and Semmann D, "How is human cooperation different?" Philosophical Transactions of the Royal Society B: Biological Sciences 365, no. 1553 (2010): 2663–2674.

[Rumm93] Rummel RJ, "How many did communist regimes murder?" Powerkills, Assessed May 27 (1993).

[Wolf01] Wolfrum E, "Geschichte als Waffe: vom Kaiserreich bis zur Wiedervereinigung," Vandenhoeck & Ruprecht, 2001.

14

Propaganda

The truth is the best picture, the best propaganda
– Robert Capa

Propaganda is amazing. People can be led to believe anything
– Alice Walker

Abstract

At this point in the book, we hope that we have established that there is no one truthful history for any narrative. That is, there may be multiple truths just as there may be multiple mistruths, depending on the contextual circumstances of the narrators. Every history, therefore, is likely pushing an agenda – whether consciously or subconsciously. This is because every narrator, no matter how impartial, brings a different set of skills, perspectives, and personal history to the task of creating the narrative. Propaganda is one common way to advance an agenda. Propaganda, when effective, taps into a collective set of sociological, political, and/or cultural points, thus engaging a large set of population in the message. Propaganda is different from hyperbole (Chapter 11) and differential emphasis (Chapter 5), although it can employ either or both as part of its mechanism. Propaganda usually invokes one or more of six key persuasive methods (logos, ethos, pathos, kairos, topos, and aesthetics), with its goal being to solidify support and/or create new support for its message. In this chapter, propaganda used for military purposes, as well as ironic propaganda will be analyzed with the goal being to help the reader more quickly identify and dissect it for what it is. This will provide the reader with enough tools to attack propaganda so that the threat of being "found out" will help dissuade most perpetrators of propaganda.

DOI: 10.1201/9788770048347-14

14.1 Introduction

By the end of the previous chapter, we hope to have shown that there is no single truthful history for any narrative. By this, we do not mean that every historical narrative is untruthful; rather, just that each truth has its own context (cultural, political, geographical, etc.) which usually makes it different from a narrative of the same history by a different narrator. This means that not only does every history have an agenda but even more so that each history *must* have an agenda, whether consciously or subconsciously advanced by the narrator. Given the choice, perhaps the former (i.e., consciously pushing an agenda) is better, especially if the author is aware of their agenda and describes it upfront. It seems defensible to say that every narrator, no matter how impartial, brings a different set of skills, perspectives, and personal history to the task of creating the narrative.

Among all the other means of bringing mistruth to a narrative, propaganda might, therefore, be the most honest. After all, when it is effective, propaganda marshals a collective set of sociological, educational, political, and/or cultural points, which means it may represent the preferences, experiences, and even subconsciousness of its target population effectively. From this perspective, then, propaganda advances a particular agenda and so is "consistent" with the overall biases, if we may use that term here, of the narrator. Unlike hyperbole (Chapter 11), propaganda does not require exaggeration. Its original meaning, in fact, was simply material that expressed a specific ideology and/or opinion. This could merely reinforce the ideology or opinions that it tapped into. However, most of us likely think of propaganda in a more negative light, where it is used to further an agenda, and in addition to reinforcing the beliefs of existing allies, also influencing the opinions of those not currently aligned with that agenda (ideology, opinion, perspective, synthesis, future plan, etc.). Propaganda is often associated with irrationality; that is, using emotional rather than intellectual content to influence its audience. Unlike differential emphasis (Chapter 5), however, propaganda may simply provide different valences to multiple perspectives on the narrative (Chapter 10), although it will employ them both simultaneously by providing a more positive valence to the desired agenda and a more negative valence to one or more opposed agendas.

In this way, propaganda often relies on the incorporation of persuasive methods, including logos, pathos, ethos, kairos, topos, and aesthetics. We review these briefly because they are important to understand not only as the reader of a historical narrative but also to report *as the writer* of a narrative. As a narrator, you should first off be aware of which types of persuasion you are using, and in most cases, you should probably let the reader know that you are employing them; that is, if you want your history to be taken seriously. The first three – ethos, pathos, and logos – go all the way back to Aristotle's *Rhetoric*. That is two and a half millennia of persuasion. Logos is of course an appeal to the logic and reason of the reader and is supported by facts and logical reasoning such as if/then/else constructs. Logos can work well when there are a lot of facts available about a historical event. Pathos, however, appeals to the emotions of the reader and can be recognized in the word pathetic, which has changed over time to focus on the emotions of sadness and sensitivity. Ethos, as the name implies, is associated with ethics, but from a traditional perspective is also associated with the credibility, reliability, and reputation of the invoked sources (e.g., citing Abraham Lincoln's view to support a point to use goodwill toward him to promote your propaganda). Note that each of these three Aristotelian approaches can be used "positively" or "negatively." For example, logos can be used to convince someone of the logic of your narrative (positive) or to convince them of the illogic of an opposing narrative (negative). Pathos can be used to create emotional investment in a perspective ("positive," called cathexis) or to create distance or detachment (negative). Ethos can be used to convince the reader of the merit of a narrative (positive) or to show them the deficiencies of an alternative narrative (negative). In each case, persuasion techniques can be used to support the overall propaganda approach, which is likely to be a combination of positive and negative approaches.

In addition to the Aristotelian persuasions are kairos, topos, and aesthetics. Kairos is associated with the timeliness of the narrative; that is, how relevant it is to the current reader. Arguments for engaging readers of the *Lais of Marie de France*, for example, are likely to be less effective in the 21st century than they were with the original medieval audience. Topos is a theme or even traditional "topic" which might include the topic of a "homeward journey" such as in Homer's *Odyssey* or more recently Sheila Burnford's *The Incredible Journey*. Aristotle viewed kairos and topos as supporting approaches for practicing logos, pathos, and ethos, but we give them their own place as mechanisms, to which we add a sixth: aesthetics. Aesthetics has become especially important since the dawn of the advertising era and is given greater energy by industrial and electronic advancements of the past century and more. That is not to say aesthetics has not been important since at least the time of Aristotle. With aesthetics, the appreciation of beauty and taste is important, and certainly, this was crucial during the times of the Romantic Poets (John Keats' *Ode on a Grecian Urn* as one example). Dialing all the way back to Aristotle's time, the Parthenon reputedly employed the so-called golden ratio, and such measures of aesthetic quality were already well-known in the world.

These six mechanisms for persuasion are often used together, and when surveying people regarding logos, pathos, ethos, and aesthetics, for example, we found that ethos was a particularly strong motivator for persuading people to reuse materials rather than simply recycle them under certain conditions [Ketk22]. Different narratives, of course, will have different relative values of persuasive techniques. We argue that the historical narrator, in most cases, should report which persuasive technique or techniques they are using – rhetoric, after all, has had its canons since the time of Cicero, and a good orator's means of persuasion were known to the audience. The positive reason to report your persuasion techniques is to try to provide the reader a guideline to search for a fully truthful narrative, acknowledging that they will have the courage, talent, and assiduity to engage the content, context, and persuasive elements in the narrative during their search. The "negative" reason to report your persuasion techniques is the threat of being found out. If you do not report the perspective you have in your attempts to persuade, your readers will figure it out anyway, and your lack of upfront ownership of it will actually discredit your otherwise perhaps quite compelling and accurate interpretation of history. In fact, this chapter is specifically intended to help your reader uncover those persuasive elements – you might think of them as persuasive biases – so please be warned that we support, hope, and trust readers of historical narratives to be able to discover and correct for propaganda in general, including mechanisms for persuasion as part of that.

14.2 Motivating Military Membership

Arguably one of the more impressive areas for successful propaganda usage throughout (and about) history is in the various types of propaganda associated with military recruitment. Superficially, motivating people to join a military organization seems almost an impossible task. Hard training, hard work, and often, if you do your job well, you get killed for it. In such a situation, of course, honor and courage are often the "positive" message, while the negative message runs from the risks associated with letting the "other side" prevail to the risks associated with being identified as a coward. In the modern world, where the "meme culture" and the Internet can produce surprising "viral" results to content, it might seem an impossible task to convince people to put their lives on the line for voluntary military service. Historically, however, it has been far easier, and perhaps even today, it is not so difficult as one might expect.

During the First World War I in England, as an example of the "negative" propaganda around military service, women were encouraged to give white feathers to men not in uniform. The white feather as a propaganda symbol arose in England due to *The Four Feathers*, a book published just over a decade before the war broke out [Maso02]. In that book, a white feather represented cowardice, and during World War I, it was also handed out to shame conscientious pacifists. This is a different approach from the perhaps more familiar "positive" propaganda associated with much military recruitment. Such positive propaganda is observed in discussions of the all-volunteer US military of today [Lope23], in which white feather negative propaganda shaming would be less likely to have the desired effect. Here, the volunteer for military service is seen to enjoy "long-term opportunities … while in uniform and thereafter – and in virtually every career field" [Ibid.]. Deputy defense secretary Kathleen H. Hicks champions military service as being in continuity with all public service, stating "We cannot afford a future of disconnection, a future without the firefighters, nurses, teachers, public servants, and service members we need to advance the common good. We should all consider how we're going to leave the world a better place than we found it." Firefighters, nurses, and teachers consistently rate in the highest echelon for respect, and so, associating military personnel with these professions is an intelligent "positive" approach.

Somewhere in between the positive and negative approaches mentioned above is the concept of civilian guilt [Mors45]. Because for most of history, military involvement was involuntary, civilians who either were not drafted or were able to obviate the consequences of being drafted would sometimes feel guilt over their nonparticipation. This might be especially problematic in conflicts that escalated more than originally anticipated (think, e.g., of the Korean and Vietnam Wars) since in contrast during a conflict anticipated beforehand to be huge such as World War II, plenty of sacrifices would be made on the home front, too. That being said, though, Morse notes that "every male civilian, consciously or unconsciously, feels guilty in his relations with soldiers" [Ibid., p. 224], here with reference to the then just-ended World War II. For this reason (and others), veterans are often reticent to bring up their service around most people, not wanting to be labeled as either heroes or victims [Merc19]. This self-imposed isolation is strongly juxtaposed with the propaganda used to recruit volunteers in a nonconscription military such as that of the United States. As such, some interesting, if not surprising, types of propaganda are employed in the attempt to draw in new recruits. Modern US "media about war, whether sponsored by the military or not, are inherently perpetuating positive messages about military/war and act as 'psychological propaganda' influencing people's perception of the institution and encouraging people to enlist" [Mart23]. Recruitment propaganda can include exploiting nihilism, anticapitalism, and even antieducation sentiment for attaching cachet to military involvement. The military is portrayed in such propaganda advanced as something "bigger than oneself," and thus, an admirable, selfless pursuit. This is a strategy that must be pursued carefully, as opposed to "defining service in terms of material rewards, [wherein] recruiters effectively commodified it, painting a picture of military life that was, if not manifestly false, then certainly extremely misleading" [Maar20].

14.3 Irony

If military propaganda runs the risk of being self-contradicting, what happens to other parts of society in which the selfless role of service and sacrifice cannot be applied? Here, propaganda can be promulgated through the use of irony. Irony can mean a lot of different things, from the plot twists of O. Henry's cosmic irony (perhaps the most famous example being *The Gift of the Magi*) to the "facts found out too late" elements of the eponymous song by Alanis Morissette. The irony is always some form of juxtaposition of the expected, and a different, often surprising, reality. Used in literature to engage the audience in the details of a story, irony can be used to provide humor and a common sense of what is truth and what is only appearance. Used negatively, however, irony can be used to distance the purveyor of propaganda from potentially negative elements of their message.

A good example of irony being used in propaganda is the 2023 movie *Barbie*, in which a message of anticapitalistic irony is used to promulgate the obvious capitalism of a movie involving a decades-old product that, according to statista.com, has had more than $12 billion in revenue over the past decade. In an era in which "meme culture" thrives, irony works well because propaganda can be disguised as antipropaganda criticism while providing just as effective brand recognition. Also, the consistent incorporation of irony into propaganda can provide a "safety valve" for the purveyor of propaganda: if a campaign goes off the rails, the purveyor can claim that they were being ironic and did not intend to offend or otherwise miss the mark.

The quotes at the beginning of this chapter speak to the power of irony in propaganda. As Alice Walker notes (perhaps with some irony, perhaps not), propaganda is considered so powerful that with it, people can be essentially led to believe anything. The other quote is most certainly involved in irony since the photographer Robert Capa probably staged one or more of his most famous photographs, including the *Death of a Republican Soldier* [Lavo16].

Capa's quote, then, is especially ironic since his "best picture" may in fact not actually be "the best propaganda." The concept of irony is indeed a tricky one, as it may give an "out" to someone who is testing the waters to see how their audience will react. A simple way of summing up the potential of irony was given by the character Chris in Season 3, Episode 6, of the 1990 television series *Northern Exposure* (aired originally November 4, 1991), where he states that "Facts don't change, truth does." Irony is a way of using facts for more than one potential truth. Since all nontrivial historical narratives have multiple perspectives and contexts, and thus multiple truths, irony is perhaps an inevitable rhetorical device for historical narration.

14.4 Ethos, Logos, Pathos, Kairos, Topos, and Aesthetics

In this chapter's introduction, rhetorical appeals or "types of persuasion" were expanded from the Aristotelian trio of elements (ethos, pathos, and logos) to include two mechanisms for persuasion (kairos and topos) along with a more modern appeal, that of aesthetics. Propaganda typically relies on the incorporation of such persuasive methods to guide the audience into agreement with the narrator.

Looking at propaganda from a Utilitarian perspective – that is where its ends are used to justify its means – the mechanisms are less important than the guidance, education, or re-education of the audience that they provide. As an example, consider the shaming of men who were noncombatants with the use of white feathers, as described earlier [Maso02]. This shaming of conscientious pacifists, which is unlikely to have the same impact today as when employed over a century ago, combined kairos (they still had "time" to sign up), pathos (the country is sad for the soldiers already at the front), and logos (the country will not win if it does not maximize its combatants). The aesthetics of the "white" feather were also likely more meaningful in early 20th-century England than they are today.

A famous doctrine that uses propaganda is Thomas Paine's *Common Sense* [Pain76]. Here, the very title gives away the approach Paine wishes to use to persuade his readers. Common sense is an expression meaning practical, sensical judgment, in other words, logos. While Paine certainly employs a wide range of rhetorical devices in *Common Sense*, it is clear that he believes his persuasiveness is consistent with that of the enlightenment which was the dominant intellectual movement in Europe at the time (*Common Sense* sold rather well in France, after all).

Gustave Le Bon's *The Crowd: A Study of the Popular Mind*, [LeBo95], rather than employing propaganda, reveals how propaganda is used to control crowds. Le Bon, like Paine, employed reason to guide his audience, but since his subject matter was about how crowd psychology moves people *away* from logos, it is an interesting combination of using logos to show how logos disappear in some crowd situations. In fact, Le Bon claims that crowd psychology leads to behavior very similar to that of a hypnotized person – can this be considered a type of pathos? Regardless of the methods employed, Le Bon shows how propaganda can be used to successfully steer the overall mindset of "the crowd." Le Bon's arguments are very familiar more than 100 years later, in no small part because of the subsequent explosion in psychology led by Freud, Piaget, James, and others. Most of us are familiar with subsequent work supporting Le Bon's thesis that crowd mentality consists of increased emotionality and decreased critical thinking. This can be considered a form of *collective pathos* that replaces individual logos.

Persuasive approaches can be employed to provide powerful, nuanced historical narratives, and we feel it is important to point out that truth-seeking writers of history can employ techniques of persuasion with the intent of seeking the truth, and not its opposite. Such narrative skill is on display, for example, in David Howarth's *1066* [Howa81]. Howarth notes that the author of the *Vita Aedwardi Regis* (a biography of King Edward III written the year after the invasion), for example, intentionally wrote about the last words of King Edward III in a vague manner: "I commend this woman and all the kingdom to your protection…Serve and honor her with faithful obedience as your lady and sister, which she is" [Ibid., p. 48]. Howarth gives *Vita*'s author credit for logos, noting that "it would have been more than the author's freedom was worth to assert that Harold was Edward's chosen heir, and so to imply that the Norman invasion was utterly unjust" [Ibid., p. 50]. Howarth cleverly explains how the mistruth of versioning (Chapter 13) arises because the author is well aware of the threat of being "too honest": William "the Conqueror" of England could hardly have been trusted to be anodyne with a more truthful, less subtle quote such as "I commend this woman and all the kingdom to your rule…Serve and honor her with faithful marriage as your lady and wife, which she is." The *Vita*'s author was skilled enough to use logos both to water down the quote and to leave enough intact for future historians to be able to infer the more likely actual quote.

Howarth continues to describe the events around the 1066 invasion using persuasive elements, including the pathos invoked by William of Poitiers: "For [William] removed from your neck the proud and cruel despotism of Harold, and killed the hateful tyrant who had reduced you to ruinous and shameful slavery" [Ibid., p.52]. This description is clearly propaganda on the part of Duke William's chaplain, and Howarth is able to show in this straightforward fashion how important propaganda was to the success of the postinvasion reduction of England. Howarth himself knows how important finding middle-ground narratives is for stripping the narrative of its propaganda, noting "To find the middle course between the two extremes, one has to rely rather heavily on the author of the *Vita Aedwardi Regis*, but that is not unreasonable...he left a dual character sketch which has the ring of truth and is often corroborated by events" [Ibid., p. 53]. In other words, a narrative that is even-handed in finding both merit and faults with its characters is less likely to be strewn with propaganda.

Howarth goes further, essentially pointing out the "Emperor's New Clothes" nature of William the Conqueror-centric, propaganda-rich histories: "Harold has had the misfortune in history to be remembered for what his foreign enemies said of him, more than for what his friends and subjects said... the Norman's verbal attacks were...the kind of political propaganda, familiar today, which even the propagandists know is untrue" [Ibid., p. 55]. In other words, propaganda lacking ethos, logos, and even pathos may work, if only you and enough other people in power say it often enough and loudly enough. Kairos, topos, and the "aesthetics" of noise, in other words, may trump the more traditional trio of ethos, logos, and pathos. Howarth employs logos to uncover this propaganda. Taking information from narratives on both sides of the conflict, Howarth deduces that a highly probable outcome of Edward III's death was an agreement between William and Harold to unite Normandy and England, with William as king and Harold as "the de facto ruler of England, with more independence than he could have had under a native king" [Ibid., p. 74]. Howarth's logos continues, with his suggestion that Harold may even have worked to make this happen "if the English had been willing to accept the idea. But they were not" [Ibid.]. The employment by Howarth of logos to uncover the other persuasive elements in the propaganda employed by the Norman conquerors is an inspiration to other historians striving to achieve a nonbiased, multilevel approach to a truthful narrative. Persuasive elements can be used truthfully.

14.5 Hegemonic Hollow Anhedonic Happiness

Are humans addicted to unhappiness? Or are they addicted to something in between happiness and unhappiness, with every episode of happiness being defined in some Manichean sense through comparison with unhappiness, and vice versa? If so, the alliterative title of this section, "hegemonic hollow anhedonic happiness," makes sense. Hegemonic because it is pervasive; hollow because it does not provide fulfillment; anhedonic because it does not provide pleasure or joy; and happiness because it is juxtaposed to something even more unhappy, such as not being able to access the information that nevertheless causes the hollowness and anhedonia.

Anhedonia is characterized by a reduced interest in formerly enjoyable pursuits. In politics and economics, powerlessness often results in anhedonia, and those in power often appear to intentionally reinforce anhedonia (it helps prevent revolutions, for one thing). Hegemonic control of society's moods can take on many forms. The lack of meaningful public discourse in the political sphere, for example, can lead to voter ennui and associated anhedonia. Reinforcement of negative emotion, called "doom scrolling" when moderated through online access of "supportive" negative information, is a recent phenomenon. However, in the context of truthfulness in history, doom scrolling is logically consistent. In doom scrolling, the scroller finds support for the validity of their anhedonia by discovering evidence of its veracity. In other words, if you feel that the world is a bad place, then finding evidence of the world actually being a bad place, at minimum, alleviates any guilt you might otherwise feel for the anhedonia. The problem with doom scrolling (and anhedonia) is that it can create a vicious cycle in which the scrolling increases your anhedonia, and this increased anhedonia increases the impetus for doom scrolling [Pas23]. The "happiness" associated with this (reinforced) anhedonia is certainly hollow.

This vicious cycle of anhedonia might help to explain the cyclical nature of populism in American politics. When the "populace" feels disconnected from the current political scene, it is relatively easy for a populist to come in, repeating the complaints of the populace, and claiming to represent them as a populist candidate. For a while, the anhedonia is accompanied by a hollow happiness, because the populace feels that someone understands. Then, when the populist has hegemony over them and does not bring about the desired, even expected, change, the happiness dissipates to be replaced by simple anhedonia until the next cycle of populism begins. Time, therefore, can be a flat circle, with the eternal recurrence of populism leading to an eternal cycle of anhedonia with and without happiness. But it does not have to be this way. The coopting that occurs with populism, wherein the anhedonic populace is taken in by the populist faction, can be replaced by a more hedonic engagement if the fundamental principles of truthfulness in historical narration can be applied.

The problem with truthfulness in narration, however, extends beyond the plurality of perspectives and the variable backgrounds and contexts of the narrators and their audience. What happens when a lie, once told, is simply represented as an "alternative fact"? Such a condition occurred when on

January 22, 2017, Kellyanne Conway defended White House Press Secretary Sean Spicer's clearly mendacious statement with the comment that Spicer was giving "alternative facts" [Blom18]. Such doublespeak – a portmanteau of *doublethink* and *Newspeak*, terms introduced in George Orwell's *1984* – unsurprisingly reminded people of Orwell's dystopian masterpiece, the sales of which increased nearly 100-fold within four days of the interview [deFr17], propelling it to number-one bestseller on Amazon.com, a full 68 years after its initial publication.

Mistruth in a historical narrative can be quite harmful, of course. Among the thousands of possible examples, the ones that are particularly egregious are those that simply deny the existence of generally accepted historical facts. One that the older of the two authors of this book has witnessed gaining momentum throughout the past few decades is that of Holocaust denial. Jean-Marie Le Pen, erstwhile leader of the French far-right Front National, has dismissed the Holocaust as a mere detail and questioned whether the gas chambers (used as part of the German death machine that killed six million Jews) actually existed [Lips12]. The fact that such claims are against the law in France has not stopped Le Pen from gaining adherents over time. One wonders how much impact the "need" for Jews (and anyone else driven by the undeniable truth of the Holocaust's narrative) to assert such an obvious truth complicates the relationship between the Jewish state (Israel) and the rest of the world. That is a subject far more complicated than we can address in this short section, but the answer is that it almost certainly complicates it and may help lead Israel to "hunker down" in its pugilism under a variety of circumstances. Does that mean that Holocaust denial contributes to Israel overreacting to events in Gaza, the West Bank, Lebanon, and Iran? Again, almost certainly, though we cannot arrogate to estimate how significant the contribution might be.

Another example of the denial of obvious historical narrative veracity is the nonfactual history that has been repeated by some people about the infamous White supremacist rally held in Charlottesville, Virginia, in August of 2017. The rally featured neo-Nazis, Ku Klux Klansmen, and neo-Confederates, provably marching with the associated German Nazi, KKK, and US Confederate flags. It is worth recognizing the propaganda value of a flag – it is aesthetic propaganda of high impact. The uniforms worn by the marchers – from Nazi to Confederate – were another form of aesthetic propaganda.

As we have mentioned previously, one aspect of having so much information at our fingertips via the Internet is the retreat of so many people into their echo chambers, filtering out so much content in order to find belonging and like-minded individuals. This filtering is also a form of self-validation and reinforcement, but its consequences can be profound if it leads to removing contrasting information that is paramount for discourse and cooperation. This was visible in a multitude of accounts of the Charlottesville rally afterward, including *The Lancet*. In a later article in this rather prestigious journal, Mary Bassett noted that an editorial two weeks after the rally [Lanc17] "seemed to endorse a view that the armed alternative-right mob reflected legitimate grievances of the neglected White working class – somehow hidden in the Nazi-inflected slogans, 'blood and soil', and 'Jews shall not replace us'" [Bass17]. If this seems off topic for a very highly-regarded medical journal, it is surely reinforced by the claim that "the absence of empathy for White distress is among the 'causes of causes'" for the Charlottesville rally which ultimately left one dead and five critically wounded. The earlier article, according to Bassett, "appeared to conclude that there has been enough talk about hate crimes, discrimination, and so forth, and further that the answer to Charlottesville is universal health coverage! It would be laughable if it were not so offensive" [Bass17]. There is a reason for the editorial in *The Lancet*, apparently. But, let us face it, if you do not feel you are at liberty to identify Nazis, the KKK, and the Confederate army as horrible, there is something wrong with truth in society. From genocide to racial hatred to institutionalized subjugation of people, these are three groups for which "multiple truths" are certainly all pejorative, right? Apparently not, and that sobering realization should only emphasize how important being able to apply the various patterns for uncovering mistruths in history, including propaganda, is for the present and future of society.

14.6 Cyber Salon – False Sense of Security

In this, the last cyber salon in the book, we address the false sense of security that is advertised with such cybersecurity approaches as malware detection software, intrusion detection systems, and automatic patching. The "truth" about cybersecurity, and especially cyber-physical security, is that complacency is perhaps just as deadly an enemy as the rogue agents who hope to exploit the vulnerabilities of your system. If a software, service, or system for protecting you from the plethora of potential rogue agents out there sounds too good to be true, well then it almost certainly is.

As with mistruths in history, mistruths in cyber-propaganda can be detected with the right set of tools. In other words, there are ways to separate propaganda from reality through vulnerability assessment. The familiar "red team" versus "blue team" approach has recently extended to "AI as red team" versus "AI as blue team" competitions (where "AI" is of course "artificial intelligence"). For you as the system defender to prevent attacks by AI, and especially generative AI, from being successful, you might need to become an "AI whisperer;" that is, a person skilled in knowing how to get AI to give desired outputs. Being more creative than the bad guys is not enough, and may not even be possible since they are clearly pooling their resources, talents, and successes. But you do have to be thorough. For some cybercriminals, the threat of being found out is a deterrent, but not always, and this means that we have to assume this threat is insufficient and that actual system protection needs to be ensured. Given this, you have to be comfortable that the approaches that you (or the services, software, and systems you are paying for) are providing actual protection, not just propaganda.

In addition to becoming an expert yourself, another way to divert the conversation around cyber-protection from propaganda to reality is to make careful measurements (or require the provider to make them as part of the contract). If the protection does not meet its claims, you will report it. Measurement, analysis, and statistical reporting are part of your repertoire of "counterthreats," and as such should be employed from the integration stage onward. To fight propaganda, you can employ the cybersecurity equivalent of every pattern for discovering mistruths (one of which was the focus of each chapter in this book). We will overview just a few of these, and superficially at that, to give you a flavor for how to proceed.

In Chapter 2, the theme of omission was considered. For countering cyber-protection propaganda, you should have a list of the types of cyberattacks you wish to have protection from and obtain in writing assurance that your provider can address each of them. A good place to start is with the Mitre Att&ck knowledge base [Mitr24]. In Chapter 3, the theme of disparity was discussed. For cyber protection, you should measure the balance between breadth and depth of coverage for each of the major attack classes (reconnaissance, privilege escalation, defense evasion, etc.). Chapter 4 presents generalization, and sometimes a cybersecurity provider will seem to generalize their past success as a guarantee of future success. Here, you should make sure to query them on the most recent types of attacks (such as generative AI). The differential emphasis discussed in Chapter 5 can be observed in some cybersecurity propaganda, as well. Make sure that the protection includes more than just the few selective types advertised. We will mention one more chapter, the one on transitive trust (Chapter 12). Here, you almost certainly would not say: "I trust the operating system and I trust the application, so I must trust running the application on the operating system right." This is because the interactions between operating systems and any software it hosts are far more complicated than simple transitivity. Oversimplification in a historical narrative can lead to mistruth by excising the nuances of the narrative, and oversimplification of a cybersecurity posture can lead to exploitation by underestimating, simultaneously, the depth and breadth of cybersecurity vulnerabilities and the impressive threat exploitation talents of the rogue agents.

14.7 Summary

One goal of the authors of this book is to help the reader change their way of thinking historically. The best historian is not the one who is right all the time. The best historian is the one who, when they are wrong, are readily identified as such because they have provided their sources, their uses of propaganda, their biases, and their own likely inaccuracies so that they can engage their audience in the never-ending work of improving history. In this chapter, we argue for at least six forms of persuasive methods in propaganda to be "searched for" by the reader, including the classical trio of logos, pathos, and ethos in addition to kairos (timing), topos (topic), and aesthetics (appearances). Aesthetics has increased in importance over time as the technologies to mass produce more compelling visual propaganda have increased (with generative AI being yet another "quantum leap" forward). Uncovering the use of these persuasive elements – or persuasive biases – is a goal of the active reader of a historical narrative.

Examples of the employment of propaganda, extending from the shaming of conscientious pacifists with white feathers in World War I England to the ironic coopting of anticapitalistic messages for capitalistic purposes by the *Barbie* movie, were then described. A further irony was cited in the likelihood that photographer Robert Capa staged the *Death of a Republican Soldier* [Lavo16]. Thomas Paine's use of vituperative logos in *Common Sense* [Pain76] was then overviewed.

In spite of our wariness to propaganda, it can be used to provide balanced, nuanced, and therefore valuable historical narratives. David Howarth's *1066* [Howa81] is one example of such a narrative of excellence. In trying to understand "both sides" of a narrative, Howarth convincingly determined that it is likely that Edward III's death was followed by an agreement between William and Harold to unite Normandy and England, with William as king and Harold as tenant-in-chief of England under Harold. Offsetting Howarth's talent and veracity, however, are some stunning examples of mistruth, such as Kellyanne Conway's "alternative facts" and *The Lancet*'s initial response to the Charlottesville march of people in Nazi, KKK, and Confederate army uniform. These latter two examples remind us that while it is important to try to understand the multiple perspectives in a historical event, it is not okay to justify genocide, racial hatred, or the institutionalized subjugation of people.

The chapter concluded with a discussion of one "truth" about cybersecurity, and especially, cyber-physical security; that is, that complacency is perhaps just as deadly an enemy as the threat agents who attempt to exploit the vulnerabilities of your software, service, or system. Rather than believe the propaganda that a cybersecurity protector provider promises, plan the means to test, measure, and analyze the protector's efficacy with sophisticated red team/blue team and other test scenarios.

References

[Bass17] Bassett MT, Krieger N, and Bailey Z, "Charlottesville: blatant racism, not grievances, on display," *The Lancet* 390, no. 10109 (2017): 2243.

[Blom18] Blommaert J, "Ergo: Exploring the world of alternative facts," *Ctrl+ Alt+ Dem* 19 (2018).

[DeFr17] de Freytas-Tamura K, "George Orwell's '1984' Is Suddenly a Best-Seller," *The New York Times* January 25, 2017.

[Howa81] Howarth D, "1066: The year of the conquest," Penguin, 1981.

[Ketk22] Ketkale H and Simske S, "Encouraging reuse in the corrugated packaging industry using persuasion and operant conditioning," *Sustainability* 14, no. 11 (2022): 6454.

[Lanc 17] The Lancet, "Charlottesville: symptomatic of broader pain," *Lancet* 2017; 390:821.

[Lavo16] Lavoie V, "Robert Capa and the turn to forensics," *Photography and Doubt*, pp. 139–156. Routledge, 2016.

[LeBo95] Le Bon G, "The Crowd: A Study of the Popular Mind," 1895, available at Beyond Books Hub, 2023.

[Lips12] Lipstadt D, "Denying the Holocaust: The growing assault on truth and memory," Simon and Schuster, 2012.

[Lope23] Lopez CT, "All-Volunteer Force Proves Successful for US Military," US Department of Defense, March 2, 2023, accessed 5 November, 2024 on https://www.defense.gov/News/News-Stories/Article/Article/3316678/all-volunteer-force-proves-successful-for-us-military/.

[Maar20] Maartens B, "Your country needs you? Advertising, public relations and the promotion of military service in peacetime Britain," *Media, War & Conflict* 13, no. 2 (2020): 213–233.

[Mart23] Martin R, "Aiming to be the Top Gun: Military Recruitment, Propaganda, and Shaping the Image of War Through Popular Media,"

Intersect: The Stanford Journal of Science, Technology, and Society 16, no. 2 (2023).

[Maso02] Mason AEW, "The Four Feathers," Macmillan, 1902.

[Merc19] Mercurio N, "Beyond "thank you": Recommended modalities for meaningful civilian-military discourse," *Journal of Veterans Studies* 4, no. 2 (2019): 1–33.

[Mitr24] Mitre Att&ck knowledge base, accessed 16 November 2024 on https://attack.mitre.org/.

[Mors45] Morse JM, "The Guilty Civilian," *The Antioch Review* 5, no. 2 (1945): 224–231.

[Pain76] Paine T, "Common Sense," R. Bell, 1776, Philadelphia.

[Pas23] Pas L, "The Influence of Depression on Doom Scrolling and Climate Change Engagement: A Mixed-Methods Study," Bachelor's thesis, University of Twente, 2023.

15

Summary and Conclusions

Only when we are no longer afraid do we begin to live
– Dorothy Thompson

The future's uncertain and the end is always near
– Jim Morrison

Abstract

By Chapter 14, with the introduction of the last major form of mistruth to be discussed (propaganda), it became clear that often several forms of mistruth are involved simultaneously. With 13 major forms of mistruth, we show how there are, at least in theory, 8191 different mistruth models for fraudulent historians to proceed. In this chapter, we discuss how hybrid mistruth models can be used to obfuscate the more dangerous threat with a more obvious and innocuous threat (something often used by recently elected politicians). We also show how sowing mistrust across the domain can be used to discredit legitimate historians. We conclude with recommendations for how to better identify, remediate, and prevent the effectiveness of mistruths, in both histories, and by appropriate repurposing, in cybersecurity systems.

15.1 Introduction

At this point in your reading, if you are not already convinced that it is of critical importance to question any and all historical narratives, then let us briefly consider a few references addressing the topic of mistruth. We start with Maurice Finocchiaro, who, in his article [Fino15], states "I formulate some problems for future research on compositional arguments: distinguishing incorrectness from fallaciousness; elaborating general principles of evaluation; ... and further historical-empirical search for such fallacies in various

DOI: 10.1201/9788770048347-15

controversies, over holism, over global warming, and over national debts." Finocchiaro thus assumes a mistruth in history and is concerned with discerning intentionality (fallaciousness) from unintentionality (incorrectness). We accept the fact that much (most?) mistruth in history is unintentional, but also have argued that it is essentially inevitable.

James Freeman extends the investigation of mistruths in history to teaching: "For pedagogical purposes, information about the frequency of a pattern of fallacious reasoning may indicate the desirability of teaching recognizing that pattern of reasoning. Students may then be forearmed against this pitfall" [Free16]. Freeman follows this up with the poignant question, "But does it tell us anything about *why* this 'popular' pitfall is a pitfall?" [Ibid.] To this question, we posit an answer: the unintentional mistruths in historical narratives are due to some combination of indolence, lack of access to sufficient reference materials, lack of balanced reference materials, time constraints, and other factors; the intentional mistruths in historical narratives, however, are framed around whatever mechanism the author thinks will be successful. In other words, intentional mistruths are crafted, and the "skill" of the liar correlates with their success in convincing people that the lie is the truth.

Zheng Wang extends the concept of mistruth in history to the process of creating, or rather forcing, analogies between different histories [Wang20]. Part of the danger is in extrapolation: "A historical analogy signifies an inference based on the notion that if two or more events separated in time are similar in one respect, then they may also be similar in others" [Ibid.]. However, the strength of each analogy is not uniform, with factors such as "the relevance of the known similarities, the amount and variety of the examples in the analogy, and the number of shared characteristics among the things being compared" [Ibid.] all requiring consideration when positing the analogy. In the context of our "patterns for mistruth," mistruth by analogy can be considered a composite mistruth, usually incorporating several of the other mistruths simultaneously. For example, an analogy between any current government and that of Nazi Germany is likely to incorporate omission (failing to cite obvious differences in governance or treatment of religious minorities, for example), disparity (emphasizing the similarities and sweeping under the rug the differences), and persuasive elements such as valence and arousal, among others. Wang noted that it is "irresponsible for scholars to spread various historical analogies and 'lessons of history,' and it is dangerous for political leaders to use historical analogies to mobilize support. These ready-to-use analogies could make people believe everything is doomed, and therefore not make strong efforts to uphold peace and to create new opportunities for reconciliation" [Ibid.]. Each era, as we have made clear throughout the book, brings its own contextualization to the narrative, and so as Wang notes, "We are not handcuffed to history, and history is not destiny" [Ibid.].

History is not destiny, and in fact, we believe that a deep study of history is crucial for preventing the so-called "history repeats itself" syndrome, and perhaps even its very ideation. While certain perspectives, processes, and practices do have cyclical behavior, each cycle has new externalities – from technologies that have changed to social mores that are no longer widely acceptable – that by definition prevent history from duplicating itself over time. Once you have internalized this tautology, you will realize that a "return" to a historical decision point is not doomed to repeat a previous historical pattern but is instead an opportunity for reevaluation and perhaps a more successful outcome if wisdom from the previous "cycle" can be applied. This is why uncovering and understanding mistruths is so valuable: with the events of the past as warning, wariness, and wisdom, a new and perhaps more cautious path forward can be forged.

15.2 What Have We Left Out?

Even a book of this length is going to leave out a lot of relevant content. We simply cannot cover everything. For example, where does the "Phantom Time Hypothesis" of 297 missing years in the Middle Ages [Illi98] fit in? Heribert Illig's *Das erfundene Mittelalter* (or *The Invented Middle Ages* in English) posits that radiocarbon dating and the paucity of information from the so-called Dark Ages (specifically, 614–911 AD) means that they did not actually exist. Can this be addressed with the patterns in this book? Is it, for example, hyperbole? Or is "conspiracy theory" another pattern for mistruth that simply is not addressed by one of the 13 patterns herein (from omission to propaganda)?

Maybe that is the wrong question to ask because, after all, the elephant in the room is the various composite mistruths that can be created by combining two or more of the 13 major patterns for mistruths elaborated in the book. A conspiracy theory may therefore combine several of the patterns, and in doing so, combine the power of each into an overall "greater" mistruth. Let us explore the hybrid possibilities briefly. If the presence or absence of each of the mistruth patterns, from omission to propaganda, is represented by a binary string, then a mistruth involving only omission is represented as 1000000000000 (the "1" for omission occurring and the "0"s for all the other patterns not occurring). A mistruth involving only propaganda is therefore represented as 0000000000001. A narrative involving both omission and propaganda is represented as 1000000000001. One involving omission, disparity, generalization, and propaganda but none of the other patterns is represented as 1110000000001. With 13 patterns, then, there are $2^{13} - 1$ (the subtraction of one is for the 0000000000000 case, where no mistruth is told) or 8191 different combinations of approaches to mistruth that can be employed, just using the patterns in this book.

It is clear from this number of possibilities that characterizing the type of mistruth in a historical narrative is less important than that of assessing the narrative for each of the 13 patterns independently. After all, 8191 is more than 630 times as large as 13, and thus, testing for each "hybrid" model, such as 1010111000101 for one example, is less important than checking for each of the 13 separate types of mistruths. In addition to being more efficient, checking for each pattern independently might help you determine whether the narrator is trying to obfuscate a more dangerous mistruth with a more innocuous one. This is a method often employed not just by historians but also by politicians, where they propose enough red herrings, often of a provocative nature, so that their opponents in trying to fight off all of the seeming insanity at once have a hard time guessing the real agenda that the politician is trying to accomplish. Hybrid methods – ones involving multiple mistruths simultaneously – are also used to sow mistrust across the entire historical domain, and thus, the narrator hopes that at least one mistruth "sticks" with the reader. This approach can undermine and/or discredit legitimate narratives since many readers might be convinced by at least one of the mistruths. If you throw enough mistruths into the mix, you may convince enough people that at least one of them has validity so as to achieve your goal of the reader believing what would otherwise be readily identified as mistruth. This can be offset, however, by careful reading focused on the patterns for mistruths described in the previous chapters. As a reader, if you assiduously try to recognize and then ignore mistruths by identifying their employment of one or more of the patterns described in this book, then you will prevent this type of "shotgun" strategy from working. To end this section with a zeugma, you owe it to yourself and the truth.

15.3 Summary of the Summaries

We admit that we have not covered everything, but at both ends of the mistruth magnitude spectrum, this is understandable. Some mistruths are so subtle that they are hard to detect, and because of the lack of surviving records, may be impossible to prove as mistruths. On the other end, some mistruths (like Holocaust denial and conspiracy theories) are so obvious and preponderous that no "pattern" is needed to uncover them. In between these two extremes are the mistruths in history that we have addressed using 13 patterns for mistruth (the bulk of Chapters 2–14). We summarize these briefly here so you can refer to them in your future historical truth-seeking.

In *Chapter 2*, the pattern for mistruth was the *omission* of credible information from the narrative of a historical event. Omission understandably occurs whenever a summary of the content must substitute for the entirety of the content, and the constant clicking and scrolling of the Internet era only makes such omission more likely both on the part of the narrator and the reader. Implicit bias, pandering to your audience, hypocrisy, and slant are all different means of promulgating mistruths through selectively omitting content.

In *Chapter 3*, the pattern for mistruth was *disparity*. Disparity is an imbalance in the flow or representation of information which can stem from a structural cause such as the difficulty of projecting from one culture into another. Seven laws of disparity were provided, relating the severity of disparity to the magnitude of differences in time, location, governance, literacy rate, source material type, quantity, and accessibility between the event and the historian.

In *Chapter 4*, *generalization* was the pattern for mistruth considered. Generalization includes *presentism* where the historical narrative of an event is interpreted with context appropriate to the time of the historian and not the event. In this chapter, a so-called Fundamental Law of Mistruth was introduced which claims that mistruth is the fault of the reporter and not the original historical persons and events. The continuum of overgeneralization, from stereotyping to profiling to outright bias, covers a wide range of misinterpretations.

In *Chapter 5*, the pattern of mistruth was *differential emphasis and evaluation*. One means of providing differential emphasis is with *selective complexity*, in which one person, interpretation, or event is presented with much more depth and/or nuance than another person, interpretation, or event. A six-step program was outlined to address these issues: (1) acknowledging the selective complexity; (2) arguing against your own point; (3) using the Hegelian dialectic to provide a richer overall synthesis of the historical reporting; (4) separating opinion from fact; (5) employing plausibility and parsimony; and (6) accepting the miraculous only within reason.

The pattern for mistruth in *Chapter 6* is a bit more subtle, or at least complicated to address. Given the limitations to accuracy in historical narratives, we highlighted in later chapters, it might seem that the concept of an *omniscient historian* is an oxymoron. We know that no historian can account for the full context of any history. From Herodotus to the Durants, historians may have different goals than simply telling the truth. The concept of a contractual history (such as Caesar's history of the Gallic wars) is shown to provide a unique opportunity for "near omniscience" of at least one side of the narrative. We made three recommendations for the would-be omniscient narrator: (1) identify your target audience; (2) provide a comprehensive bibliography, including those that influenced you even if not directly quoted; and (3) identify input that you disregarded and/or discarded.

The pattern of mistruth called *anachronism* was featured in *Chapter 7*. Anachronisms are not always obvious but may consist of a nonlinear treatment of time in the past compared to the present, often with times in the past seemingly much more compressed. Another anachronism is assuming that people today live in a time of maximum change. Finally, our perspective on the past is distorted if we struggle to remove the context of today's technologies and the social and cultural processes, or modes of behavior, that they help create.

In *Chapter 8*, some of the worst "isms" of history, including romantic nationalism, favoritism, provincialism, and racism were considered. Combined, these can be viewed as *factionalisms*. The view of some previous historical time and place being ideal, idyllic, or ideologically superior to the present is an attractive narrative, so the historian needs to be aware that this "bias" does not lead to mistruth in the narrative. Seven questions to help identify when romantic nationalism is occurring were provided:

1. Are the past, present, and future often combined into a directional narrative?
2. Does the narrative jump from the specific to the general and the converse?
3. Is the ideal portrayed as having been, at some point in the past, the literal?
4. Is one nation, ethnicity, or "people," portrayed as a "chosen people?"
5. Is one or more (dubious) claims of precedence made?
6. Is a different group's precedence rationalized or otherwise trivialized?
7. Are "universal stories" claimed as part of a national folklore, folk culture, national narrative, or national epic?

It was shown that an especially dangerous form of national romanticism involves magical thinking, which is enhanced by the "echo chamber" effect that is uniquely possible because of the Internet.

In *Chapter 9*, the pattern for mistruth described was *emboldening*. Four axes for evaluation of emboldening were defined: (1) privilege versus penury, (2) justification versus judication, (3) empowerment versus subjugation, and (4) evanescence versus permanence. Mistruth often has a temporal nature and is more or less truthful depending on how long a time scale it involves. Our perspective on emboldening is that there are always going to be "incentives" for history to be told in one manner versus another, and thus, objectivity will always be somewhat relative. From a cynical viewpoint, those who benefit from falsehood will gladly promulgate it if the benefits outweigh the risks.

In *Chapter 10*, persuasive elements such as *valence, arousal, kronos, and timing* were analyzed quantitatively. Both inclusions and omissions of the positive and negative, of incitement and prosaicness, and sequential and nonsequential timing can contribute to and/or hide mistruths in a document. This mistruth may be unintentional since no writer can reasonably include all of the context required to fully interpret their writing generations later. The role of the historian, therefore, can be argued to be the assessment of the degree of context that is left out.

Hyperbole is the mistruth pattern for *Chapter 11*. It is relatively easy to detect and is often intended for a different purpose than a factual narrative, making it one of the more "forgivable" mistruths, if such a thing can be. However, there is a danger when the hyperbole harmonizes with the preconceived biases and beliefs of their audiences; that is, when the audience wants to believe the "hype." Hyperbole, we argued, is usually used for one of three purposes: to reinforce existing beliefs, to convert the undecided, and to undermine those opposed to a particular belief.

In *Chapter 12*, *transitive trust* is the mistruth discussed. Transitive trust (and its flip side, transitive sus) is a necessity for a functional society since recommendations are so important. When we truly trust someone, we also trust their judgment, and thus, we trust what they trust. When we do not trust someone, that often has a negative impact on our trust in anyone they recommend, even when we have no direct experience with them. The relative amount of transitive trust versus transitive sus depends on the overall environment, and in historical narratives on the level of trust we have for the narrator. Transitive trust can be used to divert discussion from addressing the actual underlying problems and instead to focus on symptoms.

Next, in *Chapter 13*, the impact of *versioning* on historical truth and mistruth is considered. Just as important as understanding the differences in extant versions is identifying versions that have not been reported. But, even when all versions are available, there is usually no one correct version since there are usually multiple truths, as well as multiple mistruths, in a narrative.

As a narrator, you should trust your reader to be able to come to your opinion of truth even when it includes perspectives differing from your own (even ones you think are wrong). The best way to version, it can be argued, is to include as many relevant versions as feasible (i.e., do not include obviously fictional versions). With this approach to versioning, the "right" question to ask as a historical narrator may be "Have I left out any reasonable perspectives from my narrative?" Even if you disprove or argue against other perspectives, by including them in your narrative you make it easier for others to follow your work.

The final pattern, that of *propaganda*, was presented in *Chapter 14*. One goal of the book is to help the reader change their way of thinking about historians. The best historian is not the one who is right all the time. The best historian is the one who is readily identified as wrong when they are actually wrong because they have provided their sources, their uses of propaganda, their biases, and their own likely inaccuracies so that they can engage their audience in the never-ending work of improving history. In Chapter 14, the concept of propaganda and its persuasive power is illustrated using the "classical trio" of logos, pathos, and ethos in addition to kairos (timing), topos (topic), and aesthetics (appearances). Propaganda's benefits for drawing attention to all aspects of a narrative mean that it can be used to provide balanced, nuanced, and valuable historical narratives.

15.4 How Will This Book Change Things?

This book will not end mistruths, but it will hopefully provide the means for its readers to investigate historical narratives armed with patterns for identifying mistruths. The identification of mistruths is likely to become more difficult as the artificial intelligence (AI) revolution continues its path into the future. Generative AI, trained with increasing amounts of narratives of mixed truth and mistruth, will be used increasingly by humans in their quest to search, organize, assimilate, understand, and produce content of their own. If the AI is trained on mistruth, it will produce further propagation of the mistruth. Worse yet, because AI is produced by an intelligence structurally different from the human brain, it will produce mistruths (or "hallucinations") novel to the narrative. The 13 patterns of this book will help to combat such hallucinations.

The quote from Dorothy Thompson ("*Only when we are no longer afraid do we begin to live*") is especially compelling in the present age. Searching for and stubbornly identifying mistruths can be an unrewarding task under normal circumstances. Under conditions that exist for much of the world's people today – wherein populists, pundits, and plutocrats have so much power over the truth – it is only that much more difficult. This book should help steel your nerves to continue the fight against mistruth. As Jim Morrison wrote, "*The future's uncertain and the end is always near.*" The future of truth is always uncertain, and it can end if complacency, exhaustion, and/or despair undermine one's ability to strive for a truthful understanding. It is hard work, but we hope to have shown that it is worth it. After all, what can be more important than truth? You have the tools to defend the truth. The readiness is all.

References

[Fino 15] Finocchiaro MA, "The fallacy of composition: Guiding concepts, historical cases, and research problems," *Journal of Applied Logic* 13, no. 2 (2015): 24–43.

[Free16] Freeman JB, "Errors of Reasoning, Naturalizing the Logic of Inference," *Informal Logic,* Vol. 36, No. 3 (2016), pp. 395–426.

[Illi98] Illig H, "Das erfundene Mittelalter," Econ, 1998.

[Wang20] Wang Z, "The dangers of history analogies," *The Diplomat*, 2020.

Index

About the Authors

Steve Simske worked in a NASA CCDS (Center for the Commercial Development of Space) from 1988 to 2007, part-time after 1994. Steve worked for HP and HP Labs for 23 years and was an HP Fellow and Vice President before joining CSU as a Professor in 2018. He is an IEEE Fellow, a NAI (National Academy of Inventors) Fellow, and an IS&T (Imaging.org) Fellow. Steve won a Colorado State Teacher of the Year Award in 2022. Steve has roughly 250 US patents and this is his sixth book.

Dallen Simske received an Honors BS in History from Colorado State University in 2024. Dallen has experience in theatre, music, and teaching professions. This is Dallen's first book.

9788770048330